AF662049

THE POSITION OF WOMEN IN HINDU CIVILIZATION

THE POSITION OF WOMEN IN HINDU CIVILIZATION

From Prehistoric Times to the Present Day

A.S. ALTEKAR

MOTILAL BANARSIDASS
PUBLISHING HOUSE • DELHI

Email: mlbd@mlbd.in • Website: www.mlbd.in

12th Reprint : Delhi, ***2021***
Second Edition : Delhi, 1959

© MOTILAL BANARSIDASS PUBLISHING HOUSE
All Rights Reserved.

No part of this publication may be reproduced or transmitted in any form or by any means, electronic or mechanical, including photocopying, recording, or by way of any information storage and retrieval system, without permission in writing from the publisher.

ISBN: 978-93-90713-55-4 (Hardcover)
ISBN: 978-93-90713-50-9 (Paperback)

Printed & Published by
Rajendra P Jain *for*
Motilal Banarsidass Publishing House
A-44, Naraina Industrial Area, Phase I,
New Delhi–110 028 (INDIA)
Email: mlbd@mlbd.in
Website: www.mlbd.in

Dedicated to the sacred and beloved memory of my mother

SAU. PĀRVATĪBĀĪ ALTEKAR

who was an ideal Hindu Sādhvī

and

to that of my father

SADĀSHIVA KHANDO ALTEKAR

B.A., LL.B.

PLEADER, KARAD, MAHARASHTRA

whose life was a beautiful synthesis of dehakārya, deśakārya and devakārya

PREFACE TO THE FIRST EDITION

There are some monographs which deal with the position of Hindu women in particular periods of Indian history, but no work has as yet been written which reviews their position throughout the long history of Hindu civilisation. An attempt has therefore been made in this book to describe the position of women in Hindu civilisation from prehistoric times to the present day, and to indicate the general lines on which the various problems that confront Hindu women (and therefore men also) should be tackled in order to get a fairly satisfactory solution. Every effort has been made to utilise all possible sources of information,—Vedic, Epic, Jain, Buddhist, Smṛiti and classical Sanskrit literatures, sculptures and paintings, coins and inscriptions, narratives of foreign travellers, both ancient and medieval, accounts of European merchants and missionaries, Government blue books and reports, modern works on the feminist movement, both in the East and the West. Most of the above authorities have been consulted in the original.

The opening chapter deals with the problems relating to the childhood and education of women. Then follow two chapters (II and III), which deal with the numerous complex problems connected with marriage and married life. In the next two chapters (IV and V), the position of the widow in society has been considered. The place of women in public life and religion has been dealt with in chapters VI and VII. In chapters VIII and IX various questions connected with proprietary rights have been discussed. Fashions of dress, ornaments and coiffure are described in chapter X, and illustrated with eight plates. Chapter XI deals with the general attitude of society towards women, both in normal and abnormal times and situations.

Each chapter deals with the history and development of its topic from the earliest times to the present day, and then suggests at the conclusion the lines on which the present day problems connected with it should be solved. This method enables the reader to get a continuous and connected idea of the history of the particular topic or institution from age to age, and to realise the full nature and significance of the different forces that were governing its general development or vicissitudes. The method, however, has one defect; it does not enable the reader to have a complete and synthetic picture of the position of women in any particular age. The concluding chapter therefore takes a general review of the whole subject, and delineates in broad outlines the general position of women in its entirety in the different periods of Hindu civilisation, and discusses at full length the various causes that were responsible for the changes that were taking place from age to age. It is confidently hoped that the reader will find the subject treated in a very comprehensive manner.

A general knowledge of the position and status of women in the main civilisations of ancient and modern times, both in the East and the West, is necessary in order to get a proper perspective for the evaluation of Hindu culture with reference to its attitude towards women and their problems in the different periods of our history. Otherwise we would be too much prone to blame or praise. An effort has therefore been made in this work to enlighten the reader about the position of women in some of the important countries and civilisations with reference to most of the topics discussed in the book. This will enable him to form a correct and comparative estimate about the achievements and limitations of our civilisation regarding the woman and her problems.

The subject matter of the book bristles with controversial topics, and it is quite possible that some of my readers and reviewers may not agree with me in my conclusions. Some of them may think that I have been rather partial to ancient Hindu culture; others may hold that I have been unnecessarily severe in exposing its defects. Some may feel that the remedies suggested are too drastic, others may opine that they do not go far enough. These differences of opinion are, however, inevitable. I would assure both the reader and the critic that it has been my constant endeavour to treat the subject as impartially as possible. Limitations of our culture have not been passed over, nor its excellences magnified, nor *vice versa.* The historian can hold no brief either for the past or for the present, either for the East or for the West.

The book is mainly a research work, which documents every important statement it makes, and seeks to throw fresh light on many important and obscure points connected with the topics of enquiry. The subject matter has, however, been presented in a manner calculated to be attractive and intelligible to the general reader as well. Every effort has been made not to mar the general flow of the narrative by the introduction and discussion of original passages, or of obscure and unimportant topics. These have been all relegated to footnotes, where the scholar and the more serious reader may study them at leisure. It is therefore hoped that the book will interest both the scholar and the general reader. For the heip of the latter, dates of important events and works have also been supplied in brackets at many places.

I am grateful to Dr. S. K. Belvalkar and Principal K. V. Rangaswami Aiyangar for carefully going through the typescript and making a number of valuable suggestions. I am obliged to R. B. K. N. Dikshit, M.A., the Director General of Archaeology in India, for giving permission to reproduce the photographs of the sculptures utilised for the plates in this work. I am indebted to my wife Sau. Satyabhāmābai for offering me valuable assistance in analysing the data of sculptures and paintings for the purpose of determining the fashions in dress and ornaments.

BANARAS HINDU UNIVERSITY, A. S. ALTEKAR.
15-7-1938.

PREFACE TO THE SECOND EDITION

Though the first edition of 'Position of Women in Hindu Civilisation' was out of print for a few years, it did not become possible for me to bring out the second revised edition. There was a persistent demand for a second edition but various preoccupations prevented me from meeting it.

The first edition has been thoroughly revised and also considerably enlarged. New evidence that I could gather during the course of my subsequent studies has been utilised for this edition; it mostly confirms old conclusions though it also slightly modifies some of them. The position of nuns has been dealt with in greater details and the status of courtesans has also been considered. The section on the Purda system considers some further aspects. Three more plates have been added to illustrate dress and coiffure. The data supplied by the census of 1951 have been utilised to make the treatment quite up-to-date.

During the last 18 years several changes have taken in the position of Hindu women as far as proprietary rights, marital relations and public life are concerned. These have been fully discussed in the new edition in appropriate places. Unfortunately the legislative changes are taking place slowly and piecemeal, and the book was in the press for three years. So it was difficult to keep pace with them. As a consequence there is one slight inaccuracy on p. 363, which has been corrected in the errata. Though the bill seeking to give the daughter the same right in the patrimony as the brother is before the Parliament for several years, the matter has not yet been decided.

It is hoped that the second edition of the work will enable the cultured reader, both in India and abroad to get a clear idea of the forces that were moulding the position of women in Hindu society for the last four thousand years and thereby understand the spirit of Hindu civilisation.

I am indebted to my daughter Miss Padma Altekar, M.A. for helping me to read the proofs and to Miss Minakshi Bateshvarkar for permitting me to utilise the drawings used for Plates IX-XI.

Patna
1-5-1956.

A. S. ALTEKAR

ABBREVIATIONS AND TRANSLITERATION

ABBREVIATIONS

A. Br.—Aitareya Brāhmaṇa.

A. D. S.—Āpastamba Dharmasūtra.

A. G. S.—Āpastamba Gṛihyasūtra.

Aṅg. Nik.—Aṅguttara Nikāya.

Aś. G. S.—Aśvalāyana Gṛihyasūtra.

A. S. R.—Archaeological Survey, Annual Report.

A. S. W. I.—Archaeological Survey of Western India.

A. V.—Atharvaveda.

B. D. S.—Baudhāyana Dharmasūtra.

B. G. S.—Baudhāyana Gṛihyasūtra.

Br. Up.—Bṛihadāraṇyaka Upanishad.

E. C.—Epigraphia Carnatica.

E. I.—Epigraphia Indica.

E. R. E.—Encyclopaedia of Religion and Ethics.

G. D. S.—Gautama Dharmasūtra.

H. G. S.—Hiraṇyakeśi Gṛihyasūtra.

I. A.—Indian Antiquary.

I. M. P.—Inscriptions from Madras Presidency.

J.A.S.B.—Journal of the Asiatic Society of Bengal.

J. B. B. R. A. S.—Journal of the Bombay Branch of the Royal Asiatic Society.

J. B. O. R. S.—Journal of the Bihar and Orissa Research Society.

K. P.—Kāvyaprakāśa.

K. S.—Kāṭhaka Saṁhitā.

Kss.—Kathāsaritsāgara.

Mbh.—Mahābhārata.

M. Nik.—Majhima Nikāya.

M. S.—Maitrāyaṇīya Saṁhitā.

Par.—Parāśarasmṛiti.

Par. Mād.—Commentary of Mādhavāchārya on Parāśara Smiṛiti.

P. G. S.—Pāraskara Gṛihyasūtra.
Rjt.—Rājataraṅgīṇī.
R. V.—Ṛigveda.
Sam. Nik.—Samyutta Nikāya.
S. Br.—Śatapatha Brāhmaṇa.
S. B. E.—Sacred Books of the East Series.
SCS.—Smṛitichandrikā, Saṃskārakāṇḍa.
SCV.—Smṛitichandrikā, Vyavahārakāṇḍa.
Ś. G. S.—Śānkhyāyana Gṛihyasūtra.
S. I. E. R.—South Indian Epigraphical Reports.
T. Ar.—Taittirīya Āraṇyaka.
T. Br.—Taittirīya Brāhamaṇa.
Thg.—Therīgāthā.
T. S.—Taittirīya Saṁhitā.
V. D. S.—Vasishṭha Dharmasūtra.
VMS.—Vīramitrodaya, Sanskāraprākaśa.
VMV.—Vīramitrodaya, Vyavahāraprākaśa.
Yaj.—Yājñavalkyasmṛiti.

TRANSLITERATION

The following are the main points to be noted in the scheme of transliteration followed in this work.

आ	ā	ई	ī	ऊ	ū
ऋ	ṛi	ए	e	ऐ	ai
ओ	o	औ	au	ङ्	ṅ
च्	ch	छ्	chh	ञ्	ñ
ट्	ṭ	ठ्	ṭh	ड्	ḍ
ढ्	ḍh	ण्	ṇ	श्	ś
ष्	sh	स्	s	*Visarga*	ḥ

Anusvāra

Current words like Brahmana and modern names like Shivaji, Tarabai, etc. are usually written without any diacritical marks.

CONTENTS

LIST OF PLATES

(BOUND AT THE END OF THE BOOK)

CHAPTER I

CHILDHOOD AND EDUCATION

One of the best ways to understand the spirit of a civilisation and to appreciate its excellences and realise its limitations is to study the history of the position and status of women in it. Civilisation is to a great extent the result of a society's capacity to control some of the strongest and most selfish impulses embedded in the human nature. No class of similar importance and extent as that of women was placed in the infancy of society in a position of such absolute dependence upon men, and the degree in which that dependence has been voluntarily modified and relaxed naturally serves as a rough test of the sense of justice and fairplay developed in a community. The marriage laws and customs enable us to realise whether men regarded women merely as market commodities or war prizes, or whether they had realised that the wife is after all her husband's valued partner whose cooperation was indispensable for happiness and success in family life. The rules about sex morality enable us to know the ethical tone of the society and ascertain how far men were prepared to be themselves judged by the standard they had set for women. The degree to which women were given a voice in the settlement of their marriages and the management of their households, and the extent to which their proprietary rights were recognised, illustate man's capacity to control the natural love of self, pelf, power and possession, which is so firmly implanted in every human heart. The sense of sympathy that is developed in a community can very well be tested by the treatment it metes out to the widow. The genuineness of its appreciation of the value of education can be ascertained by finding out whether its benefits were extended to the fair sex. The progress in fine arts like music and dancing depends a good deal on the facilities given to women for specialising in them. A study of their dress and ornaments gives us an idea of the wealth of a community and enables us to obtain a glimpse of its progress in trade, mining and metallurgy and the skill in inlaying, tailoring and embroidery.

The degree of freedom given to women to move about in society and to take part in its public life gives a good idea of the nature of its administration and enables us to know how far it had realised the difficult truth that women too have a contribution of their own to make to its development and progress. How far a religion stands for justice and fairplay and how far it has succeeded in exploding prejudices and shibboleths of a primitive age can be seen from the position it assigns to women in its ritual and theology. The nature of its philosophy can well be ascertained from the observations of its philosopher about the nature and worth of the fair sex.

The history of the position and status of women is therefore of vital importance to the student of Hindu civilisaton. The subject is a very wide and comprehensive one, for we shall have to ascertain not only the general estimate formed about women in the different periods of our long history, but its actual effects also upon the diverse spheres of their activities during the different stages of their life. The best way to begin our enquiry is to study the condition of women during their childhood and to find out the general arrangement made about their training and education. This will at once disclose to us the concern of society for women and the steps it was taking for properly starting them in life.

The history of Hindu civilisation can be taken back to prehistoric times. The data for some ef the subsequent centuries are still incomplete and unsatisfactory; nevertheless we can trace the development of women's position through the subsequent periods with a fair amount of confidence and reliability. We shall, therefore, begin our narrative in each chapter with the earliest possible period and bring it down to the present age, and conclude by indicating the lines on which further development should take place in future in view of the tendencies in the past and the needs of the present.

In ancient times in all patriarchal societies the birth of a girl was generally an unwelcome event. Almost everywhere the son was valued more than the daughter. He was a permanent economic asset of the family. He lived with his aged parents and did not migrate like the daughter to another family after the marriage. He perpetuated the name of his father's family. As he grew into adolescence and youth, he could offer valuable co-operation to his family, when it had either to defend itself or to attack an enemy, The daughter, on the other hand, had no fighting value whatever. It is no doubt true that women have potential military value: by giving birth to sons they contribute indirectly to the fighting strength and efficiency of their community. The primitive man, however, could not take such a long view of the situation. In actual fighting, he found the woman a handicap rather than a help. He therefore hardly ever welcomed the birth of a daughter. Sometimes he abandoned her after her birth; sometimes he even killed her. Details of these unfortunate practices can be gathered from standard works on sociology like Westermarck's *History of Human Marriage*.

The available evidence shows that in India too in early times the daughter was not as welcome as the son. The latter was preferred to the former even in the Indo-Iranian age.[1] The same was the case in the Vedic period. The *Atharvaveda* contains charms and rituals to ensure the birth of a son in preference to that of a daughter (III, 23; VI, 11). The latter's birth, however, was not a source of consternation to the family in the Vedic and Upanishadic ages. Nay, we find one of the early Upanishads recommending a certain ritual to a householder for ensuring the birth of a scholarly daughter.[2] It is true that this ritual did not become as popular as the Puṁsa-

1. Geieger, *Civilisation of the Eastern Iranians*, pp. 53-4.

2. अथ य इच्छेद् दुहिता मे पंडिता जायेत, तिलौदनौ पाचयित्वा अश्नीयातामिति। *Bṛih. Up*. IV. 4. 18. While commenting upon this passage, Saṅkara on doubt explains पांडित्यम् as गृहतंत्रविषयम् but that was because his age held that women were ineligible for Vedic studies.

vana one, prescribed for procuring the birth of a son; but it clearly shows that cultured parents were often as anxious for daughters as they were for sons. Some thinkers have even pointed out that a talented and well behaved daughter may be better than a son (*Sam. Nik.*, III 2, 6). In cultured circles such a daughter was regarded as the pride of the family.[1] In lower sections of society where the custom of the bride-price prevailed, the birth of a daughter must have been a welcome event; we have, however, no literature preserved reflecting their views.

The reasons why daughters were relatively less unpopular in ancient India during the early centuries are not difficult to understand. They could be initiated in Vedic studies and were entitled to offer sacrifices to gods; the son was not absolutely necessary for this purpose. The marriage of the daughter was not a difficult problem; it was often solved by the daughter herself. The dread of a possible widowhood did not very much weigh upon the mind of parents; for, as will be shown later, levirate and remarriage were allowed by society and were fairly common.

As time passed on, the above circumstances gradually changed. The importance of ancestor-worship increased and sons alone were regarded as eligible for offering oblations to the manes; daughters could not perform this very important religious duty. Child marriage came into vogue from about the beginning of the Christian era, and soon thereafter both levirate (*niyoga*) and widow remarriage were prohibited. Inter-caste marriages began to be disapproved by society; and there came into existence hundreds of sub-castes all insisting upon mutual exogamy. The field of choice for the selection of a suitable son-in-law thus became very narrow, intensifying thereby the anxiety of the daughter's father about the selection of a proper bridegroom. If a cruel fate inflicted widowhood upon the daughter, the calamity would break the

1. कन्येयं कुलजीवितम् । *Kumārasambhava*, VI, 63.

parent's heart. Remarriage being no longer possible, parents had to bear the heart-rending pain of seeing their daughter wasting herself in an interminable widowhood. The growing prevalence of the Satī custom from about the 5th century A.D. added to the poignancy of the grief; parents had often to pass through the terrible ordeal of seeing their daughters burning themselves alive on the funeral pyres of their husbands. To become a daughter's parent thus became a source of endless worry and misery.

As a natural consequence of the above circumstances, in the literature belonging to the later periods of Hindu civilisation passages about the undesirability of the birth of daughters become more numerous. In the Brāhmaṇa literature there is one passage observing that while the son is the hope of the family, the daughter is a source of trouble to it.[1] A similar idea occurs in the *Mahābhāratā* also.[2] The *Rāmāyaṇa* tells us that when Sitā came of age and her marriage had to be arranged her father's anxiety became as intense as that of a poor man, who suddenly loses all his little money.[3] The epic goes on to observe that a daughter's father, even if occupying a position as exalted as that of the king of gods, has to put up with insults not only from his equals but also from his inferiors.[4] Even when he succeeds in making a very good selection of the son-in-law, his anxiety does not terminate; he has to wait anxiously to find out whether the marriage will eventually be a happy one.[5] Under these circusmtances it was but natural that an 11th century writer should have observed that there is a world of

1. सखा ह जाया कृपणंहि दुहिताज्योतिर्हि पुत्रः परमे व्योमन् । *A.Br.*VII, 18.

2. आत्मा पुत्रः सखी भार्या कृच्छ्रं तु दुहिता नृणाम् । I, 173, 10.

3. पतिसंयोगसुलभं वयो दृष्ट्वा तु मे पिता ।
चिन्तामभ्यगमद्दीनो वित्तनाशादिवाधनः ।

4. सदृशाच्चापकृष्टाच्च लोके कन्यापिता जनात् ।
प्रधर्षणमवाप्नोति शक्रेणापि समो भुवि ॥ II, 119, 35-6.

5. पुत्रीति जाता महतीह चिन्ता कस्मै प्रदेयेति महान्वितर्कः ।
दत्त्वा सुखं प्राप्स्यति वा न वेति कन्यापितृत्वं खलु नाम कष्टम् ॥
Pañchatantra, Mitrabheda 5.

difference between the son and the daughter; the former is bliss itself incarnate, the latter is the root of misery.[1] It is also possible that the poignant pain felt by the parents at the time of their first separation from their daughter after her marriage may be also partly responsible for the general dislike for a daughter.[2]

It will be thus seen that if there are passages in later literature showing that the birth of a daughter was unwelcome, the reason was not so much the hatred of her sex as the all-engrossing anxiety to see that she was well placed in life and enabled to lead it in comfort and happiness. It has further to be pointed out that the prevailing view that the daughter is less desirable than the son, though popular, was not accepted by all social thinkers. There were some among them who realised that it was causing great harm to society and felt that it ought to be counteracted. They therefore championed the daughter's cause and pointed out that patricides have been a monopoly of the male sex; no father is ever known to have been killed by a daughter either to history or to legend. There are cases on record where daughters like Kuntī[3] and Lopāmudrā[4] have saved their parents from dire calamities. In marriage it is the daughter, and not the son, who enables the father to get the great merit of *prithvī-dāna* or the gift of the earth. She is thus really better than the son. One should not be, therefore, elated by the birth of a son and depressed by the advent of a daughter (*Kathāsaritsāgara*, 28, 27 ff.) To a cul-

१. शोककन्दः क्व कन्या हि क्वनन्दः कायवान्सुतः । *Kss.* 28, 6.

२. केनापि कृता धर्म्यानाभिमता मे स्थितिरियं यदङ्गभूतानि अंकलालितानि अपरित्याज्यान्यपत्यानि अकांड एवागत्य असंस्तुतैर्नीयन्ते । *Harshacharit*, IV.

3. Kunti's father, king Kuntibhoja, had become very nervous when the angry sage Durvāsas came to stay with him as his guest; Kuntī, however, uudertook the onerous responsibility of attending upon the guest and keeping him in good humour. She performed her task with remarkable success. *Mbh.* III, 304.

4. In order to save the family from the ire of Agastya, Lopāmudrā consented to marry the sage, fully conscious of her ability to persuade him in course of time to lead the normal life of royal comfort. *Ibid.* III. 59.

tured parent both should be equally welcome. There can be no doubt that these arguments were definitely advanced to counteract the harm that was done by the prevailing tendency to depreciate the birth of a daughter. Owing, however, to the circumstances above described, they did not carry the day.

It must be, however, added that the feeling of dejection and dissatisfaction at the birth of a daughter was a fleeting one; it did not lead to female infanticide in ancient India. There are no references to this evil custom in the Vedic, epic or classical literature. Weber had wrongly concluded that a passage in the Yajurveda referred to the custom of the exposure of new-born daughters. It is, however, now generally admitted by Indian and European scholars that Weber's interpretation of the passage in question is wrong. It will appear from the passage and its translation given below[2] that it merely refers to the traditional habit of Hindu midwives of keeping the child aside on the ground if it was a daughter, and of lifting it up in joy if it was a son. The passage has no reference to the abandonment of unawanted daughters. How a mistake in translation sometimes gives rise to an unfounded theory would become clear from the present instance.

If female infanticide had at all been practised, it must have been confined to a very small section of society. If the evil had been fairly common, Smṛiti writers would certainly have denounced it very vehemently. When we note how eloquent they grow in condemning the conduct of a father who would accept bride-price for his daughter in marriage, we cannot but

1. In the story of the demon Baka, the father while declining to sacrifice his daughter to save himself or his son, says:
मन्यंते केचिदधिकं स्नेहं पुत्रे पितुर्नराः ।
कन्यायां चैव तु पुनर्मम तुल्यौ उभौ मतौ ॥ *Mbh.*, I. 145. 36.

2. Cf. अवभृथमवयन्ति । परा स्थालीरस्यन्ति । उद्वायव्यानि हरन्ति । तस्मात्स्त्रियं जातां परास्यन्ति उत्पुमांसं हरन्ति । *T. S.* VI, 5, 10; *M. S.*, IV, 6, 4.

"They go to the final bath; they deposit pots (called *sthālī*; the woad being feminine in gender), but lift up vesssels for Vāyu (*aalled graha*, the word being masculine in gender); therefore they keep aside a daughter at birth, a son they lift up."

conclude that they would have consigned to the most dreadful hell those parents who were guilty of exposing their daughters at birth, because they were unwelcome. Smṛiti writers regard the destruction of an embryo as the most heinous crime; the murder of a child born alive could not have escaped their thundering denunciation.

The custom of infanticide of girls crept into some sections of Hindu society during the medieval period. We have seen above that at this time the daughter was regarded as the root of all misery and the source of unending trouble by the average householder. The temptation to do away with her became too irresistible in some uncultured sections of society. The female infanticide, however, never obtained a footing in cultured families. At the advent of the British rule the custom seems to have prevailed to a slight extent in some lower sections of society, but its extent has been very much exaggerated due to the prejudiced, if not malicious, reports of some foreign writers. That the evil was confined to a microscopic minority in society will become abundantly clear when we note how the census figures show that the females between the age period I-5 have exceeded the males of the same age. This will become clear from the following table:—

Age distribution of 10,000 of each sex in India.

Year	No. of boys under 5	No. of girls under 5
1931	1458	1665
1921	1202	1306
1911	1327	1433
1901	1254	1339
1891	1409	1527

The sex distribution per thousand of children under 5 years of age was 489 males to 511 females in 1941 and 500 males to 500 females in 1951.

Statistics therefore convincingly demonstrate that even in the 19th century the infanticide of girls must have been a very very rare practice ; it has now completely disappeared.

Let us now resume the story of the fortune of the daughter in ancient India. We have already seen how the passages, showing that the birth of a daughter was an unwelcome event, were a natural result of the greater anxiety which the parents felt for her well-being and happiness. Once the temporary feeling of disappointment was over, the family took as keen an interest in the daughter as it did in the son. On his return from a journey the father used to recite a prayer (*mantra*) for the welfare of his daughter just with the same solicitude as he did for the happiness of his son (*Āp. G. S.*, XV, 12-3). Stories in Sanskrit dramas and novels show that daughters received from their parents and other relations the same affectionate treatment as sons. Nay, some of them like Devayānī were too much fondled and became spoilt children. Goddess of Fortune was regarded as residing in the person of the unmarried daughter; so she, and not the unmarried boy, was regarded as an object of good men. Unmarried girls were, therefore, among the persons selected to receive Rāma on his return to Ayodhyā from his long exile and to offer him the coronation ablution (*abhisheka*). It is interesting to note that Rāma receives this important religious bath first at the hands of unmarried girls, and then of his trusted generals and ministers(*Rāmāyaṇa*, VI, 131, 38 and 61).

To impart education to children and to help them in settling in life are the two main duties of parents. Both of them were well discharged with reference to the daughter for several centuries in ancient India. Let us first consider the case of education.

Down to about the 3rd century B. C. girls could remain unmarried till the age of 16; this will be shown in the next chapter. The period before marriage was utilised for imparting education to them. Till about the beginning of the Christian era *Upanayana* or the ceremonial initiation into Vedic studies was

1 नित्यं निवसते लक्ष्मीः कन्यकासु प्रतिष्ठिता । *Mbh*, XIII, 11,14 (B.) See also *Vishṇusmriti*, 99,4.

as common in the case of girls as it was in the case of boys; this will be shown in Chapter VII. The initiation ceremony was followed by a period of discipline and education, which was regarded as very essential to secure a suitable match. The *Atharvaveda* observes that a maiden can succeed in her marriage only if she has been properly trained during the period of studentship (*brahmacharya*).[1] That women are, like Śūdras, ineligible for Vedic studies is the view of a later age; in prehistoric times lady poets themselves were composing hymns, some of which were destined to be included even in the Vedic Saṁhitās. According to the orthodox tradition itself as recorded in the *Sarvānukramaṇikā*, there are as many as twenty women among the 'seers' or authors of *Ṛigveda.* Some of these may have been mythical personages; but internal evidence shows that Lopāmudrā, Viśvavārā, Sikatā Nivāvari and Ghoshā, the authors of the *Ṛigveda* 1. 179, V. 28, VIII. 91, IX. 81. 11-20, and X. 39 and 40 respectively, were women in flesh and blood, who once lived in Hindu society. The authors of X. 145 and 159 are undoubtedly ladies, though it may be doubted whether their real names were Indrāṇī and Śachī, as recorded by tradition. Among the authors and scholars to whose memory a dialy tribute of respect is enjoined to be paid at the time of *brahmayajña*, a few ladies also are seen to figure; they are Sulabhā Maitreyī, Vaḍavā Prāthiteyī, and Gārgi Vāchaknavī (*Āś. G. S.*, III, 4,4). These ladies must have made real contributions to the advance of scholarship; otherwise their names would not have been recommended for daily remembrance by posterity for all time to come. It is a great pity that we should know nothing about these lady scholars except their names; their works have been all lost, probably for ever.

Women students were divided into two classes, *Brahmavādinīs* and *Sadyodvāhās*. The former were lifelong students of theology and philosophy; the latter used to prosecute their studies till their marriage at the age of 15 or 16. During the eight or

1. ब्रह्मचर्येण कन्यानं युवाविन्दते पतिम् । XI, 5, 18.

nine years that were thus available to them for study, they used to learn by heart the Vedic hymns prescribed for the daily and periodical prayers and for those rituals and sacraments in which they had to take an active part after their marriage. There is ample evidence to show that, like men, women also used to offer regularly their Vedic prayers both morning and evening. For instance, in more than one place in the *Rāmāyaṇa* Sītā is described as offering her daily Vedic prayers.[1] When writing came into general vogue, girls were initiated into the three R's as a matter of course.

Brahmavādinīs used to aim at a very high excellence in scholarship. Down to about the 4th century B. C. Vedic and philosophical studies attracted the main attention of society. We therefore find ladies also naturally cultivating these subjects with great devotion and enthusiasm. Besides studying the Vedas, many of them used to specialise in Pūrvamīmānsā, which discussed the diverse problems connected with Vedic sacrifices. This science is a very dry and difficult one, perhaps even more abstruse than mathematics; but still a very large number of ladies used to take deep interest in it. A theologian named Kāśakṛitsana had composed a work on Mīmānsā called Kāśakṛitsnī; lady scholars, who used to specialise in it, were designated as Kāśakṛitsnās (*Mahābhāshya*, IV, 1, 14; 3, 155). If lady scholars in such a technical branch of study were so numerous as necessitate the coining of a special term to designate them, is it not reasonable to conclude that the number of women, who used to receive general education, must have been fairly large ?

When the reaction against the Vedic sacrificial religion gave a stimulus to philosophical speculations at about 800 B. C., lady scholars did not lag behind in taking an active interest in the new movement. Yājñavalkya's wife Maitreyī belonged to this class. She was more interested in finding out the way to

1. *E.g.* संध्याकालमनाः श्यामा ध्रुवमेष्यति जानकी ।
नदीं चेमां शुभजला संध्यार्थं वरवर्णिनी ॥ V. 15, 48.

immortality than in setting new fashions in dress and ornaments[1]. In the philosophical tournament held under the auspices of king Janaka of Videha, the subtlest philosophical questions were initiated for discussion by the lady philosopher Gārgī, who had the honour to be the spokesman of the distinguished philosophers at the court. She launched her attack on Yājñavalkya, the newly arrived philosopher, with an admirable coolness and confidence. 'Just as an experienced archer', says she, 'would get ready to attack his enemy with two piercing arrows kept at hand, so I assail you with two test questions. Answer them if you can.' The topics of her enquiry were so abstruse and esoteric in character, that Yājñavalkya declined to discuss them in public. The searching cross-examination of Yājñavalkya by Gārgī shows that she was a dialectician and philosopher of a high order (*Br. Up.*, III, 6 and 8). Ātreyī was another lady student of Vedānta; she was reading under the sages Vālmīki and Agastya. Some of these lady philosophers used to remain unmarried throughout the life in order to carry on their spiritual experiments unhampered.

The admission of women to the Buddhist Order gave a great impetus to the cause of female education among the ladies in commerical and aristocratic families. Like the *Brahmavādinīs* in Brahmanical circles, several ladies in Buddhist families used to lead a life of celibacy with the aim of understanding and following the eternal truths of religion and philosophy. Some of them like Saṅghamitrā went even to foreign countries like Ceylon and became famous there as teachers of the Holy Scriptures. Among the authoresses of the *Therīgāthā*, who were all believed to have obtained the salvation, 32 were unmarried women and 10 married ones. Among the former Subhā, Anopamā and Sumedhā belonged to rich families and are said to have been wooed by princes and rich merchants. When a large percentage of girls were leading a life of celibacy,

1. येनाहं नामता स्यां किं तेन (अतिप्रभूतेनापि वित्तेन) कुर्यामिति ।

Br. Up., II, 4.

in pursuit of religion and philosophy, it is but natural to presume that the general average of intelligence and education among them must have been high.

According to the Jain tradition, Jayantī, a daughter of king Sahasrānīka of Kauśāmbī, remained unmarried and received ordination at the hand of Mahavīra after being convinced by him in discussion.[1] A Jātaka refers to the story of a Jain father having four clever daughters touring about in the country and challenging all and sundry for a debate on philosophical matters.[2]

Many educated women used to follow teaching career either out of love or out of necessity. Sanskrit language found it necessary to coin a special word in order to distinguish them from wives of teachers. The latter, who were not necessarily scholars, were called Upādhyāyānīs, but women who were themselves teachers, were called Upādhyāyās. Women teachers must have been fairly numerous in society; otherwise a new term would not have been coined to designate them. It may be pointed out that the tradition of lady scholars is known to Purāṇas as well; the *Bhāgavata*, for instance, refers to two daughters of Dākshāyaṇa as experts in theology and philosophy.[3]

The modern reader, on being told that female education was fairly widespread, will naturally enquire whether there was a system of co-education, or whether lady students were taught separately. The historian has to confess that in the present state of our knowledge this question is difficult to answer. In the Vedic age education was mostly centred in the family; brothers, sisters and cousins probably studied together under the family elders. Subsequently, when specialisation became the order of the day, students had to leave

1. *Bhagavatisūtra*, Gujarati edition, Vol. III, p. 257.
2. No. 301.
3. तेभ्यो दधार द्वे कन्ये वयुनां धारिणीं स्वधा ।
उभे ते ब्रह्मवादिन्यौ ज्ञानविज्ञानपारगे ॥ IV. 1. 64.

their homes and often to go to distant places to study under celebrated teachers. When there were competent lady teachers (*āchāryās*) available, parents must have naturally preferred to send their daughters to read under them. But the number of these could not have been very large. In technical subjects like theology, philosophy and medicine most of the experts were usually males, and advanced lady students used to go to them for their studies. This is clear from the example of Ātreyī in the *Uttararāmacharita*, who was reading under Vālmīkī along with Lava and Kuśa, the sons of Rāma. The stories of Kahoda and Sujātā, Ruru and Pramadvarā, narrated in the Purāṇas, would also point to co-education and to love-marriages sometimes resulting from it. But the number of lady students going to distant places for higher education was not large; the Jātakas, for instance, do not refer to lady students going to Takshaśilā for education. It would however seem that co-education in higher studies was not unknown even in the 8th century A. D., for Bhavabhūti in his *Mālatīmādhava* represents Kāmandakī as being educated along with Bhūrivasu[1] and Devarāta. The percentage of girls receiving co-education was however not large. Usually, ordinary girls who did not go in for higher education were educated in their own families by their fathers, uncles or brothers or by local lady teachers. It has to be remembered that, down to the 4th century A. D., there were no public schools even for boys. Writers like Hārīta lay down that girls should be usually taught at home by their male relations.[2] They probably refer to the practice of about the 5th century B. C. We should not forget that higher female education was generally confined to cultured and well-to-do families.

1. अयि किं न वेत्सि यदेकत्र नो विद्यापरिग्रहाय नानादिगन्तवासिनां साहचर्यमासीत् । Act 1.

2. द्विविधाः स्त्रियो ब्रह्मवादिन्यः सद्योद्वाहाश्च । तत्र ब्रह्मवादिनीनामग्नीन्धनं वेदाध्ययनं स्वगृहे च भैक्षचर्येति । सद्योवधूनां तूपस्थिते विवाहे कथंचिदुपनयनमात्रं कृत्वा विवाहः कार्यः । Quoted in *VMS*, p. 402.

It is not easy to determine the extent of education among women from the Vedic to the Sūtra period (down to *c.* 300 B.C.). We have seen how parents were often anxious to have scholarly daughters born in their families; ordinary well-to-do families could hardly have neglected the education of girls. Upanayana ritual was also obligatory for them; this must have ensured the imparting of a certain amount of Vedic and literary education to all the girls in the Brāhmaṇa, Kshatriya and Vaishya classes. The custom of child marriage had also not yet become common. We may therefore conclude that most of the girl in the well-to-do families used to be given a fair amount of education down to *c.* 300 B. C.

Grown up and educated girls naturally played an important part in the management of their parent's households. The important duty of receiving guests and looking after their comforts was usually entrusted to them. This work solely devolved upon them when their parents were out of station. We find Śakuntalā and Kuntī discharging this function in their father's households before their marriage. The latter was quite an adept in this task; she could extort admiration even from such a notoriously irascible guest as Durvāsas, who, being pleased with her attention and devotion, gave her a valuable boon unasked.

Our sources enable us to have only a glimpse of the recreations of girls during the Vedic and epic periods. Music and dancing formed the principal indoor games. Public and dramatic concerts were often organised and girls used to go out to see them along with their elders or lovers.[1] In fashionable circles game with the ball (*kandukarīdā*) seems to have been the chief out-door physical exercise. Śāntā and Kuntī are, for instance, represented as spending their leisure hours in this game in the *Mahābhārata* (V, 93, 63; III, 112, 16). Players can so regulate this game as to have just the amount of exercise they want. The *Rāmāyaṇa* represents girls as going in the

1. *Kamasutra*, III, 1.

evening to gardens for playing and talking with their friends;[1] but this was probably possible only in towns and cities. We have some references to girls going out to swim[2] as well, it is not, however, easy to say what percentage of girls knew this very useful art. Girls used to play a number of courtyard games like 'hide and seek' and 'run and catch', which are graphically described in the *Kāmasūtra* (III, 3). These gave very good physical exercise to the players and were well calculated to help their general development and give a suppleness to their limbs. Though not very often mentioned in literature, these games have been very popular with all classes of society since very early times. They were, however, played usually before the marriage.

The cause of women's education suffered a good deal after *c.* 300 B. C. on account of the new fashion of child marriage that then began to come into vogue. It will be shown in the next chapter how on account of a number of causes the marriageable age of girls began to be gradually lowered in successive centuries. By the beginning of the Christian era pre-puberty marriages became the order of the day. Naturally this meant a serious handicap to advanced studies, which could not be obviously finished before the ages of 12 or 13, which was the new marriageable age. Even the initiation ritual (*Upanayana saṁskāra*), so necessary for endowing woman with the proper Aryan status, was first reduced to a mere formality and then dropped out altogether.[3] This put an end to their Vedic education. They became unable to recite even the hymns of daily prayer. It is no wonder that they should have lost the status of the regenerate classes (*devijas*); like the Śūdras they were in course of time naturally regarded as

1. नाराजके जनपदे उद्यानानि समागताः ।
सायाह्ने क्रीडितुं यान्ति कुमार्यो हेमभूषिताः ॥ II. 67. 13

2. जलक्रीडायां तद्दूरतोऽप्सु निमग्नः समीपमागत्वा स्पृष्ट्वा चैनां तत्रैवोन्मज्जेत् ॥ *Kāmasūtra* III. 4. 6.

3. See Chap. VII for detailed evidence in this connection

unfit for reciting or even hearing Vedic prayers. By about the 8th or 9th entury A.D. the marriageable age of girls was further lowered to 9 or 10; this gave practically a death-blow to any education worth the name. No doubt two or three years were still available, when some primary education could have been imparted, but both the girls and their guardians used to devote their attention during this period more to the problem of marriage than to that of education.

We have seen above how the admission of women into the order had given an indirect encouragement to the cause of female education in the pre-Mauryan period. Nuns continued to figure in the Buddhist monastic life down to the 3rd. century A. D., but do not seem to have distinguished themselves as authoresses or preachers. Nunneries went out of vogue in Buddhism from about the 4th century A. D.; neither Buddhist nuns nor scholars nor authoresses are mentioned either by Fa Hien or by Yuan Chuang, who have given a detailed account of Buddhism of India in their times. Female education therefore received no helping hand from Buddhism during the period 300 B. C. to 800 A. D.. It is interesting to note that in modern Burma and Ceylon, nunneries do not impart education to girls as monasteries do to boys.

During the first millenium of the Christian era there undoubtedly flourished in Hindu society a few famous lady scholars and poetesses. Among the authors from whose works selections have been made by Hāla in his anthology of Mahārāshṭrī poems (*Gāthāsaptaśatī*), there are seven poetesses, their names being Revā, Rohā, Mādhavī, Anulakshmī, Pahaī, Vaddhavahī and Śaśiprabhā. Some Sanskrit anthologies also have preserved the memory of a few distinguished poetesses, who appear to have composed poetry of a really high order. Śīlabhaṭṭārikā, we learn, was famous for her easy and graceful style, noted for a harmonious synthesis of sense and sound. Devī was a well-known poetess of Gujarat, who continued to enchant her readers on earth even when she had herself gone to heaven. Vijayāṅkā's fame was second only to that of Kālidāsa. She seems to have attained a really high position among Sanskrit writers, for a distinguished critic and poet like Rājaśekhara compares her to goddess Sarasvatī herself. Nature was not very kind to this gifted lady, because it had chosen to give her a blue-black complexion. Rājaśekhara boldly declares that even masters of Sanskrit verse were clearly in the wrong when they declared that Sarasvatī, the goddess of learning, was all fair in complexion. For in that case, how could poetess Vijayāṅkā, the incarnation of that goddess, have had a complexion resembling the blue, rather than the white lotus ?[1] This is of course all a play of poetic fancy, but it proves beyond all doubt that Vijayāṅkā was a celebrated poetess. Rājaśekhara's wife, a Kshatriya by caste, was a good literary critic and poetess. The recently published drama *Kaumudīmahotsava*, whose central theme is an important political revolution at Paṭalīputra, has proceeded from the pen of a lady courtier; it shows that cultured ladies used to take a good deal of interest in the complications of contemporary history and politics. Mārulā, Morikā and Subhadrā are other poetesses referred to in Sanskrit anthologies.[2] The umpire in the fateful controversy between Śaṅkarāchārya and

1. शब्दार्थयोः समो गुंफः पांचाली वृत्तिरिष्यते।
शीलभट्टारिकावाचि बाणोक्तिषु च या सदा ॥
सूक्तीनां स्मरकेलीनां कलानां च विलासभूः।
प्रभुर्देवी कवी लाटी गतापि हृदि तिष्ठति ॥
सरस्वतीव कर्णाटी विजयांका जयत्यसौ।
या वैदर्भगिरां वासः कालिदासादनन्तरम् ॥
नीलोत्पलदलश्यामां विजयांकामजानता।
वृथैव दण्डिनाप्युक्तं सर्वशुक्ला सरस्वती ॥

These verses are attributed to Rajaśekhara in the *Suktimuktāvalī*.

2. शीलाविद्यामारुलामोरिकाद्याः काव्यं कर्तुं संति विज्ञाः स्त्रियोऽपि।
शारङ्गधरपद्धति

पार्थस्य मनसि स्थानं लेभे खलु सुभद्रया।
कवीनां च वचोवृत्तिचातुर्येण सुभद्रया ॥ काव्यमीमांसा।

It is likely that Śilā and Vidyā in the first quotation are identical with Śilabhaṭṭārikā and Vijayaṅkā, mentioned earlier above.

Maṇḍanamiśra was the latter's wife.[1] Obviously she must have been very well grounded in literature, philosophy and theology; otherwise she would not have been accepted as the sole judge in this momentous controversy. Some women were attracted by medical studies also; the majority of these, like our lady doctors to-day, specialised in women's diseases. A treatise on this subject written by a lady doctor, whose name appears as Rūsā in the Arabic garb, was translated in the eighth century A. D. into Arabic at the order of Khalifa Harun.[2] Obviously the most authoritative works on the subject seem to have been written by lady doctors.

Unfortunately we do not know anything about the status and family circumstances of the above lady poets, philosophers and doctors. Very probably some of them belonged to rich and cultured families, which could make special arrangements for girls' education even after their marriage, and some to Kshatriya circles, where the custom of child marriage did not take root for a long time even after it had become well established in the rest of society. In the 9th century A. D., higher education of women was confined to royal, official, rich and well-to-do families and to the class of dancing girls.[3] It may be pointed out that most of the heroines of Sanskrit dramas written in this period, who are represented as fairly educated, belong to the classes mentioned above.

Cultured and rich families were naturally few in society. They had sufficient resources to enable them to employ special teachers like Bṛihannaḍā, Gaṇadāsa and Haradatta for their daughter's education. Ordinary families, however, could not afford to do this and their daughters, who had to be married

1. विधाय भार्यां विदुषीं सदस्यां विधीयतां वादकथा सुधीन्द्र ॥
Sankaradigvijaya, VIII. 51.

2. Nadvi, *Arab aur Bharat ke Sambandha*, p. 122.

3. पुरुषवद्योषितोऽपि कवीभवेयुः । श्रूयन्ते दृश्यन्ते च राजपुत्र्यो महामात्रदुहितरो गणिकाः कौटुम्बिकभार्याश्च शास्त्रप्रहितबुद्धयः कवयश्च ।
Kāvyamīmānsā, p. 53.

at this time at about the age of 10 or 11, could therefore hardly receive any education. Asahāya, a commentator on *Nāradasmṛiti* who flourished in the 8th century A. D., justifies the theory of the tutelage of women on the ground that their intellect is not developed like that of men on account of their not having the benefit of proper training and education.[1] This observation makes it clear that education had become fairly rare among women in general in the 8th century A. D. It is hazardous to make any statement about the exact extent of literacy among women at about 1000 A.D., for we have no data like modern census reports to guide us. Literacy among men at this time was about 30 per cent,[2] that among women could not have very probably been more than 10 per cent.

The cultivation of fine arts like music, dancing and painting was encouraged in the case of girls since very early times. Musical recitation of the Sāma hymns was originally the special function of ladies.[3] It is clear that they must be specialising in music in the early Vedic period; otherwise this important duty would not have been assigned to them. Some legends in the Vedic literature make caustic references to women's partiality to music. Once Devas and Asuras both wanted to win over the Goddess of Speech; gods succeeded in their effort because they were clever enough to realise that the best way to achieve their object was to sing and dance before her. The author of the legend cannot resist the temptation of observing that women can be easily won over by one who sings melodiously and dances gracefully before them (*Ś. Br.*, III, 2, 4, 6).

In the post-Vedic period also society went on encouraging music and dancing in the case of girls. Among the arts which ladies in cultured families were expected to cultivate, the *Kāmasūtra* assigns the most prominent place to dancing and

1. शास्त्राध्ययनानधिकारित्वात् शास्त्रमात्रोपजीविधर्माधर्मज्ञानाभावा-दस्वातंत्र्यम् । On *Nāradasmṛiti*, X 30.

2. Altekar, *Education in Ancient India*, (4th edi.), pp. 213-4.

3. पत्नीकर्मैव वै तेऽत्र कुर्वन्ति यदुद्गातारः ।

S. Br., XIV, 3, 1, 35

music, both vocal and instrumental (1,3,16). Other arts which they were recommended to master were painting, gardening, garland-making, toy-making, house decorations, etc. (*Ibid.* 1, 3, 1). Heroines of Sanskrit dramas and poems like Priyadarśikā, Śakuntalā and Kādmbarī written during the first millennium of the Christian era, are well versed in most of these arts.[1] Not infrequently, maidens used to give a dance in the court before a select audience without incurring thereby any social opprobrium.[1] The dance teacher was a regular officer in the royal court and some queens like Lokamahādevī are known to have been experts in fine arts.[2] It is clear that higher sections of society used to take all possible care to develop the aesthetic sense of girls.

Girls in ruling families used to receive some military and administrative training also. If such were not the case, dowager queens like Nayanikā of the Sātavāhana dynasty (2nd. century B. C.), Prabhāvatī Guptā of the Vākāṭaka family (4th century A. D.), Vijayabhaṭṭārikā of the Chālukya house (7th century A.D.) and Sugandhā and Diddā of Kashmir (10th century A. D.) could not have successfully administered extensive kingdoms during the minority of their sons. It will be shown in chapter VI that in the Chālukya administration (*c.* 980-1160 A. D.), queen governors and officers were quite common. The due discharge of these administrative duties presupposed a good training on proper lines. In ordinary Kshatriya families ladies used to receive a fairly good amount of military training. Women guards of kings, referred to in dramas, belonged to this class; they were usually experts in the use of the bow and the sword. South Indian inscrip-

1. Cf. एवमतिक्रान्ते शैशवे वयसि पितुर्नियोगात्प्राप्तं नैपुण्यं पुण्यकर्मारंभेषु जाता प्रवीणा वीणासु निराकुला कुलाचारेषु कुशला शलाकालेख्येषु प्रबुद्धा प्रबंधालोचनषु चातुरानाथजनविचिकित्सासु । *Nalachampu*, III.. गीतनृत्यवाद्यादिषु विशिष्टकन्यकोचितं सर्वं शिक्षयित्वा ।

Priyadarśikā, I, p. 10.

2. *S. I. I.*, IX. I, p. 273.
3. Stenzler, *Ocean of Stories*, IX, p. xiv.

tions of the medieval period disclose the existence of many Kshatriya heroines defending their hearths and homes in times of danger. Women from Karnatak seem to have led the way in this matter. A heroine from Mysore is known to have died in a village affray at Siddhanhalli in 1041 A. D. In 1264. A.D. another Karnatak heroine was honoured by the government of the day with the reward of a nose jewel in recognition of her bravery in overpowering a dacoit. A Nilgund inscription records a military expedition led by a feudatory queen. In 1446 a Mysore heroine died in Shikoga Taluka fighting to avenge the murder of her father.[1]

It is quite well known that Rajput princesses were adepts in the use of the sword and the spear. They could lead the armies and direct the government in the hour of need. Kūrmādevī, a queen of king Sāmarasī, took over the administration of her kingdom on her husband's death and repulsed the attacks of Kutub-ud-Din. Javāhirdevī, a queen of king Saṅgā, died fighting at the head of her army, while defending Chitor after her husband's death. Rajput history is full of such instances and they need not be all enumerated here.

This tradition of giving military training to girls continued in the Maratha royal families, which were ruling over a considerable part of India during the 17th and 18th centuries. Rani Bhimābāī, the daughter of Yeshwantrao Holkar, told Sir John Malcolm that it was an incumbent duty on a Maratha princess to lead her troops in person, when there was no husband or son to do so. Tārābāī, the founder of Kolhapur state, used to lead her army and direct her government. The example of queen Lakshmībāī of Jhansi, who excited the admiration even of her opponents by her remarkable bravery and sound generalship, is well known. The late princess Kamalābāī Scindia, the sister of the present Maharaja of Gwalior, was an adept in all military excercises. Her father was but carrying out the old Maratha tradition when he laid down detailed directions in his

1. See *S. I. E. R.*, for 1921, No. 73; *E. C.*, I, No. 75, *A. S. R.*, for 1928-9, p. 117, *E. C.* Vol. VII, Shikarpur No. 2.

will in this connection.

Could women become economically independent as a result of their training ? Those who followed the medical or the teaching line could of course become economically self-reliant. The same was the case with singers and dancers. For ordinary women spinning and weaving were of great help in times of difficulty. Textile industry was a very important and prosperous one in India down to 1850 A. D. It was organised and conducted mainly as a cottage industry and so it afforded good scope to women in financial distress. In early Buddhist literature (*c.* 300 B. C.), we come across ladies assuring their dying husbands that they need not worry about the financial future of their families;[1] for they could earn the necessary income by spinning and weaving cotton and woollen yarn and piece goods. The *Arthaśāstra* of Kauṭilya lays down that the state should provide special facilities to destitute women to enable them to earn a living by spinning.[2] From medieval commentators we learn that spinning continued to be the mainstay of poor widows at that time as well.[3] It may be pointed out that cloth was much costlier in ancient and medieval India than what it is to-day; Indian fabrics were beside in great demand throughout the three continents down to the beginning of the last century.[4] Women in distress, who resorted to spinning as a means of maintenance, had therefore ample scope for work and got fair wages.

Let us now survey the state of female education during the last 700 years. During the Muslim rule the percentage of literacy among Hindu women went further down with a great rapidity. Rich and cultured families were as a rule ruined

1. कुसलाहं गहपति कप्पासं कंतितु वेणिमोलिखितुं सक्काहं गहपति तवच्चयन दारके पोसितुम्। *Ang. Ni.*, III, p. 293.

2. याश्चानिष्कासिन्यः प्रोषितविधवा न्यंगाः कन्यका वा आत्मानं बिभृयुः ताः सोपग्रहं (कर्तन) कर्म कारयितव्याः। *Arthaśāstra*, II, 23.

3. मृतपत्निकाया अनपत्याया असति भर्तृधनादौ दायिके च कर्तनादिना। केनचिदुपायेन जीवन्त्याः। Medhātithi on *Manu*, V, 157.

4. Moreland, *India at the Death of Akbar* p. 179.

by the new political revolution; they were no longer in a position to make special arrangements for the education of their daughters. Some new Hindu families also no doubt rose to eminence with the rise of Islam, but their number was generally small and they did not, as a rule, possess sufficient culture to induce them to take active steps for the fostering of education among the girls of their households. The daughters in Rajput, Nair and Zamindar families could read and write; the same was the case with Jain nuns, who were generally in a position to read their own scriptures. These, however, were exceptional cases. Society had a general prejudice against female education; it was believed that a girl taught to read and write would become a widow[1]. Ordinarily only prostitutes and dancing girls could read and write. The decline of literacy among women was so marked and rapid that by the beginning of the 19th century hardly one woman in a hundred could read in Madras and Mālwā. In the former province in 1826 A. D. only 1,023 girls were attending schools as against 1,57,664 boys. According to the then population of the Presidency the percentage[2] of girls receiving some kind of education was only $\frac{1}{2}$. It may, therefore, be stated that at the advent of the British rule female education had practically disappeared from Hindu community. Nay, it was regarded as a source of moral danger, if not as an actual vice, since only dancing girls could normally read and write. In their families the old tradition to teach reading and writing to the new generation was continued.

The cultivation of the fine arts also declined during this period. Music teachers were usually men not very famous for high character, and Hindu families were not rich enough to engage them. By the beginning of the 19th century singing, dancing and writing were regarded as achievements fit only for the class of dancing girls. Ladies of orthodox families would have been shocked, if a report had spread that they were

1. Stark, *Vernacular Education in Bengal*, p. 43.
2. *Indian Education Commission, 1882*; *Report of the Madras Provincial Committee*, p. 5,

aquainted with any of the above mentioned arts.

Hindu women during the last millennium were usually unlettered, but they could not be described as uncultured. In fact, books being rare and costly, traditional wisdom and culture could be learnt more easily from the lips of a preacher than from the pages of a manuscript. Every village had its own religious teacher (*purāṇika*), whose vernacular discourses on religion, philosophy and culture were listened to with wrapt attention by all the matrons of the village. Though unlettered, they thus became better and more faithful custodians of ancient traditions and culture than even literate men.

We have seen above that the literacy among Hindu women had reached its nadir by about 1850 A. D. Subsequent to the assumption of the Indian administration by the British Crown, Government began to take some steps for the promotion of education among girls. Progress during the first forty years was very very slow. By the end of the last century, however, public opinion also began to support its cause, mainly owing to its vigorous championship by the school of social reform. Not much progress, however, was made for a long time, primarily because girls were married at the age of 9 or 10. Their education could thus continue only for three or four years, as it had to be suspended after marriage. The terrible havoc caused by the plague at the begining of the present century tended to raise the marriageable age of girls to 12 or 13. Among the educated middle classes in cities it has now advanced to 18 or 19, chiefly owing to the influence of economic factors. In 1929, a legislation was passed fixing 14 as the minimum age for the marriage of girls; this has been raised to 18 in 1955.

The raising of the marriageable age of girls has helped the cause of the female education in a remarkable degree. We have seen above that the lowering of that age to 9 or 10 by the 8th or 9th century A. D. was the main cause of the decline of education among girls. As this cause is being now gradually removed, we may expect a corresponding advance in the progress of female education. Economic conditions also are helping its spread. Since the second World War, an earning and therefore educated wife has become an economic necessity in lower middle class families. Services of educated women are still in great demand; these circumstances also are helping the growth of female education. An idea of the progress that female education has been making during the last thirty years can be gathered from the fact that the number of girl scholars, which was 1,230,698 in 1924-25, rose to 2,890,246 in 1934-35 and to nearly 37 lakhs in 1947. The progress in higher education is remarkable; the number of girl scholars in the secondary and collegiate education has risen from 108,660 and 14,435 in 1937 to 2,32,136 and 24,466 respectively in 1947. Much leeway, however has yet to be made; only 16·5 per cent. of the girls of the school going age are attending schools, and of these only 13 per cent reach the 4th class. The ratio[1] of literate women to men is 1 : 4.

While the female education is still in its infancy, a serious effort should be made to solve some of its complex problems. Fortunately these do not exist as far as primary education is concerned; the knowledge of the three R's and of elementary history, geography and drawing is as much necessary for boys as it is for girls. Marriage also does not now interrupt the course of primary education.

As far as the secondary and college education is concerned, we have to solve two thorny and difficult problems. The first is about co-education and the second is about the curriculum. The exigencies of the situation have in a way forced us to reconcile ourselves to co-education, and therefore to a common curriculum. Outside big cities, there are few schools and colleges intended for girls, and so guardians are practically forced to send their daughters to institutions primarily intended for boys. The curriculum also is therefore a more or less common one. Even when there are special schools and colleges

1. Report of the Educational Commissoner with the Government of India on the Progress of Girls' Education for the year 1934-5 (Published in April, 1937).

for girls, they usually follow the course laid down for boys. For, the institutions have to send their students for examinations to universities, which have so far, with rare exceptions, failed to introduce a different curriculum for lady students.

The difficulty in answering the question as to whether there should be a different curriculum for girls in high schools and colleges primarily arises from the fact that neither the scholars nor their guardians know definitely at the outset whether the students concerned are going to be housewives or are going to follow a career. In the case of a girl scholar intending to follow the latter alternative, it is clear that she will have to receive the same education as the boy student. A woman who wants to become a pleader or a doctor must obviously get the same education which a male pleader or doctor receives.

The number of women who will be thus going in purely for a career will, however, not be a large one. They should attend men's colleges and follow a common curriculum. The vast majority of girl scholars, however, will eventually be destined to become housewives and schools and colleges for girls should be primarily intended to meet their needs with a special curriculum of their own. The education imparted in them should be such as will make the recepients efficient wives and mothers, and also enable them to become earning members of their families in their spare time, or in case of need and adversity.

In Hindu society at present, normally speaking, the marriage of a girl cannot be convenienty postponed to beyond the age of 20. We should, therefore so draft the courses of female education, that they should be over before that time. Primary education should take four years and be over at the age of 10. The secondary course should extend over seven years only; if we adopt the mother tongue as the medium of instruction and slightly reduce the curricula in subjects like geography, mathematics and history, it will be possible to finish the course in seven years' time. Hygiene, nursing, domestic science, music, sewing, knitting and house-decorations should figure prominently in the school curriculum as subjects alternative with mathematics, geography and the second language. The secondary course would be over at the age of 17. It should be followed by a college course extending over three years, which would be thus completed when the scholar is about 20. It will be easy to frame three years' courses in subjects like (A) Arts and Teaching, (B) Domestic Science, Medicine and Midwifery, (C) Music, Painting, and Photography, (D) Tailoring and Embroidery, which will be self-sufficient, and enable girl scholars not only to become efficient and cultured house-wives, but also to earn some money both in their spare time and in the case of need. In the last three groups there should be included a paper on Literature or History as well. Course in Groups A and B will be obviously below the B .A., the B.T. or the M.B.B.S. standards. Those girls, however, who have taken a diploma in these subjects, should be allowed to appear as private candidates for the B.A., B.T., and Intermediate M.B.B.S. examinations. This would remove the difficulty in the way of a girl scholar who has joined the women's college, but who eventually desires to devote a few more years to education in order to attain the highest efficiency in her subject. The recasting of secondary and higher education of girls on the above lines would remove the defects in the present system and cater for the needs both of those who want to settle down in family life, as also of those who want to follow a career. It is of course true that a cut in the normal curriculum has been suggested in the courses for girls, but that is necessary in order to equip them for their normal functions of intelligent and efficient wives and mothers. As the matters stand to-day, girls have to pass the same examinations as boys and to learn house-keeping at home as well, all the while having less physical strength than their brothers. This certainly puts too much strain upon them and is injurious to the future well-being of the race.

1. Steps have been taken in some Universities on somewhat similar lines. In the Hindu University, Banaras, girl students can offer Music, Domestic Science and Fine Arts for their B. A. degree. At M. S. University in Baroda also, special emphasis is being given on these subjects in the case of girl students.

CHAPTER II

Marriage and Divorce

Marriage is a very important event in the life of a woman. Matrimony in course of time is followed by maternity, and its recurrence makes the woman periodically helpless and absolutely dependent on her husband for some time. Marriage, therefore, determines the fate of a woman to a much greater extent than it does the destiny of a man. A good marriage is a welcome protection for the woman, a bad one is worse than a painful chain. Marriage and the problems connected with it form an important topic in the history of woman. We shall see in this chapter how the institution of marriage was evolved in ancient India, what forms it assumed in course of time, what was the marriageable age, how the marriage was settled and celebrated and how far it was irrevocable.

The Evolution of Marriage

Being of hoary antiquity Hindu literature has naturally preserved some traces of promiscuity existing in prehistoric times. The *Mahābhārata* informs us that in the land of the the Uttarakurus[1] and in the city of Māhishmatī[2] the institution of marriage did not exist. It may be, however, added that Uttarakuru is very probably a mythical country, not existing on terrestrial globe, and that the evidence about Māhishmatī consists of an observation made by its Pāṇḍava conqueror Sahadeva during his short stay there in the course of a hurricane military campaign. It may not be worth more than the proverbial traveller's tale. According to the Great Epic it was the sage Śvetaketu who decreed that promiscuity should be sup-

1. यत्र नार्यः कामचारा भवन्ति । XII, 102, 26 (B).
2. स्वैरिण्यस्त्र नार्यो हि यथेष्टं विचरन्त्युत । II, 32, 40.

planted by regular marriage.[1] Whether the state of promiscuity, here referred to as existing in prehistoric times, is a mere possibility intellectually conceived, or whether it actually did exist in some sections of society in certain parts of the country, we do not know. There are a few passages in the epic showing that a state of promiscuity may not have been an impossibility at an early period. They disclose an astounding laxity in sexual morality. It must, however, be noted that most of these passages have a context and are not to be taken at their face value. Thus Śarmishṭhā observes that there is no difference between one's own husband and the husband of a friend;[2] but we must note that this is an argument advanced by a woman driven into desperation by the unnatural punishment of eternal maidenhood inflicted upon her. When eventually king Yayāti yields to Śarmishṭhā's importunities and is taken to task by Śukra, his father-in-law, he observes that duty and chivalry rendered it necessary for him to comply with Śarmishṭhā's re-

1. अनावृताः किल पुरा स्त्रिय आसन्वरानने ।
कामाचारविहारिण्यः स्वतंत्राश्चारुहासिनि ॥ ४ ॥
तासां व्युच्चरमाणानां कौमारात्सुभगे पतीन् ।
नाधर्मोऽभूद्वरारोहे स हि धर्मः पुराऽभवत् ॥ ५ ॥
प्रमाणदृष्टो धर्मोऽयं पूज्यते च महर्षिभिः ।
उत्तरेषु च रम्भोरु कुरुष्वद्यापि दृश्यते ॥
स्त्रीणामनुग्रहकरः स हि धर्मः सनातनः ॥ ७ ॥
अस्मिंस्तु लोके न चिरान्मर्यादेयं शुचिस्मिते ॥
स्थापिता येन यस्माच्च तन्मे विस्तरतः श्रृणु ।
बभूवोद्दालको नाम महर्षिरिति नः श्रुतम् ॥ ९ ॥
श्वेतकेतुरिति ख्यातः पुत्रस्तस्याभवन्मुनिः ।
मर्यादेयं कृता तेन धर्म्या वै श्वेतकेतुना ॥ १२ ॥
तदा प्रभृति मर्यादा स्थितेयमिति नः श्रुतम् ।
व्युच्चरन्त्याः पतिं नार्या अद्यप्रभृति पातकम् ॥ ४४ ॥
भ्रूणहत्यासमं घोरं भविष्यत्यसुखावहम् ।
भार्यां तथा व्युच्चरतः कौमारब्रह्मचारिणीम् ॥
पतिव्रतामेतदेव भविता पातकं भुवि ॥ ४७ ॥ *Mbh.* I, 128.

2. समावेतौ मतौ राजन् पतिः सख्याश्च यः पतिः ॥ *Ibid*, 1, 76, 28.

quest.[1] The astounding proposition here advanced by him is, however, nothing but an untenable defence put forward by an accused who is at a loss to know how to defend himself. The traces of promiscuity that we get in the epic have to be referred to pre-Vedic times; for we find the institution of marriage well established in the *Ṛigveda*.

Not only was marriage well established in the Vedic age, but it was also regarded as a social and religious duty and necessity. This was the case even in the Indo-Iranian period. According to the Avesta oblations offered unto gods or ancestors by a maiden or a bachelor are unacceptable to them (*Ashi Yashta*, *c*, X, 54). A Vedic passage says that a person, who is unmarried, is unholy.[2] From the religious point of view he remains incomplete and is not fully eligible to participate in sacraments. This continues to be the view of the society even now; the modern practice of keeping a betel nut by one's side in the absence of the wife or the older one of having her image to indicate her symbolical presence at the time of a sacrament both are due to the same belief. Marriage opened a new period of holy life which was to be led at the altar of truth and duty.[3] The couple was to take particular care in properly performing the rituals connected with the Gārhapatya fire kindled at the time of their marriage. Prescribed sacrifices to gods and manes were to be regularly offered. And finally the couple was to perpetuate the race by raising and training a numerous progeny, so that oblations may for ever continue to be offered to gods and ancestors. A later age, which had developed the system of the four Āśramas, pointed out that the whole society depends upon the householder for its maintenance; the Brahmachārī, the Vānaprashtha and the Saṁnyasī can hardly exist without active help from a zealous and conscientious class of householders.

1. ऋतुं वै याचमानाया न ददाति पुमानृतुम् ।
भ्रूणहेत्युच्यते ब्रह्मन् स इह ब्रह्मवादिभि: ॥ *Ibid.* I, 7754.
2. अयज्ञियो वा एष योऽपत्नीक: । *T. Br.*, II, 2, 2, 6.
3. ऋतस्य योनौ सुकृतस्य लोके । *R. V.*, X, 85, 24.

The householder is as necessary for society as the breath is for the body.[1]

Such being the views of society about marriage since very early times, it was naturally regarded as normally necessary and desirable for all. According to the Avesta bachelors are spiritually inferior to married men, and among the latter those without children to those who have them (*Fargard* IV, 130-3). The Vedic age shares the same views. It must be, however, observed that down to about 500 B. C., though marriage was regarded as highly desirable for both men and women, society did not insist that it should be performed at all cost, even if there were insuperable impediments in arranging a suitable match. The Vedic literature often refers to the spinster; *amājūḥ* one who grows old in one's parent's house, is the significant expression used to denote an old maid. The usual cause that compelled maidens to remain unmarried was some serious physical defect or disease. Such, for instance, was the case of Ghoshā, who could not marry till she was cured of her skin disease by the favour of gods Aśvins. In the age of the Upanishads hundreds of youths began to enter the monastery without caring to marry, and some maidens like Sulabhā began to follow their example with a view to achieve spiritual salvation.[2] The commentary on the *Therīgāthā* shows that some women used to join Buddhist Saṁgha before their marriage; their number, however, was not very large.

By about 300 B. C. marriage came to be regarded as obligatory for girls. Several causes induced society to subscribe to this view. In the first place there was a reaction produced in society by maidens joining the Buddhist and Jain orders either without a genuine spiritual urge or without a free and sponta-

1. यथा वायुं समाश्रित्य वर्तन्ते सर्वजन्तवः ।
तथा गृहस्थमाश्रित्य वर्तन्ते सर्वं आश्रमाः ।। *Manu*, III, 77.

2. साहं तस्मिन्कुले जाता भर्तर्यसति मद्विधे ।
विनीता मोक्षधर्मेषु चराम्येका मुनिव्रतम् ।।

Mbh., XII, 325, 103.

neous permission of their elders. Some of these were unable to live up to their high ideals, and their lapses were furiously commented upon by the public. Social thinkers began to feel that it would be better to prevent such abuses by making marriage obligatory for all girls. Socondly, the marriage of girls came to be compared to the *upanayana* of boys at about this time. If *upanayana* was obligatory for boys, marriage which was its counter part, ought to be absolutely binding on girls. As we shall soon see, marriageable age of girls was reduced to 13 or 14 by this time; girls found themselves already married before they attained an age when they could exercise an intelligent choice in the matter. The *Mahābhārata* informs us that it was the sage Dīrghatamas, who laid it down that women ought never to remain unmarried in future.[1] Elsewhere the epic illustrates the same principle by a naive story. Subhrū was the daughter of sage Kuṇi. Her father wanted to give her in marriage, but she would not consent. She remained unmarried for all her life, practising severe penance. At the time of her death, however, she learnt to her great surprise that she could not go to heaven because her body was not consecrated by the sacrament of marriage. With great difficulty she then induced sage Śriṅgavat to marry her, stayed with him for one night and was then enabled to go to heaven (IX, 33). A late Sūtra goes to the extent of declaring that the corpse of a maiden can be burnt only after a formal marriage even after the death.[2]

The epic is undoubtedly right in emphasing the great necessity of marriage for girls in the above legend; for there are more pitfalls in the path of an unmarried woman than those in the way of an unmarried man. As a consequence of the new theory which made marriage obligatory for girls, negligent parents must have become more alert in arranging the marriage of their daughters. It must, however, be admitted that this theory

1. अपतीनां तु नारीणामद्यप्रभृति पातकम् । 1,114,36

2. तथैव कन्यां च मृतां प्राप्तयौवनां तुल्येन पुंसा प्राप्तगृहवत्तां दहेत् ।
Baudhāyana Sūmārta Stra, V, 9,

tended to crush the literary and spiritual ambitions of the gifted section of the fair sex. Further, it has to be pointed out that it led to grave abuses when pre-puberty marriages began to be insisted upon from about the beginning of the Christian era. Some Smṛitis like Yama|began to advocate the unfortunate view that since marriage was compulsory for girls, parents should marry them even to undesirable persons, if suitable bridegrooms were not available before the time of puberty[1]. This rule made the lot of a defective deformed or diseased girl very pitiable. She could not naturally get a good husband and her father had yet to marry her. He had therefore to spend heavily in marrying her to a person, who was almost certain to discard her, and contract a fresh marriage with a more suitable bride. It must, however, be added that even if a defective girl is kept unmarried, her lot is by no means happy. As years roll on and the parents die, her brothers do not care for her, and scoundrels and selfish persons in society are not few in number who delight in spreading thorns in her way.

It is interesting to note that marriage was made obligatory for girls in contemporary Persia as well. Matrimony however was not regarded there as necessary for the spiritual salvation of men. For a woman there is no offspring except by intercourse with a man and no lineage proceeds from her. But for a man without a wife, when he shall recite the Avesta as it is mentioned in the Vendidād, there may be a lineage which proceeds onwards to the future existence (*Pahlvi Texts*, Part I, pp. 322-3). In India also students were regarded as the spiritual children of their teachers, and women teachers had practically disappeared from the scene by the beginning of the Christian era. But women's incapacity to leave behind a spiritual lineage has not been advanced as argument for making marriage obligatory for them.

1 दद्याद् गुणवते कन्यां नग्निकां ब्रह्मचारिणे ।
अपि वा गुणहीनाय नोपरुन्ध्याद्रजस्वलाम् ॥
Quoted in *SCS*, p. 216,

In India also marriage was made obligatory for women and not for men. One of the reasons may perhaps have been the possibility of men leaving a spiritual or intellectual lineage behind them. The real reason for this differential treatment, however, seems to have been the recognition by society of the simple fact that an unmarried woman has to face greater risks in society than an unmarried man. Public opinion also is much less sympathetic to a woman who has gone astray even unwillingly, than to a man who leads a vicious life deliberately. Smṛiti writers should, however, have recognised some exceptions to the general rule. This would have avoided its abuse in an age when pre-puberty marriages became the order of the day, and given scope to talented girls to master their favourite subjects and to spiritually minded women to try seriously for the realisation of their dreams. In that case the number of lady scholars would not have dwindled down and a Mirābāi would not have been compelled to lead a married life much to her own and to her husband's sorrow.

Forms of marriage

The eight forms of marriage recognised by Smṛitis are well known. There are, however, several other varieties and customs of marriage prevailing in the lower sections of Hindu society, which find no recognition in the Dharmaśāstra literature. Thus among the Levā and Kadvā Kunbis of Gujarat, the marriage season comes only once in the course of twelve years and lasts for three days only. During this short period even girls in the cradle have to be married; for pre-puberty marriages are insisted upon. Gazetteers have recorded several other strange customs prevailing among backward tribes in different districts and provinces. These, however, are the traces of the earlier primitive practices, which exist, not on account of, but in spite of Hinduism and its culture. They are also fast disappearing at present. It is therefore not necessary for the purpose of the present work to examine and discuss them.

A critical survey of the well known eight forms of marriage

is very interesting and important from the sociological point of view. We shall first consider the unapproved ones among them, for they take us back to prehistoric times. Paiśācha, Rākshasa and Āsura unquestionably belong to this group. There is a difference of opinion abut the Gāndharva or love marriage; some writers approve and praise it, while others regard it with disfavour. The parties themselves were conscious of a certain irregularity in their conduct, but they knew that they were within the law.

The Paiśācha form of marriage, which is the most condemned one, is undoubtedly of the greatest antiquity. In this marriage the bride is either duped, very often by making her overdrunk, or physically overpowered by the bridegroom in order to make her yield to his passion. To mesmerise a woman by talisman or magical practices and carry her away was also regarded as a Paiśācha form of marriage in medieval times.

Surprise has been expressed by several writers that force or fraud should thus have been legalised, and the bridegroom allowed to compel the unfortunate woman to live with him as his wife. This objection is based upon the ignorance of the simple fact that our Smṛitis preserve the relics of several prehistoric customs. They have included Paiśācha marriage in their list, firstly because old tradition knew of it, and secondly because it was sometimes resorted to by backward tribes. They wanted to stamp out this practice and have therefore mentioned it only for the purpose of its strong condemnation. There was a further reason for its legal recognition. From about the beginning of the Christian era society began to insist upon absolute virginity in the case of brides. Virgins, who had the misfortune of being criminally assaulted, had therefore hardly any chance of an honourable marriage with any other person. The only way in which law-writers could help them was by compelling the culprits to marry the parties they had wronged. This obviously is not a satisfactory arrangement, but no other alternative was available. A regard for the future prospects of the unfortunate victim was thus a further reason for the mention of the Paiśācha marriage. Much against their wishes, Smṛiti writers were compelled to recognise it. It may, however, be added that two of the early Dharmaśāstra writers, Vaśishṭha and Āpastamba, do not recognise Paiśācha marriage at all. They mention only three unapproved forms, Gāndharva, Rākshasa and Āsura. They seem to have subscribed to the modern view that a culprit should not be allowed to be benefitted by his wrong.

The Rākshasa marriage, or as it is more appropriately described by one authority, the Kshātra marriage, takes us back to prehistoric times when women were regarded as prizes of war. In this marriage the victor carried away the bride and married her. The fight was necessary either because women offered real resistance on account of the ill-treatment which they received from their husbands in primitive society, or because parents were unwilling to lose the services of their daughters, or because it was regarded as a point of honour for a warrior that he should have for his wife a woman, whom he could point out also as a trophy of war. The last point has been emphasised by Śrikṛishṇa, when he proceeds to appease the anger of Baladeva and justify the conduct of Arjuna in forcibly carrying away Subhadrā, who, though fallen in love with Arjuna, was about to be married to a son of Dhṛitarāshṭra. 'Arjuna', says Śrikrishṇa, 'did not like Brāhma marriage, because brides are treated there as objects of gift like cattle. Purchase of bride, being a disreputable procedure, was altogather out of question. Since Subhadrā had fallen in love with him, to carry her away relying upon the power of his own arms was the only honourable course left open for Arjuna."[1] This argument gives a good glimpse of the warrior mentality, which favoured the Kshātra marriage. It is interesting to point out that Śrikṛishṇa had himself acted upon

1. प्रदानमपि कन्यायाः पशुवत्कोऽनुमन्यते ।
विक्रयं चाप्यपत्यस्य कः कुर्यात्पुरुषो भुवि ॥
एतान्दोषांस्तु कौन्तेयो दृष्टवानिति मे मतिः ।
क्षत्रियाणां तु वीर्येण प्रशस्तं हरणं बलात् ।
अतः प्रसह्य हृतवान्कन्यां धर्मेण पाण्डवः ॥ I, 245, 5-6.

this theory at the time of his marriage with Rukmiṇī.

Examples of Kshātra marriages preserved in ancient Indian tradition are not many. In Ṛigveda (I,116) Vimada is described as having won his bride in battle. The *Mahābhārata* informs us that Bhīshma defeated the king of Kāśī and carried away his daughter, Ambā, as a bride for his brother Vichitravīrya. It is, however, necessary to point out that this procedure of Bhīshma has been later condemned in the epic by Śiśupāla.[1] It is clear that though the Kshātra marriage continued to be recognised by Smṛitis and epics, it had ceased to be approved even by enlightened Kshatriyas in the 3rd century B.C. It is not to be supposed, however, that even in the earlier period it was the normal or the usual form of marriage among the Kshatriyas; some warriors used to have recourse to it if need arose. Normally Kshatriya marriages too were settled otherwise than by an appeal to arms.

The traces of Kshātra marriage, however, still remain in the marriage customs and procedure prevailing in some parts of the country. Thus in the marriage songs of Gujarat and U. P., which are sung at the time of the departure of the bride for her new home, the bridegroom is compared to a robber and liberally showered with abuses. It is not possible to suppose that all these abuses are intended for the invisible evil spirits which are supposed to be hovering about the couple. Some of them at least are clearly intended for the bridegroom who is carrying away the bride like a conqueror. In many tribes the formality of chase is still preserved, though the marrige union is previously arranged by mutual consent. In such cases the drama of the

1. को हि धर्मिणमात्मानं जानञ्ज्ञानविदां वरः ।
कुर्याद्यथा त्वया भीष्म कृतं धर्ममवेक्षता ॥
अन्यकामा हि धर्मज्ञा कन्यका प्राज्ञमानिना ।
अंबा नामेति भद्रं ते कथं सापहृता त्वया ॥
तां त्वयापहृतां भीष्म कन्यां नैषितवान्नृपः ।
भ्राता विचित्रवीर्यस्ते सतां धर्ममनुस्मरन् ॥ I, 64, 22 ff.

1. *Statistical Account of Bengal*, Vol. XVI, p. 258.

mock chase or fight, that is enacted, is not in honour of force, but in honour of the institution of marriage, which has superseded it.

The next form of marriage that we shall now consider is the Āsura Vivāha, under which the husband used to get a bride by paying a reasonable price for her. The idea probably was that it would be disgraceful for a girl and her family if she was given in marriage for nothing. It would mean that she was not worth any price and that her family had no status and respectability. The origin of the name of this form of marraige is uncertain. Marriage by purchase was the order of the day among ancient Assyrians, and this circumstance may have been responsible for the name Āsura being given to that form of marriage where a bride-price was paid. The price paid by the bridegroom was originally a compensation to the bride's family for the loss of her service, but a portion of it soon began to be returned to the bride as a marriage gift. The bride-price was usually paid in cash or kind. In some uncivilised communities, bridegroom agrees to serve his would be father-in-law for a number of years in lieu of the payment of the bride-price. This custom is not referred to anywhere in the Hindu tradition or literature.

The Āsura marriage is undoubtedly better than the Kshātra one, for it presupposes a recognition by society of the fact that woman has a value and has to be paid for. It therefore helped the improvement of the lot of the wife. The average husband became naturally unwilling to ill-treat his wife out of mere frivolity; very often she used to cost him dearly and to find another substitute for her was not always an easy economic proposition.

There are a few cases of Āsura marriages recorded in ancient Indian tradition. In Vedic times, the custom of the bride purchase was known, but not held in esteem; the son-in-law in such cases was described as a *vijāmātā* or a disreputable son-in law.[1]

1 अश्रवं हि भूरिदावत्तरा वां विजामातुरुत वा वा स्यालात् ।

R. V., I, 109, 2.

To Pāli literature also the custom is not unknown; the father of Isidasī, one of the nuns of the *Therīgāthā*, had received a bride-price for her in her marriage (Vv. 120 and 153). The *Dhammapada* also mentions the custom (v. 215 and commentary). In the epics we find that at the time of the marriages of Kaikeyī, Gāndhārī and Mādrī a heavy bride-price had to be paid to their guardians. It must be, however, pointed out that though the custom undoubtedly prevailed in some sections of the community, it was vehemently condemned by the leaders of society. Those who followed it knew that what they were doing was not commendable. This would be quite clear from the great hesitation which Śalya felt in informing Bhīshma[1] that if he wished to secure his sister Mādrī as a bride for Pāṇḍu, he would have to pay a good bride-price. He opens the topic apologetically: "There is a family custom with us which whether good or bad, I have got to follow. You also know it. Why then do you want me to say in so many words that you should pay a bride-price ? It is quite clear from the tone and contents of this speech that Śalya recognised the custom as undesirable, though he had not the moral courage to give it up in order to set a better example for his successors. Perhaps the greed of money was too strong for the feeble inner voice.

The writers of Dharmaśāstra literature almost lose their temper in condemning the custom of the bride-price. Baudhāyana warns the guardians that they will go to the most terrible

1. पूर्वैः प्रवर्तितं किंचित्कुलेऽस्मिन्नृपसत्तमैः ।
साधु वा यदि वासाधु तन्नातिऽक्रान्तुमुत्सहे ॥
व्यक्तं तद्भवतश्चापि विदितं नात्र संशयः ।
न च युक्तं तथा वक्तुं भवान्देहीति सत्तम ॥
कुलधर्मः स नो वीर प्रमाणं परमं च तत् ।
तेन त्वां न ब्रवीम्येतदसंदिग्धं वचोऽरिहन् ॥
तं भीष्मः प्रत्युवाचेदं मद्रराजं जनाधिपः ।
धर्मं एषः परो राजन्स्वयमुक्तः स्वयंभुवा ॥
नात्र कश्चन दोषोऽस्ति पूर्वैर्विधिरयं कृतः । I, 1229 ff.

hell if they sell daughters in marriage, and points out to the husband that a purchased bride would not become a legal wife at all.[1] She continues to remain in her father's *gotra*, and sons born of her do not become entitled to offer oblations to her husband's ancestors.[2] The *Padma-purāṇa* advises that even the face of a person, who has sold his daughter in marriage, should not be seen.[3] A fifteenth century inscription from Tanjore district records an agreement among the Brāhmaṇas of that area to the effect that they would excommunicate anybody who would accept bride-price in marriage (*S. I. I.*, Vol. I, No. 56). This will show that the custom prevailed among Brāhmaṇas also sometimes; we find the Peshwas warning the Brāhmaṇas of the town of Wai in Maharashtra against practising it.

The custom of bride-price has thus been vehemently condemned by the leaders of society almost in every age. That this should have been necessary shows, however, that the evil was very deep-rooted. The prevalence of child marriages since the beginning of the Christian era has further helped its growth. When brides were grown up and educated, they had naturally some voice, direct or indirect, in the settlement of their marriage and so could not be sold to the highest bidder. When, however, they began to be married at the tender age of 10 or 11, it became easy for avaricious and uncultured guardians to settle the marriage more with a view to get the highest bride-price than with the aim of finding the most suitable bridegroom. The custom of bride-price has therefore become commoner in the

1. क्रीता द्रव्येण या नारी सा न पत्नी विधीयते ।
सा न दैवे न सा पित्र्ये दासीं तां कवयो विदुः ।।
शुल्केन ये प्रयच्छन्ति स्वसुतां लोभमोहिताः ।
पतन्ति नरके घोरे घ्नन्ति चासप्तमात्कुलम् ।। I, 11, 20-1.

2. क्रयक्रीता च या कन्या न सा पत्नी विधीयते । *Atri*, 384.
तस्यां जाताः सुतास्तेषां पितृपिण्डो न विद्यते ।

3. कन्याविक्रयिणां ब्रह्मन्न पश्येद्वदनं बुधः ।
दृष्ट्वा चाज्ञानतो वापि कुर्यान्मार्तण्डदर्शनम् ।।

Brahmakhaṇḍa. 24, 26.

lower sections of society during the last fifteen hundred years as a result of the lowering of the marriage age. Its vehement denunciation has succeeded in stamping it out only from the higher classes of society. The spread of education and the raising of the marriageable age are, however now eradicating the evil even from the lower strata of society.

The Gāndharva marriage now comes up for consideration. This was a love marriage, pure and simple. From the Vedic age, the Gandharvas were well-known for their amorous disposition, and a marriage which was consummated before the due performance of the sacred rituals, naturally came to be known after them.

Authorities are not agreed as to whether love unions should be included within the category of approved marriages. The *Baudhāyana Dharma Sūtra* refers with approval to the view of some thinkers that love unions ought to be commended, as they presuppose reciprocal attachment.[1] The *Kāmasūtra* regards them as ideally good;[2] so also did an earlier thinker named Angiras, quoted by Bhavabhūti in the Mālatī-Mādhava.[3] The *Mahābhārata* in one place includes the Gāndharva union within the group of the approved marriages (XIII, 44). Manu seems to be indecisive in the matter (III,23-25). The same, is the case with Nārada. He declines to place Gāndharva marriage either among the approved or among the blameworthy forms and calls it *sādhāraṇa* or ordinary. Later writers disapprove both the Gāndharva marriage and the self-choice by the bride (*svyaṁvara*). Owing to the introduction of child marriages

1. गान्धर्वमप्येके प्रशंसन्ति सर्वेषां स्नेहानुगतत्वात् ।
B. D. S., 1. 11, 13, .7

2. सुखत्वादबहुक्लेशादपि चावरणादिह । III. 5. 61.
अनुरागात्मकत्वाच्च गान्धर्वः प्रवरो मतः ।।

3. इतरेतरानुरागो हि दारकर्मणि पराध्यं मंगलं गीतश्चायमर्थोऽगिरसा
यस्यां मनश्चक्षुषोरनुबंधस्तस्यामृद्धिर्भवति । Act II.

4. एषां तु धर्म्याश्चत्वारो ब्राह्माद्याः समुदाहृताः ।
साधारणः स्याद् गांधर्वश्चयोऽधर्म्यास्तथाऽपरे ।। XV. 44.

both these had become impracticable in their days.

In the Gāndharva marriage parties fall in love with each other and immediately proceed to consummate their contemplated marriage. Religious rituals etc. do not precede the union. A passage interpolated in the *Mahābhārata* in later times no doubt represents Śakuntalā as calling a priest for the performance of the religious rites before proceeding to consummate her marriage.[1] This version of the story is inconsistent with the one given by Kālidāsa in his *Śākuntala*; it further contradicts the definition of the Gāndharva marriage as given in the epic itself. When Kaṇva proceeds to express his approval to his daughter of her love marriage, he incidentally defines the Gāndharva marriage as a love union brought about without any recitation of Mantras.[2]

In course of times, as the hold of religion increased, Gandharva ceased to be one of the ideal forms of marriage; it was included in the list of unapproved forms. But as long as post-puberty marriages were in vogue, Gāndharva marriages could not be altogother stopped. It was however, laid down that even in Gāndharva marriages the ritual should be performed after the union.[3] The possible objection that the marriage Mantras refer to a *kanyā* or a virgin and so could not be recited in such a case was met by laying down that the term *kanyā* is to be understood in a general way as referring to a bride and not necessarily to a virgin.[4] The subsequent formal celebration of the marriage served the purpose of its proper announcement to society; it also gave an opportunity to relations and friends to share its joy.

1. शासनाद्विप्रमुख्यस्य कृतकौतुकमंगलः ।
जग्राह विधिवत्पाणिमुवास च तया सह ॥ I, 94, 38

It may be pointed out that this passage is omitted as an interpolation in the Bhandarkar Institute edition of the epic.

2. क्षत्रियस्य तु गान्धर्वो विवाहः श्रेष्ठ उच्यते ।
सकामायाः सकामेन निर्मन्त्रः श्रेष्ठ उच्यते ॥ IV, 94, 60

3. गान्धर्वेषु विवाहेषु पुनर्वैवाहिको विधिः ।
कर्तव्यश्च त्रिभिर्वर्णैः समयेनाग्निसाक्षिकः ॥

Devala quoted by Kullūka on *Manu*, VIII, 226.

4. See the commentary of Kullūka on *Manu*, VIII, 226.

Brāhma, Daiva, Prājāpatya and Ārsha are the four approved forms of marriage. It is only in a marriage by one of these forms that the union is completed from the religious point of view by bringing about the change in the *gotra* of the bride at the end of the Saptapadī ritual. It was held that in the case of the four other forms just discussed above; the bride never passes into the family or Gotra of her husband.

Among these Ārsha ranks the last. In this marriage the father of the bride is permitted to accept a cow and a bull from his son-in-law for facilitating the performance of sacrifices, which require the cow's milk. There is, however, no reason why he should not have called upon his son, who was to inherit all his property, to make the necessary provision in this respect. The truth is that this gift, which the son-in-law gave to his father-in-law, is a relic of the bride-price, which was once very common. It would appear that some families like those of Śalya, for instance, were determined not to lose their time-honoured right of receiving the bride-price; a compromise was eventually arrived at by permitting them to receive only a pair of cow and bull, ostensibly for the purpose of getting milk for religious sacrifices. We can now understand why Ārsha form is usually placed last in the list of approved marriages. Nay, some writers continued to regard it as a variety of Āsura marriage; they maintained that the gift of a pair of cow and bull was nothing less than a bride-price in disguise. This historically correct view is opposed by Jaimini and Śabara, who had to defend loyally the compromise that had been arrived at. The former points out that the gift given by the son-in-law, being for religious purposes, could not be regarded as bride-price. The latter observes that prices of articles vary in the market according to their quality; in Ārsha marriages all sons-in-law offer the same present to their fathers-

2. ब्राह्मादिषु विवाहेषु या तूढा कन्यका भवेत् ।
भर्तृगोत्रेण कर्तव्या, तस्याः पिण्डादिका क्रिया ॥
गांधर्वाविवाहेषु पितृगोत्रेण धर्मवित् ॥

Mārkaṇḍeya Purāṇa, quoted in *P. M.* I. 2. pp. 63-4.

in-law, and so it cannot be called bride-price.[1] These arguments, while undoubtedly true of the character of Ārsha marriages in the days of Smṛitis, do not disprove the theory that they are a refined relic of Āsura marriages.

When a daughter was offered in marriage to an officiating priest by the sacrificer, the marriage was designated as a Daiva one. It was given this name, because the marriage was settled while a sacrifice to Devas (gods) was being performed. This form of marriage did not, however receive an unstinted approval of Smriti writers; they felt that while a sacrifice to gods was being offered, neither the sacrificer nor any of his priests should think of secular matters like possible matrimonial alliances.

Vedic sacrifices, which were fairly popular down to the 4th century B. C., often lasted for several weeks. The sacrificer had to invite a large number of priests to perform various duties in their connection. During this close and prolonged association, he would often be very favourably impressed by the culture, character and attainments of some one among the priests, and would decide to solve the marriage problem of his grown-up daughter by offering her to him. These were the days of post-puberty marriages; owing to the close association during the sacrifices, daughters also could get an opportunity to form an estimate of their future husbands and guide their parents in the choice. Daiva marriages disappeared with Vedic sacrifices. Later tradition has not preserved any instances of the earlier period. The case recorded in the *Bṛiaddevata* is not really an instance of this marriage; for there the sage Śyāyāśva does not himself marry the sacrificer's daughter, but selects her for his son (V, 54-55).

Brāhma and Prājāpatya are the only two forms of marriage

1. क्रयस्य धर्ममात्रत्वम् । *Pū. M.*, VI. 15. नासौ क्रय इति । क्रयो ह्युच्चनीचपण्यो भवति । नियतं त्विदं दानम् । Śabara on *Ibid.* Mitramiśra refutes this argument by referring to the fixed price that was paid for the Soma plant. He defends Ārsha marriage on the ground धर्मनिमित्तो ह्यसौ संबंधो न लोभनिमित्तः ॥ *VMS*, p, 850,

that now remain to be considered. The distinction between the two is not very clearly explained by Smṛitis. We are told that in the Brāhma marriage, the bride, properly bedecked and ornamented, is offered to a bridegroom who is specially invited for the purpose, while in Prājāpatya, the bride is offered according to due rites, but with an injunction to the couple that they should be always inseparable companions in the discharge of their religious duties.[1] These definitions do not really state the difference between the two forms. It is sometimes argued that the injuction to the couple in the Prājāpatya marriage to remain inseparable companions in the performance of religious duties renders polygamy impossible and prohibits the husband from entering into the Vānaprastha or Sanyāsa stage without the consent and company of his wife.[1] This view, however, is not correct, for the same corollaries can be drawn from the usul exhortation in the Brāhma marriage, enjoining the husband and the wife to be inseparable companions of each other in all their activities in the spheres of religion, love and wealth. Brāhma and Prājāpatya are synonymous words and it is quite possible that the Brāhma marriage was originally identical with the Prājāpatya one. This conclusion is supported by the fact that two of the early writers, Vasishṭha and Āpastamba, do not mention Prājāpatya marriage at all; they refer to only three approved forms, Brāhma, Daiva and Ārsha. Prājāpatya was

1. आच्छाद्य चार्चयित्वा च श्रुतिशीलवते स्वयम् ।
आहूय दानं कन्याया ब्राह्मो धर्मः प्रकीर्तितः ॥
सहोभौ चरतां धर्ममिति वाचानुभाष्य च ।
कन्याप्रदानमभ्यर्च्य प्राजापत्यो विधिः स्मृतः ॥ *Manu* III, 27,30.

Hārita, quoted by Hemādri in Vol, IV, p. 647, includes the gift of a pair of clothes to the bridegroom as an element of Prājāpatya; but this must have been quite common in all approved forms of marriage; cf, विधिवद्वस्त्रद्वयं दत्वा अनया सह धर्मंश्चर्यतामिति प्राजापत्यः ।

1. यद्यपि ब्राह्मादिषु अपि सह धर्मचर्या भवति तथापि आ अन्तादनया सह धर्मश्चरितव्यो नाश्रमान्तरं प्रवेष्टव्यं नापि स्त्र्यन्तरमुपयन्तव्यमिति मन्त्रेण समयः क्रियते । एवं ब्राह्मादेः प्राजापत्यस्य विशेषः । आच्छाद्यालंकृतामिति समानम् ।
Haradatta on *G. D. S.*, I, 4, 5,

added later, probably to make the number of the forms of marriage eight. Smṛiti writers therefore naturally faill to bring out the difference between the two.

In the Brāhma marriage, the father carefully selects the son-in-law, invites him to his house and offers him his daughter according to proper religious rites, along with such presents as he can conveniently give on account of natural affection. The definition of the Brāhma marriage, as given above, occurs in Smritis which were written when girls were married at a young age; the bride is therefore naturally seen figuring as an object of gift and not as an active agent. It should be pointed out that the talk of the gift of the bride was a mere formality in a religious ritual; it did not invest the husband with any right of ownership either over the wife or over her children, as has been pointed by several writers.[1] It did not at all authorise the husband to treat his wife in any way he liked. He had to take an oath that he would be always very closely associated with his new partner in life in all its spheres. The phraseology of the bride being an object of gift was introduced in the marriage ritual simply because the word *'dāna'* had very holy associations in Hindu mind. One can give a *dāna* only to a properly qualified person; so the bridegroom-elect had to be a good and suitable husbad. What one receives as a sacred gift in the presence of the Divine Fire is really a trust, for the proper discharge of which one is responsible to the Creator of the Universe. The hold and influence of religion being what they were, the conception of the bride being a sacred gift freely given to the bridegroom in the presence of gods for the proper dischage of religious and social duties and obligations was the best guarantee against any possible tendency in the husband to ill-treat his wife, or to become unfaithful to her.

1 गवाद्राविव भार्यायां स्वत्वभावेन तस्यामुत्पन्नेऽपत्ये तदभावात् ।

Vyavahāramayūkha, p. 92.

दानं क्रयधर्माश्चापत्यस्य न विद्येते । विवाहे........दानं धर्मार्थमेव श्रूयते । क्रयशब्दः संस्तुतिमात्रः । *A. D. S.*, II· 6. 3. 10-11.

It is true that to the modern mind the conception of the bride being a gift to the bridegroom given at the marriage may not appear as a high or happy one. Historically speaking, however, it may be pointed out that this conception marked a great advance over the earlier practice which freely permitted the father to sell his daughter in marriage. To give away a daughter to the best available bridegroom out of sole regard for her happiness without receiving any consideration whatsoever thus recorded a marked ethical advance. The interests of the bride were safe-guarded by making the whole transaction a religious one, and by prescribing an oath for the husband to be for ever true, kind and considerate to his partner. In course of time several sacred and lyrical associations came to cluster round the Brāhma marriage, and it became most popular and sacred. If its ritual is to be amended, it should be in the direction of making the bridegroom also offer himself to the bride as a free, sacred and unconditional gift. A marriage can become happy only when each party dedicates its entire existence for promoting the happiness and welfare of the other.

The conception of marriage as a secular contract did not arise in ancient India. In the Vedic literature (*T.Br.*, II, 3.10), we have the story of Sītā Sāvitrī, who is seen refusing to marry Soma, who had fallen in love with her, unless he accepted certain conditions of her own. There is also the story of Urvaśī, who agrees to marry Purūravas only if certain conditions of hers were satisfied. When there was a breach, we find the nymph deserting her human lover. These stories presuppose a tendency to regard marriage as a contract, but it did not make much progress. Marriage was regarded as a sacred religious union brought about by divine dispensation; it was felt that the mutual vows which the parties took in the presence of Sacred Fire sufficiently emphasised all the points that could possibly have been included in a marriage contract. The marriage sacrament united the parties in an indissoluble union, and the husband and the wife each prayed that their love and friendship should be lasting, genuine and indisoluble. Complete unity of interest left no room for a contract.

THE AGE OF MARRIAGE

Girls were married at a fairly advanced age in the Vedic period. The precise age is not stated, but from the Avesta we learn that maidens were usually wedded at the age of 15 or 16 in ancient Persia (*Vendidād*, 14, 15). The same was certainly the case in the Vedic period. The very term for marriage, *udvāha*, 'carrying away (of the bride)' presupposes a post-puberty marriage, for it shows that immediately after her marriage, the bride went to her husband's house to live as his wife. A perusal of the marriage hymn (X,85) shows that the bride was fully mature and quite grown up at the time of the marriage; she is expressly described as blooming with youth and pining for a husband.[1] A hope is expressed that the bride would forthwith take over the reins of the household from her parents-in-law.[2] This would have been possible only in the case of grown up brides, at least 16 to 18 years in age.

In the Vedic literature there are several references to unmarried girls growing old in their parents' houses, and the *Atharvaveda* is full of charms and spells intended for compelling the love of a reluctant man or woman. At least some of these spells must have been used by maidens and bachelors not succeeding in winning the affection of the party desired. There are references to lovers following their sweethearts, giving them presents and yearning for mutual company. In one case we have the reference to a maiden pining for a husband approaching a youth anxious for a wife.[3] Under such circumstances, children

1 अन्यामिच्छ प्रफर्व्यां संजायां पत्या सृज । X, 85, 22.
सूर्यां यत्पत्ये शंसन्तीं मनसा सवितादात् । X, 85, 9.

2 साम्राज्ञी श्वशुरे भव सम्राज्ञी श्वश्रवां भव । X, 85, 46.

3 एयमगन्पतिकामा जनिकामोऽहमागमम् ।
अश्वः कनिक्रदद्यथा भगेनाहं सहागमम् ॥ *A. V.* II, 30, 5.
अभि त्वा योषणोदिश जारं न कन्याऽनूषत । *R. V.*, IX, 56, 3.

of maidens were not unknown to society, and we get references to their occasional exposures as well. Indra is sometimes represented as rescuing them.[1]

Verses 27-9 and 37 of the marriage hymn describe the consummation of the marriage. The facts mentioned in the last paragraph make it clear that this event must have happened immediately after the marriage. It has been argued by some writers that the marriage hymn, which is a composite one, narrates different events that may well have taken place at widely separated intervals of time; we can therefore well assume that the consummation took place several months or years after the celebration of the marriage. There is, however, no evidence to support this conjecture; the description of the bride as blooming with youth and pining for a husband makes it altogether improbable and unacceptable.

Some other arguments advanced to prove the existence of child marriages in the Vedic age may be briefly considered here. It is true that in two passages of the *Ṛigveda* (1, 51, 13 and 1, 116,1) the word *arbha* has been used to denote the bride and the bridegroom. This expression, however, denotes tenderness rather than childhood, for Vimada who has been described as an *arbha* bridegroom is seen to be defeating his rival in battle and winning his bride. This is possible only in the case of a full-grown youth. In another place we find a wife praying for hair growing at the time of puberty;[2] orthodox tradition itself, however, states that the cause for this prayer was not her childhood, but a skin disease from which she was suffering. Similarly in another hymn, we find a wife asserting to her husband that

1. उत त्यं पुत्रमग्रुवः परावृक्तं शतक्रतो ।
उक्थेष्विन्द्र आभजत् । *R. V.* VI, 30, 6.

See also *R. V.* IV, 19, 9; *V. S.*, XXX, 6.

2. इमानि त्रीणि विष्टपा तानीन्द्र विरोहय ।
शिरस्तस्योर्वरामादिदं मे उपोदरे ॥
असौ च या न उर्वरादिमां तन्वं मम ।
अथो ततस्य यच्छिरः सर्वास्ता रोमशा कृधि ॥ VII, 91. 5-6.

she is fully developed physically and has abundant marks of complete puberty on her person. This statement is not, however, made to remove the misapprehension of an ignorant husband; the wife makes it in the privacy of the bedroom to excite the passion of her husband, who had previously expressed his exuberant appreciation of her amorous skill.[1] There is thus no data to rebut the force and evidence of the passages and circumstances mentioned in the last two paras, which go to prove that marriage in the Vedic age took place when the parties were fully grown up.

The case continued to be the same down to about the 5th century B. C. The Gṛihya Sūtra literature composed at about this time lays down that the consummation of the marriage should take place on the fourth succeeeding day. *Chaturthī-karma*, 'the event of the fourth day' long continued to be the technical name for the ritual prescribed at the consummation of the marriage. Some Gṛihya Sūtras also provide for the contingency of the bride being in her monthly course during the marriage ceremony. It is true that in a few works of this class it is laid down that the bride should be a *nagnikā* at the time of her marriage. This term has been no doubt interpreted by some later commentators as denoting a girl of five or six, who has no sense of bashfulness and moves about without properly covering her body.[2] This, however, is not the real or original meaning of the word. The *Mahābhārata* describes a bride of 16 as *nagnikā* and one Gṛihya Sūtra lays it down that the *nagnikā*[3]

1. Husband;—आगधिता परिगधिता या कशीकेव जङ्गहे ।
ददाति मह्यंयादुरी याशूनां भोज्या शता ॥
Wife:—उपोप मे परामृश मामे दभ्राणि मन्यथाः ।
सर्वाहमस्मि रोमशा गान्धारीणामिवाविका ॥ I, 126 6-7.

2. यावन्न लज्जयाङ्गानि कन्या पुरुषसन्निधौ ।
योन्यादीन्यवगूहेत तावद्भवति नग्निका ॥
पुराण in *SCS.*, p. 213.

3. त्रिंशद्वर्षः षोडशवर्षां भार्यां विन्देत नग्निकाम् । In *VMS*, q. 766.

bride should-also be a virgin at the time of her wedding.[1] Such a requirement in the case of a girl of five would be superfluous. As pointed out by Mātridatta, the term *nagnikā* therefore really refers to a woman who is fit to welcome her husband in privacy, immediately after her marriage[2]. When child marriages came into vogue, the meaning of the term was changed and it was maintained that it denotes a girl playing in dust without properly clothing herself.

The evidence from the epics and the Buddhist literature also shows that down to about 400 B. C. brides in cultured families used to be about 16 at the time of their marriage. They are often described as eagerly pining for being united with husbands.[3] Nuns like Viśākhā and Kuṇḍalakeśā, who had entered the nunnery before their marriage, are represented as being either of the age of 16 or of the age of discretion when their marriages were being contemplated. Brides in the Jātakas are also usually seen to be grown up. We often come across love affairs there; in one place we find a maiden named Paṭachara eloping with her lover, because her parents would not sanction her contemplated marriage.[4] Sītā, Kuntī and Draupadī were fully grown up at the time of their marriages, which were consummated immediately.

There is some ambiguity in the present version of the *Rāmāyaṇa* about the age of Sītā at the time of her marriage. In her talk with Rāvaṇa at the time when he had come to abduct her, she informs him that she was 18 at the time of her hus-

1. नग्निका सजाता ब्रह्मचारिणी। *H. G. S.*, I, 19,2,

2. तस्माद्वस्त्रविक्षेपणार्हा नग्निका मैथुनार्हेत्यर्थः।

Mātridatta on the above

3. राजगृहे तु एका सेट्ठिधीता सोळसवस्सुद्देसिका अभिरूपा अहोसि दस्सनाय। तस्मिं च वये थिता नारियो पुरुसज्झासाय होंति पुरिसलोला।

Commentary on *Dhammapāda 102*.

A passage in *Sam Ni.*, 37, 3. 1 points out that one of the evils to which women are subject is the necessity to go to the homes of their husbands, when they are young (*dahara*). The term *dahara*, does however refer to childhood, because *Vimānavatthu*, 31, 5, refers to a *dahara* wife as being pure and chaste as well.

4. *Therīgāthā* No. 47 commentary.

band's banishment, and that her marriage had taken place twelve years earlier[1]. This would lead to the conclusion that Sītā was a child of 6 at the time of her wedding. This passage is, however, a spurious one; that Sītā, who was very anxious for her husband's safety should have discussed her history with Rāvaṇa, an absolute stranger, appears extremely improbable. The Bālakāṇḍa, on the other hand, states that the marriages of Rāma and his brothers were consummated immediately after the return of the marriage party to Ayodhyā.[2] Similarly, while narrating the story of her marriage to Anasūyā, Sītā describes to her the great anxiety of her father when she had attained an age fit for being united to a husband.[3] It is therefore clear that Sītā was a youthful maiden when she was married, and the passage in Araṇyakāṇḍa, suggesting that she was a child of six at her marriage, is a later interpolation. It is true that Bhavabhūti also represents Sītā to have been quite a child in her marriage in several passages;[4] herein, however, he was influenced by the practice of his age, rather than by the evidence of any earlier and genuine tradition.

Marriages at a lower age began to be advocated from about the 4th century B. C. The writers of the Dharmasūtras, who flourished from *c.* 400 B. C. to *c.* 100 A. D., begin to advise that marriages of girls should not be delayed long after their puberty. Two of them, *viz.*, Vaśishṭha and Baudhāyana, are prepared to recommend that girls may be kept unmarried for a period of three years after their puberty, if there are difficulties in properly settling their marriages, and Manu and Kau-

1. III, 47, 4 and 10.

2. अभिवाद्याभिवाद्यांश्च सर्वा राजसुतास्तदा ।
रेमिरे मुदिताः सर्वा भर्तृभिः सहितं रहः । I, 77, 14.

3. पतिसंयोगसुलभं वयो दृष्ट्वा तु मे पिता ।
चिन्तामभ्यगमद्दीनो वित्तनाशादिवाधनः । II, 119, 34.

4. अविवाहसमयाद् गृहे वने शैशवे तदनु यौवने पुनः ॥
शिशुर्दधती मुखम् । *Uttararāmacharit*, I, 37 and I, 20.

ṭilya (IV, 2) concur with them.[1] But Gautama[2] and Vishṇu (24,41) insist that marriages must be celebrated within three months of the time of puberty. It is clear that they were in favour of pre-puberty marriages in normal circumstances. Opinion was obviously divided at this time. Some thinkers pointed out that life was transitory, and if marriage was intended to ensure the continuance of the family, the bride should not be too young when it is performed. Others contended that absolute chastity was to be most desired, and so we should select a bride, who should not have even dreamt of sexual love.[3] It is, however, necessary to point out that even those, who allowed a short period of three months after the puberty, do not shower any curses upon the guardians, if they fail to perform the marriages within the ninety days period of grace. Manu, who normally contemplates a prepuberty marriage, goes to the extent of permitting the father to keep the daughter unmarried, even to the end of her life, if a suitable husband cannot be procured.[4]

The institution of nunnery in Jainism and Buddhism and the instances of several grown up maidens taking holy orders against their parents' desire and some of them later falling from their high spiritual ideal must also have strengthened the

1. त्रीणी वर्षाण्युदीक्षेत कुमारी ऋतुमती सती ॥ *B. D. S.* IV. 1,14.
कुमारी ऋतुमती त्रीणि वर्षाण्युदीक्षेत ।
ऊर्ध्वं त्रिभ्यो वर्षेभ्यः पतिं विन्दत्तुल्यम् । *V. D. S.* XVII. 59.
त्रीणि वर्षाण्युदीक्षेत कुमारी ऋतुमती सती ।
ऊर्ध्वं तु कालादेतस्माद्विन्देत सदृशं पतिम् । *Manu,* IX, 90.

2. त्रीन्कुमारी ऋतूनतीत्य स्वयं युज्येतानिन्दितेन उत्सृज्य पित्र्यानलंकारान् । *G. D. S.* XVIII, 20.

3. नातिबालां वहन्त्यन्ये अनित्यत्वात्प्रजार्थिनः ।
वहन्ति कमिष्यास्तस्यामन्तः शुद्धिव्यपेक्षया ॥
अपरान्वयसंभूतां संस्वप्नादिविवर्जिताम् ।
कामो यस्यां निषिद्धश्च केचिदिच्छन्ति चापदि ॥ *Mbh.* XIII, 79,14.15.

4. काममामरणात्तिष्ठेद् गृहे कन्यर्तुमत्यपि ।
न चैवैनां प्रयच्छेत्तु गुणहीनाय कर्हिचित् ॥ *Manu,* IX, 89.

view of those who favoured marriages at about the time of puberty. If a girl is married before her personality is fully developed, there was no danger of her joining a nunnery. We may therefore conclude that during the period 400 B.C. to 100 A.D. the marriageable age was being gradually lowered, and the tendency on the whole was to marry girls at about the time of puberty. There was, however, no uniformity in practice current in society. The *Kāmasūtra*, which belongs to the end of this period, presupposes the existence of both the post-puberty and pre-puberty marriages (III, 2-4). The stories in the *Kathāsaritsāgara*, which depict the social life of about this time, refer both to child marriages brought about by parents and to love marriages arranged by the parties themselves (Chaps. 24, 124).

It is sometimes argued that girls used to be married not at about the age of 14 or 15 during the Mauryan period, but at the much younger age of 6 or 7. This contention is based upon Megasthenes, Fragment LI, where he states that among the Pāṇḍyas, who lived in Madura and Tinnevelly districts, girls used to be married at the age of 6. At the outset it may be pointed out that the Greek ambassador does not make this statement about the girls at Pāṭaliputra, of which he had first-hand information, but about the brides in Pāṇḍya country, which he had never visited. He had no first-hand information about South India and he makes this statement on the authority of a hearsay report, which gravely asserted that girls in that country could conceive at the age of 7, because of a favour conferred upon its women by Heracles of Greece, when he had visited it (*Arrian*, chap. ix). The marriage at the age of 6 and conception at the age of 7 are as true as Heracles' visit to south India. The data from Greek authors do not thus invalidate the conclusion, reached above, that girls were usually married at about the age of 14 or 15 during the Mauryan period.

We have seen above that there was a conflict of opinion in society during the period 400 B.C.-100 A.D. about the desirability of pre-puberty marriages. Soon after 100 A.D. this conflict ended and society definitely decided in favour of pre-puberty marriages. An undue premium came to be placed upon absolute chastity; in order to prevent the theoretical possibility of unchastity in any bride whatsoever, it decreed that marriages should always be performed before puberty[1]. Society was anxious that there should be no room whatsoever even for the possibility of any reports arising reflecting upon the character of its maidens.[2] As we have already shown (*ante*, p. 15), at about this time Upanayana of girls came to an end and they had to follow no course of education worth the name. As a natural consequence girls of 15 or 16, who were not married, must have begun to find time hanging heavily upon them. Parents also must have felt that since girls were not pre-occupied with completing any educational course, it would be desirable to get them married soon after, or at about the time of their puberty. The birth of a son to ensure the continuity of the family and offer oblations to the manes was always welcome; an early marriage meant a son soon after puberty and was thus felt to be preferrable.[3] That this may mean an undue physical strain on the girl-mother was unfortunately not realised.

From about 200 A.D. pre-puberty marriages became the order of the day. Yājñavalkya, who wrote at about this time, insists that girls should be married before the age puberty; otherwise every month their guardians will be guilty of the destruction of an embryo.[2] Yama, who came abut 400 years later, states that even if a suitable match is impossible, the girl should be married before she comes of age even to an unsuitable

1. See *ante* p. 54 note No. 3.

2. तस्माद्विशल्ययितुमिच्छसि मां यदि त्वं
वत्से तदुन्मिषति नूतनयौवनेऽस्मिन् ।
न स्वेच्छमर्हसि चिरं खलु कन्यकात्व
मासेवितुं सुलभदुर्लभदुष्प्रवादम् ॥ *Kss*, 34, 229.

3. ऋतवो बहवस्ते वै गता व्यर्थाः शुचिस्मिते । Mbh, I, 94, 65.

4. अप्रयच्छन्समाप्नोति भ्रूणहत्यामृतौ ऋतौ । I, 13.

husband.[1] What a difference between the views of Manu and Yama ? The former was willing to allow a girl to remain unmarried even to the end of her life, if a proper husband could not be secured. The latter did not mind a girl being chained to an unsuitable and undeserving husband for her whole life, if there was the least danger of the fatal line of the age of puberty being crossed before the marriage.

It was not always possible to celebrate a marriage in every case just on the eve of puberty. If it was postponed to the last moment, there was the danger of crossing the fateful line. Not content, therefore, with prohibiting post-puberty marriages, Smṛiti writers of the period 500-1000 A.D. began to encourage marriages *much before* the time of puberty. They held that a girl should be regarded as having attained puberty at the age of 10 and therefore her marriage should not be postponed beyond that age.[2] At this time the ritual of marriage in the case of girls was regarded as corresponding to that of *upanayana* in the case of boys; if the eighth year was the proper time for the latter, it ought to be the ideal time for the former also. A girl of 8 was Gaurī and was therefore the most suitable one for marriage.

The Vedic marriage mythology referred to Soma, Gandharva and Agni as the earlier divine husbands of the bride; her human husband was the fourth one. Writers of this period began to advocate the view that the different divine husbands get jurisdiction over the girl when different signs of impending puberty manifest themselves at different ages. They pointed out[3] that

1. दद्याद्गुणवते कन्यां नग्निकां ब्रह्मचारिणे ।
अपि वा गुणहीनाय नोपरुन्ध्याद्रजस्वलाम् ॥

Quoted in *SCS.*, p. 216.

2. अष्टवर्षा भवेद् गौरी नववर्षा तु रोहिणी ।
दशवर्षा भवेत्कन्या अत ऊर्ध्वं रजस्वला ।
प्राप्ते तु दशमे वर्षे यस्तु कन्यां न यच्छति ।
मासि मासि रजस्तस्याः पिता पिबति शोणितम् ॥ *Br. Yama*, III. 21-22.

3. रोमकाले तु संप्राप्ते सोमो भुंक्ते तु कन्यकाम् ।
रजःकाले तु गन्धर्वो वह्निस्तु कुचदर्शने ॥
तस्मादुद्वाहयेत्कन्यां यावन्नर्तुमती भवेत् । Samvarta in *SCS*, 321.

one should forestall them all by marrying the girl at the age of 8 or 9.

The custom of pre-puberty marriages became common among the Brāhmaṇas alone in the beginning; one writer even of the 17th century A. D. observes that the Kshatriyas are not expected to follow it.[1] Life was more ephemeral in the case of the members of the fighting classes than it was with the rest of the community; they naturally refused to follow the new custom, which would have enormously increased the number of child widows in their community. We can therefore well understand how, in spite of the universal and terrible condemnation of the post-puberty marriages by Smṛiti writers from *c.* 200 A.D. child marriages did not come into vogue among the Kshatriyas for a long time. Heroines of most of the Sanskrit dramas written during the period 300-1200 A. D. are grown up brides at the time of their marriages; this is so because they mostly belong to Kshatriya circles. There are many historic examples of grown up marriages among the Rajputs during the medieval period. This will now cause no surprise to the reader. In the Deccan also during the Vijayanagar rule while pre-puberty marriages were common among the Brāhmaṇas, post-puberty ones were frequent among the non-Brāhmaṇas[2].

Post-puberty marriages continued as local customs also in some of the areas that continued to be under the influence of the old pre-Aryan culture. This, for example, is the case in Malbar to the present day. A 15th century commentator observes that among the people of this province, the attainment of puberty before the marriage is not regarded as a blemish[3]. The influence of the matriarchate is responsible for Malbar's bold stand against child marriages.

1. 'यस्तु तां वरयेत्कन्यां ब्राह्मणो ज्ञानदुर्बलः ।' अत्र ब्राह्मणोपादानाद् ब्राह्मणस्यैवायं निषेधो न क्षत्रियादीनाम् । *VMS.*, p. 771.

2. Venkataramanayya, *Studies in Vijayanagar History*, p. 390.

3. केरलदेशे कन्याया ऋतुमतीत्वं न दोषाय ।

Madhava on *Par.*, i, p. 19.

In the course of time the advocates of pre-puberty marriages did not remain content with the girl's marriage at 8 or 9. There was an extreme section among them that clamoured for a still lower age. It is represented in *Brahma Purāṇa*, which recommends that a girl should be married at any time after the age of four.[1] Texts like those of Manu, which permitted a girl to remain unmarried even throughout her life if a suitable husband was not available, were explained away as emphasising the importance of a proper selection of the bridegroom and not as permitting any post-puberty marrioge.[2]

The analogy of *Upanayana* was also utilised for lowering the marriage age to this ridiculous extent. Parents anxious to ensure a rapid progress of their sons in education were advised to perform their *Upanayana* at the age of 5; marriage was the substitute for *Upanayana* in the case of girls, and so it could well be performed at the same early age.

It may be, however, pointed out that the extreme views above referred to, did not become popular for a long time. We learn from Alberuni that during the 11th century A.D. the normal age of a Brāhmaṇa bride was 12 (II,p.131). Parents in the lower sections of society, where the pernicious custom of the bride price prevailed to a great extent, were the first to take advantage of the permission to marry girls at the age of 5 or 6 for their own selfish ends. Their example was later on followed by other classes, and the custom of very young marriages thus began to be more and more common. The ramification of the caste system into hundreds of sub-castes and the prohibition of intermarriages among them from about the 8th or the 9th century A.D. further accentuated the evil of child marriages. The selection of a

1. चतुर्थाद्वत्सरादूर्ध्वं यावन्न दशमात्ययः ।
तावद्विवाहः कन्यायाः पित्रा कार्यः प्रयत्नतः । 165,8.

2. 'काममामरणात्' इति । तद् गुणवति सति गुणहीनाय निषेधपरम् । न तु सर्वथा गुणहीननिषेधपरम् । ऋतुमत्यपि तिष्ठेदिति वचनं उक्तरीत्या न स्वार्थे तात्पर्यवत् । Mādhava on *Par.*, I. ii, p. 78.

suitable bridegroom was becoming progressively more difficult, as the field of choice was being further and further narrowed down by the rise of new water-tight sub-castes. Parents did not like to take the risk of losing a good bridegroom at hand by postponing the marriage to a later date. Paradoxical though it may appear, it seems that the Satī custom, which became fairly popular at this time, helped the cause of early marriages to some extent. If the father died and the mother followed him on his funeral pyre, there would be a father-in-law at least to look after the young orphans, if they were already married. So why not provide them with an additional guardian of natural affection by marrying them at an early age ? This reason for the child marriages prevailing in Bengal was given to Merchant Fitch by the Bengalis with whom he discussed the problem in the 16th century.[1] Thy joint family system prevailing in society was also favourable for early marriages. Marriages could be performed long before the husband became an earning member, because his parents, uncles or elder brothers used to take care of his wife and children till the time he began to earn. The economic condition of the country was fairly satisfactory and it did not therefore necessitate the postponement of marriage to the time the husband became an earning member. Naturally therefore society became more and more conscious of the advantages of early marriages and oblivious to their drawbacks. It further found that child marriages gave a good opportunity to the bride to know gradually the natures and idiosyncrasies of the different members of the joint family of her husband, to note almost imperceptibly their likes and dislikes, and to entertain an affection for him before the sex instinct had been aroused. There was further no chance of any scandals arising as was admittedly the case in the earlier era of post-puberty marriages. Nor need the parents entertain any apprehensions of a daughter slipping into a nunnery against their wishes. Of course society knew that under the system of child marriage there was the

1 - Dasgupta *Bengal in the 16th century A. D.*, pp. 128 131.

danger of widowhood overcoming a bride before she came of age. But such a calamity was believed to be a decree of fate, which could not be set at nought by any human efforts.

The popularity of early marriages therefore went on increasing in medieval times. Some enlightened rulers like Akbar disliked them and recommended to their subjects that marriages should be performed after the attainment of puberty (*Ain-i-Akbari*, p.277). The advice, however, produced no effect. A number of foreign travellers and merchants tell us that boys and girls were married in India several years earlier than the time of puberty. Fitch, a 16th century English trader, has noted that boys and girls were married at Murshidabad in Bengal at the age of 10 and 6 respectively (Dasgupta, p. 131). Manucci tells us that during the 17th century girls were often married before they were able to speak, but never after the age of 10 (Vol. III, pp. 59-60). According to Tavernier, the usual marriage age was 7 or 8 (Vol. II, p. 197). One of the Brāhmana generals of the Peshava was filled with great anxiety because his daughter's marriage could not be arranged at the age of 9. 'If the marriage is postponed to the next year', he writes from the battlefield, the bride will be as old as 10. It will be a veritable calamity and scandal.'

8 or 9 was the usual marriageable age of girls at the advent of the British rule. With the introduction of western ideas and civilization the educated sections of society began to feel the necessity of deferring marriages to a more advanced age. Social conferences began to advocate the cause of post-puberty marriages during the nineties of the last century, but their efforts were not appreciably successful till the beginning of the 20th century. The terrible havoc caused by the plague, advanced the marriageable age of girl from 8 to 12 or 13. Society, however, was still afraid to cross openly the fateful age of puberty. The gradual disruption of the joint family system, the progressive realisation of the usefulness of female education, and above all, the hard necessities of the economic struggle for existence eventually induced the advanced sections of Hindu society to throw over-board the

Smṛiti injunctions, and to openly adopt post-puberty marriages. If, on account of economic factors, youths find it necessary to postpone marriages to the age of 24 or 25, they have naturally to choose their partners in life who are at least 16 or 17 at the time of the marriage. The Sarda Act, which laid down 18 and 14 as the minimum legal age of marriage for boys and girls respectively, followed the actual practice of the advanced middle classes of society: The second World War caused a further rise in the marriageable age of girls. The inflation which it has caused since 1942 has made it almost impossible for the middle classes to balance their budgets with only one earning member in the family Several new lines of employment became available to women with the opening of Rationing and other new departments. It used to be debated formerly as to whether married women should seek employment or not; now they began to accept them as sheer economic necessity in a large number of cases. Now a days marriages are often settled after ascertaining whether the bride can be an earning member of the family. This has necessitated a higher education for girls and thereby increased the marriageable age to about 20 or 21 in the case of the middle classes. Of course early marriages still prevail in lower sections of the community, and working on the data of the census of 1921, the Age of Consent Committee of 1929 computed that about 39% of girls were married before the age of 10. The censues of 1941 and 1951 showed that percentage of girls who were married before the age of 14 was 17 and 14 respectively. But the factors favouring late marriages will soon begin to operate even in the ease of lower classes and in less than a generation post-puberty marriages will become the order of the day.

The passing of the Sarda Act in1929,penalising the marriages of girls before the age of 14,produced a reaction in the orthodox section of Hindu society, some members of which procceded to openly break the law. Their protests and propaganda, however, did not help the cause of the child marriage to any appreciable degree. The fact is that all those secular causes,which favoured the custom of the child marriage, are rapidly disappearing now. The joint family system is disintegrating, the economic struggle is becoming hard, and the theory that girls need not be educated like boys has ceased to appeal to society. The injunction of the later Smṛitis prescribing pre-puberty marriages is of course there, but the thoughtful section of Hindu society feels that it should be now set aside in favour of the view of the earlier Dharmaśāstra writers, who permitted the postponement of girls' marriages to about the age of 16 or 17. In accepting and following the theory of post-puberty marriages Hindu society is merely returning to the old custom of the Vedic and Epic times. It need not therefore be regarded as anti-religious at all. The main reason that was responsible for popularising post-puberty marriages in the early period of Hindu history was the great concern which society felt over the question of gitls' education. Precisely the same reason is now helping the cause of post-puberty marriages. In the past a few ladies known as Brahmavādinīs used to remain for ever unmarried, as they were anxious to devote themselves entirely to the cause of learning and religion. The phenomenon is repeating itself in modern times. Today also we have some ladies in society, who prefer to remain unmarried, because they want to devote themselves to the cause of education and social service. The short-lived Servants of Women Society of Poona had laid it down that its members should remain unmarried, so that they should find it possible to devote themselves wholly and solely to the cause of the Society. In the Passive Resistance movement of Gandhiji there were several women who after discarding marriage, had devoted themselves whole-heartedly to the cause of the country.

When the pendulum is now moving towards the direction of late marriages, it is necessary to point out that they also have their own defects and draw-backs. The marriage of a girl at the age of 10 is undesirable as her marriage at the age of 30. There should be post-puberty marriages, no doubt, but they should not be normally postponed to beyond the age of 19 or 20. We have shown in Chapter I (*ante*, pp. 27-28) how the escondary and higher education of girls can be finished before this time. One Dharmasūtra writer has pointed out that both the bride and the bridegroom ought to be in the prime of their youth at the time of their marriage; not a single hair of theirs should have grown gray at that time. This point has to be remembered when the marriage age is being gradually raised every decade. Society therefore must be vigilant and should not countenance any tendency to postpone girl's marriage beyond the age of 19 or 20.

In the Vedic and Upanishadic periods when post-puberty marriages were the order of the day, religious and spiritual ideals were held in high veneration by the community; they used to permeate the atmosphere of society and raise up its moral tone. This used to help grown-up maidens and youths in following the strict rules and discipline of the Brahmacharya life. Unless there is a similar or corresponding atmosphere in society, it will not be able to reap the full advantages of post-puberty marriages. If youths and maidens, who have to remain unmarried till an advanced age, have to live in a society full of temptation and characterised by a vitiated taste, their late marriages would not be much better than the child marriages of the last century from the eugenic point of view.

Before concluding this section it may be pointed out that child marriages were quite common in Europe also for a long time. In ancient Rome maidens were married at the age of 10 or 12 (Muller, *Family*, p. 260). In the age of chivalry girls were often married at the age of 5, simply because marriage was a matter of military tactics and territorial alliances. The rule of the Church, that boys and girls should be married at the age of 15 and 12 respectively, was openly flouted.[1] In England, especially in the upper classes, child marriages were common in Tudor times. Some-times they were preformed when the parties were only 4 or 5; they were, however, voidable before the time of consummation

1. J. L. Daves: *A Short History of Woman*, pp. 237-61.

(Muller, p. 114). Child marriges were less common among the working classes. Though in actual practice, late marriages became common in England by 1850 A.D., still down to 1929, the minimum legal age of marriage continued to be 12 for girls and 14 for boys. In that year the Parliament raised it to 16 both in the cases of girls and boys, partly as a reaction to the introduction of the Sarda Bill in the Indian Legislature.

THE SETTLEMENT OF MARRIAGE

Let us now see what part the bride took in the settlement of her marriage. It naturally varied in different periods. In early times when brides were 16 or 17 at the time of their marriage, they had a more or less effective voice in the selection of their partners in life. The Vedic literature does not refer to parents controlling the marriages of their sons and daughters, though they must doubtless have played an important part in arranging and financing them. On the other hand we have references to beautiful brides selecting their own husbands.[1] Kshatriya circles in society even conceded to grown-up brides the exclusive right of selecting their own consorts, as is proved by the custom of *svayaṁvara* or self-choice.

The *svayaṁvara* marriages of Sāvitrī, Damayantī and Rukmiṇī are well-known.[2] In later times when the custom of

1. भद्रा वधूर्भवति यत्सुपेशाः स्वयं सा मित्रं कृणुते जने इत्।

R. V., X, 27, 1

2. It is often customary to refer to the marriages of Sītā and Draupadī as having taken place by *svayaṁvara*. This is, however, a mistake. The selection of the husband in their cases depended, not upon their choice, but upon the ability of the suitor to satisfy the specific conditions previously laid down. Very often it resulted in the maiden being married to a person she did not like. This happened in the case of Ambā, who had to marry Vichiravirya much against her own wish. She is seeing cursing her father for making her a *vīryaśulkā*, liable to be carried away by anybody who possessed the necessary valour. Aṁbā felt bitterly on the point and states that the lot of a *vīryasūlkā* maiden is none better than that of a prostitute, who has to offer herself to every customer; cf:—

धिग्भीष्मं धिगहो मे मंदं पितरं मूढचेतसम्।
येनाहं वीर्यशुल्केन पण्यस्त्रीव प्रचोदिता॥

Mbh, V. 175. 31

early marriages came into vogue, the *svayaṁvara* custom naturally died down. Girls of 8 or 9 could hardly be expected to make any intelligent choice. We find that *Agnipurāṇa* tolerates the custom,[1] but *Brahmapurāṇa* definitely disapproves of it.[2] Post-puberty marriages were in vogue in Kshatriya circles down to the middle ages, and hence *svayaṁvara* custom survived there till the 12th century A.D. Hence it is referred to in Sanskrit poems and dramas, which mostly deal with the life in royal and aristocratic families.

When society had conceded to grown up brides the right to choose their own husbands, it was but natural that love marriages, arranged by the parties themselves, should have taken place with fair frequency. Some theorists went to the extent of advocating that it is not the father or the mother, but the bride herself, who has the right of giving herself away in marriage.[3] This theory did not find general acceptance, but forward girls like Devayānī or Kuraṇgī took full advantage of it and proposed themselves. Sometimes love marriages were consummated before the performance of the ritual; these were known as Gāndharva marriages; we have discussed them alreay before (*ante*, pp. 42-43).

Details of how love marriages were usually arranged can be gathered from Sanskrit drama and fiction and the *Kāmasūtras* of Vātsyāyana. The Dharmaśāstra literature is silent on the topic, partly because it disapproved of Gāndharva marriages, and partly because most of it was composed when child marriages had come into vogue rendering love unions impossible. Referen-

1. अवण्डया स्त्री भवेद्राज्ञा वरयंती स्वयंपतिम्। 226.4

2. यस्माद्वृतवती चेयं पतिं पितृमती सती।
स्वतंत्रा धर्ममुत्सृज्य तस्माद्भवतु निम्नगा ॥ Chap. 219

3. See for instance the arguments of Dushyanta and Sūrya to Śakuntalā and Kunti respectively when trying to win them over—
आत्मनो बन्धुरात्मैव गतिरात्मैव चात्मनः।
आत्मनैवात्मनो दानं कर्तुमर्हसि धर्मतः। *Mbh.* I, 94,24.
न ते पिता न ते माता गुरवो वा शुचिस्मिते।
प्रभवन्ति प्रदाने ते भद्रं ते शृणु मे वचः। *Ibid*, III, 3, 8.

ces in Vedic literature to lovers yearning for each other, moving in each other's company, exchanging mutual presents, using spells for ensuring reciprocal affection have been already given, (*ante*, pp. 58-9) and they will enable the reader to get some idea of how love marriages used to take place at that time. The most detailed and circumstantial description is to be found in the *Kāmasūtras* of Vātsyāyana (III, 5). Love would start with the accidental meeting of the parties in a garden or a show. Sometimes these meetings used to be deliberately brought about by their friends or guardians, who were anxious to see them united in wedlock. When once the hearts were stirred, the passion became stronger by subsequent meetings and associations. The girl would go to see her lover with her friends and vice versa. The parties would often play together and go to see a show or a fair in each other's company. The lover would tell stories to his sweetheart, and the latter would play music for the recreation of the former. Both would often go together for sport in water at the time of bath. On such occasions they were usually accompanied by some friends or trusted servants. Mutual exchange of gifts was a normal procedure. A confession of love followed in course of time and it was tested by pretended illness. In some cases the parties would unite together and the formal marriage would follow with the consent of the elders, which was always presumed. Usually, however, even in love marriages, brides did not regard themselves free to take the final step, as they felt that such a procedure would smack of disrespect to their parents.[1] They would urge their lovers to make the formal proposal to their guardians, as they were confident of its outcome. Thus Suvarchalā confessed to Śvetaketu that she had fallen in love with him, but asked him to make the formal request to her father.[2] A heroine

1. मा भूत्स कालो दुर्मेधः पितरं सत्यवादिनम्।
अवमन्य स्वधर्मेण स्वयंवरमुपास्महे ॥ *Rāmāyaṇa*, I, 32, 20.

2. मनसापि वृतो विद्वन् शेषकर्ता पिता मम।
वृणीष्व पितरं मह्यमेष वेदविधिः स्मृतः ॥ XII, 224, 38.

in the *Kathāsaritsāgara*, with abashment writ large on her face, prayed her lover to open the topic to her father, as she did not feel free to give herself away.[1] This procedure was no doubt an improvement over the alternative one, whereunder the bride took the final step on her own responsibility. The known love of a grown up daughter would naturally induce the father to give his consent, even if he may not be very enthusiastic about the proposed union. If he felt that the match was unsuitable, he would usually take steps at an earlier stage to discourage the growing intimacy, and thus prevent the marriage.

It is difficult to say how many marriages were preceded by courtship as above described during the time when post-puberty marriages prevailed. The percentage of such love marriages, however, was probably not very high. They seem to have been confined to Kshatriya and well-to-do classes. In the vast majority of cases, even when parties were quite grown up, their marriages were usually arranged by parents, of course with due regard to their desires expressed or implied. Such, for instance, is usually seen to be the case in Jātaka stories. The father, and more particularly the mother, were anxious to find out whether their choice met with the approval of their daughters or not. In many stories of the *Kāthāsaritsāgara*, parents are seen anxiously enquiring which of the bridegrooms tentatively selected by them met with their daughters' approval.[2]

When from *c.* 200 A.D. child marriages became the order of the day, the state of affairs changed. Girls of 10 or 12 were incapable of exercising any choice worth the name, and so the whole responsibility gradually fell upon the father. The Hindu father has been always trying to discharge this responsibility with a solicitude, that has justly become proverbial. He passes

१. तयाऽप्यूचे स विनमद्वक्त्रया मुनिपुंगवः।
एषा यदीच्छा भवतो नर्मालापो न चेदयम्॥
तद्देव दाता नृपतिः पिता मे याच्यतामिति॥ २७, ८१-२.

२. एषां चतुर्णां वर्णानां पुत्रि कोऽभिमतस्तव।

sleepless nights when his daughter approaches the marriageable age. He does not mind even the insults that he has sometimes to pocket while searching for a proper son-in-law. In order to secure a very desirable match, he often spends much more than what is the legitimate share of his daughter in the ancestral property. If she is very young, he cannot have the benefit of her mature views; but his wife's guidance in the matter usually ensures a selection that meets with his daughter's approval, when grown up. Long association with each other before the rise of sex consciousness usually results in a genuine mutual attachment between the couple.

In the absence of the father, the responsibility of arranging the marriage would devolve upon the grand-father, brother or uncle of the daughter. The mother is usually placed last in the list of marriage guardians, the reason being that she was not usually the administratrix of her husband's property. Being a widow she had no facilities to take an initiative in the matter. In the final selection of the son-in-law, her voice, however counted a good deal.

The classical Sanskrit literature written after *c.* 500 A.D. shows that society regarded it as unmannerly that girls should proceed to choose their partners without being authorised by their guardians. In the *Kādambarī* of Bāṇa Mahāśvetā regards such a procedure as highly objectionable. The father alone was regarded as having the sole authority to dispose of his daughter in marriage.[1]

The dowry system did not stand as an impediment in daughter's marriage in ancient India. In prehistoric times women were regarded as chattel and so it was the bride's father, and not the bridegroom's, who was regarded as justified in demanding a payment at the time of marriage. The bridegroom carried away the bride and deprived her family of her services. He could not have dreamt of demanding a further dowry or donation. Such a request, if ever made, would have been summarily turned down

1. प्रभवति निजस्य कन्यकाजनस्य महाराजः । *Mālatimādhava* p. 50.

as preposterously unreasonbale. The wife in these early times used to get no proprietary rights in her husband's family. Nor had her father-in-law to provide any expensive education to her husband.

Dowry system, therefore, was generally unknown in early societies, and the same was the case with ancient Hindus. In rich and royal families some gifts used to be given to sons-in-law at the time of marriage. Thus the *Atharvaveda* once incidentally refers to royal brides, bringing with them the dowry of a hundred cows.[1] Draupadī, Subhadrā and Uttarā also brought with them rich presents of horses, elephants and jewels at the time when they left their parents' homes after their marriages. The Jātakas often describe how very valuable presents were given to the bridegroom when rich merchants like the father of Viśākhā sent their daughters to their husband's homes. Inscriptions often refer to rich marriage presents given at the time of the marriages of princes. In *Raghuvaṅśa* (VII, 32) we find the king of Vidarbha sending handsome presents with his sister Indumatī at the time of her departure with her husband after her marriage. These presents, however, can hardly be called dowries, for they were voluntarily made after the marriage out of pure affection. There are no references either in Smṛitis or in dramas to the dowry, *i. e.*, to a pre--nuptial contract of payment made by the bride's father with the bridegroom or his guardian. If the custom had prevailed to anything like its present extent, it would have been very vehemently condemned by Smṛiti writers like the counter custom of the bride-price. We meet with no such condemnation. Smṛitis, no doubt, recommend that the bride should be given in marriage along with suitable ornaments, but their number and price is left entirely to the discretion and ability

1. नास्य जाया शतवाही कल्याणी तल्पमाशये। V. 17, 12.

In अश्रवं हि भूरिदावत्तरा वा विजामातुरुत धा वा स्यालात्। (*R.V.*, I, 109, 2.) the generosity of a brother-in-law is extoled. There may be a possible reference here to a brother giving a handsome dowry for his sister, but this interpretation is by no means free from doubt.

of the bride's father. A prenuptial contract in this respect is neither contemplated nor countenanced.

The dowry system is connected with the conception of marriage as a *dāna* or gift. A religious gift in kind is usually accompanied by a gift in cash or gold. So the gift of the bride also was accompanied by a formal and small gift in cash or ornaments. The amount of this gift was a nominal one for a long time, and did not create any impediments in the settlement of marriages. It is only in medieval times and in Rajputana that we find the dowry system assuming alarming proportions. This, however, happened only in the case of royal and aristocractic families. The extraordinary pride, which the Rajputs took in their ancestry, was mainly responsible for this development. A Rajput youth of the bluest blood would be desired as a son-in-law by a large number of people, and so his price in the marriage market would sore high. The dowry system had become a positive evil of great magnitude in Rajputana from about the 13th or 14th century A.D.

In ordinary families, however, the amount of the dowry was a nominal one. It was a voluntary gift of pure affection and presented no impediment in the settlement of the daughter's marriage till the middle of the 19th century. It is only during the last 50 or 60 years that the amount of the dowry has begun to assume scandalous proportions. A good education, a lucrative appointment, or a good footing in a learned profession improved enormously the social and economic position of a youth, and made him immensely attractive as a son-in-law. He naturally acquired a high price in the marriage market. There were no such factors in the pre-British period, when society was mostly agricultural and government appointments were not so lucrative as they are at present. So naturally anything like the present scandalous dowry system did not exist. It is now high time for Hindu society to put an end to this evil custom, which has driven many an innocent maiden to commit suicide. There are signs to show that this custom is becoming unpopular and odious, but public opinion must assert itself more emphatically. The youth must rise in rebellion against it. The custom is really as heinous as the counter custom of bride-price, which has been so vehemently condemned by our culture. Proper female education, marriages at an advanced age, mainly settled by the parties themselves, and the awakening of the public conscience seem to be the only remedies that will eventually stamp out the custom.

For a long time astrological considerations like the tallying of horoscopes played no part in the settlement of marriage. Gṛihya Sūtras and Dharma Sūtras nowhere suggest or recommend that horoscopes of the parties to be married should be consulted before deciding upon their marriage. The reason is quite simple. In their days the science of astrology was quite in its infancy and had yet to evolve or borrow the zodiacal signs. Complicated horoscopes of the modern type did not exist and had not to be consulted down to about 400 A.D. From the dramas of Bhāsa it appears that astrologers of the 3rd century A. D. were only concerned about the auspiciousness of the marriage day. Certain lunar mansions (*nakshatras*) were regarded as auspicious and parents used to take the precaution of celebrating marriages on their days. Astrology played no further part in the marriage ceremony. The subject, however, made rapid progress during the period 400-900 A.D.; it then began to play an important part in the making and breaking of matches. Horoscopes came into vogue at this time and began to be consulted at the settlement of marriage.

A reference to parents of brides consulting an astrologer for the marriages of their wards occurs perhaps for the first time in the *Daśakumāracharit*, written in the 7th century A.D.[1]

QUALIFICATIONS OF THE PARTIES

Let us now consider the question of the qualifications of the bride and the bridegroom. Wealth, beauty, health, intelligence and good family were the main considerations in the selection of

1. लक्षणज्ञोऽयं कार्तान्तिक इत्यमुष्मै कन्याः कन्यावन्तः प्रदर्शयाम्बभूवुः।
(p. 219 Nirṇayasagar Ed).

the bride and the bridegroom. Naturally opinion was not unanimous about the relative importance to be attached to each of these factors, and we find different advocates claiming superiority for each of them. In actual practice different persons must have been swayed by different considerations.

Dumb, deaf, blind or lame persons were naturally regarded as undesirable spouses. Marriages with them were however not regarded as invalid, probably because it was realised that they too have the sex instinct and are perhaps in greater need for a partner in life than ordinary individuals. Levirate was current in early times and so even impotency was not regarded as an insuperable impediment. The instance of Pāṇḍu shows that in such cases the wife could get issues by levirate. Manu includes children of impotent persons among his list of heirs.[1] When, however, levirate went out of vogue on account of its strong condemnation by the reformist school, marriages with impotent persons were declared to be invalid by writers like Parāśara and Nārada.[2] Both these jurists allow the wife of an impotent person to remarry. When, however, remarriages went out of vogue, this remedy became unavailable.

The present day rule, which prohibits marriages between persons of the same *gotra*, was unknown to society for a long time. The very conception of *gotra* as a group of persons connected with one another by spiritual or blood relationship was unknown in the Vedic age. The word *gotra* occurs in the Vedic literature, but it is used there in the sense of a cow-pen. The prohibition of *sagotra* and *sapravara* marriages does not go back to a period much earlier than *c.* 600 B. C. The Purāṇas are unaware of this bar; Vāsudeva and Devakī for instance both belonged to the same Sātvata stock and had therefore probably the same *gotra*. It is very likely that the introduction of the bar

1. यद्यर्थिता तु दारैः स्यात्क्लीबादीनां कथंचन।
तेषामुत्पन्नतन्तूनामपत्यं दायमर्हति॥ IX, 203.

2. अपत्यार्थं स्त्रियः सृष्टाः स्त्री क्षेत्रं बीजिनो नराः।
क्षेत्रं बीजवते देयं नाबीजो क्षेत्रमर्हति॥ *Nārada*, XII, 19.

of *sagotrata* to the marriage is due to the influence of a cognate custom prevailing among the non-Aryans, which interdicted marriages among the worshippers of the same totem. It is also likely that the marriages among *sagotra* persons may have been prohibited with a view to discourage clandestine love affairs among persons closely related to each other.

The prohibition first appears in the Gṛihya Sūtra literature and is subsequently accepted by later writers. A *sagotra* marriage was very seriously viewed by Smṛiti and Nibandha writers, who could never think of validating it by the theory of the *factum valet.* The modern law courts also regard it as illegal. There is however no point in continuing this ban now; *gotras* were originally merely surnames and members of the same *gotra* have no real tie of consanguinity. And even if we suppose that there originally existed such a tie, it would be hardly rational or eugenic now to prohibit marriages on that account. For, members of any particular *gotra* existing to-day are removed by hundreds of generations from its original founder.

It may be passingly pointed out that the modern idea that the members of a *gotra* are descended from one and the same Ṛishi is not historically true. Some *gotra* founders like Vasishṭha, Viśvāmitra, Bhāradvāja etc. were no doubt Ṛishis, but an analysis of the *gotra* names shows that many of them had nothing to do with any family progenitor. Some *gotra* names are territorial in their significance; compare for instance, Gandhāra, Panchāla, Kauśāmbeya, etc. Many of them are professional like Meshapa, Hastipa, Hotā, Yājaka etc. Some of them are based on personal defects like Matsyagandhi, Kāṇa, Dīrghajangha, etc. Some of them refer to personal idiosyncracies; thus Jayaviśvambhara was obviously the way in which some particular individual used to greet his visitors; it became first his nickname and then his descendants also began to be known by it; thus this *gotra* was brought into existence. It will thus be seen that *gotras* are really not all connected with a descent from any Vedic Ṛsihi; to argue that persons of the Kauśāmbeya *gotra* should not intermarry would be as reasonable as to argue that there should be no intermarriages among the residents of Poona or Calcutta. The bar of the *sagotratā* to the marriage was removed by the legislature in 1946 and it is a reform in the right direction.

Marriages among near relations were discouraged. It was laid down that the parties to a marriage should not be *sapiṇḍas*, i.e. related to each other within seven generations on the father's side and five generations on the mother's side. Very often, however, the *sapiṇḍatā* was contracted to five and three generations respectively. In the Deccan, however, the custom was long established of the marriage of a person with his maternal uncle's daughter though it conflicted with the rule of *sapiṇḍatā* mentioned above. Medieval writers further lay down that one should not marry one's wife's sister's daughter or one's paternal aunt's sister as a kind of parental relation existed between the above parties.[1] There was also a prejudice against marrying two sisters to one person. This latter injunction was often transgressed in practice, espacially when an elder sister had died leaving behind a child.

The caste also did not raise any insurmountable barrier in the way of marriage for a long time. Even in the days of Manu the system was much more flexible than it is today, both as regards inter-marriages and inter-dining. The question of intercaste marriages cannot be discussed here in detail; we may however observe that *anuloma* marriages *i. e.*, marriages of males of higher castes with females of lower ones were not uncommon in society down to the eighth century A.D. Even orthodox Smṛiti and Nibandha writers regarded them as legal, though not comenedable, down to the 14th century A.D. Dharmaśāstra authors further lay down rules governing the shares of inheritance of sons born from wives of different castes.[2] Nor do they

1. दंपत्योर्मिथः पितृमातृसाम्ये विरुद्धसंबन्धः ।
यथा भार्यास्वसुर्दुहिता पितृव्यपत्नीस्वसा च । *Nirṇayasindhu.*

2. नानावर्णस्त्रीसमवाये दायं दशांशान्कृत्वा चतुरस्त्रीन्द्वावेकमिति यथाक्रमं विभजेत् । *B. D. S.*, II. 2, 19.

forget to enlighten us about the different periods of ceremonial impurity to be observed in case the relation dying happens to be of a different caste.[1] That rules on these points should be found necessary to be laid down shows that inter-caste marriages of the *anuloma* type were not infrequent at least among the Brāhmaṇas, Kshatriyas and Vaiśyas.

Epigraphical and literary evidence shows the same thing. The Brāhmaṇa king Agnimitra of the Śuṅga family had married a Kshatriya princess named Mālavikā in *c.* 150 B.C. A fifth century inscription records how a Brāhamaṇa of a respectable family, Soma by name, had married a Kshatriya lady 'in accordance with the precepts of Śrutis and Smṛitis',[2] and not out of any frivolity; the Vākāṭaka minister Hastivarman was descended from him. At about the same time a Kadamba ruler, though a Brāhmaṇa by caste, gave his daughter in marriage to the Guptas, who were Vaiśyas. As the bride belonged to a higher caste than the bridegroom, this was not only an inter-caste but also a *pratiloma* marriage, which is very vehemently condemned by Smṛiti writers. The founder of the Pratīhāra family, king Harichandra (*c.* 550 A. D.), had both a Brahmana and a Kshatriya wife.[3] The father of poet Bāṇa had a Śūdra wife as well, and her children were living in the same household. Rājaśekhara, a poet laureate at the Gurjara Pratīhāra court, had married a cultured Kshatriya lady in *c.* 860 A. D. In the *Kathāsaritsāgara* we often find the daughter being asked by her father as to which of the suitors belonging to the four castes met her approval.[4] When Brāhmaṇa Aśokadatta was married to a princess, the author of

1. ब्राह्मणस्य क्षत्रियविट्शूद्रेषु सपिंडेषु षड्रात्रत्रिरात्रैकरात्रैः
2. सोमस्ततः सोम इवापरोऽभूत्स ब्राह्मणः क्षत्रियवंशजासु।
श्रुतिस्मृतिभ्यां विहितार्थकारी द्वयीसु भार्यासु मनो दधार॥
A. S. W. I., Vol. IV, p. 140.
3. तेन श्रीहरिचंद्रेण परिणीता द्विजात्मजा।
द्वितीया क्षत्रिया भद्रा महाकुलगुणान्विता॥ *E. I.*, XVIII, p. 87.
4. एषां चतुर्णां वर्णानां पुत्रि कोऽभिमतस्तव। 53, 108.

the above book records his hearty approval of the union; 'the marriage between the princess and the Brāhmaṇa youth appeared to mutual advantage like the union of learning with modesty.[1]

It was from about the 10th century A. D. that intercaste marriages began to go out of fashion. Alberuni (*c.* 1020 A.D.) observes that the Brahmanas of his day no longer availed themselves of the permission to take wives from the three lower castes. Kalhaṇa, the 12th century Brahmana historian of Kashmir, had to record the marriage of a sister of king Saṅgrāmarāja (1003-1028 A.D.) with a Brahmana youth. The marriage evidently shocked him, and he does not fail to express his regret that the king should not have realised how he was bringing his family into disgrace by such an intercaste union.[2] Several 16th and 17th century travellers have noted how intercaste marriages were quite unknown to the contemporary Hindu society.

Intercaste marriages were permitted down to the 10th century because the cultural differences between the members of the different twice-born castes were not many or far-reaching. They all performed *upanayana*, and observed the various sacraments laid down for them. They were all non-vegetarians; even Brahmanas used to eat meat when they took part in Vedic or ancestral sacrifices. Things began to change gradually, and by about the 9th century, the cultural gulf between different castes became too wide to permit of happy and harmonious inter-marriages. Under the influence of growingly rigorous notions of puritanism Brahmanas gave up Vedic sacrifices and meat-eating; not content with one daily bath, they began to have two or even three ablutions a day. Sandhyā prayers could never have been more than two in the earlier times, now a third one was

1. तयोस्तु सोऽभूद्राजन्यपुत्रीविप्रेन्द्रपुत्रयोः ।
संगमोऽन्योन्यशोभायै विद्याविनययोरिव ॥ 25, 171.

2. पर्याप्तं तस्य भीरुत्वं कियदन्यत्प्रकाश्यताम् ।
असमैर्यौनसंबन्धैश्चक्षमे यशसः क्षतिम् ॥ VIII, 10.

added at the midday. A number of new *vratas* came to be prescribed. The Brahmana community as a whole used to conform to the new standard as much as possible. Other castes, however, could not only not follow the new standard, but found it difficult to maintain the old one. Thus all the *dvijas*, *i. e.*, Brahmanas, Kshatriyas and Vaiśyas, were authorised to study the Vedas. From Alberuni, however, we learn that the Vaiśyas had ceased to avail themselves of this privilege long before the 10th century, and even as regards Kshatriyas, although a few of them were still studying the Vedas, marriage and other ceremonies were performed in their case with Pauranic and not with Vedic prayers and formulae. This shows that the rule permitting Vedic studies to them had practically become a dead letter. Kshatriyas and Vaiśyas could not accept the prohibition of meat-eating, laid down and followed by Brahmanas. When the cultural differences between the Brahmanas and other castes had become so wide, inter-caste marriages were found to be highly undesirable. How could, for instance, the marriage between a vegetarian and a non-vegetarian be found feasible ? Marriages between Brahmanas and non-Brahmanas first went out of vogue. When Brahmanas made their own group endogamous, other castes followed suit, and in course of time intercaste marriages even of the *anuloma* type, though permitted by Smṛitis, disappeared from society.

Who can deny that the prohibition of intercaste marriages was a reform in the right direction when it was introduced ? The cultural disparity, which was its main cause, is however now diminishing owing to the wide spread of a homogenous culture and education. If we consider the question of intercaste marriages in modern Hindu society from the cultural and sociological view point, as, distinguished from the theological one, we shall have to conclude that their revival would not be against the spirit of Hinduism, if the parties contracting them are of the same cultural level and outlook. The few intercaste marriages that are taking place now a days usually satisfy this condition. They cannot become more frequent until the cultural differences between different castes and sub-castes substantially disappear. Our social reformers should not forget that the observation of the *Mahābhārata* still holds good, *viz.* an alliance of friendship or of marriage is possible between those two parties only who are evenly matched as far as character, education, culture and wealth are concerned.[1]

MARRIAGE RITUAL AND CEREMONY

Let us now consider the marriage ritual. Its detailed description is not necessary for the purpose of this book; only a few points of cultural and sociological interest will be noted here.

Betrothal and marriage were the two main parts of the marriage ceremony. Naturally there was not much difference in time between the two events when post-puberty marriages were the order of the day. When, however, child marriages came into vogue, several months, and even years, would sometimes elapse between betrothal and marriage. This would often lead to peculiar complications. During the interval a better party may, for instance, become available. In such a case, Smṛitis generally allow the former contract to be rescinded, but with due compensation to the party aggrieved. Or, one of the parties may die. If it was the bride, the bridegroom was always at liberty to select a different consort. But what if the bridegroom-elect were to die? Smṛitis differ on the point. Some of them allow the bride to be married to a different person. They point out that betrothal is not marriage, and that the latter is complete and binding only after the actual performance of the ritual.[2] Some, however regarded even a betrothed bride as a widow, if the bridegroom-elect died before the actual marriage. Manu holds this view; he, however,

1. ययोरेव समं वृत्तं ययोरेव समंश्रुतम्।
तयोर्मैत्री विवाहश्च न तु पुष्टविपुष्टयोः॥ I. 131.10.

2. अद्भिर्वाचा प्रदत्तायां म्रियेतोर्ध्वं नरो यदि।
न च मन्त्रोपनीता स्यात्कुमारी पितुरेव सा॥
Vasishṭha in *SCS*, p. 219.

allows the bride to be united with her brother-in-law but by *niyoga* only.[1] This ultra-puritanical view did not meet with public approval; it is in fact opposed to what Manu himself has stated in an earlier part of his works.[2] There is no evidence to show that betrothed girls were regarded as widows by Hindu society, if the persons to whom they had been affianced happened to die before the performance of the marriage.

We shall now briefly survey the marriage ritual in so far as it is necessary to understand its aims and ideals. When the hands of the two parties were being united in wedlock, they were informed that the union was being brought about at the behest of the god Sun. In the marriage sacrifice oblations were offered unto Pūshan, Bhaga and Aryaman, because they were the presiding deities over prospertity, good luck and conjugal fidelity respectively. These were sought to be ensured for the new couple by the nuptial sacrifice. The parties then touched each other's heart; they may be two in person, but henceforward they ought to be one in heart. Then they ascended a stone, and the prayer was offered that their mutual love should be as firm and steadfast as the stone they were treading upon. At night they were shown the Polar Star and Arundhatī; the bridegroom was to be as steadfast in love as the former and the bride was to be as chaste as the latter. In the important ritual of *saptapadī*, the bride and the bridegroom took seven steps together, and it was hoped and prayed that their future life should be full of love, brilliance, opportunities, prosperity, bliss, progeny and holiness. Finally, the husband and wife took mutual vows that each would further and fulfil the hopes, desires and ambitions of the other in the spheres of religion, love and

1. यस्या म्रियेत कन्याया वाचा सत्ये कृते पतिः।
तामनेन विधानेन निजो विन्देत देवरः॥
यथाविध्यधिगम्यैनां शुक्लवस्त्रां शुचिव्रताम्।
मिथो भजेताप्रसवात्सकृत्सकृदृतावृतौ॥ IX, 69, 70.

2. पाणिग्रहणिका मन्त्रा नियतं दारलक्षणम्।
तेषां निष्ठा तु विज्ञेया विवाहात्सप्तमे पदे॥ VIII, 227.

worldly prosperity. A prayer was offered at the end that the affectionate union of the couple should never be dissolved.[1]

After the conclusion of the marriage, the ritual required the parties to observe a *vrata* for three days, during which they could increase mutual acquaintance, but were to observe strict celibacy. It is laid down that during this period the couple was to sleep in the same room, but on different beds, and were to abstain from consummating their marriage. The idea was to emphasise at the outset on the mind of the young couple that self control was as much necessary in married life as it was before. Some writers have recommended this *vrata* for a longer period, if very capable children were desired (*B.G. S., I*, 7, 9), while others have complained that this ordeal, even if for three days only, puts too strong a strain upon the self-restraint of the newly married couple.[2] The period of three days' celibacy seems to have been selected as a golden mean between extreme views. If, however, a couple felt unequal to the ordeal, the marriage was allowed to be consummated on the first night.[3] According to Nārāyaṇa, a commentator on the *Aśvalāyana Gṛihya Sūtra*, this custom prevailed among the Vaidehas of Northern Bihar.[4]

The modern Garbhādhāna or Dvirāgamana ritual, which is performed when the bride attains puberty, is unknown to the Sūtras, which take it for granted that a marriage would be ordinarily consummated on the 4th night, as both the bride and

1. See *Aś G. S.* and *B. G. S.* for the details of marriage ritual.
2. This is the view of Bābhravya as quoted by the *Kāmasūtra* III, 2, 4-5. He pleads that during the period of three nights the couple should be allowed to approach and converse with each other on the understanding that they would not consummate the marriage. Cf:—

त्रिरात्रमवचनं हि स्तंभमिव नायकं पश्यन्ती कन्या निर्विद्येत परिभवेच्च तृतीयमिव प्रकृतिम् इति बाभ्रवीयाः। उपक्रमेत विस्रंभयेच्च न तु ब्रह्मचर्यमतिवर्तेतेति वात्स्यायनः॥

III, 2, 4-5.

3. यद्यशक्तः कुलाचाराद्वा तद्दिन एव धृतिहोमादि चतुर्थीकर्मान्तं कर्म क्रियते।
Tālavakara quoted by Chandrakānta on *G. G. S.*, II. 3, 22.

4. वैदेहेषु सद्य एव व्यवायो दृष्टः।

On *Aś G. S.*, 1. 7. 2

the bridegroom were quite grown up. Writers of a later age, who were acquainted only with child marriages, could not naturally understand this assumption. Some of them, therefore, explain away Chaturthīkarma as a ritual unconnected with the consummation of marriage,[1] while others like Mitramiśra adopt the more convenient course of omitting it altogether from their description of the marriage (*VMS*, p. 843).

When girls were married at the age of 9 or 10, the consummation of the marriage naturally took place some years afterwards. A separate Sanskāra called Garbhādhāna came to be prescribed for the occasion. It was performed on the attainment of puberty by the bride. From Alberuni we learn that this Sanskāra had become common in the 11th century A.D. (II, p. 156). The reader will find its description in a medieval digest like the *Smritichandrikā*.

When did the marriage become complete and binding ? We have seen already that betrothal was not deemed sufficient for the purpose. The majority view is that the parties become husband and wife at the end of the *saptapadī*, when the bride also passes into the *gotra* or the family of the husband.[2] The minority view is that it becomes complete only on its consummation.[3] In early times when post-puberty marriages were in vogue, the difference between the two views was more or less academical, as the consummation followed on the 4th night at the latest. In later times when child marriages became the order of the day, the question assumed a vital importance. If the marriage was incomplete before its consummation, a girl would be at liberty to marry again as a maiden, if her husband died before that event. Society, however, did not unforunately accept this view, and

1. See Śaunaka in *VMS*, p. 845.

2. पाणिग्राहणिका मन्त्रा नियतं दारलक्षणम्।
तेषां निष्ठा तु विज्ञेया विवाहात्सप्तमे पदे।
Manu, VIII, 227.

3. विवाहे चैव निवृत्ते चतुर्थेऽहनि रात्रिषु।
एकत्वमागता भर्तुः पिण्डे गोत्रे च सूतके ॥
Manu as quoted by Chandrakanta on *G. Gr. S.*, II, 3, 13.

held that the marriage should be deemed to be complete with the performance of the *saptapadī*. As a natural consequence the problem of child widows arose in an acute form when girls began to be married at the age of 8 or 9. We shall discuss it in due course in Chapter V.

DIVORCE

There is no doubt that the later Dharmaśāstra literature as a whole (200-1200 A.D.), while liberally permitting the husband to remarry during the life-time of the first wife, refuses the remedy of divorce to the wife even when completely forsaken by the husband. Like early Christianity Hinduism also held that the marriage union was indissoluble; Manu advances the extreme view that the wife's marital tie and duty do not come to an end even if the husband were to sell or abandon her.[1]

If, however, we examine carefully the earlier Dharmaśāstra literature, we find that divorces were permitted before the beginning of the Christian era under certain well-defined circumstances. It is interesting to note that even Manu himself observes elsewhere in his book that a wife is not to blame if she abandons a husband, who is impotent, insane, or suffering from an incurable or contagious disease.[2] This abandonment of the husband practically amounted to a divorce, for Manu permits such a wife to remarry if her previous marriage was not consummated.[3] The children of the new union were legal heirs to

1. न निष्क्रयविसर्गाभ्यां भर्तुर्भार्या विमुच्यते ।
एवं धर्मं विजानीमः प्राक्प्रजापतिनिर्मितम् ॥

Manu, IX, 46.

2. उन्मत्तं पतितं क्लीबमबीजं पापरोगिणम् ।
न त्यागोऽस्ति द्विषन्त्याश्च न च दायापवर्तनम् ॥

IX, 79.

3. या पत्या वा परित्यक्ता विधवा वा स्वयेच्छया ।
उत्पादयेत्पुनर्भूत्वा स पौनर्भव उच्यते ॥
सा चेदक्षतयोनिः स्याद् गतप्रत्यागतापि वा ।
पौनर्भवेन भर्त्रा सा पुनः संस्कारमर्हति ॥

IX, 175-6.

their parents. In actual practice, however, down to about the beginning of the Christian era, divorces and remarriages took place now and then in all sections of society even after the consummation of the first marriage. The *Atharvaveda* in one place refers to a woman marrying again,[1] very probably in the lifetime of her first husband; it lays down a ritual intended to unite her permanently in heaven with her husband. Her second marriage of course presupposed a divorce. Dharmaśūtra writers (400 B.C. to 100 A.D.) lay it down that a Brāhmaṇa woman should wait for her husband gone out on a long journey for five years; Kauṭilya reduces this period to ten months only (III 4). If the husband did not return within that time and she was unwilling or unable to go out to join him, she should regard him as dead and unite herself with another member of the same faimly or *gotra*.[2] Similar permission is given by the *Arthaśāstra* of Kauṭilya which requires judicial permission before contracting the second marriage.[3] Jurists differ only about the period of waiting, which however never exceeds eight years. Parāśara's permission to remarry given to the wife of a person, who is impotent or has become a religious recluse or is boycotted, clearly presupposes the possibility of divorce from the earlier marriage.[4]

Kauṭilya gives detailed rules of divorce intended for the

1. या पूर्वं पतिं वित्वाऽथान्यं विन्दतेऽपरम्।
पंचौदनं तावजं ददातो न वियोषतः॥
समानलोको भवति पुनर्भुवाऽपरः पतिः।

IX, S. 27-8

2. प्रोषितपत्नी पञ्च वर्षाण्युदीक्षेत। ऊर्ध्वं पञ्चभ्यो वर्षेभ्यो भर्तृसकाशं गच्छेत्। यदि धर्मार्थाभ्यां प्रवासं प्रत्यननुकामा स्याद्यथा प्रेते एवं वर्तितव्यं स्यात्। अत ऊर्ध्वं समानोदकपिण्डर्षिगोत्राणां पूर्वः पूर्वो गरीयान्।

V. D. S., XVII, 67.

3. अन्ततः परं धर्मस्थैर्विसृष्टा यथेष्टं विन्देत।

III, 4.

4. नष्टे मृते प्रव्रजिते क्लीबे च पतिते पतौ।
पञ्चस्वापत्सु नारीणां पतिरन्यो विधीयते॥

IV, 24.

couples who found it impossible to live with each other. They were, however, applicable only to Āsura, Gāndharva, Kshātra and Paiśācha marriages. These marriages, though commoner among the lower sections of society, were not unknown among Brāhmaṇas and Kshatriyas; divorce therefore must have prevailed among higher classes also to some extent. According to Kauṭilya, if the husband or the wife hated each other, divorce was to be granted. If a man, apprehending danger from his wife, sued for divorce, he had to return to her whatever presents he may have received at the time of marriage. If it was the wife who was the complainant, she had to forfeit her proprietary rights in her husband's family. No divorce, however, was permitted, if the marriage were performed by any of the four approved forms (III, 3).

How far these rules of divorce were availed of, it is difficult to say. Recorded cases of divorce are not to be met with in Brāhmanical tradition. In Buddhist literature, however, we meet with a few. Thus we are told that a woman named Kāṇā refused to return to her husband, when she learnt that he had contracted a second marriage during her absence. At the request of the Buddha, she was taken in adoption by a certain king, who married her to a nobleman (*Dhammapada*, II, 82 and comm.). The nun Isidasī had several divorces in her earlier life. She was first married to a merchant in Ayodhyā, who abandoned her within a month. Then her father married her to another person, who also disliked her and sent her back in an equally short time. She was then married to a third worthy, but this time the marriage did not last even for a fortnight (*Therīgāthā*, 72 and comm). *Majhima Nikāya* refers to a family where the elders were anxious to divorce a discarded wife even against her wish and marry her to a new husband.[1] It seems that parents in the lower sections of society were not accustomed to

1. इमस्सेव सावत्थिया अञ्ञातरा इत्थी ञातिकुलमागमासि। तस्सा ते ञातिका सामिकं आच्छिन्दित्वा अञ्ञस्स दातुकामा। सा च नेच्छति। Vol. II. p. 109.

waste their time in inducing unwilling sons-in-law to accept unwanted wives; they would rather bring about a second marriage, though the woman concerned may not be enthusiastic about it.

The recorded cases of divorce, however, are few, and we have evidence in the Buddhist literature itself to show that divorce was rather unusual in cultured sections of society. Thus in the Kaṇhadipāyana Jātaka (No. 444), a woman points out to her husband that though she felt no love for him, she refrained from a new marriage because it was not the custom in that family for a wedded wife to take a new husband. It is therefore clear that women in higher classes of society were very unwilling to take advantage of the custom of divorce, prevailing among the lower classes.

At about the 5th century B.C. a wave of asceticism passed over Hindu society. Though there was a good deal of opposition to it, the ideal of renunciation and puritanism, which it assiduously advocated, became eventually very well grounded in society by about the beginning of the Christian era. As one of its natural consequences society began to hold that a girl could be given in marriage only once. To divorce one husband and to marry another, because the marital life was not happy, began to appear as a grossly sensual procedure. Society, therefore, held that even if the husband were a moral wreck, or were grievously ill-treating his wife, the latter could not claim any relief by way of divorce. It may be pointed out that the Roman Catholic Church also holds the same view even today, as it regards marriages as indissoluble. In England down to the middle of the last century, a divorce could be had only by an Act of Parliament. During the long period of 140 years between 1715 and 1855 A.D., only about 180 persons could get relief through Parliamentary legislation.

We may, however, point out that divorce went out of vogue only in the higher sections of Hindu society. The *Śūdrakamalākara*, written in the 17th century, expressly permits it to Śūdras

1 *Report of the Royal Commission on Divorce and Matrimonial Causes, 1912*, p. 11.

and other lower castes.[1] In the middle of the last century the Panchayats of several castes in Gujarat used to grant divorce. The Bombay High Court in the beginning recognised this right, but later on pronounced the custom as invalid on the ground of its being opposed to the spirit of the Hindu Law.[2] In actual practice at present, however, divorces are not difficult to obtain in the lower sections of Hindu society.

In recent years some educated ladies have begun to advocate the legal recognition of divorce in Hindu community. This demand is to a large extent a natural outcome of the present Hindu law of marriage, which is very unfair to the fair sex. Man is permitted practically to divorce his first wife by contracting a fresh marriage. He can even evade his legal responsibility of maintaining the discarded wife under the plea that she refuses to stay with him. How can a self-respecting woman stay with a husband, who has transferred all his affection to a new wife and who will at best treat her only as an unpaid and unwanted maid-servant ? The number of young women, who have been in this way deserted by their husbands merely out of frivolity or whimsicality, is not small. The deserted wives cannot remarry, for neither law nor religion consents to sever their nominal marital tie with their heartless husbands. Some of them change their religion in order to contract a new legal marriage.

This state of affairs is undoubtedly unsatisfactory; it is against the spirit of what is best in Hindu culture. There are two ways of improving the situation. The first and the best one is to render polygamy altogether illegal. It may be pointed out that some cultured classes in Hindu society; *e.g.*, the Nāgara Brāhmanas of Gujarat, have voluntarily foresworn the privilege of polygamy; it is high time for all sections of Hinduism to imitate their noble example. If this is done and polygamy becomes illegal, the cases of deserted wives, who pass their

1. न शूद्रायाः स्मृतः कालो न च धर्मव्यतिक्रमः।
विशेषतोऽप्रसूतायाः स्त्रियाः संवत्सराद्विधिः॥
Nārada in *Śūdrakamalākara.*

2. Steele, *Law and Custom of Hindu Castes*, p. 26.

days in misery while their husbands are leading merry married lives with new consorts, will disappear altogether.

If, however, this step cannot be taken, divorce should be allowed in cases of proved and extreme hardship. In the interest of the solidarity of society and of the purity of morals, it is desirable that deserted wives should be allowed the remedy of divorce, *if they desire it.* It should not be, however, granted at the instance of their husbands; for that would enable them to evade their legal responsibility of maintaining their unwanted wives. The latter may find it difficult to marry or maintain themselves after the divorce.

Should divorce be allowed on wider grounds like cruelty, insanity, long imprisonment, continued adultery etc. is a difficult question to answer. There can be no doubt that in the present state of the mentality of Hindu society, permission for divorce for the above reasons would be generally detrimental to the interests of women. Even child widows do not find it easy to contract a new satisfactory marriage. Among divorced wives, not even ten per cent. may succeed in arranging a good second marriage. The remaining 90 per cent would be unable to remarry; divorce may merely result in depriving them of their legal right of maintenance against their husbands.

The introduction of divorce for reasons usually admitted as sufficient in the west would thus not be in the interest of women themselves. Experience in western countries shows that liberalisation of divorce laws usually leads to a slacker sex-morality. In recent years in most of the western countries the rate of divorce has been increasing continuously like the velocity of a falling body, and the present tendency both in Russia and England is to restrict the facilities once granted. There is no doubt that the best interests of society require that the marriage tie should be normally regarded as permanent and indissoluble. This is possible only if the ideal of marriage is very high. Both the husband and the wife have to develop self control and a high sense of responsibility. They have to realise that human nature being what it is, temperamental differences are bound to arise now and then in daily life, and they cannot be got rid off by divorce and a second marriage. Happiness in family life is possible only if the husband and the wife are prepared to make great sacrifices in order to accommodate themselves to each other. Divorce should be the last remedy in very exceptional cases.

Among the educated sections of the Hindu society there is a growing feeling that the remedy of divorce should be legally available, and the Indian Parliament has now provided for it under certain circumstances. The Hindu Marriage and Divorce Act of 1955 now allows divorce if there is a change of religion or cruelty, rendering staying with the other party unsafe. If there is lunacy for five years, or if one of the parties has a communicable venerial disease for the same period, divorce can be claimed. It is also possible if there is a desertion for five years, or if the husband keeps a concubine or if the wife becomes a concubine. If there is idiocy or impotency at the time of the marriage, it can be declared to be null and void *ab initio*. The Act also permits Sagotra as well as inter-caste marriages, both of the *Anuloma* and *Pratiloma* types.

It may be pointed out that some State Governments had passed legislation prohibiting polygamy and allowing divorce earlier. Bombay and Madras had passed these measures in 1947 and 1948 respectively. The grounds on which divorce was allowed were more or less similar to those allowed by the Act of the Indian Parliament,

CHAPTER III.

MARRIED LIFE.

In this chapter we shall take a comprehensive survey of the married life. After indicating the treatment which the bride received in her new home from her elders, we shall discuss her duties in the household, the relations that existed between her and her husband and the ideals that they were both expected to follow. We shall then consider the custom of polygamy and the evils that naturally resulted from it. The chapter will conclude with a note on the history and prevalence of polyandry.

Early in the history of our civilisation brides naturally received affectionate and respectful treatment in their new homes as they were grown up and educated at the time of marriage. The Vedic marriage hymn lays down that the bride should immediately take the reins of the household from her elderly relations.[1] Her views were usually to prevail in the household management.[2] Perhaps these statements have to be taken with a grain of salt, being of the nature of the eulogy and glorification of the new bride. Probably they refer to the wife of the eldest son in the family, who has become its *de facto* head owing to the old age of his parents, his unmarried brothers and sisters being still under his guardianship. Nevertheless we may well conclude from them that the elders of the Vedic age treated the brides with very great consideration, regard and affection. They on their part used to observe proper decorum and treat their elders with utmost deference and reverence.[3] They could,

1. सम्राज्ञी श्वशुरे भव सम्राज्ञी अधि देवृषु।
R. V., X, 85. 46.

2. यथा सिन्धुर्नदीनां साम्राज्यं सुषुवे वृषा।
एवा त्वं सम्राज्ञ्येधि पत्युरस्तं पुरेत्य च।
A. V., XIV, 1, 43.

3. यथैवादः स्नुषा श्वशुराल्लज्जमाना विलीयमानैति।
K. S., 31. 1.

however, join them at the common table, and take part in conversation.[1]

Such continued to be the case down to *c.* 500 B.C. We must of course allow for individual temperaments. In the days of the Buddha, when brides were still about 16 at the time of marriage, we come across some cases of daughters-in-law seeking refuse in nunneries in order to escape from the tyranny of their mothers-in-law. We sometimes find the latter striking their daughters-in-law in rage with a pestle and with fatal results.[2] As against these cases, however, it has to be noted that we sometimes find mothers-in-law also donning monastic robes in order to escape the ill-treatment of their daughters-in-law (*Dhp*, 115; *Thg*, XLV and comm.). There is a case on record where even a father-in-law was lounded out of his house by his four energetic daughters-in-law (*Dhp*, 324 and comm.). One daughter-in-law had a resourceful brain; she cunningly led her mother-in-law into a tank haunted by crocodiles, and the expected result followed (*Jātaka*, No. 432). We also come across a son resolving not to marry because of his observation that wives usually tend to domineer over their parents-in-law instead of showing due deference to them.

The above cases of ill-treatment of daughters-in-law and parents-in-law are however, abnormal ones. We may well conclude that down to *c.* 500 B.C., when brides were grown up and educated at the time of their marriage, they received good and considerate treatment from their elders. They, on their part, used to show them proper respect. A Buddhist nun, while describing her married life, says:—

My salutations morn and eve I brought,
To both the parents of my husband, low

1. तस्माज्ज्यायांश्च कनीयांश्च स्नुषा च श्वशुरश्च सुरां पीत्वा विलाल-पत आसते।

M. S., II, 4, 2.

2. *Vivādavatthukathā* quoted in *J. A. S. B.* 1933, p. 59; *Thg*, XLV.

Bowing my head and kneeling at their feet,
According to the training given to me.
(*Therīgāthā*, English translation, p. 158.)

The behaviour here described has been the normal one with Hindu daughters-in-law since very early days.

When child and illiterate brides became the order of the day, the tone of the treatment which was given to them by their elders in their new homes began to change. Their legal status also had changed by this time. They had ceased to be queens in their new households; they were now regarded as pupils of their husbands, who themselves were still in the student stage. Being very young, inexperienced and nervous, they were naturally prone to commit mistakes in their household work and duties, and their mothers-in-law, who also were uneducated and narrow-minded, began to feel the temptation of showing their power and authority too strong. The daughter-in-law had not for a long time the consolation of even a glance or a word affection of her husband. She had no opportunity to meet him in privacy, as her marriage could not for a long time be consummated on account of her being very young. The extent of the ill-treatment of the daughter-in-law is probably exaggerated, but there is no doubt that it did exist. We must, however, note that it was an age of authority; sons, daughters, daughters-in-law had all of them to bow down before the orders and decisions of their elders. The latter, however, though sometimes stern in their behaviour, had usually the welfare of their wards at their heart.

More vital for the wife's happiness is the treatment which she receives from her husband. Since Indo-Iranian times the husband and the wife were regarded as the joint-owners of the household. The Vedic word for the couple, *dampatī* etymologically means the joint owners of the house. The Avesta (Yashṭa, 15, 4) describes the husband and the wife as *nmāno-paiti* and *nmāno pathnī*, showing thereby that they were equal partners and joint owners of the common household. In actual practice, however, joint government or dyarchy, with absolutely equal rights and privileges to either half, is an impossibility in all spheres of life. Domestic government is no exception to this rule. Discord, disorder and deadlocks will arise in domestic management on some occasions if the husband and the wife are each allowed an absolutely equal power, and happen to possess conflicting and opposing views. To resolve these deadlocks, ultimate supreme authority has to be given to one of the two parties, and in patriarchal societies it is naturally the husband who is invested with it. In India also the case was the same. In the Hindu household the husband is the senior partner and the wife is under his general guidance.

According to the Avesta a good wife is one, who is obedient to her husband. The Vedic marriage ritual, however, does not enjoin the duty of obedience upon the wife. Both parties take the same vows. The original Christian marriage ritual, it is interesting to note, specifically enjoined the duty of obedience upon the wife. She took the oath that she would *love and obey* her husband till the death, while the latter merely averred that he would *love and cherish* her. This deliberate differentiation in oath was a natural corollary of the theory adumbrated in Paul, V, 22, that the husband is the head of the wife as Christ is the head of the Church. It is interesting to note that even in 1928 A.D., the British Parliament refused to sanction the proposal to delete the reference to obedience from the wife's oath. The Church of England, however, has in a way sanctioned the new proposal by deciding to take no action against a clergyman administering the new oath, requiring both the husband and the wife to love and cherish each other. The theory of the wife's subordination is thus dying very slowly even in the west.

Though supreme authority was clearly vested in the husband, the wife's position was one of honorable subordination. In the Vedic and epic society we find that the wife was treated with utmost courtesy and regard. It was well recognised that the wife was the ornament of the house (*R. V.* 1, 66, 3); nay, the wife herself was the home.[1] The home management was under her direct charge and ordinarily, her views were to prevail there.[2] It was she who used to rouse the servants and assign them their proper duties (*R. V.* 1, 124, 4), and thus arrange for the normal running of the household. Early Indian literature does not recognise, even theoretically, the power of physical correction in the husband. In practice also it was probably very rarely exercised in the Vedic and epic times.

When the era of child and illiterate brides came, the situation naturally changed. The marriage came to be regarded as the bride's *upanayana*, the husband as her preceptor, and the stay at his place as the counterpart of the stay at the teacher's house (*gurukula*). So, like the teacher, the husband also was endowed by later writers[3] with a limited power of physical correction over the wife, if she were guilty of a mistake or an offence. It may be pointed out that this power was conceded to the husband in the west also almost to an unlimited extent down to recent times. The calmness with which Chaucer describes the punishments inflicted on rebellious wives by their stern husbands is startling. We see a husband going to a doctor, making arrangements for the treatment of broken bones, and then beating his wife with a petle and breaking her legs for the offence of disobeying him by visiting a forbidden place.[4] In medieval Russia, the bride's father supplied his son-in-law with a new whip as a

1. जायेदस्तं मघवन्त्सेदु योनिः।

R. V., III, 53. 4.

2. यथा सिन्धुर्नदीनां साम्राज्यं सुषुवे वृषा।
एवा त्वं सम्राज्ञ्येधि पत्युरस्तं परेत्य च॥

A. V.. XIV. 1, 43.

3. भार्या पुत्रश्च दासश्च प्रेष्यो भ्राता च सोदरः।
प्राप्तापराधास्ताड्याः स्यू रज्ज्वा वेणुवलेन वा॥

II, 6, 14, 16-20.

पृष्ठतश्च शरीरस्य नोत्तमांगे कथंचन।
अतोऽन्यथा प्रहरन्प्राप्तः स्याद्राजकिल्बिषम्॥

Manu, VIII, 299, 300.

4. Abraham, *English Life and Manners in the later Medieval Ages*, p. 126.

symbol of his authority, and it was hung over the bridal bed. There was a proverb current in Germany during the 15th century to the effect that a woman and an ass existed only to be beaten (Hall, *Women in Soviet Russia*, p. 75). In England it was as late as in 1891 A.D., that the husband's right to inflict corporal punishment on his wife was first denied by the law courts. A sessions judge in Madras Presidency had recognised this right in 1936, but his view was overruled by the High Court. The above facts will show that we need not feel very much surprised if Hindu Smṛitis, written 2000 years ago, have recognised the husband's right to inflict a mild punishment on his wife, warning him at the same time that he would be a liable in a court of law if he overstepped the proper limits in the matter.

The normal relations between the husband and the wife were determined by the principle that there should be an absolute identity in their aesthetic, material and moral interests. This principle was recognised in the Vedic age, and is approved by later Dharmaśāstra writers like Manu and Āpastamba.[1] It is also emphasised in the marriage vow taken by the couple that they would invariably cooperate with each other in the realisation of their aims and ambitions in the spheres of live, wealth and spirituality. Social conscience was outraged if a couple did not honestly live up to its marriage vows.

The principle of the absolute identity of the interests of the couple followed as a natural corollary from the recognition of the fact that the husband and the wife are the complements of each other. 'Man is only one half,' says a Vedic passage, he is not complete till he is united with a wife and gives birth to children.[2] The wise have observed, says Manu, that the

1. जायापत्योर्न विभागो दृश्यते। पाणिग्रहणाद्धि सहत्वं कर्मसु। तथा पुण्यफलेषु। द्रव्यपरिग्रहेषु च।
2. अर्धो ह वैष आत्मनस्तस्माद्यावज्जायां न विन्दते अर्धो ह तावद्भवति अथ यदैव जायां विन्दतेऽथ प्रजायते तर्हि सर्वो भवति।
S. *Br.*, V, 1, 6, 10.

husband is identical with the wife and vice versa.[1] It was therefore natural that the happiness of each should be regarded as depending upon the other. If there was complete harmony between the two, the house would be a heaven, if there was discord, it would be a hell.[2] Wife is the keystone of the arch of the husband's happiness. The house may be full of sons, daughters and daughters-in-law; but it is quite empty to a person if his wife is not there to supervise over it.[3] She is the surest solace to the husband, however trying his worries and miseries may be.[4] She is the only friend, who never forsakes him in adversity. You may be in a forest, still your comfort is assured if your wife is by your side; in fact a home without wife is a orest.[5] Wife alone is the husband's trust friend, consel and companion.[6] Without her he cannot go to heaven either; so, at the time of the symbolical ascent to heaven in the sacrificial

1. विप्राः प्राहुस्तथा चैतद्यो भर्ता सा स्मृतांगना।

IX, 45.

2. आनुकूल्यं हि दम्पत्योस्त्रिवर्गोदयहेतवे।
अनुकूलं कलत्रं चेत्त्रिदिवेन हि किं ततः॥
प्रतिकूलं कलत्रं चेन्नरकेण हि किं ततः।
गृहाश्रमः सुखार्थाय पत्नीमूलं हि तत्सुखम्॥

Padmapurāṇa, Uttarakhaṇḍa, 223, 36-7.

यदा भार्याच भर्ता च परस्परवशानुगौ।
तदा धर्मार्थकामानां त्रयाणामपि संगतम्।

Mārkaṇḍeya Purāna, 67-71.

3. पुत्रपौत्रवधूभृत्यैराकीर्णमपि सर्वतः।
भार्याहीनगृहस्थस्य शून्यमेव गृहं भवेत्॥

M bh, XII. 4, 4.

4. न च भार्यासमं किंचिद्विद्यते भिषजां मतम्।
औषधं सर्वदुःखेषु सत्यमेतद्ब्रवीमि ते।

Ibid, III. 58, 29.

5. न गृहं गृहमित्याहुर्गृहिणी गृहमुच्यते।
गृहं तु गृहिणीहीनं कान्तारादतिरिच्यते॥

Mbh, XII, 144, 6.

6. गृहिणी सचिवः सखी मिथः प्रियशिष्या ललिते कलाविधौ।

Raghuvanśa, VIII, 67.

ritual he has to wait till his wife comes to accompany him.[1]

The husband is therefore to treat his wife as his dearest friend. The wife is the companion friend of a man, says a Vedic passage, and the *Mahābhārata* concurs with it.[2] Buddhist thinkers also have accepted the same view.[3] Naturally therefore the husband cannot even think of pleasure, if his wife cannot participate in it.[4] Human beings are imperfect and the wife may be sometimes cross. The husband must, however, put up with her.[5] To maintain and support his wife is the most sacred duty of the husband, which must be discharged at all costs; otherwise, he would have no right at all to be called a husband.[6] Above all, he must be true to his vow of conjugal fidelity; its violation is the greatest sin he can commit.[7]

The wife on her part had corresponding duties and obligations. She must be true to her husband in her marriage vows and lead the life of an ideal *pativratā*. She must try her utmost

1. स रोक्ष्यञ्जायामामन्त्रयते, जाये एहि स्वो रोहावेति। रोहावेत्याह जाया। तस्माज्जायामामन्त्रयते। अर्धो ह वैष आत्मनो यज्जाया।।
Ś. Br., *V*, 2, 1, 10.

2. सखा ह जाया।
A. Br., VII, 3, 13.
पुत्र आत्मा मनुष्यस्य भार्या दैवकृतः सखा।
Mbh., I, 374,73
पुत्रः प्रियाणामधिको भार्या च सुहृदां वरा।
IV, 22, 17 (B).

3. पुत्ता वत्थू मुनिस्सानं भारिया च परमसखा।
Sam. N., I, 6, 4.

4. नाकल्पां नारीमभिरमयेत्।
G. D. S., I, 8, 29.

5. अप्रियोक्तोऽपि दाराणां न ब्रूयादप्रियं बुधः।
रतिं प्रीतिं च धर्मं च तदायत्तमवेक्ष्य च।।
Mbh, I, 98, 39.

6. भरणाद्धि स्त्रियो भर्ता पालनाद्धि पतिः स्मृतः।
गुणस्यास्य निवृत्तौ तु न भर्ता न पुनः पतिः।।
Ibid, XII, 272, 37.

7. अन्योन्यस्याव्यभीचारो भवेदामरणान्तिकः।
एष धर्मः समासेन ज्ञेयः स्त्रीपुंसयोः परः।।
Manu, IX, 101.

to promote her husband's happiness.[1] Neither the father nor the mother, neither a son nor a friend, can do for a woman what a husband will. The help these can give is limited, the help the husband can offer is unlimited.[2] Her real happiness is centred in her husband.[3] The average Hindu wife will say with Sāvitrī that if separated from her husband, she will desire neither pleasure nor prosperity nor heaven; she will prefer death to separation from him.[4] She will therefore follow him in adversity as well as in prosperity.

The household management is primarily her duty, to be discharged in consultation with her husband.[5] She is to frame a proper annual budget and regulate the daily expenditure according to it. If the husband is spendthrift, it is her duty to put a gentle check on his extravagence. She is to make purchases when provisions are cheap, and to store them properly for consumption throughout the year. She is to be the paymaster of the household. She is to look after the general needs and comforts of the servants by giving them old clothes and articles. General supervision over cattle and agriculture comes within her jurisdiction, if the family is an agricultural one. If it is poor, she is to help her husband by taking her own share in the manual labour of the household management. Spinning, weaving and rope-making are to occupy her spare time. If the

1. सा हि स्त्रीत्यवगन्तव्या यस्यां भार्या नु तुष्यति।
Mbh. XII, 144, 20.

2. न पिता नात्मजो नात्मा न माता न सखीजनः।
इह प्रेत्य च नारीणां पतिरेको गतिः सदा॥
मितं ददाति हि पिता मितं भ्राता मितं सुतः।
अमितस्य च दातारं भर्तारं का न सेवते॥
Rāmāyaṇa, II, 27, 6; II, 40, 3.

3. नातंत्री वाद्यते वीणा नाचक्रो वर्तते रथः।
नापतिः सुखमेधेत या स्यादपि शतात्मजा॥
Ibid, II, 37, 30.

4. न कामये भर्तृविनाकृता सुखं न कामये भर्तृविनाकृता श्रियम्।
न कामये भर्तृविनाकृता दिवं न भर्तृहीना व्यावसामि जीवितुम्॥
Mbh., III, 297. 53.

5. The rest of this para is based on the *Kāmasūtra* IV, 1.

family is well-to-do, knitting, embroidery, kitchen-garden, and household decorations are to engage her leisure hours. If the husband is away, she is to shoulder the whole responsibility of the household, and discharge it with due regard to any instructions that he may have left behind. In times of difficulty, she is to be her husband's counsellor; if he is unable or unwilling to follow the plain path of duty, she is to bring him round by sweet yet effective words.[1] That Hindu wives could do this successfully, would be clear from the example of Draupadī, who won over Dharma to her own views by her clever and persuasive eloquence. Several Rajput ladies have emulated her example in the medieval period.

A Sanskrit poet has described the ideal conduct of a housewife in an interesting way. She was to be open-hearted to her husband, respectful to his brothers and sisters, devoted to his mother, affectionate towards his relations, considerate towards the servants, smiling even to her cowives, courteous to her husbands' friends, and hateful to his enemies.[2]

A wife, who discharged all these duties, was the true *pativratā*. Sanskrit literature is full of passages in her praise. The sanctity of gods, sages and holy places is all centred in her. The world is sanctified by her existence, and there is no sin that would not evaporate by her mere presence.[3] A tear falling from

1. काव्यं यशसेऽर्थकृते कान्तासंमिततयोपदेशयुजे।

Kāvyaprakāśa I,2.

2. निर्व्याजा दयिते ननांदृषु नता श्वश्रूषु भक्ता भव।
स्निग्धा बंधुषुवत्सला परिजने स्मेरा सपत्नीष्वपि॥
पत्युर्मित्रजने सनम्रवचना खिन्ना च तद्द्वेष्टृषु।
स्त्रीणां संवननं नतभ्रु तदिदं श्रेष्ठौषधं भर्तृषु।

Bālarāmāyaṇa, IV, 44.

3. पृथिव्यां यानि तीर्थानि सतीपादेषु तान्यपि।
तेजश्च सर्वदेवानां मुनीनां च सतीषु वै॥
सतीनां पादरजसा सद्यःपूता वसुन्धरा।

Brahmavaivarta-purāṇa, 35, 119 and 127.

her eye, when wronged, uproots even a mighty tyrant like Rāvaṇa.[1]

The ideal love and harmony between the husband and the wife have been beautifully described by Bhavabhūti. The dearest friend, the essence of all kinship, the fulfilment of all desires, a veritable treasure, the very life itself,—all these is a husband to the wife and vice versa.[2] Their love is uniform both in prosperity and adversity, and adjusts itself to surrounding circumstances; it affords the best solace to each other's heart; old age does not diminish its flavour; when the veil of reserve drops down in course of time, it develops into an ever-abiding affection.[3]

The aim of the Hindu marriage is to help the full growth and development of the husband and the wife and to promote the preservation and progress of society and its culture by enjoining upon the couple the procreation of children and their proper education. Children, especially sons, were also indispensable for offering the monthly oblations to the manes, residing in heaven.

Motherhood therefore has been the cherished ideal of every Hindu woman. The birth of a son immediately heightens her status. Kisā Gautamī was not well treated for some time after her marriage; things changed for the better the moment a son was born to her (*Thg.*, 63 and comm.). Devout prayer is offered in the marriage ritual that the couple may be blessed with sons and grandsons (X, 85, 42). Childlessness was regard-

1. प्रवादः सत्य एवायं त्वां प्रति प्रायशो नृप।
पतिव्रतानां नाकस्मात्पतन्त्यश्रूणि भूतले॥
VI, 114, 65.

2. प्रेयो मित्रं बन्धुता वा समग्रा सर्वे कामाः शेवधिर्जीवितं वा।
स्त्रीणां भर्ता धर्मदाराश्च पुंसामित्यन्योन्यं वत्सयोर्ज्ञातमस्तु॥
Mālatīmādhava, Act, VI, 18.

3. अद्वैतं सुखदुःखयोरनुगुणं सर्वास्ववस्थासु यत्।
विश्रामो हृदयस्य यत्र जरसा यस्मिन्नहार्यो रसः॥
कालेनावरणात्ययात्परिणते यत्स्नेहसारे स्थितं।
भद्रं तस्य सुमानुषस्य कथमप्येकं हि तत्प्राप्यते॥
Uttararāmacharit, Act, VI, 39.

ed as a great misfortune,[1] and every effort was made to overcome it. What a childless woman looks on, gods do not accept. India then needed more and more men and women to develop the country, and so the ideal was of a large family. The Vedic father was anxious for ten sons; the number was reduced to eight in the Smṛiti period.

The apotheosis of the mother has reached a greater height in India than anywhere else. The son could never abandon his mother, even if she was boycotted socially and religiously. He was to respect her more than father.[2] Of course, there are also passages which place the father and the preceptor higher than the mother (*Manu*, II, 145-6), but these are probably due to later sacerdotal influence. Eventually Hindu culture solved the problem of the relative superiority of these three by classing them all together as *atigurus* or supreme worthies (*Vishṇu*, 31, 1-2).

The widow could not inherit the property of her husband after his death; it passed on to her sons. Yet decorum required that they should live under the protecting care of their mother after the death of the father. They could not think of partition during her lifetime (*Manu*, IX, 104). She was in fact their *de facto* guardian. Relations between the mother and her children were very tender; people felt old not when their hair had grown gray, but when their mother was no more.[3] Mothers were never more unhappy than when away from their children. Kuntī was separated from her sons, when they were banished for thirteen years. In her message to Kṛishṇa at the end of that period she observes that neither widowhood nor

1. या वाऽपुत्रा पत्नी सा परिवृत्ती। सा निर्ऋतिगृहीता तद्यदेवास्या नैर्ऋतं रूपं तदेवैतच्छमयति।

Ś. Br., *V*, 3, 1, 13.

2. गुरूणां चैव सर्वेषां माता परमको गुरुः।

Mbh. I, 211, 16.

3. तदा स वृद्धो भवति तदा भवति दुःखितः।
तदा शून्यं जगत्तस्य यदा मात्रा वियुज्यते॥

Mbh. XIII, 268, 30.

poverty have caused her that much affliction as her separation from her dear sons.[1]

It may be pointed out that ancient Indian history knows of no matricides. In this connection an interesting anecdote is given in Amitāyurdhyāna Sūtra. Ajātaśatru, who wanted to kill his father by starvation, discovered that his plan was not succeeding because a step-mother of his was surreptitiously carrying him nourishment by smearing honey to her person. When he decided to kill this step-mother, his ministers remonstrated and said, 'Bad kings, 18,000 in number, have killed their fathers, but we have yet not heard of any, who has killed his mother'. Upon this, we are told, Ajātaśatru gave up his plan (*S. B. E.*, XLIX, Part II, p. 163).

The only matricide known to Indian tradition is Paraśurāma. In his case the legend is probably invented to emphasise the duty of obeying the father. It may be pointed out that the first boon, which Paraśurāma asks of his father after carrying out his fiendish command, is his mother's resurrection with the proviso that she should never recollect her murder.[2]

A few lines may be conveniently devoted here to the delineation of the family ideal. The words of a Vedic sage may be quoted in this connection. 'The husband and the wife are to be of one mind; the matron is to be noted for the sweetness of speech; brothers and sisters are to be of one accord; sons are to be smart and intelligent so as to carry on and further the work of the father'.[3] The Vedic age required the house-

1. न मां माधव वैधव्यं नार्थनाशो न वैरिता।
तथा शोकाय भवति यथा पुत्रैर्विना भवः॥
Ibid V, 90, 69.

2. स वव्रे मातुरुत्थानमस्मृतिं च वधस्य वै।
Mbh., III, 117, 18.

3. अनुव्रतः पितुः पुत्रो मात्रा भवतु संमनाः।
जाया पत्ये मधुमतीं वाचं वदतु शंतिवाम्॥
मा भ्राता भ्रातरं द्विषन्मा स्वसारमुत स्वसा।
संम्यञ्चः सव्रता भूत्वा वाचं वदत भद्रया।
A. V., III, 30, 2-3.

holder to tend three sacred fires, Āhavanīya, Gārhapatya and Dākshiṇeya. Social thinkers of a later age pointed out that this can be best done only by showing proper respect to parents, by promoting the welfare and happiness of the wife, children and servants, and by offering willing and effective help to self-sacrificing public workers (*Ang. Ni.*,IV, p. 44).

The above picture of the ideal family life is indeed very attractive. Let us now see how far the ideal was attained in actual life in ordinary families. We shall confine ourselves here mainly to the relations between the husband and the wife.

There is no doubt that the average Hindu wife lived up to the ideal. Sītā voluntarily exiling herself in order to share her husband's afflictions and Gāndhārī refusing to use her eyes, lest she should enjoy a pleasure denied to her consort, are but typical examples of the average devoted Hindu wife. Hundreds and thousands of others have followed similar courses, but they were too humble in society to be known to history or tradition. The conjugal fidelity of the Hindu wife is proverbial. She has stood the most trying test. She has lived up to the ideal of Sītā and Sāvitrī.

Did husbands in ancient India carry out their conjugal duties as devotedly as their spouses ? Did they live up to the high ideal laid down for them ? Did they make a serious effort to carry out the obligations laid down in marriage vows ? It is not easy to answer these questions confidently for the community as a whole. But it has to be admitted that the percentage of those who honoured the marriage vows more by the breach than by the observance was much greater in the case of husbands than it was in the case of wives. Of course we are not to generalise from stray cases of brutal husbands; nor are we to draw hasty conclusions from some caustic popular sayings like 'One may save oneself even by sacrificing one's wife'. Such sayings are cynical observations of a few persons with an abnormal mental constitution; they do not reflect the opinion or indicate the practice of the society as a whole. There are several instances to show that such theories were not followed in practice by the average husband. We have, for instance, the story of Bakāsura where the husband refuses to follow the advice of his wife, who persistently implored that she should be sacrificed in order to save the family. In the *Madhyamavyāyoga* of Bhāsa the head of the family is in a similar predicament, but he also does not think of surrendering his wife in order to save himself or his family.

In the presence of the sacred Fire the husband promised his wife that he would never forsake her in his pursuit of pleasure, wealth and spirituality. Our complaint is that the delinquents who violated this vow were not severely dealt with by society. It tolerated polygamy; it did not for a long time give any proprietary rights to the widow; later on when renunciation of the worldly life became popular, it did not condemn the action of those persons who used to desert their wives in persuit of their spiritual ideals. All this affected the position of the wife very adversely.

It is true that monogamy normally prevailed in Hindu society. The word *dampatī* 'two joint owners of the household' excludes a third person from the conjugal life. The ritual too does not provide for the association of more than one wife in the normal sacrifice. The Vedic gods also are monogamous. In practice, however, polygamy often prevailed in the rich and ruling sections of society. It was fairly common among kings and nobles, who often found it a useful instrument in strengthening their political power by contracting numerous but judicious matrimonial alliances. The rich probably regarded plurality of wives as a proof of their wealth, reputation and social position. References to polygamy are fairly numerous in the Vedic literature. The *Ṛigveda* in one place compares a person attacked on all sides by his enemies to a husband troubled by his jealous wives.[1] The *Atharvaveda* has numerous charms to enable a co-wife to monopolise the love of the common

1. सं मां तपन्ति अभितः सपत्नीरिव पर्शवः।

R. V., R, 105, 8.

husband (e. g., III, 18). The coronation ritual presupposes four wives for the king, and in practice he may have had more. Father Manu is said to have had 10 wives, and king Hariśchandra of the *Aitareya Brāhmaṇa* had only a hundred. Even the philosopher Yājñavalkya had two. There are some observations in the late Vedic literature to show that polygamy was well established in certain sections of society.[1] In later times also society thought it to be nothing unusual that men should have several wives; it however regarded it as a grievous sin if a woman transgressed her husband and transferred her affection to another person and married him.[2] Polygamy, of course, was a luxury beyond the means of the poor. A rich man can support several wives; a poor man finds it difficult to maintain even one.[3]

The main reason, however, for the occasional occurrence of polygamy even among ordinary classes was the great anxiety that was felt for the preservation and continuance of the family. For offering the prescribed oblations to ancestors so as to secure their continuance in heaven, a son was absolutely necessary, and so society permitted the husband to take a second wife, if the first one was barren. Nay, we find some writers laying down that it was the duty of the wife to urge her husband to contract

1. यदेकस्मिन्यूपे द्वे रशने परिव्ययति तस्मादेको द्वे भार्ये विन्दते।

T. S., VI, 6, 4, 3.

It has been observed that in several primitive societies, wives often urge the husbands to add to their number with a view to lighten their domestic labour. When marriage means for the woman chiefly doing her husband's work, she desires to share him with others. The situation changes when a higher conception of marriage is evolved (J. L. Davies, *A short History of Woman*, p. 146).

2. न चाप्यधर्मः कल्याण बहुपत्नीकता नृणाम्।
स्त्रीणामधर्मः सुमहान्भर्तुः पूर्वस्य लंघनम्॥

Mbh, I., 169, 36.

3. सपत्न्यो हि भवन्तीह प्रायः श्रीमति भर्तरि।
दरिद्रो बिभृयादेकामपि कष्टं कुतो बहूः

KSS., 49, 208.

a second marriage, if she had failed to present a son to him (*Kāmasūtra*, IV, 2).

Sufficient time, however, had to be allowed to pass in order to make it certain that the wife was really barren. Ten years at least had to elapse before barrenness could be presumed. In case daughters alone or very short-lived children were born, a further period of waiting for three or four years was prescribed.[1] A concession that was intended to be given only in exceptional cases, however, came soon to be regarded as the normal right of the husband. Leaders of society, however, tried to nip this tendency in the bud. One of them grows eloquent in describing the inequity of the procedure, if a husband abandons his wife with whom he has solemnly promised to live for ever.[2] Another expressly prohibits a second marriage, if the first wife had already given birth to a son.[3] A third one declares that a man who marries a second wife without a just cause, will be guilty of a sin, which can never be atoned.[4] A fourth one grows so indignant that he pronounces such a person as unfit even to become a witness in a court of law (*Nārada*, 1, 180).

Unfortunately, however, this condemnation of the second marriage did not produce the result desired. Supersession of the first wife began to become more common in well-to-do families from the beginning of the Christian era. The lowering of the marriageable age, that took place at this time, helped this undesirable tendency. Husbands would not always like to be bound down by the choices made by their parents, when they had not even

1. अप्रजां दशमे वर्षे स्त्रीप्रजां द्वादशे त्यजेत्।
मृतप्रजां पंचदशे सद्यस्त्वप्रियवादिनीम्॥
B.D.S., II, 2,4,6.

2. पाणिबन्धं स्वयं कृत्वा सहधर्ममुपेत्य च।
यदा यास्यंति पुरुषाः स्त्रियो नार्हन्ति याप्यताम्॥
Mbh., XII, 272,36.

3. धर्मप्रजासंपन्ने दारे नान्यां कुर्वीत।
A.D.S., II, 5,11,12.

4. एवं हि त्यजतां भार्यां नराणां नास्ति निष्कृतिः।
Mbh., XII, 58,13.

entered their teens. Wives too were not cultured or educated enough to succeed in rivetting their husbands' affections and dissuading them from the contemplated second marriage. The inevitable result followed. Supersessions on flimsy grounds began to become common in some sections of society. What pains one most is that they should have been justified by some Smṛiti writers. We have seen above that some of our early thinkers tried their best to discourage this tendency by condemning it in no uncertain terms. Even when they allowed a second marriage for the continuation of the family, they laid it down that it should be performed only with the consent of the first wife.[1] The husband was further required to look after her in the proper manner, and give her a suitable allowance if she desired to live separately.

Other Smṛiti writers, however, have taken quite a different stand. They have propounded the astounding doctrine that the husband has the right to discard his wife any moment she proves herself disagreeable to him.[2] This is a monstrous principle and we feel pained to find that some of our Smṛiti writers should have ever propounded it. This principle, along with the lowering of the marriageable age of girls, produced disastrous consequences for the happiness of women. In spite of their anxiety to do everything to please their husbands, devoted wives began to be sometimes superseded, even when they had given birth to sons. Smṛitis have no doubt laid down that such wives should be given a maintenance. It was not, however, easy for them to live in a kind of judicial separation; for a section of the public was

1. या रोगिणी स्यात्तु हिता संपन्ना चैव शीलतः।
सानुज्ञाप्याधिवेत्तव्या नावमान्या च कर्हिचित्॥
Manu, IX, 88.

2. सद्यस्त्वप्रियवादिनी।
Manu IX, 81.

It is true that we sometimes find one and the same work like *Manusmṛiti* laying down that a husband should wait for a long time in order to be sure that his wife is barren, and also permitting supersession on the flimsy ground of the wife being disagreeable. This is due to the blending of the earlier and later tradition in the same work.

always inclined to spread baseless scandals about their character if they followed such a course.[1]

It is, however but fair to point out that in contemporary times almost everywhere similar license was given to the husband in the matter of discarding his wife. At Rome, a woman could be divorced because she was childless, or disagreeable, or for any other similar reason. Women were allowed divorce, but they suffered socially if they availed themselves of this permission (*Story of Women*, p. 86).

Owing to the growing helplessness of women on account of their illiteracy and ignorance, they became easier prey to ill-treatment and tyranny. The disappearance of divorce, permitted by earlier writers under certain circustances, further embittered their life. We have seen above (*ante*, p. 85), how one woman refused to go to live with her husband on learning that he had contracted a second marriage during her absence, and how she eventually married a different person. Now things had changed completely. Manu no doubt states that the husband should contract a second marriage only with the consent of the first wife, but his permission was merely a formal affair. If the wife refused to give it, the husband could still carry out his plan of the second marriage. If after that event a self-respecting wife found it impossible to live with her husband, and proceeded to leave his household, she was to be compelled to stay with him. The only concession that Manu shows to her is to permit her to stay with her parents, provided she did not claim any maintenance (IX, 83). All this treatment laid down for the wife is a natural consequence of Manu's theory that marriage establishes the supremacy of the husband over the wife.[2] This view

1. सतीमपि ज्ञातिकुलैकसंश्रयां जनोऽन्यथा भर्तृमतीं विशङ्कते।
अथ तु वेत्सि शुचिव्रतमात्मनः पतिकुले तव दास्यमपि क्षमम्।

Sākuntala, Act V, 19 and 27.

2. प्रदानं स्वाम्यकारणम्।

V, 152.

soon became quite popular; we find Kālidāsa subscribing to it.[1]

It is no wonder that under such circumstances unreasonable demands should have been made on wives. The husband may be self-willed, he may be even vicious; the wife must nevertheless worship him as a god.[2] Such husban ds of course may not have been many; what is surprising and painful is that they should have got some advocates even among Smṛiti writers. The impudence with which ludicrously absurd stories are sometimes narrated in later literature to illustrate the life of the ideal wife, who followed the above gospel, is indeed astonishing. Anasūyā was a very obedient wife and an ideal *pativratā*, says the *Mārkaṇḍeyapurāṇa*. At her husband's bidding she once proceeded to carry him on her own shoulders to the house of a dancing girl. On the way the love-lorn husband kicked an angry sage, who was passing near him, and the latter forthwith cursed him to die before the sunrise. Anasūyā proceeded to render the curse inoperative by prohibiting the sun from rising. The luminary could not of course disobey the command of a *pativratā*. The earth was plunged into darkness and gods got alarmed and intervened. They eventually succeeded in pacifying the angry sage, who was then induced to take back his curse.

It is no doubt true that such stories are intended to illustrate the power of a *pativratā* and her unswerving devotion to her husband in the most trying circumstances. They are not to be taken too literally. Nevertheless, the fact that their imaginary plots should have been conceived on these lines shows that the position of the wife *vis-a-vis* her husband had changed very greatly to her disadvantage by about the 4th century A.D.[3] The situa-

1. उपपन्ना हि दारेषु प्रभुता सर्वतोमुखी।

Śākuntla, V. 26.

2. विशील: कामवृत्तो वा गुणैर्वा परिवर्जित:।
उपचर्य: स्त्रिया साध्व्या सततं देववत्पति:॥

Manu, V, 154.

Cf., also the statement in the *Daśakumārcharita*, p. 178, N. S. Ed.)

स्त्रीधर्मश्चैष यददुष्टस्य दुष्टस्यवाभर्तुर्गतिर्गन्तव्येति।

3. Some passages in Buddhist literature show that even in the 3rd century B.C. the slave type of wife, who would quietly bear

P. T. O.

tion worsened with the abuse of the very guarded permission given to the husband to take a second wife. The concession was intended only for certain specific and unusual circumstances. But soon men began to think more of the permission than of the qualifying conditions. When this tendency manifested itself in society, it was the clear duty of Smṛiti writers to condemn it in the most unqualified manner. In stead of discharging it, many of them virtually proceeded to encourage frivolous irresponsibility in men by permitting them to marry a second time, if the first wife were guilty merely of unpleasant speech. This shows a light-heartedness, which is hardly creditable to any writers who profess to guide society.

The different angles of vision with which the question of the remarriage of the widow and the widower was viewed at this time also show a growing callousness to the feelings and sentiments of women, and an inordinate anxiety to avoid the least inconvenience and discomfort to men. We shall see in Chapter V how widow marriages were completely frowned out of existence by about 600 A.D. The rising tide of asceticism, which was mainly responsible for this development, did not however affect the position of the widower at all. Nay, strangely enough the prospects of his immediate remarriage brightened up. The earlier times did not hold that a widower could not discharge his religious duties except by marrying a second time. The *Aitareya Brāhmaṇa* expressly states that a widower can continue his Vedic sacrifices even if he remains unmarried; his devotion (*śraddhā*) will be his figurative wife.[1] Vishṇu (*c.* 100 A.D.) does

(*Continued from the last page*)

all the ill-treatment of her husband, was regarded as the best one by some thinkers who preferred her to a wife, who would be her husband's companion. (*Jātaka*, No. 269.) The available evidence shows, however, that this theory was not generally subscribed to before the Christian era. The prevalence of child marriages was responsible for its becoming popular in latter times.

1. तदाहुरपत्नीकोऽप्यग्निहोत्रमाहरेदिति। आहरेदित्याहुः। यदि नाहरेदनद्धा पुरुषः। तदेषाभियज्ञगाथा गीयते। यजेत् सौत्रामण्यामपत्नीकोऽप्य सोमपः। मातापितॄणामनृण्यार्थाद्यजेतेति वचनाच्छ्रुतिः। अपत्नीकः कथमग्निहोत्रं जुहोति। श्रद्धा पत्नी सत्यं यजमानः श्रद्धा सत्यं तदित्युत्तमं मिथुनम्।
A. Br., VII. 9-10

not regard remarriage as a religious necessity; he points out that an image of the dead wife can well serve the sacrificial purpose.[1] Śri-Rāmchandra concurred with this view, for when separated from Sītā, he performed his sacrifices with an image of his wife by his side. He did not deem it necessary to marry a second time in oder to have a living wife with him during the performance of his sacrifices. In course of time, however, widowers, who would spend their remaining life in cherishing the memory of their departed wives, began to become rarer and rarer. A second marriage for the widower was soon declared to be a religious necessity by some obliging Smṛiti writers. After describing the funeral of the wife, Manu immediately proceeds to inform the bereaved husband that he ought to marry again.[2] How could household sacrifices be properly performed without the presence and cooperation of a wife ? The texts which permitted the performance of the sacrifices with the effigy of the dead wife were explained away with the usual ingenuity of commentators. The wife can never be represented; she must be always present in person. She had to do personally some work in the sacrifice like the pounding of the rice etc.; obviously this could not be done by an effigy. So the second marriage was an absolute religious necessity for the widower.[3] It would not have been difficult to show that the same

1. मृतायामपि भार्यायां वैदिकाग्निं न हि त्यजेत्।
उपाधिनापि तत्कर्म यावज्जीवं समाचरेत्।
Quoted by Aparārka on *Yaj.*, I, 89.

2. भार्यायै पूर्वमारिण्यै दत्वाग्निं विधिपूर्वकम्।
पुनर्दारक्रियां कुर्यात्पुनराधानमेव च॥
V. 168.

3. Cf. Aparārka on *Yāj.*, I, 89:—
'उपाधिनापि तत्कर्म' इत्यस्यार्थः कुशमय्या कांचनमय्या वा पत्न्या कार्यसमाप्तिः कार्येति। न। पत्न्या अप्रतिविधेयत्वात्। यत्पुनः "अन्ये कुशमयीं पत्नीं कृत्वा तु गृहमेधिनः। अग्निहोत्रमुपासन्ते यावज्जीवमतन्द्रिताः" इति वचनं तदग्निहोत्रस्तुत्यर्थं न स्वार्थविधायकम्।

would be the case for the widow as well. The son was an imperative necessity for offering oblations to the manes, and it could well have been argued that a widow should lose no time in marrying again for ensuring the continuance of the family. No Smṛiti writer, however, has cared to take this stand.

We shall conclude this chapter with a few words on polyandry in ancient India. This custom was practically unknown to Hindu society. In the Vedic marriage hymn Sūryā is married to Aśvins; the latter, however, are not two persons but a twin deity. The marriage of lady Rodasī (sky) with Maruts (Storm-gods, is figurative.[1] it is intended to show the close connections between the sky and the storm. It is also true that there are some passages in Vedic literature where the wife is mentioned in connection with husbands in plural. The plurals in these cases are, however, either generic or used *majestatis causa.*[2] In later Vedic literature it is pointed out in several places how polyandry is not permissible, though polygamy is legal.[3] Smṛitis nowhere contemplate the possibility of polyandry, when they discuss the rules of marriage.

It is only in the *Mahābhārata* and some Purāṇas that we come across a few stray cases of polyandry. The most well-known case is that of Draupadī, who was married to five Pāṇḍava brothers. Kuṇālaka Jātaka (No. 536) also refers to a polyandrous marriage of a princess named Kaṇhā. Kṛishṇā was another name of Draupadī and the Kaṇhā of this Jātaka is identical with her as is shown by the fact that the names of her husbands are identical with those of Pāṇḍavas. Draupadī's polyandrous marriage seems to have been a historic

1. *R. V.*, I. 167, 6.
2. पुनः पतिभ्यो जायां दा अग्ने प्रजया सह।
R. V., X. 85, 38.

स्योनं पतिभ्यो वहतुं कृणु त्वम्।
A V., XIV, 1,61.

3. यन्नैकां रशनां द्वयोर्यूपयोः परिव्ययति तस्मान्नैका द्वौ पती विन्दते।
T. S. VI, 6, 4, 3

Cf. also, *A. Br.*, III, 23, *G. Br.* II, 3, 19.

event; otherwise the author of the *Mahābhārata*, who is at his wit's end to justify it, would have quietly kept silence over it. Polyandry, however, seems to have been rarely practised even in the days of the *Mahābhārata*. Kuntī was pained to find that her well-meant direction to her sons that the brothers should evenly divide what they may have obtained should result in a polyandrous marriage.[1] Drupada also stood aghast at the polyandrous proposal of Yudhisṭhira.[2] The latter could justify it only on the convenient excuse of family tradition.[3] He no doubt refers to an earlier polyandrous marriage of Jaṭilā, but whether it was a historical event may well be doubted. The *Mahābhārata* proceeds to give several fantastic reasons in justification of Draupadī's marriage; only one of them may be given by way of illustration. Draupadī got five husbands in this life because in one of her previous existences she had five times uttered the prayer to God, 'Give me a husband' (I, 213). Later writers were so much upset by Draupadī's polyandry that they refused to believe in it. The *Tantravārtika*, for instance, maintains that Draupadī's marriage with five royal brothers is to be understood only figuratively. Draupadī was not a lady in flesh and blood; she stood for royal glory (*rājya-lakshmī*), and her marriage with five brothers is only intended to show that they were jointly ruling their kingdom with absolute accord. Or, we may suppose, that the brothers were really married to five different ladies, but they were so much alike in person and character, that they came to be described under the common

1. कुटीगता सा त्वनवेक्ष्य पुत्रान् प्रोवाच भुंक्तेति समेत्य सर्वे ।
पश्चाच्च कुन्ती प्रसमीक्ष्य कृष्णां कष्टं मया भाषितमित्युवाच ।।
Mbh., *I*, 206, 2.

2. सोऽयं न लोके वेदे वा जातु धर्मः प्रशस्यते ।
लोकधर्मविरुद्धं त्वं नाधर्मं धर्मविच्छुचिः ।।
Ibid, 27.

3. सूक्ष्मो धर्मो महाराज नास्य विद्मो वयं गतिम् ।
पूर्वेषामानुपूर्व्येण यातं वर्त्मानुयामहे ।।
Ibid, I, 210, 29.

name Draupadī. Or, we should understand the situation in this way : Draupadī was really the wife of Arjuna who had won her by his skill in archery, but the epic describes her as the common wife of all the five brothers with a view to emphasise the extraordinarily cordial relations that existed among them.[1]

The fact is that polyandry was not in vogue among the Aryans even in the Vedic age; whether it existed in any earlier period among them is also very doubtful. Its unexpected occurrence in the *Mahābhārata* has surprised and puzzled its readers, and so later commentators have sought to explain it away as best as they could. Polyandry is still current to some extent among a few non-Aryan tribes of Kashmir and Tibet, and it is probable that the Pāṇḍavas were following a custom which they may have borrowed from either of these provinces. This would suggest that they belonged to a stock of Aryans different from that of the Kauravas, and that they entered India via the Gilgit pass in Kashmir or through Nepal. It is of course not possible to discuss the *pros* and *cons* of this interesting theory in this work.

1. Vol. I, pp. 191-192 (English Translation).

CHAPTER IV.

THE POSITION OF THE WIDOW, PART I.

The position of the widow in society is one of the most important topics which the historian of woman has to discuss and elucidate. The treatment which she receives is often an index to the attitude of society towards women as a class. What was the general lot of the widow ? Was she allowed to survive her husband, or was she compelled to die with him ? If permitted to survive, could she marry again if she so desired ? Did she receive a humane and considerate treatment from the family and society ? Could she hold or inherit property, so that she could lead an honourable and independent life after her husband's death ? These are the main topcis which we have to discuss in connection with the position of the widow. Of these, the question of the proprietary rights will be discussed in the ninth chapter. Here we shall take up the problems of Satī, levirate, remarriage, and tonsure. Of these, the question of the Satī custom will engage us in this chapter and the rest will be discussed in the next, which will close with a general survey of the position of the widow from age to age.

THE CUSTOM OF SATĪ (SUTTEE).

In prehistoric times there prevailed a belief in several societies that the life and needs of the dead in the next world are more or less similar to those in this life. It therefore became a pious duty of surviving relations to provide a dead person with all the things that he usually needed when alive. Especially when an important personage like a king, a nobleman or a warrior died, it was felt that his usual paraphernalia should be 'sent' with him. He would of course require his wives, horses and servants in the next world, and it would therefore be necessary and desirable to kill these all, and burn or bury them with him. Such a belief should have given rise to the custom of burning or burying the husband also along with the wife. Man, however, wielded supreme power in society almost everywhere and was not prepared to sanction a custom adverse to his own interest and comfort. It may, however, be pointed out that in Ashanti, kings' sisters were allowed to marry handsome youths among commoners, but they were compelled to commit suicide on the death of their royal consorts.

The custom of the sacrifice of the widow at the funeral of her husband was widely prevailing in ancient times. There is no direct evidence to show that it prevailed in the Indo-European age, but the fact that it was practised among the Gauls, the Goths the Norwegians, the Celts, the Slaves and the Thracians would justify the inference that it was probably well established among the Indo-Europeans. It was quite common among the Scythians. In China if a widow killed herself in order to follow her husband to heaven, her corpse was taken out in a great procession.[1]

The general prevalence of this custom among the primitive warlike tribes is not difficult to understand. Fighting races are very jealous of their women and often prefer to kill them, rather than take the risk of their going astray after their husbands' death. There was also the general belief, already referred to, that the warrior will require in his next life all those things that were near and dear to him in this existence. It was therefore as reasonable to bury his clothes, bows, arrows and horses as to inter his wife. The wife is usually the dearest relation of a man, and the visitations of a chief's ghost were popularly attributed to his desire to be united with his quondam queen. Why not lessen these dreaded visitations by burning or burying her along with his remains? This custom also made the life of the patriarch very safe; it practically eliminated all possibility of any one among his numerous mutually envious wives intringuing against

1. Tawney : *Kathāsaritsāgara*, Vol. IV, Terminal Essay on Suttee by Penzer.

his life. They all knew that even if successful, they had no chance of surviving him. They were, therefore all care and attention to see that no preventible accident intervened to shorten the husband's life.

Whatever the real reasons may have been, we find, as shown already, that the custom of sacrificing the wife at the husband's death existed among the Aryans in the Indo-European period. By the time they entered India, it had, however, gone out of vogue. We do not find it mentioned in the *Avesta*. Nor is it referred to in the funeral hymns of the *Ṛigveda*, where it would certainly have been mentioned if it had been in existence. It is true that in the great controversy that raged at the time of the legal prohibition of the Satī custom by Lord William Bentick, it was argued that the custom had a Vedic sanction. It was maintained that the funeral hymn in the *Ṛigveda* refers to widows ascending the funeral pyre. The case, however, could be rendered plausible only by fraudulently changing the last word of the stanza from *agre* into *agneḥ:* The verse in question refers to women with their husbands living coming forward to annoint the corpse before it was consigned to flames, and contains no reference whatsoever to any widow immolating herself on her husband's funeral pyre.[1]

It was also argued that a passage in the Aukhya Śākhā of the *Saṁhitā* quoted in the 84th *anuvāka* of the *Nārāyaṇīya Taittirīya Upanishad* refers to a prayer by a widow to god Fire that she was about to follow the *anugamana-vrata* or the Satī custom and that she may be able to bear the ordeal and reap the promised reward[2]. The *Nārāyaṇīya-upnishad* is however a late

1. इमा नारीरविधवाः सपत्नीरांजनेन सर्पिषा संविशन्तु।
अनश्रवोऽनमीवाः सुरत्ना आरोहन्तु जनयो योनिमग्रे ॥

R. V., x,18,7.

Even when the last word is changed into *agneḥ*, it is only a forced construction that can detect in this stanza a reference to the widow immolation.

2. अग्ने व्रतानां व्रतपतिरसि पत्यनुगमनव्रतं करिष्यामि तच्छकेयं तन्मे राध्यताम्।

P. T. O.

work; the passage from the Aukhya Śākhā quoted in it is otherwise not known to us from any other source. We cannot therefore conclude from it that the Satī custom was recognised as a ritual in the Vedic period.

The *Artharvaveda*, however, shows that the funeral ritual of the Vedic age preserved some formalities reminiscent of the archaic custom of Satī. It shows that it was still customary for the widow to lie by the side of her husband's corpse on the funeral pyre; she was, however, asked to come down, and a prayer was offered that she should lead a prosperous life enjoying the bliss of children and wealth.[1] It is therefore clear that the Vedic age expected the widow rather to remarry than to immolate herself.

The reasons that led to the discontinuation of the Satī custom in the Vedic age can only be inferred. Probably the finer cultural outlook, that the Vedic Aryans had developed by this time, had convinced them that the custom was a barbarous one; probably they found themselves in minority in India and felt the compelling necessity to increase their population in order to ensure their political domination. In stead of allowing widows to be burnt, they thought that it would be better to encourage them to live and increase the population by levirate or remarriage.

Whatever the reasons may have been, it is undisputed that the Satī custom had gone out of vogue among the Aryans at the time they had entered India. We find no traces of it whatsoever down to *c*. 400 B.C. The Brāhmaṇa literature (*c*. 1500 B.C. to *c*. 700 B.C.) is silent about it. The Gṛihyasūtras (*c*. 600 to *c*. 300 B.C.) describe numerous rituals and Sanskāras, but the custom

(Continued from the last page.)

इह त्वाऽग्ने नमसा विधेम सुवर्गस्य लोकस्य समेत्यै।
जुषाणोऽद्य हविषा जातवेदा विशामित्वा सत्वतो नय मां पत्युरन्ते।

Wilson's Collected Works, II, pp. 295-6.

1. इयं नारी पतिलोकं वृणाना निपद्यत उप त्वा मर्त्यं प्रेतम्।
धर्मं पुराणमनुपालयन्ती तस्य प्रजां द्रविणं चह धत्त॥

xviii, 2,I.

of Satī does not figure among them. From the details of the funeral ritual and procedure given in them, we find that the widow was to be brought back from the funeral pyre, either by her husband's brother or disciple, or by an old trusted servant.[1] From the *Taittirīya Āraṇyaka* we find that while returning from the funeral pyre, the widow took away from her husbad's hand objects like bow, gold, jewels, etc., which were burnt along with the widow in an earlier age. A hope was then expressed that the widow and her relatives would lead a happy and prosperous life.[2] It is clear that the custom of Satī had died down long ago.

The Buddhist literature also is unaware of the custom of Satī. If it had existed in the days of the Buddha, one feels certain that the great Śākya sage would have started a vehement crusade against it. He who opposed sacrifices to gods, because dumb animals were immolated therein, would certainly have been exasperated by a custom which entailed the burning of human beings alive. So we may well conclude that even in Kshatriya circles the custom was not prevalent in *c.* 500 B.C. Megasthenes and Kauṭilya both do not mention the custom. The authors of the Dharmasūtras (*c.* 400 B.C. to *c.* 100 A.D.) and the writers of the early Smṛitis like those of Manu and Yājñavalkya (*c.* 100 A.D. to *c.* 300 A.D.) have laid down detailed rules about the duties of women and widows. None of them, however, even hints that it would be commendable for a widow to burn herself alive with her dead husband on his funeral pyre.

1. तामुत्थापयेद्देवरः पतिस्थानीयोऽन्तेवासी जरद्दासो वा 'उदीर्ष्व नारि अभि जीवलोकम्' इति।

A. G. S., IV, 2, 18.

2. धनुर्हस्तादाददाना मृतस्य श्रियै ब्रह्मणे तेजसे बलाय।
अत्रैव त्वमिह वयं सुशेवा विश्वाः स्पृधोऽभिजातीर्जयेम ॥

VI, 1.

The verse is repeated twice more with the change of the first word into मणिम् and सुवर्णम्।

We begin to get stray references to the custom of Satī from about 300 B. C. The *Mahābhārata*, a major portion of which was composed at about this time, records only a few cases of Satī. The most important among them is that of Mādrī. But in her case, it is interesting to note that the assembled sages try their best to dissuade her from her resolve. Mādrī, however, is unmoved by their arguments. She says that she is determined to die with her husband, firstly because she was the cause of his death, secondly because she would be unable to control her passions, and thirdly because she might find it difficult to treat evenly her sons and stepsons. No argument of any religious merit is assigned by her or by anybody else.[1]

In the Mausala-parvan of the *Mahābhārata* we find that four wives of Vasudeva, Devakī, Bhadrā, Rohiṇī and Madirā, ascend his funeral pyre.[2] When the news of Kṛishṇa's death reaches Hastināpura, five of his wives, Rukumiṇī, Gāndhārī, Sahyā, Haimavatī and Jambavatī ascend the funeral pyre, of course without their husband's body. Satyabhāmā retires to forest for practising penance.[3]

As against the above few cases of Satī, we have scores of instances of widows surving their husbands. The wives of Abhimanyu,[4] Ghaṭotkacha and Droṇa do not become Satīs. There is a talk of Draupadī being consigned to flames along with

1. अहमेवानुयास्यामि भर्तारमपलापिनम्।
न हि तृप्तास्मि कामानां ज्येष्ठा मामनुमन्यताम्॥
वर्तेयं न समां वृत्ति जात्वहं न सुतेषु ते।

I, 138, 71-2.

2. *Mbh*, XVI, 7. 18.

3. *Ibid*, XVI. 7. 73-4.

4. In the *Kādambarī* Bāṇa expressly refers to the case of Uttarā in justification of the conduct of Mahāśvetā in deciding to survive her lover. We, however, find Uttarā represented as burning herself with her husband Abhimanyu in the Bali island version of the *Māhabhārata*. The reason of the discrepancy is obvious; the Bali island version belongs to a time when the custom of Satī had become popular.

Kīchaka, but that was merely for the sake of revenge.[1] If four wives of Vasudeva became Satī, there were thousands of Yādava widows who survived their husbands and accompanied Arjuna to Hastināpura. In the 11th book of the epic we have the spectacle of hundreds and thousands of dead heroes being burnt along with their costumes, weapons and chariots; in not a single case, however, do we find a widow burning herself along with the remains of her husband (Chaps. 31-33). The *Veṇīsaṁhāra* no doubt refers to the case of a Satī on the Kaurava battlefield (Act IV), but it is quite clear that it is due to the anachronism of its author. The epic itself states that all the widows of the fallen heroes remained behind and offered them funeral oblations.[2]

In the original portion of the *Rāmāyaṇa* there is no case of Satī. In the Uttarakāṇḍa (17, 14) we find Vedavatī's mother becoming a Satī; but this story is more legendary than historical and the book where it occurs is admittedly a later addition, being as modern as about 500 A.D. In the original kernel of the epic, we find that when Rāvaṇa by means of his magic raised before the eyes of Sītā the illusion of the fall of Rāma, she expressed the wish to be burnt along with her husband (VI, 32, 32). This passage also is probably a later interpolation, for none of the wives of Daśaratha or Rāvaṇa are represented in the epic as accompanying their husbands on the funeral pyre.

Purāṇas refer only to a few cases of Satī. This shows that by about 400 A.D. when the Purāṇas were given their present form, the custom was gradually coming into general vogue. It

1. ददृशुस्तु ततः कृष्णां सूतपुत्राः समागताः।
हन्यतां शीघ्रमसती यत्कृते कीचको हतः।
अथवा नैव हन्तव्या दह्यतां कामिना सह।
मृतस्यापि प्रियं कार्यं सूतपुत्रस्य सर्वथा॥

IV, 23, 4 ff.

2. Later on they are represented as plunging into the Gangā and being reunited with their husbands in heaven. At best, this would be a case of suicide. The procedure has no affinity with the custom of Satī.

does not prove its antiquity. It is interesting to note that some of the Satī cases in Purāṇas are the imaginary creations of a later age, and go against the earlier tradition. Thus the *Mahābhārata* is unaware of any Yādava widows having burnt themselves on their husband's funeral pyres; according to the *Padmapurāṇa*, however, all of them became Satīs (Uttarakāṇḍa, chap. 279). The vast majority of the widows that figure in Purāṇas survive their husbands.

The earliest historical instance of Satī is that of the wife of the Hindu general Keteus, who died in 316 B.C. while fighting against Antigonos. Both the wives of the general were very anxious to accompany their husband on the funeral pyre, but as the elder one was with child, the younger one alone was allowed to carry out her wish. Greek writers tell us that she was led to the pyre by her brother, and that shewas all gleeful even when the flames enveloped her person. Some Greek historians tell us that the custom was prevalent among the Kathians (Kaṭhas) of the Punjab. It was, however, still confined only to a few Kshatriya circles, for it is not noticed by Greek writers in connection with other fighting tribes, which stubbornly opposed Alexander and many members of which died while fighting with the invader.

The custom was gradually struggling into existence in the early centuries of the Christian era. Hence, as shown above, we get stray references to it in the later portions of the *Rāmāyaṇa* and the *Mahābhārata*, and in the present version of some Purāṇas. *Vishṇusmṛiti* (*c.* 100 A.D.) thinks the custom to be not illogical; it advanced the view that in spite of diversity of Karman, a widow can, though other relations cannot, go the way of the departed soul by dying after him.[1] The custom, however, was not yet regarded as a religious duty. Vishṇu himself does not recommend it; he merely mentions it. He is in fact one of

1. मृतोऽपि बान्धवः शक्तो नानुगन्तुं प्रियं जनम्।
जायावर्जं हि सर्वस्य याम्यः पन्था विरुध्यते॥
20, 36.

the earliest writers to recognise the widow as an heir to her husband; he allows her to remarry also (17, 43).

The custom began to become gradually popular from c. 400 A.D. It is known to Vātsyāyana, Bhāsa, Kālidāsa and Śūdraka. Vātsyāyana points out (VI, 2. 53) how clever dancing girls gain ascendancy over the mind of their lovers by swearing that they would burn themselves on their funeral pyres. From the *Dūtaghaṭotkacha* and *Ūrubhaṅga* of Bhāsa, it appears that the dramatist differed from the *Mahābhārata* in holding that Uttarā, Duśśalā and Pauravī died on the funeral pyres of their husbands, Abhimanyu, Jayadratha and Duryodhana respectively. In the *Kumārasambhava* (Canto IV) Ratī is about to burn herself after her husband's death; it is only a voice from the heaven that dissuades her from her resolve. In the *Mṛichchhakaṭika* the wife of Chārudatta wants to burn herself before the arrival of the expected news of her husband's execution (Act. X). To turn to historic cases of the period, we find that the wife of general Goparāja, who fell in 510 A.D. while fighting for his country against the Hūṇas, immolated herself on her husband's funeral pyre.[1] In 606 A.D. the mother of king Harsha chose to predecease her husband by committing herself to flames, when it was declared that there was no chance of her husband's recovery. At about this time a Nepalese queen, named Rājyavatī, is also seen becoming a Satī.

Some Smṛiti writers of the period now begin to refer to the practice. They do not, however, hold it as an ideal for the widow; they allow it only as a second alternative and regard ascetic life as preferrable to it. Such is the case with Bṛihaspati, Parāśara (IV, 26-8) and the author of *Agnipurāṇa*.[3]

1. भक्तानुरक्ता च प्रिया च कान्ता भार्यावलग्नानुगताग्निराशिम् ॥
C. I. I. Vol. III, p. 93.

2. शरीरार्धं स्मृता भार्या पुण्यापुण्यफले समा।
अन्वारूढा जीवती वा साध्वी भर्तृहिताय सा ॥
Quoted in *Vivādaratnākara*, p. 442.

3. भर्त्राग्नि या विशेन्नारी सापि स्वर्गमवाप्नुयात्।
221, 23.

There were, however, several thinkers, who were altogether opposed to the idea of giving even a qualified recognition to the custom. Thus Medhātithi admits that the custom has been mentioned by *Aṅgirassmṛiti*, but maintains that it has no authoritative value, for it is opposed to an express Vedic text which prohibits suicide to all.[1] Virāṭa takes a more decisive stand and positively prohibits the custom. He points out that the widow can do some good to her husband, if she survives and offers him the prescribed oblations at the Śrāddha; if she ascends the funeral pyre, she will be only incurring the sin of suicide.[2] Devaṇabhaṭṭa, a 12th century writer from south India, maintains that the Satī custom is only a very inferior variety of Dharma and is not to be recommended at all.[3] To the poet Bāṇa (*c.* 625 A.D.), however, belongs the credit of offering the most vehement, determined and rational opposition to this inhuman custom. 'To die after one's beloved' says he, is most fruitless. It is a custom followed by the foolish. It is a mistake committed under infatuation. It is a reckless course followed only on account of hot haste. It is a mistake of stupendous magnitude. It does no good whatsoever to the dead person. It does not help him in ascending to heaven; it does not prevent him from sinking into hell. It does not at all ensure union after death; the person who has died goes to the place determined by his own Karman, the person who accompanies him on the funeral pyre goes to the hell reserved for those who are guilty of the sin of suicide. On the other hand, by surviving the

1. पुंवत्स्त्रीणामपि प्रतिषिद्ध आत्मत्यागः। यथैव 'श्येनेन हिंस्याद्भूतानि' इति अधिकारस्य अतिप्रवृद्धद्वेषान्धतया सत्यामपि प्रवृत्तौ न धर्मत्वम् एवमिहापि (अनुमरणस्य) न शास्त्रीयत्वम्। किं च तस्माद् ह न पुरायुषः प्रेयादिति प्रत्यक्षश्रुतिविरोधोऽयम् अतोऽस्त्यव पतिमनुमरणे स्त्रियाः प्रतिषेधः।

On *Manu*, V, 157.

2. अनुवर्तेत जीवन्तं न तु यायान्मृतं पतिम्।
जीवद्भर्तुर्हितं कुर्यान्मरणादात्मघातिनी॥

Quoted by Aparārka on *Yāj.*, I, 87.

3. तद्धर्मान्तरमपि ब्रह्मचर्यधर्माज्जघन्यं निकृष्टफलत्वात्।

Vyavahārakāṇḍa, p. 598.

deceased, one can do much good both to oneself and to the departed by offering prescribed oblations for his happiness in the other world. By dying with him one can do good to neither'.[1]

It is clear that Bāṇa was struck with horror by the tendency to eulogise the Satī custom, shown in some quarters in his days, and was anxious to offer the most determined opposition to it. Tantra writers also joined him in the crusade. They pointed out that woman was the embodiment of Supreme Goddess, and boldly declared that if a person burnt her with her husband, he would be condemned to eternal hell.[2]

Unfortunately this crusade sponsored by wise thinkers failed to have any effect. The custom continued to gain in popularity mainly among fighting classes. Ascetic ideals were gaining the upper hand in society; the conduct of a widow boldly burnning herself with the remains of her husband appeared to it as the most glorious example of supreme self sacrifice. The theory of Karman also was modified so as to support the Satī custom. There was no doubt that normally a relation could not join a dead person in the other world by dying after him, as the Karman of the two persons would lead them to different destinations. The Satī, however, was an exception; the merit of her self-sacrifice was more than sufficient to annihilate her husband's sins and raise him to heaven to live in eternal union with his wife.

1. यदेतवनुमरणं नाम तदतिनिष्फलम्। अविद्वज्जनाचरित एष मार्गः। मोहविलसितमेतद्वरभसाचरितमिदं यदुपरते पितरि भर्तरि भ्रातरि वा प्राणाः परित्यज्यन्ते। स्वयं चेन्न जहति न परित्याज्याः। उपरतस्य तु न कमपि गुणमावहति। न तावदुस्यायं शुभलोकोपार्जनहेतुः, न निरयपातप्रतिकारः, न परस्परसमागमनिमित्तम्। अन्यामेव स्वकर्मफलपाकोपचितामसौ अवशो नीयते भूमिम्। असावपि आत्मघातिनः केवलमेनसा संयुज्यते। जीवंस्तु जलाञ्जलिदानादिना बहूपकरोत्युपरतस्यात्मनश्च मृतस्तु नोभयस्यापि।

Kādambarī, Pūrvārdha, p. 308

2. भर्त्रा सह कुलेशानि न दहेत्कुलकामिनीम्।
तव स्वरूपा रमणी जगत्याच्छन्नविग्रहा।
मोहाद्भर्तुश्चितारोहाद् भवेन्निरयगामिनी॥

Mahānirvāṇatantra, X, 79-80.

From about 700 A.D. fiery advocates began to come forward to extol the custom of Satī in increasing numbers. Aṅgiras argued that the only course which religion has prescribed for a widow is that of Satī.[1] Hārīta maintained that the wife can purify her husband from the deadliest of sins, if she burns herself with his remains. The two will then happily reside in heaven for three and a half crores of years.[2] A passage interpolated in *Parāśarasmṛiti* observes that just as a snake-charmer forcibly drags out a snake from a hole by force, in the same manner the Satī takes out her husband from hell and enjoys heaven with him for three and a half crores of years.[3] Even if the wife had led a dissolute life, it would not matter; her immolation, even if not voluntary, will ensure a permanent seat in heaven both to her and her husband.[4]

The views advocated by these writers gradually began to produce some effect on society. During the period 700-1100 A.D., Satīs became more frequent in northern India and quite common in Kashmir. The history of Kashmir during this period teems with the cases of Satīs in royal families. Kalhaṇa, the historian of the province, is surprised to find that even notoriously

1. साध्वीनामिह नारीणामग्निप्रपतनादृते।
नान्यो धर्मोऽस्ति विज्ञेयो मृते भर्तरि कुत्रचित्॥
Quoted by Aparārka on *Yāj*, I, 87.

2. तिस्रः कोटयर्धकोटी च यानि रोमाणि मानुषे।
तावत्कालं वसेत्स्वर्गे भर्तारं यानुगच्छति॥
व्यालग्राही यथा व्यालं बिलादुद्धरते बलात्।
एवमुद्धृत्य भर्तारं तेनैव सह मोदते॥
IV, 31-32.

This passage is an interpolation, because two verses earlier, Parāśara permits a widow to remarry.

3. ब्रह्मघ्नं वा सुरापं वा कृतघ्नं वापि मानवम्।
यमादाय मृता नारी सा भर्तारं पुनाति हि॥
Vṛiddhāhārīta 201.

4. अवमत्य तु याः पूर्वं पतिं दुष्टेन चेतसा।
वर्तन्ते याश्च सततं भर्तॄणां प्रतिकूलतः॥
भर्त्रानुमरणं काले याः कुर्वन्ति तथाविधाः।
कामात्क्रोधाद्भयान्मोहात्सर्वाः पूता भवन्ति ह॥

Mādhava attributes these verses to the *Mahābhārata* at Parāśara, IV, 33; they, however, do not occur in the epic.

unchaste queens like Jayamatī, the wife of king Uchchala, should be seen immolating themselves on their husband's funeral pyres.[1] The custom of Satī was so deep-rooted in the ruling families of Kashmir, that not only regularly married wives, but even concubines used to follow it. Kings Kalaśa and Utkarsha were, for instance, followed both by their wives and concubines (*Rājataraṅgiṇī*, VII, 858). It seems that the principle of dying after a beloved relative was extended to relations other than the husband as well; we sometimes come across mothers, sisters and sisters-in-law burning themselves with the dead relation (*Ibid*, VI, 1380; VIII, 448; VII, 1486). Cases are also on record of ministers, servants and nurses burning themselves with their masters (*Ibid*, V, 206; VII, 481; VII, 490; VIII, 1447). This reminds us of the *harikari* custom of Japan. Kalhaṇa records the case even of a cat, which out of affection for its royal master Sussala, voluntarily threw itself on his funeral pyre (VII, 2441). In the stories of the *Kathāsaritsāgara*, (which was written in *c.* 1100 A.D. in Kashmir,) the custom of Satī is quite common. Its great prevalence in the valley of Kashmir is probably due to its proximity to Central Asia, which was the home of the Scythians, among whom the custom was quite common.

There is evidence to show that outside Kashmir also the custom of Satī and *Anumaraṇa* was getting gradually more popular in northern India. The mother of Harsha, queen Yaśomatī, did not care to wait till the death of her husband; when his case was pronounced to be hopeless, she gave away her ornaments, took a sacred bath, put on all the marks of a lady with her husband living (*avidhavāmaraṇachihnamudvahantī*) and entered the funeral pyre. When her husband Prabhākaravardhana died, some of the royal officers, including the physician, entered the fire.[2] In the 4h Act of the *Veṇīsaṁhāra* we find the mo-

1. दौश्शील्यमप्याचरन्त्यो घातयन्त्योऽपि वल्लभान् ।
हेलया प्रविशन्त्यग्निं न स्त्रीषु प्रत्ययः क्वचित् ॥

Rājataraṅginī, VIII, 366.

२. *Harshacharit*, Book V

ther of a dead hero coming on the battlefield to enter his funeral pyre along with her daughter-in-law.[2]

Down to *c.* 1000 A. D. Satīs were rare in the Deccan. Sulaiman, an Arabian merchant who had spent some time on the western coast of India at the beginning of the 10th century, states that it was only sometimes that queens used to mount the funeral pyres of their consorts; there was no compulsion; it was entirely left to them to choose (Elliot and Dowson, Vol. I, p. 6).

As far as the extreme south of India is concerned; the Satī was more an exception than a rule down to *c.* 1000 A.D. The queen of only king Bhūta Pāṇḍya of the Saṅgam age is known to have followed the custom (*Puram*, 246-7). Her historicity is, however, a matter of uncertainty. Among the members of the Pallava, the Chola and the Pāṇḍya ruling families, so well known to us from numerous inscriptions, we do not come across any cases of Satī down to *c.* 900 A.D. It is therefore clear that the custom was yet to obtain a footing in South India.

We have already observed that the Satī was originally a Kshatriya custom. The accounts of the Greek historians make it clear that it was confined only to fighting classes in the 4th century B.C. The *Bṛihaddaivata*, while recognising the validity of the custom among the Kshatriyas, doubts whether it could be permissible for other castes to follow it.[2] The *Padmapurāṇa* extols the custom to the sky, but expressly prohibits it to Brāhmaṇa women. It declares that any person, who will be guilty of helping a Brāhmaṇa widow to the funeral pyre, will be guilty of the dreadful and unatonable sin of the murder of a Brāhmana[3] (*brahmahatyā*).

1. हा अतिकरुणं वर्तते। एषा वीरमाता समरविनिहतं पुत्रं श्रुत्वा रक्तांशुकनिरसनया समग्रभूषणया वध्वा सहानुम्रियते।

2. वर्णानामितरेषां तु स्त्रीधर्मोऽयं भवन्न वा।

VII, 15.

3. न म्रियेत समं भर्त्रा ब्राह्मणी ब्रह्मशासनात्। प्रव्रज्यागतिमाप्नोति मरणादात्मघातिनी॥ नरोत्तम उवाचः–सर्वासामेव जातीनां ब्राह्मणः शस्य उच्यते। पुण्यं च द्विजमुख्यन अत्र किं वा विपर्ययः॥ भगवानुवाचः—ब्राह्मण्या साहसं कर्म नैव कार्यं कदाचन। निश्शेषेऽस्या वधं कृत्वा स नरो ब्रह्महा भवेत्॥

Srishṭikhaṇḍa, 49, 72-3.

The Brāhmaṇa community, however, was accustomed to pride itself on following the most ascetic and self-denying code of life; eventually it began to feel that it should not allow itself to be outdistanced by the Kshatriyas in the custom of Satī. The custom therefore began to be followed by a few Brāhmaṇa families soon after 1000 A. D. We have seen already how there are express commands in earlier texts prohibiting a Brāhmaṇa widow from following the new fashion of suicide, but commentators of this period began to explain them away with their proverbial ingenuity. It was argued that when death by mounting the funeral pyre of the husband was apparently prohibited to a Brahmaṇa widow, what was meant was that she should not take the step merely under a temporary sense of overwhelming grief. It should be the result of full and mature deliberation.[1] Or, the intention may be to interdict death by mounting a separate funeral pyre; a Brāhmaṇa widow must be always burnt along with her husband's remains on the same pyre[2]. These arguments are advanced by south Indian commentators of the 12th and 14th centuries; it is therefore clear that the custom had by this time spread to south India and penetrated into the Brāhmaṇa community as well.

We have shown above how the literary evidence from the works of Bhāsa, Kālidāsa, Bāṇa, Śūdraka and Kalhaṇa tends to show that the Satī custom was getting gradually popular in the royal families of northern India during the period 200 to 1000 A. D. It is however rather strange that only a few epigraphical records from Northern India of this period should be referring to the actual cases of the Satī. Negative evidence is never conclusive, but it is only reasonable to expect that the court panegyrists

1. तस्माद्विधितः प्रवर्तमानाया ब्राह्मण्या अनुगमनान्निषेधो न विद्यते। शोकादिप्रवृत्तायास्तु विद्यते एव।

Aparārka on *Yāj*.,I, 87.

2. अस्य निषेधस्य पृथक्चितिनिषेधत्वात्। अत एवोशनाः। पृथक्चितिं समारुह्य न विप्रा गन्तुमर्हति।

Mādhava on *Parāśara* IV, 31.

would not have failed to mention the cases of Satī, when they were eulogising the kings and queens of their royal families. As it is, only a few epigraphs refer to the Satī cases even in Rajputana, which later became a stronghold of the Satī custom. The earliest among these is that of the mother of the Chāhamāna king Chaṇḍamahāsena, who became a Satī in 842 A.D. The next case is that of Sampalladevī, who became a Satī at Ghatiyala in Rajaputana in 890 A.D. We have no other recorded cases of Satī in Rajputana records prior to 1000 A.D. The Chedi king Gāṅgeyadeva is stated to have obtained salvation at Prayāga at the root of the holy Vaṭa tree along with his 100 wives in *c.* 1020 A.D. The language of the record however suggests that the old king and his 100 queens simultaneously drowned themselves at the confluence of the Gaṅgā and the Yamunā[1]; it was not the case of the Satī custom. It may be therefore doubted whether the Satī custom had become common even in the Rajput royal families of northern India before the 10th century. Kashmir is of course an exception.

The Satī custom had however obtained the status of a well recognised but optional practice in Hinduism; for we find it travelling to the islands of Java, Sumatra and Bali along with the Hindu emigrants.

The enthusiastic advocacy of the Satī custom by medieval commentators began to have an appreciable effect on society only after about 1300 A. D. About twenty cases of Satīs are referred to by records in Rajputana between the period 1200 and 1600[2]; most of these are of ladies belonging to the royal or Kshatriya families. In Mahākośala, the Satī stones near Saugar show that widows belonging to the weaver, barber and mason classes were often becoming Satīs during 1500-1800 A.D.[3] Among the Karnatak inscrip-

1. प्राप्ते प्रयागवटमूलनिवेशबन्धौ सार्धं शतेन गृहिणीभिरमुत्र मुक्तिम् ॥

E. I., XII, p. 211, V. 12.

2. *Bhandarkara's List*, No. 227, 394, 407, 413, 423, 615, 616, 713, 935, 980, 1009 and 1242.

3. Hiralal, *Inscriptions from C. P.*, p. 53.

tions published in the *Epigraphia Carnatica* there are only 11 cases of Satīs during the period 1000-1400 A.D., but 41 during the period 1400-1600 A.D. Most of these Satīs, however, belonged to the Nāyaka and the Gauḍa classes, which formed the main fighting community of southern India. Two of them belonged to the Jain sect[1]; it is clear that some Jains had also begun to feel that they ought not to lag behind Hindus in the matter. Inscriptions, however, record only very few cases of Brāhmaṇa widows becoming Satīs; it is obvious that the lifting of the canonical ban had not yet succeeded in popularising the custom in the priestly order.

Among the ruling Rajput families of northern India the custom became firmly established by this time. The average Rajput princess welcomed the opportunity to become a Satī and would not allow her husband to be cremated alone. Bards, ministers and relatives would often expostulate, but without any success. So, generally at the death of almost every Rajput king or nobleman, those among his widows, who were not with child or who were not required to direct the government as regents, used to ascend the funeral pyre. Their number was sometimes appallingly large. When Raja Ajitsingh of Marwar died in 1724, 64 women mounted his funeral pyre. When Raja Budhsingh of Bundi was drowned, 84 women became Satīs.[2] The example of Rajputs was emulated by the Nāyakas of Madura. When two rulers of this family died in 1611 and 1620, we are told that as many as 400 and 700 women ascended the funeral pyres. These numbers are probably exaggerated by missionary reporters; it is, however, clear that a large number of women used to become Satīs at the death of each member of the Nāyaka family.

Amaradas, the 3rd Sikh Guru (1552-1574 A.D.) had condemned the Satī custom, and it was not followed by the Sikhs for a long time. When, however, they developed into a fighting

1. *Ep. Car.*, Vol. VIII, Sorab Nos. 106 and 261, dated 1376 and 1408 respectively.

2. Tod : *Annals*, vol. II, p. 837.

community, they did not like to lag behind the Rajputs in following time-honoured martial traditions, which enjoined Satī as a matter of course. The Satī custom became common in Sikh aristocracy in spite of its prohibition by the Gurus. Thus when Ranjit Singh died, four queens and seven concubines of his ascended the funeral pyre. During the troublesome period following his death, princes and generals fell in quick succession and almost everyone of them was accompanied by his wives and concubines. Three women died with Maharaja Kharag Singh, five with Basant Singh, eleven with Kishori Singh, twentyfour with Hira Singh and 310 with Suchet Singh.

The Maratha ruling families claimed Rajput descent and so could not remain immune from the influence of the custom. Satī, however, was rather an exception than a rule with them. When Shivaji died, only one of his wives became a Satī. The same was the case with Rajaram. The queen of Shahu was compelled to burn herself owing to the political machinations of her mother-in-law, Tarabai. There are very few other cases of Satīs recorded among the annals of the Maratha ruling families at Satara, Nagpur, Gwalior, Indore and Baroda. Among the members of the Peshwa family, only Ramābai, the widow of Madhavarao I, became a Satī. It is clear that the custom did not become popular among them, as it did among the Sikh princes and generals.

Numerous Satī stones that are to be seen in almost all parts of India belonging to the 17th and the 18th centuries, show that the Satī custom was frequently followed by the commoners as well. There are, for instance, 51 Satī stones in the Saugar district ranging in date from *c.* 1450 to 1824 A.D., attesting to the women of all classes including weavers, barbers and masons becoming Satīs.[1] It would appear that about 2% widows used to become Satīs at this time.

Muslim rulers as a general rule did not like the custom. Humayun wanted to prohibit it in the case of the widows, who had passed the child-bearing age (*J. A. S. B.*, 1935, p. 76).

1. Hiralal, *Inscriptions from C. P.*, p. 51.

He, however, could not take any adequate steps in the matter. In the 22nd year of his reign Akbar translated his opposition to the custom into action by appointing inspectors to see that no force was used to compel widows to burn themselves against their will. As a consequence, Satīs became rare in the territories contiguous to Agra. Many Muslim administrators had made it a rule that no widow should be allowed to mount the funeral pyre without the permission of the local Government officer. This provision did not materially check the custom, as the prescribed permission could be usually obtained without much difficulty.

That the practice of Satī was mainly a medieval development is also proved by the circumstance that its detailed procedure has not been described even by those few late Smṛitis, which recommend the practice. We get detailed information on the point only from some late medieval Purāṇas and foreign merchants and travellers. The ritual is described in detail only in very late digests like the *Nirṇayasindhu*[1] and the *Dharmasindhu*[2] written after the 17th century.

The Satī was an object of the highest veneration, and so was taken out to the accompaniment of music in a grand procession through the town to the cremation grounds. She was given a bath, and then she put on her person all the insignia of *saubhāgya* or married bliss.[3] She used to carry with her *kumkuma*, mirror, comb and betel leaves which were the insignia of *saubhāgya*. Very often she used to give away her ornaments and belongings to her friends and relations, who used to keep

1. Part III, Uttarārdha, p. 623.
2. Pp. 483—4.
3. स्नानं मंगलसंस्कारो भूषणाञ्जनधारणम्।
गन्धपुष्पं तथा धूपं हरिद्राक्षतधारणम्॥
मंगल च तथा सूत्रं पादालक्तकमेव च।
शक्त्या दानं प्रियोक्तिश्च प्रसन्नास्यत्वमेव च॥
नानामंगलवाद्यानां श्रवणं गीतकस्य च।
कुर्यादथ स्वकां भूषां विप्राय प्रतिपादयेत्॥

Padmapurāṇa, Pātālakhaṇḍa, 102, 67 ff.

them as sacred mementos. Then she used to take final leave of her relations. Some travellers have narrated that people used to entrust to her messages to their dead relations in heaven; whether such was really the case may well be doubted. Ascending the funeral pyre, she used to place her husband's head on her lap. Then the pyre was lighted.

Usually there was *sahamaraṇa*, *i. e.*, the widow mounted the same pyre that was prepared for her husband. If there were several widows, the practice differed. Sometimes the favourite wife was selected for the honour of *sahamaraṇa*, others being burnt on separate pyres; sometimes all were placed on the same pyre, their petty jealosies if any, being reconciled during the last fateful moments of their life

If the husband had died on a distant battle-field, joint cremation was impossible. In such cases the widow used to mount a separate pyre, along with her husband's turban or shoes as a substitute for his body.

Even widows intensely anxious to follow their husbands were likely to recoil and jump out under the agony of the flames of fire. So special funeral arrangments were made in the case of a Satī. The funeral pyre was piled in a deep pit in many parts of the country, especially in the Deccan and Western India. This rendered an escape impossible. A Mysore inscription refers to a lady going out to become a Satī as going forth to the fire pit to die (*E. C.*, Vol. IV, 2, Hg. No. 18). Barbosa and Linscholen have also referred to this method. In Gujarat and northern U. P., a wooden house, about 12 feet square, was constructed and the widow was tied to one of its pillars. In Bengal the widow's feet were tied to posts fixed into the ground; she was thrice asked whether she really wished to go to heaven, and then the pyre was lighted. Where burial was practised, the widow was interred along with her husband. This was the case in Andhra province in the 16th century.

Was any force exercised to compel unwilling widows to mount the funeral pyre ? A straight reply like 'yes' or 'no' cannot be given to this question. There can be no doubt that in some cases unwilling widows were forced to burn themselves. Kalhaṇa has recorded the cases of two Kashmir queens bribing their ministers in order to induce them to come to the cremation ground for dissuading them from their apparently voluntary resolution to accompany their departed husbands. Queen Diddā adopted this strategem and was saved by her minister Naravāhana (VI, 195). Garga, the wily minister of queen Jayamatī, had a fiendish heart; he took the bribe all right, but deliberately delayed going to the cremation ground. The poor queen had to allow herself to be burnt in pursuance of her so-called voluntary resolve (VIII, 363). Medieval travellers record many cases of force being exercised, and their accounts must be true at least in some cases. Manucci tells us that Kshatriya women were burnt even against their wishes (III, p. 65); he himself rescued one such woman, who was eventually married to a European friend of his. Nicoli Conti informs us that financial pressure was often exercised, the widow being informed that she would lose her right to Strīdhana, if she decided to survive (*J. A. S. B.*, 1935, p. 256). Bernier has narrated the pathetic case of a child widow of 12 being burnt against her will at Lahore (pp. 363-64). In the case of Jaimall, one of Akbar's officers, his son wanted to forcibly immolate his mother; she was eventually saved only by the intervention of Akbar (*Akbarānmā*, 28th year). Sometimes the unfortunate widows, who were forced to become Satīs, used to recoil and run away from the funeral pyre. They were then regarded as untouchables and were not accepted back by their castes and families. They had to throw themselves on the mercy of low caste men, who used to assemble at the funeral when they suspected that the widow was likely to recoil at the 11th hour. Some times they were rescued by European traders, who used to marry them. It is a pity that in spite of such instances society should not have realised the enormous inequity of the custom.

The failure of society in this respect is partly attributable to the fact that in the vast majority of cases widows were willing parties to their immolation. A Karnatak inscription, belonging to the 11th century, tells us how a lady named Dekabbe would not listen to the earnest entreaties of her parents not to mount her husband's pyre (*E. C.*, IV, Hg. No. 18). Muktabai, the daughter of Rani Ahalyabai of Indore, became a Satī in 1792 in spite of the weeping and heart-rending entreaties of her old and saintly mother. Tavernier, a 17th century traveller, narrates how a widow of 22 went to the governor of Patna to get his permission, and how she held her hand in the flame of a torch till it was burnt to cinders in order to convince the officer that she was a willing party, and was not afraid of fire (pp. 414-7). Ibn Batuta, a 14th century traveller, tells us how he fainted to see the unbelievable courage of a dauntless widow, who gleefully embraced the devouring flames of the funeral fire (p. 191). Bernier, while describing a case of which he was an eye witness, states that it is impossible to describe the brutish boldness or the ferocious gaity depicted on the woman's countenance; her step was undaunted, her conversation was free from all perturbation; her easy air was free from all dejection, her lofty courage was void of all embarrassment. She took a torch and with her own hand and lighted the fire. It appeared to be a dream, but it was a stern reality (pp. 312-3). Pietro della Valle was also impressed by the courage of the average Satī. 'If I knew (of a lady about to become a Satī), I will not fail to go and see her and honour by my presence her funeral with that compassionate affection, which such a great conjugal fidelity and love seem to deserve' (*Travells*, II, p. 266).

That it is a religious duty for a woman of sufficient courage and resolution to accompany her husband was so deep-rooted a conviction in medieval times, that we sometimes come across cases of betrothed but unmarried women insisting to mount the funeral pyres of their would-be husbands. Mustaqui has recorded one such case; the betrothed husband died in trying to save his sweetheart from a serpent, which eventually bit him with fatal effects. Though not yet married, the girl insisted on becoming a Satī and burnt herself on the funeral pyre of her lover (*J. A. S. B.*, 1935, p. 259).

The present writer is not inclined to disbelieve the above accounts of foreign travellers. For his own sister Mrs Indirabai Madhav Udgaonkar showed an indescribable fortitude in carrying out her long-formed and oft-announced resolution not to survive her husband when on 17-1-1946 she committed herself to flames within 24 hours of her husband's death, in spite of the pressing entreaties of all her relations Nothing,—not even the presence of a sucking child, would dissuade her from taking a step which she believed to be dictated by her duty and Dharma as a *pativratā*.

The available evidence shows that, barring a few exceptions, most of the widows, who used to become Satīs, were free agents in their choice. The average Rajput or Kshatriya lady ascended the funerel pyre with the same reckless courage with which her husband used to embrace death on the battle field, when leading a forlorn hope against very heavy odds. It is probable, however, that in some cases the force of public opinion may have been felt to be too strong. It is equally clear that young and childless widows in particular may have in some cases decided to terminate their life with their husbands, because they feared that it would be too dreary for them. Remarriage was out of question, and even for their maintenance they had to depend upon not very sympathetic relations.[1] Grown up widows like the mother of king Harsha would feel that the purpose of their life was over, that they had nothing more to achieve or enjoy, and that it was therefore in the fitness of things that they should accompany their beloved spouses. The vast majority of widows, who terminated their life on their husband's funeral pyres, did so out of genuine love and devotion to their husbands whom they also revered as God. They believed that the course

1. Compare, for instance, the following extract from a 13th century Tamil inscription which contains the passionate outpourings of the heart of a young widow, afraid of the woes and ill-treatment in store for her:—'If she lived after her husband, she would be the slave of her cowives (who apparently had sons and were therefore going to be *de facto* owners of the family property). Whosoever said that she ought not to die,...those, who did not bind her, and throw her into fire, and kill her would get the sin of prostituting their wives.' *S. I. E. R.*, 1907, p. 77.

they were following was in the best spiritual interest both of themselves and their husbands. A stern sense of duty, a stoical contempt of physical pain, and the hope of an eternal union with their beloved husbands in heaven sustained them through the terrible ordeal on the burning pyre. Naturally society held them in reverence and immortalised their memory by suitable memorials, as it does in the case of heroes who deliberately and cheerfully sacrifice their lives in the cause of their religion or mother-land out of a sense of duty and patriotism, often after undergoing long and excruciating pain on the dismal and desolate battle field.

What was the percentage of widows who ascended the funeral pyre, when the course came to be fervently recommended by later Purāṇas? It is difficult to answer this question for the period 1300-1800, as there are no statistics for it. We have no doubt numerous Satī stones scattered throughout the country, but it is difficult to utilise them for determining the percentage. There is no doubt that it was high in the warrior families of Rajputana. It may have been as high as 10% per cent.

As far as the general population is concerned, perhaps one widow in a thousand became a Satī, when the custom was in its greatest vogue. Public opinion and government had not begun to assert themselves against the custom in the first quarter of the 19th century; we may therefore well presume that the prevalence of the custom at this time was more or less the same as it was during the preceding four or five centuries. Government records of this period show that in the presidencies of Bombay and Madras, the average annual number of Satīs was well below 50. In the Poona dominion of the Peshwa the annual average was about 12 during the period 1800 to 1812. Tanjore district had the worst reputation for Satīs, but its record was of only 24 cases during the eighteen months preceding 1817. In Central India only 3 or 4 cases of Satīs used to take place annually.[1] It is quite possible that these statistics may be incomplete.

1. The statistics in this and subsequent paragraphs are taken from Edward Thomson's *Suttee*, London, (1926).

But even if we suppose that the actual number of Satīs was twice the number officially recorded, the conclusion becomes inevitable that only an infinitesimal number of widows in the general population were immolating themselves. It is clear that not more than one widow in a thousand used to mount the funeral pyre in the Deccan and Central India.

In Bengal the Satī custom was more prevalent; this would clearly appear from the following table of Satī statistics, prepared by the British government:—

Name of the Division.	*Number of Satīs during the years* 1815-28.
Calcutta Division, predominently Hindu	5099
Dacca Division, predominently Muslim	610
Murshidabad Division, predominently Muslim	260
Patna Division, predominently Hindu	709
Bareily Division, predominently Hindu	193
Benares Division, predominently orthodox	1165

The above table will show that the percentage of Satīs in the Hindu population of Bengal was much larger than what obtained in the presidencies of Bombay and Madras, or even in the division of Benares, which was the greatest stronghold of orthodoxy.[1] There is therefore some force in the view that undue advantage was taken in Bengal of the helpless and grief-stricken condition of the widow in order to induce her to become a Satī by some coparceners, who stood to gain by her elimination as an heir. The Dāyabhāga law, which permitted even the childless widow to become an heir to her husband, was thus not an unmixed blessing to the weak-minded section of the women of Bengal. The

1. The annual number of Satīs in Bengal, during the years 1815 to 1828, is as follows:—

Year	Number	Year	Number	Year	Number
1815	378	1820	598	1825	639
1816	442	1821	654	1826	518
1817	707	1822	583	1827	517
1818	839	1823	575	1828	463
1819	650	1824	572		

Bengal, however, then included U. P., Bihar, Orissa and Assam.

Mill and Wilson, *History of British India,* IX, p. 271.

cases of force or undue influence, however, could not have been many. The annual average of Satīs in the Calcutta Division was about 370. This Division was at that time probably having a population equal to the whole of the then Bombay presidency, and its statistics also were very probably compiled much more accurately. It would therefore appear that Satīs were only twice as common in Bengal as they were in Bombay or Madras. In the latter provinces usually one widow in a thousand became a Satī. In Bengal the ratio was probably double, but not higher. Most of the Satīs in Bengal and U. P. were from the Brāhmaṇa caste. It is clear that the lifting of the canonical ban on the Brāhmaṇa widows to become Satīs had greatest effect in the Gangetic plain.

We have already observed that the Satī custom could not have been in much greater vogue in the Hindu and Muslim periods than it was in the first quarter of the 19th century. Available statistics clearly show that outside ruling and priestly families the custom did not make a wide appeal. The fact was that the advocacy of the custom in later Smṛitis and Purāṇas failed to make a wide appeal to Hindu community. Though it admired and even deified the Satī as an example of supreme devotion and sacrifice, it really disliked the custom. It had not, however, the moral courage at this time to start a crusade against the custom, as Bāṇa had done in the 7th century. Its religious leaders believed implicitly in the authority of later Smṛitis and Purāṇas and would not countenance any open agitation against a custom sanctioned by them. Society therefore tried to check the custom by individual persuasion. Usually relations would try their best in dissuading a widow from becoming a Satī. Thus when the father-in-law of Narayanrao Peshwa died, his wife desired to follow him on the pyre. She was, however, dissuaded by her relations. Ahalyabai Holkar, who embodied the orthodox Hindu culture of the age, did not herself become a Satī, and tried her best, though without success, to dissuade her daughter from becoming one. Towards the beginning of the 19th century, the Brāhmaṇa government of Poona and the Maratha government of Savantwadi had issued official orders, definitely disapproving and discouraging the custom.

When therefore Lord William Bentick issued his famous regulation in December 1829, making the custom illegal in British India, there was not much opposition to the proposal. It undoubtedly created a stir in the orthodox community, and its journal the *Chandrikā* wrote vehemently against the step. But the appeal to the Privy Council to annual the new regulation could get only 800 signatures. The new regulation was welcomed by the enlightened Hindu public opinion, and its mouthpiece the *Kaumudī* went on defending the action of the government. A memorial was presented to the Governor-General thanking him for his humane regulation. Raja Ram Mohan Roy, the Morning Star of Asian Renaissance, went to England and pleaded before the members of the Parliament and Privy Council that the new regulation should not be annulled. Strengthened by this advocacy, the authorities in England rejected the memorial of the pro-Satī party in 1832.

The credit for the suppression of the Satī custom belongs, however, undoubtedly to Lord Bentick, who resolved to take the step in spite of the almost general opposition of his subordinate English officers. Enlightened Hindu opinion came to support him only when he had promulgated the regulation. Left to itself, it would certainly have taken a few decades more to stamp out the custom.

Though the custom of Satī was prohibited in British India in 1829, it continued to linger in Rajputana, its greatest stronghold, for about thirty years more. At the deaths of Maharana Jivan Singh of Udaipur in 1838 and of Maharaja Man Singh of Jodhpur in 1843, several women mounted the funeral pyre. Jaipur first agreed to prohibit the custom in 1846 and other Rajput states gradually followed. Udaipur was the greatest stronghold of the orthodox Rajput tradition and the last public case of a legal Satī took place there in 1861 at the death of Maharana Sarup Singh in 1861. But even the Rajput public opinion had by this time so strongly ranged itself against the custom that not a single one among the legal wives of the Maharana felt it necessary to accompany her husband. Frantic efforts were made to induce at least one of them to become a Satī in order to 'preserve the honour of the Sisodias by preventing its chief being burnt all alone'. All of them however flatly refused to mount the funeral pyre. Eventually a slave girl was induced to become a Satī and was burnt with the remains of the Maharana. The incident will show how firmly even the Rajput public opinion had ranged itself against the custom by this time.

Since 1861 A.D., no case has occured of a public legal Satī. During the subsequent years some Hindu widows, who intensely believed that it was their bounden religious duty to accompany their husbands, have tried to ascend their funeral pyres, but have been usually prevented from achieving their object by the public and the Police. Foiled in this attempt, some of them often shut themselves in a room and put an end to their lives by igniting their saris.

CHAPTER V

POSITION OF THE WIDOW, PART II
LEVIRATE, REMARRIAGE, TONSURE, ETC.

Section, 1 : *Niyoga or Levirate*

We have seen in the last chapter that widows were not permitted or required to die with their husbands on the funeral pyres down to *c.* 300 B.C. How then were they expected to lead their remaining life ? There were three courses open for them. They could either pass their remaining life in widowhood, or have some children by levirate (*niyoga*), or remarry regularly. The first was of course the most honourable course, but there were many who followed the second or the third alternative. We shall consider in this section the history of the custom of Niyoga, which appears so strange and unacceptable to the modern mind.

It may be observed at the outset that the custom of levirate was quite common in ancient times in several civilisations. It was prevailing in Sparta. Among the Jews a widow would become her husband's brother's wife without any ceremony; if he refused to marry her, she would spit in his face (Spencer, *Sociology*, I, p. 661). The Old Testament also declares that if a woman becomes a widow, 'her husband's brother shall go unto her and take her to wife, and perform the duties of a husband's brother unto her' (Deuternonomy, 25, 5-10). The marriage of Hamlet's mother with Claudius and of Henry VIII with Katherine indicate an earlier custom of Niyoga, eventually developing into a regular remarriage with a borther-in-law.

The reasons for the prevalence of this custom are not difficult to make out, if we would understand the primitive ideas about women and children. The woman was everywhere regarded as a species of property, which passed into the husband's family on her marriage. She was married no doubt to a person, but also in his family. So if her husband died, his brother or any other near relation would take her to wife, or raise children on her.[1] This usually happened when a person died without leaving any male issue behind. To die without a son was regarded as a great spiritual calamity, and it was the sacred duty of a brother to see that a son was raised on his sister-in-law to perpetuate his brother's memory and to ensure him a seat in heaven. If this was not done, there was also the danger of the widow marrying a stranger and being lost to the family.

In early societies, a son by levirate was always preferred to a son by adoption. An adopted son pre-supposed a tremendous legal fiction, for which society was not yet ripe. A Vedic sage declares that an adoptive son born of another is no son at all.[2] He was an absolute stranger; he had no blood of the family running in his veins. A son by Niyoga, on the other hand, had the blood of the mother. He had of course not the blood of his father, but he had at least that of a near relative. A son born of Niyoga therefore resembled a real son as nearly as possible. We can now well understand why in the list of subsidiary sons given in Dharmasūtras, a son by Niyoga usually occupies the second position, coming immediately next after the real or *aurasa* son. The custom was in fact fairly common in early times in India. Several heroes of the *Māhabhārata* and Purāṇas were born of Niyoga. 'If a woman loses her husband', says the great epic, 'she marries her brother-in-law'[3].

Under the system of Niyoga if a woman's husband was dead or incapable of procreating children, she was allowed to have conjugal relations with her brother-in-law or some other near relation till she got some children. The brother-in-law of the woman was regarded as the most eligible person for this duty. In modern times we find that a brother is often very anxious to

1. *G. D. S.*, II, 10, 27, expressly refers to this argument of the advocates of the Niyoga custom : Cf:—

कुलाय हि स्त्री दीयते इति उपविशन्ति।

2. न शेषो अग्ने अन्यजातमस्ति।

R. V., VII, 5,7.

3. नारी तु पत्यभावे वै देवरं कृणुते पतिम्।

XIII, 12, 19.

give his son in adoption to his widowed sister-in-law; for if the latter were to adopt a stranger, an undesirable person was likely to be introduced as a claimant to the family property. To prevent a similar complication, it was felt that the appointment of a widow for the purpose of Niyoga should be primarily with her brother-in-law. If it was made with a stranger, it was apprehended that he may exercise a great influence over the son born from him, and eventually manage to get the child's share in the family virtually transferred to himself. Probably such cases had happened in society; for it has been expressly laid down that property considerations should never be a motive for Niyoga.[1] If the appointment was with the brother-in-law of the widow, there was likely to be as much affection between the sons born of Niyoga and other coparceners of the rising generations, as normally exists among brothers and cousins. Of course the appointment must have naturally aroused uneasiness and resentment in the mind of the firs t wife of the brother-in-law; but her feelings did not count for much at the time we are talking of. It was further regarded as most important that the son by Niyoga should resemble the real son as much as possible. He would have the maximum amount of the blood of the family running in his veins, only if the appointment of the widow for Niyoga was made with her husband's brother. If the appointment was with a stranger, the son would have only half the blood of the family in his veins.

Later Smṛiti writers allow only one son to be raised by Niyoga, but the earlier practice was quite different. At her husband's pressing entreaties, Kuntī raised three sons by Niyoga. Pāṇḍu however was not satisfied with that number and pressed his wife to have some more. Kuntī protested against the suggestion, pointing out that the custom permitted only three sons by Niyoga and no more.[2] In Kshatriya circles it was re-

1. लोभान्नास्ति नियोगः।

V. D. S., XVII, 57.

2. पाण्डुस्तु पुनरेवैनां पुत्रलोभान्महायशाः।
प्राविशद्दर्शनीयार्थी कुन्ती त्वेनमथाब्रवीत्॥ P.T.O.

garded as vitally necessary to have a large number of sons, and in prehistoric times there seems to have existed practically no limit to the number of sons that could be raised by Niyoga. King Vyushitāśva had seven such sons and King Bali had as many as 17, six from his crowned queen and eleven from a Śūdra wife (*Mbh*, I, 127, 113). Three was, however, the normal nu b.r of sons usually permitted. Kuntī's sister, Śrutasenā, had, for instance, got this number of sons by Niyoga (*Ibid*, I, 126). But a woman will not always have three successive sons; some girls are likely to intervene. Permission to have three sons by Niyoga therefore practically amounted to a remarriage.

The custom of Niyoga was fairly common down to *c.* 300 B.C. After that time it began to meet with considerable opposition, because society felt that such temporary unions were undesirable from several points of view. A school of reformers arose, which opposed this custom tooth and nail. It was led by Āpastamba, Baudhāyana and Manu. Āpastamba argued that the son by Niyoga would belong to the begetter and so would be of no spiritual benefit to the woman's husband.[1] Baudhāyana concurred with him. Manu condemned the custom as beastly and declared that it was no longer permissible to follow it.[2] It is, however, interesting to note that in spite of their vehement condemnation these writers have laid down detailed rules about the Niyoga procedure. It is therefore clear that the advocacy of the new school was for a long time ineffective. Among the Dharmasūtra writers, Vasishṭha and Gautama do not join the crusade against

नातश्चतुर्थं प्रसवमापत्स्वपि वदन्त्युत ।
अतः परं स्वैरिणी स्याद्बन्धकी पञ्चमे भवेत् ॥

I, 132, 63-4.

1. रेतोधा पुत्रं नयति परेत्य यमसादने ।

II, 6, 13, 8.

2. अयं द्विजैर्हि विद्वद्भिः पशुधर्मो विगर्हितः ।
ततः प्रभृति यो मोहात्प्रमीतपतिकां स्त्रियम् ।
नियोजयत्यपत्यार्थं तं विगर्हन्ति साधवः ॥

IX, 66. ff.

Niyoga started by Āpastamba and Baudhāyana; they permit Niyoga to the widow at her option, with the only proviso that she should not choose a stranger if a brother-in-law was available. Kauṭilya permits an old king to raise a new son by Niyoga, if his own son turned out to be wicked or incompetent.

If the reformers of the period 400 B.C. to 200 A.D. failed to stamp out the custom, they succeeded at least in restricting its scope. Formerly three sons were allowed; now some thinkers (referred to by *Manu*, IX, 61) permitted two, while the majority was in favour of one only. A woman, who had children, was prohibited from having recourse to Niyoga (*B. D. S.*, II, 1, 20). At least one year must elapse after the husband's death before Niyoga could be permitted. If a widow was unwilling, she was not to be compelled to submit to Niyoga. This provision seems to have been laid down to prevent an unscrupulous brother-in-law from forcing himself on an unwilling sister-in-law.[1] Financial considerations were not to be a motive for Niyoga.[2] It would appear that sometimes a person would be anxious to raise a son upon a widow in order to get a share in her family's property. No doubt the new child was to be the heir, but it was expected that it would naturally be under the influence of its real father. At present we very often find a person getting an effective control over the property of another family by giving his son in adoption to it. The same very often happened in the case of Niyoga. So the Dharmasūtra writers warn that economic motives should be excluded from Niyoga. Niyoga was to be regarded as a matter of duty, and not as an occasion for license. The parties were not to meet after the conception had taken place. It is clear that the desire for a son and not any craving for carnal pleasures was to be the governing factor (*Nārada*, XII, 80-88).

The school which was opposing Niyoga began to grow stronger

1. अनियुक्तो भ्रातृभार्यां गच्छंश्चान्द्रायणं चरेत् ।

Garuḍapurāṇa, I, 105-42

2. लोभान्नास्ति नियोगः ।

V. D. S., XVII. 57.

and stronger in course of time. The ascetic tendency was getting the upper hand in society. It disliked and discouraged Niyoga. Society had developed a finer sense of the marriage ideal and conjugal fidelity; it began to feel that the Niyoga procedure was primitive and beastly. Adoptive son, it was felt, should be preferred when a real son was out of question. Adoption may involve a legal fiction, but it did not transgress recognised canons of morality. It was also realised that the Niyoga custom was detrimental to the purity and peace in family life. A brother would cultivate the habit of looking upon his sister-in-law as a prospective wife of his own. Very often this would lead to serious complications. The earlier wife would naturally not take kindly to the 'appointed' widow; there would arise interminable disputes between the two which would ruin the peace of the family. Coparceners also did not like that additional sharers in the family property should arise in this irregular manner. In the *Dūtavākya* of Bhāsa, Duryodhana refuses to recognise Pāṇḍavas as heirs because they were born of Niyoga.[1] The Niyoga custom was thus felt to be more and more undesirable in course of time and the public opinion became very strong against it. It therefore went out of vogue soon after *c.* 600 A.D. It is recognised by Nārada, Yama and Parāśara, who flourished at about this time. Bṛihaspati however opposes this custom and Asahāya, the 8th century commentator on Nārada, observes that though sanctioned by Dharmaśāstra, Niyoga and re-marriage are both tabooed by society.[2] Purāṇas, written soon after this period, include Niyoga among the customs prohibited for the Kali age.[3]

There can be no doubt that leaders of Hindu society took

1. परात्मजानां पितृतां कथं व्रजेत्।
V. 21.

2. धर्मशास्त्रोक्तमपि लोकाचारव्यवहारे परित्यक्तम्।
I. 39.

3. ऊढायाः पुनरुद्वाहं ज्येष्ठांशं गोवधं तथा
कलौ पञ्च न कुर्वीत भ्रातृजायां कमंडलुम्॥
Ādityapurāṇa.

a step in the right direction in stamping out the custom of Niyoga. It was a relic of barbarism and was quite incongruous and incompatible with higher ideas and ideals of marriage, that were held before society. It cannot be, however, gainsaid that Niyoga served a useful purpose in its own days. Men are disinclined to marry widows, though they expect virgins to marry widowers. The custom of Niyoga solved the widow's difficulty to some extent by permitting the brother-in-law to raise issues on his sister-in-law under certain circumstances. Niyoga served as a half-way house between a formal remarriage and an absolute celibacy, especially in earlier days when three sons were allowed to be raised under it. Of course it indirectly encouraged polygamy, but we should not forget that society was already tolerating it. It also helped in improving the economic condition of the widow. When she had no son, she could get no share in the family property. When she got a son by Niyoga, she could get a share, if not as an heiress, at least as the guardian of her minor son.

Those, who opposed the custom of Niyoga, no doubt stood for the ideal of purity and constancy in sex relations. They should have, however, realised that if Niyoga was to be forbidden, regular remarriage ought to be allowed in the case of those widows, who found the ideal of celibacy too difficult to follow. This step, however, was not taken. As we shall see in the next section, both Niyoga and remarriage were forbidden to widows at about the same time. This resulted in a great hardship, eapecially because by this time child marriages had come into vogue, giving rise to a large class of virgin widows. Hypnotised by the ascetic ideal, which had now become popular, leaders of society failed to afford adequate relief to the widow, when they took the undoubtedly correct step of forbidding Niyoga.

Svami Dayanand Sarasvati, the founder of the Arya Samaja, has permitted Niyoga to his followers. He took this step probably because he felt that the mentality of Hindu society being deadly opposed to remarriage, the only way to give relief to the widow was by reviving the practice of Niyoga, which had a Vedic sanction. The members of the Arya Samaja have, however, shown no inclination to revive the archaic custom. They prefer the more straightforward and refined custom of widow remarriage.

SECTION 2 : WIDOW REMARRIAGE.

Side by side with Niyoga, the widow remarriage also prevailed in Vedic society. The suggestion that the proposal for a remarriage was made to the widow at the funeral of her husband is preposterous; it is based upon a wrong interpretation of a Vedic stanza.[1] There is however no doubt that widow remarriages used to take place not infrequently in the Vedic age.

In one place the *Atharvaveda* refers to a woman marrying a second time. It lays down a ritual to secure the union of the new couple in heaven.[2] It is therefore clear that the author of this hymn did not regard the conduct of the widow who remarried, as in any way disreputable; had he regarded it as

1. उदीर्ष्व नार्यभिजीवलोकं गतासुमेतमुपशेष एहि।
हस्तग्राभस्य दिधिषोस्तवेदं पत्युर्जनित्वमभिसंबभूथ ॥

R. V., X, 18,8.

The verse seeks to dissuade the widow from burning herself on her husband's funeral pyre by following the archaic Satī custom, which had gone out of vogue. Its correct translation is as follows :—'Oh lady, get up, come back to the world of the living; you are lying by the side of a dead person. As far as thy wife-hood to thy husband, who had seized thy hand (in marriage) is concerned, you have lived it out completely.' Those, who see in this verse a proposal for marriage, translate the last line in the following way :—'Thy wife hood to me, who has seized thy hand and who is thy lover, has now commenced.' This is, however, a wrong translatlon. It is, however, surprising to find that Sāyaṇa should support this interpretation; cf:

त्वं हस्तग्राभस्य पाणिग्राहवतो दिधिषोः पुनर्विवाहेच्छोः पत्युरेतज्जनित्वं जायात्वमभिसंबभूथ आभिमुख्येन सम्यक्प्राप्नुहि।

On *Tai. ran*, VI, I.

2. या पूर्वं पतिं वित्त्वा अथान्यं विन्दते पतिम्।
पञ्चौदनं च तौ अजं ददतो न वियोजतः ॥
समानलोको भवति पुनर्भुवा अपरः पतिः।
योऽजं पञ्चौदनं दक्षिणाज्योतिषं ददाति ॥

IX, 5, 27-8.

objectionable, he would not have recommended a ritual to facilitate her union with the second husband in heaven. A widow's son (*daidhīshavya*) is referred to in a passage in the *Taitirīya-saṁhitā*, probably suggesting the existence of the widow-marrage.[1]

In the passage of the *Atharaveda* referred to above, there is no suggesti on to the effect that the widow in question is to marry only her brother-in-law. It would therefore appear that some widows in the Vedic age used to marry outside the circle of their late husband's families. The usual procedure for the widow, however, seems to have been to marry a younger brother-in-law, who was very often unmarried at the time. It is therefore difficult to determine whether in a particular place the reference is to a regular remarriage with an unmarried brother-in-law, or merely to a Niyoga relation with him. References like those in Ṛigveda X, 40, 2 seem to contemplate Niyoga rather than a regular marriage with the brother-in-law.[2] References to regular remarriages of widows in Vedic literature are few, probably because Niyoga was then more popular than remarriage. At this period, however, a widow could get as many as three sons by Niyoga; so the Niyoga relationship practically amounted to a remarriage.

Though actual instances of widow remarriages, that can be clearly distinguished from Niyoga are few, they must not have been infrequent in society. For the Dharmasūtras (*c.* 400 B.C. to *c.* 100 A.D.) allow remarriage even when the death of the husband was only presumed and not proved. Thus Vasishṭha says that even a Brāhmaṇa lady with living children need wait only for five years, if her husband, gone out on a journey, does not return. *If she is unwilling to go to him*, she should marry a near relative; only she should not wed outside the family, if there is an eligible person within it.[3] Vasishṭha is not here referring to

1. *T. S.* II, 2. 4. 4.
2. को वां शयुत्रा विधवेव देवरम्।

R. V., X, 40, 2.

3. प्रोषितपत्नी पञ्च वर्षाण्युदीक्षेत। ऊर्ध्वं पञ्चभ्यो वर्षेभ्यो भर्तृसकाशं गच्छेत्। यदि धर्मार्थाभ्यां प्रवासं प्रत्यननुकामा स्यात् यथा प्रेते एवं वर्तितव्यं स्यात्।

P. T. O.

Niyoga, for he extends this permission even to women having living children. Kauṭilya (III, 4) and Nārada (XII, 88 ff.) have laid down similar rules. The former reduces the period of waiting to a few months only, and allows even women married by regular religious rites to enter into a fresh wedlock.[1] This permission was availed of even in high class families. Uḍupī was a widow, and she practically compelled Arjuna to marry her. In Uchchaṅga Jātaka, a lady when given an option of choice between a husband, a son and a brother, chooses the last mentioned one, observing that she can easily get another husband or son, but not another brother.[2] In Nanda Jātaka (No. 39) we come across a husband shuddering at the prospect of his youthful wife marrying again after his death, and not giving any share of his property to his son. In the Vessantara Jātaka, however, we find a dying husband urging his wife to remarry and not to waste away her youth (VI. 495). It is a different matter that she does not follow this advice.

Widow remarriages were, however, gradually coming into disrepute during the period 300 B.C. to 200 A.D. When urged to make peace on the last day of the war, Duryodhana says that he is disinclined to enjoy the earth as a man is to marry a widow.[3] Dharmasūtra writers usually place the son of a widow low in their scheme of succession. In *Aṅguttara Nikāya* we see

एवं ब्राह्मणी पञ्च प्रजाता अप्रजाता चत्वारि। अत ऊर्ध्वं समानोदकपिण्डर्षिगोत्राणां पूर्वः पूर्वः गरीयान्। न तु खलु कुलीने विद्यमाने परगामिनी स्यात्।

XVII, 67.

It is true that while commenting upon *Yājñavalkya*, I. 69, Viśvarūpa explains this passage as urging the wife to repair to her husband and not as permitting a second marriage. This interpretation is clearly in conflict with its concluding portion and is due to the commentator being influenced by the contemporary practice.

1. जीवितार्थमापद्गता वा धर्मविवाहात्कुमारी परिगृहीतारमनाख्याय प्रोषितं श्रूयमाणं सप्त तीर्थान्याकांक्षेत संवत्सरं श्रूयमाणमाख्याय। III, 4.

2. उत्संगे देव मे पुत्ते पथे धावंतिया पती।

3. क्षीणरत्नां च पृथिवीं हतक्षत्रियपुंगवाम्।
न ह्युत्सहाम्यहं भोक्तुं विधवामिव योषितम्॥

IX, 31, 45.

a lady assuring her husband on his death bed that she would never remarry after his death, but would look after the household and children.[1]

Owing to the growing influence of the ascetic ideals, the opposition to widow remarriage began to grow stronger and stronger from *c.* 200 A.D. Vishṇu recommends celibacy to the widow. Manu lays down that a widow should never even think of remarriage after her husband's death.[2] Nārada (*c.* 500 A.D.) can think of a girl's marriage only once (XII, 28). Elsewhere, however, he allows a woman to remarry if her husband had expired, or entered a monastery, or gone out on a long journey. Parāśara concurs with this view.[3] Medhātithi's view that the verse of Parāśara refers to a woman seeking service for her maintenance and not to her contracting a fresh marriage[4] is rendered altogether untenable by the inclusion of impotency as one of the causes for her doing so. The verse does contemplate a second marriage.

The contradictory provisions, that we sometimes come across in works like *Nāradasmṛiti* of this period, would show that though widow marriages were getting unpopular in Brāhmaṇa community, they were still common among the other classes. The famous emperor Chandragupta Vikramāditya, (*c.* 375-414 A.D.), who was probably a Vaiśya by caste, had married his elder brother's wife after the death of her husband. Kumāragupta, a son of this union, became an heir to the Gupta empire.

1. सिया खो पन ते गहपति एवमस्स, नकुलमाता गहपतानी ममच्चयेन अञ्ञं घरं गमिस्सति।

III, p. 295.

2. न तु नामापि गृह्णीयात्पत्यौ प्रेते परस्य वै।

V. 157.

3. नष्टे मृते प्रव्रजिते क्लीबे च पतिते पतौ।
पञ्चस्वापत्सु नारीणां पतिरन्यो विधीयते॥

Nārada, XII, 97; *Parāśara*, IV, 28.

4. यत्तु नष्टे मृते···इति तत्र पालनात् पतिमन्यमाश्रयेत सैरंध्रकर्मादिना आत्मवृत्त्यर्थम्।

On Manu, V. 163.

It is important to add that the opponents of the widow remarriage of this period were not against the remarriage of child widows. The prevalence of early marriages at this time had raised the problem of the child widow, and it was at first sympathetically solved by society. Social thinkers represented in the later portion of the *Mahābhārata* declare that no derogation would attach to a child widow if she married again; her sons would be fully entitled to offer oblations both to gods and manes.[1]

The earlier writers of the Dharmaśāstra also adopt a sympathetic attitude towards the child widow. Thus Vasiṣṭha states that if merely the marriage ritual is performed and the marriage itself is not consummated, the girl should be married again.[2] Baudhāyana holds the same view (II, 2, 4, 7). Laghu-Śātātapa holds that such a girl is really a virgin, and she should marry again as a matter of course[3].

In the absence of definite data, it is difficult to state what percentage of widows used to avail themselves of the opportunity of remarriage when it was permitted to them. Probably women with chidren did not usually think of remarriage. Among the rest also, many had a genuine love for their departed spouses and would not therefore think of remarriage. They tried, and tried with admirable success, to wade through the dreary life of widowhood, supported by their devotion to their husbands and such consolation as religion could afford. The percentage of the widows, who were remarrying may have been about 25%.

From about 600 A.D. the prejudice against the widow remarriage began to become deeper and deeper. Smṛiti writers from this period onwards begin to condemn them vehemently.

1. पुनर्भूरपि सा कन्या सपुत्रा हव्यकव्यदा। XIII, 55, 7.

2. पाणिग्राहे मृते बाला केवलं मन्त्रसंस्कृता।
सा चेदक्षतयोनिः स्यात्पुनः संस्कारमर्हति॥ XVII, 66.

3. उद्वाहिता च या कन्या न संप्राप्ता च मैथुनम्।
भर्तारं पुनरभ्येति यथा कन्या तथैव सा॥ V. 44.

Passages in earlier works clearly permitting them began to be explained away as referring to a bygone age. The *Ādityapurāṇa* declares that widow remarriage is not · › be performed in the Kali age.[1] A widow's son could not be invited for a Śrāddha. Referring to the permission for his sacared initiation given by earlier texts, Laghu-Aśvalāyana states frankly that it may have been a good and valid custom in a former age, but it can no longer be followed in the present times.[2] Mādhava, while commenting upon the famous text in Parāśara permitting remarriage observes that it is no longer valid in the Kali age.

From about 1000 A.D. the prohibition of remarraige began to be extended even to the cases of child widows. Devaṇabhaṭṭa (*c.* 1150 A.D.) states that the texts sanctioning remarriages in such cases have no application to the present age[3]. A section of the puritanical school tried to extend the denotation of the term widow. It was argued that girls betrothed verbally, nay even mentally, should be regarded as married. If perchance their husbands died before the performance of the marriage ritual, they should be regarded as widows and become ineligible for remmariage.[4] If by mistake a person married such a 'widow', he was to perform a penance and abandon her. The marriage was invalid *ab initio*.[5] Luckily this absurd doctrine did not appeal to society; it continued to be guided by Manu's

1. ऊढायाः पुनरुद्वाहं ज्येष्ठांशं गोवधं तथा।
कलौ पंच न कुर्वीत भ्रातृजायां कमण्डलुम्॥

2. युगान्तरे स धर्मः स्यात्कलौ निन्द्य इति स्मृतः ।
XXI, 14.

3. एवं च यानि संस्काराद्रूर्ध्वमक्षतयोन्याः पुनरुद्वाहपराणि तानि युगांतराभिप्रायाणीति मन्तव्यम्।
SCS., p. 221.

4. सप्त पौनर्भवाः कन्या वर्जनीयाः कुलाधमाः।
वाचा दत्ता मनोदत्ता कृतकौतुकमंगला॥
Kāśyapa *in SCS.*, p. 202.

5. अज्ञातस्तु द्विजो यस्तु विधवामुद्वहेद्यदि।
परित्यज्य च वै तां च प्रायश्चित्तं समाचरेत्॥
Laghu-Aśvalayana, XXI, 6.

sensible opinion that no marital tie arises before the marriage ritual is actually performed.

Though this move to extend the meaning of the term widow failed, widow remarriages disappeared almost completely from society from about 1100 A.D. Even child widows could not be married. This prohibition, however, became operative only in the higher sections of Hindu society. As far as its lower strata were concerned,—and they form more than 80 per cent of the community,— remarriages continued to be current among them. It was only in the last century that out of a desire to increase their respectability, some lower classes began to impose upon themselves the prohibition of widow marriage. The tendency has now disappeared.

Let us now examine the consequences of the prohibition of Niyoga and remarriage. The school advocating the recognition of the right of inheritance of the widow got an additional ground in its favour when they ceased to remarry. If widows were not to remarry or have any Niyoga relations, it was but fair that they should be conceded a share in the property of their husbands, to whom they were showing signal fidelity in most trying circumstances. Another consequence, and a sad one, followed the discontinuance of the widow remarriage. Many young widows found it a hard ordeal to lead a life of enforced celibacy and began to prefer to die with their husbands, rather than live behind them. The custom of Satī therefore became more general. Some widows, however, had not the courage to go through this inhuman fiery ordeal; nor had they sufficient strength of mind and character to live up to the high ascetic ideal prescribed for them. It is sad to record that they were driven to lead the life of a concubine or *avaruddhā strī*. The *Kāmasūtra* informs us that a widow, unable to lead a celibate life, used to approach a rich person, who used to accept her as mistress without the formality of any religious marriage.[1] If she found it difficult to pull on well

1. विधवा त्विन्द्रियदौर्बल्यादातुरा भोगिनं गुणसंपन्नं विन्देत । सौख्यार्थिनी किलान्यं विन्देत । IV, 2.

with him, she would have recourse to another person. It is difficult to state what percentage of widows was driven to this sad life, but probably it was not high.

This development should have induced society to change its attitude towards widow remarriage. The ascetic ideal of life had, however, acquired a complete ascendancy over the social mind. A large number of Jain, Buddhist and Hindu monks and nuns were following that ideal, and it was felt that widows also should do the same. Leaders of society should, however, have realised that what a few men and women could do out of intense religious conviction, could not be prescribed for a whole class. They should have realised that if the average widower found it difficult to pass his life without a second marriage, the average wiodow could not be in a different predicament. Society had, however, ceased to be guided by reason at this time, and had come under the complete sway of authority .Smṛiti texts, and Smṛiti texts too of the most recent date, which interdicted remarriage, were its sole sources of inspiration. Ancient authorities, which clearly permitted the widow remarriage, were silently ignored or ingeniously explained away.

Leaders of thought of the Hindu society in the medieval period were the writers of law digests and the saints of the Bhakti school. The former were too much under the influence of later Smṛitis to recommend a course opposed of their injunctions. The latter could hardly have championed the cause to the widow remarriage, as they were completely under the influence of the ascetic ideal. The prejudice of Hindu society against widow remarriage began to become deeper and deeper. Nay, it could never conceive the possibility of a respectable widow embarking on a course of remarriage. Tragic cases of girls being widowed at the age of 8 or 9 were often happening in society; but people regarded them as decrees of an unscrutable Providence and bowed down to them. Parshurambhau Patwardhan, one of the Peshwa generals, had the misfortune of his daughter being widowed at the age of 8; contemporary documents show that he thought it extremely unreasonable that scuh girl widows should not be allowed to remarry. But he could not break away from the tradition and get his daughter remarried.

It was only with the advent of western ideas during the second quarter of the last century that some leaders of thought began to realise the inequity of compelling widows to lead a life of enforced celibacy. Ishvarchandra Vidyasagar was the chief among them, and he succeeded in getting the necessary legislation passed in the Imperial Council in 1856, permitting widow remarriage under certain conditions. This legislation, however, was too much in advance of time, and did not succeed in giving any appreciable impetus to the cause of widow remarriage. Social reformers, who were championing this cause, were not all sincere in their advocacy. Many of them expressed public apology for their association with widow marriages, and some of them refused to follow the gospel they preached, when eventually occasions arose for them to contract a second marriage. In these days social and religious boycott was a terrible weapon, which leaders of orthodox thought could use with tremendous effect. So, for a decade or two, even ardent social reformers did not dare tc follow what they preached. More than 99 per cent. of widows also were honestly holding the view that it would be a great sacrilege for them to depart from the established custom. Women are proverbially conservative, even in matters that adversely affect their own welfare.

The cause of the widow remarriage has begun to make appreciable progress since the beginning of this century. Many sincere workers have come forward to devote themselves to it. The terrible havoc caused by the plague at the beginning of the 20th century made the problem acute. With the wider spread of western education, reason began to reassert itself; Smṛiti texts began to lose their hold, and reformers could point out earlier and more authoritative works which permitted widow remarriage. The angle of vision of society of looking to the problem is rapidly changing; the thinking section now frankly recognises that the cause of the widow marriage is a just one, deserving the sympathy and support of all humane persons. The ascetic and puritanical atmoshphere, which is a *sine qua non* for the successful working of the ban on widow marriage, has now compleley disppeared from society, probably never to return. The age of reason has returned which refuses to preseribe a course for the widows, which widowers are unwilling and unable to follow. The authority of later Smṛitis, which prohibit the widow marriage, is being questioned in the light of the earlier Smṛitis and Śrutis, which permit it. The closer study of social data and statistics is revealing that society becomes an unconscious party to great moral inequities by refusing its sanction to remarriages. All these factors are now operating with full force and helping the cause of the widow remarriage. There is, however, much uphill work still to be done; the number of widows under the age of 15 was as high as 3, 16, 926 in the census of 1931, it has only slightly dicreased in the census of 1951. It cannot be denied that alarge number of them may be anxious and yet unable to remarry.

TONSURE

The custom of the tonsure of widows, which is a very ugly and unfortunate one, is of recent origin and growth. The motive underlying it was to make the outward appearance of the widow in harmony with the ideal of renunciation (*saṁnyāsa*), that she was expected to follow. Monks and nuns used to shave their heads; it was felt that widows should do the same. It was hoped that this would help in creating an ascetic atmosphere around her, so necessary for her resolution to lead a celibate life. The procedure was calculated to destroy the beauty of face; it was thought that it would incidentally afford the widow a greater protection against the unwanted attentions of undesirable characters.

We have seen above that both Niyoga and remarriage were permitted to the widow down to *c.* 500 A.D. The custom of tonsure could obviously have not arisen upto that time. Among the duties of widows which are described at great length in early Smṛitis, the shaving of the head does never figure. Some authorities interdict the decoration of the hair;[1] this shows that the hair was there on the head and was not shaved. The widowed daughters-in-law of Dhṛitarāshṭra are expressly described in the epic as having the hair on the head decently arranged.[2] There was clearly no tonsure in vogue. Epigraphic evidence shows that during widowhood, the curly hair of women used to become straight[3]; this shows that only the oiling of hair was stopped. It is thus clear from the above data that widows used to keep their hair, but they were not allowed to oil, decorate or arrange them in any luxurious or fashionable manner.

When precisely the custom of tonsure came into vogue is not easy to determine. Epigraphic and Smṛiti evidence cited above shows that the custom was not in vogue down to the 9th century A.D. Some Smritis like that of Vedavyāsa, which are probably later than this period, begin to recommend that if a widow does not become a Sati, she should tonsure her head.[4] It was argued that the braid of hair, if continued by the widow, would result in the husband being put in bondage through it in the other world.[5] The prohibition of Niyoga and remarriage, which began to be fully operative at this period, gave a further impetus to the custom. Medieval writers like Mādhava and Anantadeva recommend the custom, and it is referred to by several European merchants and travellers from the 16th century downwards. It was quite common in the kingdom of Vijayanagar. We may, therefore, conclude that the custom

1. न कुर्यात्केशसंस्कारं गात्रसंस्कारमेव च।

Brahmavaivartapurāṇa 83, 101.

2. एतास्तु सीमन्तशिरोरुहा या शुक्लोत्तरीया नरराजपत्न्यः।
राज्ञोऽस्य वृद्धस्य परं शताख्याः स्नुषा नृवीराहतपुत्रनाथाः॥

XV, 27. 16.

3. सरलितप्रचुरालकजालकाः।

Pehova inscription of Madanapāla, *c.* 900 A. D., *E., I.*, Vol. I, p. 246.

4. जीवन्ती चेत्त्यक्तकेशा तपसा शोषयेद्वपुः॥

I, 53.

5. विधवाकबरीबन्धो भर्तृबन्धाय जायते।
शिरसो वपनं तस्मात्कार्यं विधवया सदा॥

Skandapurāṇa, Kāśikhaṇḍa, 4.74 ff.

became general from about 1200 A.D. Probably it was first confined to the Brāhmaṇa class, and was then gradually extended to the rest of society. It was, however, more common in southern than in northern India.

Among Jains and Buddhists, nuns used to be shaved. The custom of the tonsure of widows seems to have been borrowed from this practice. At any rate it smacked of a heterodox tendency to some orthodox thinkers, and they proceeded to oppose it on that account tooth and nail. This was the case with the Śrīvaishṇavas of southern India, many of whose Saṃhitās prohibit tonsure of women in express and decisive terms.[1] The prohibition extends to both maidens and widows. The question of the tonsure of maidens would arise only if they wanted to become nuns, availing themselves of the permission given in Buddhism and Jainism. The opposition of Śrīvaishnavas to the custom was most vehement; they declare that a woman who shaved her head would go to the most terrible hell; she would become a Chaṇḍālī in a subsequent life. The most advisable course for a widow, therefore, was to continue to have her hair till her death. This opposition, however, was of no avail, for eventually the custom spread even among the Vaishṇavas of south India.

The custom to tonsure was quite common till the end of the last century. A widow was regarded as impure and ineligible for association with religious rites and functions as long as she had

1. जन्मरोमणि या नारी क्षुरकर्म समाचरेत्।
कन्या वा विधवा वापि रौरवं नरकं व्रजेत्॥

Śambhusaṁhitā.

भर्तृहीना तु या नारी मुंडयित्वा समाचरेत्।
श्रौतस्मार्तानि कर्माणि चाण्डालीं योनिमाप्नुयात्॥

Manusaṁhitā, (different from *Manusmṛiti*).

स्त्रीणां तु भर्तृहीनानां वैष्णवीनां वसुन्धरे।
यावच्छरीरपातं हि प्रशस्तं केशधारणम्॥

Hayagrīvassaṁhitā.

The above quotations are given in *I. A.*, Vol. III, pp. 136-37. The date of these works is probably *c.* 1000 A. D. Their originals have not yet been published.

not removed her hair. Orthodox people would not take any water or food touched by her.

Hindu reformers launched a most determined attack against the custom in the nineties of the last century. Prin. Agarkar's articles against the custom created a ferment in Maharashtra. Society began to realise that the custom, far from protecting widows, was often exposing them to the mercies of most unscrupulous persons. The custom began to disappear rapidly in the first quarter of the 20th century. At present it has practically died down in towns and cities. It still lingers in rural areas, but there also its days are numbered.

A Resume

Let us now take a general resume of the position of the widow from age to age. We find that down to *c*. 300 B.C., her position on the whole was fairly satisfactory. The prehistoric custom of Satī having died down, she was not required to immolate herself on the funeral pyre of her husband. If she was disinclined to lead a life of celibacy, she could either contract a second marriage or have recourse to Niyoga, the latter hardly differing from the former in earlier times. The custom of tonsure was absolutely unknown. Her only disability was a proprietary one; as we shall see in the chapter IX, she was not regarded as an heir to her husband's property. This was, however, more or less a theoretical disability. Niyoga and remarriage being common, it was very rare for a widow not to have a son; so what she could not claim as an heir to her husband, she could get as a guardian of her minor son.

From *c*. 300 B.C. the position of the widow began to deteriorate. Satī custom began gradually to come into vogue in Kshatriya circles. Secular and religious Hindu thinkers opposed its rivival, and for some centuries they were able to check its spread. Eventually, however, their opposition proved of no avail and the custom spread to all sections of the community. Society began to come under a progressively greater influence of ascetic views and ideals and as a result, the customs of both Niyoga and remarriage began to become gradually unpopular at about the beginning of the Christian era. Widows, not inclined to lead a celibate life, could however have recourse either to Niyoga or remarriage down to *c.* 500 A.D. Thereafter, however, the force of public opinion made it difficult for them to do so. Niyoga came to be definitely forbidden for the present age. Remarriages of child widows continued to be permitted till about 1000 A.D., but soon thereafter even this concession was withdrawn.

Widows came to be regarded as inauspicious; they could not be present at the marriages of even their own children. They had to lead a dreary life of enforced celibacy, and society did not show much sympathy to them. Many widows waded through their unwanted life, supported by such solace as religion could afford them. Some summoned the necessary fortitude and preferred to escape from life through the frightful door of the Satī custom, which consequently began to become commoner. A few found it impossible to follow either course and lapsed into a life of ignominy and immorality.

The only direction in which a change for the better took place in the condition of the widow after *c.* 200 A.D. was the question of the rights of inheritance. When a large number of widows were leading a life characterised by high moral fervour, remaining true to the memory of their departed consorts, society found it necessary to make provision for their suitable maintenance. Joint families, of which they were members, were no doubt morally bound to provide for their maintenance, but it was felt that widows should be given a life estate in the property of their late husbands in order to enable them to lead a peaceful and retired life. This concession, however, was given only to those widows, whose husbands had separated from the joint family. It was only Bengal, which extended it to all widows. This question, however, will be discussed at length in Chapter IX.

From *c.* 1000 A.D. the condition of the widow further deteriorated. The custom of tonsure came into vogue. The motives for its adoption may have been good, but its consequences were often disastrous. The custom of Satī now began to appeal more and more to all classes of society. As a consequence, sometimes even unwilling widows were driven to follow it owing to the force of public opinion. Sometimes on rare occasions even child widows were burnt, lest they should go astray and bring disgrace to their families. Society had become quite callous. It is true that a very large number of widows voluntarily ascended funeral pyres, but society had no moral right to hold up a custom for admiration, which was likely to result in the burning alive of even a few innocent and unwilling human beings. Reason, however, had ceased to weigh with Hindu society at this time, as it did before in an earlier age. Authority counted for everything, and authority too of the most recent texts.

The above survey will show that it was but natural that widowhood should have been regarded with the greatest apprehension by Hindu women. The widow did not receive much intelligent sympathy from society as a whole. If she continued to live in the family of her husband, she had to work as a drudge; if she lived separately, she was given a pittance as her maintenance.[1] She had to spend her life with her head shaven and arms bared; she was an outcaste on festive occasions,—a bad omen, her very sight being regarded as most inauspicious.[2] A lady apprehending to be widowed observes in the *Mahābhārata* that a widow is pounced on all sides by the wicked like a piece of flesh by the birds of prey.[3] The greatest danger that can overcome a woman is widowhood, says the *Rāmāyaṇa*.[4] In the earlier period,

1. अन्नार्थं तण्डुलप्रस्थं अपराह्णे तु सेन्धनम्।
वसनं त्रिपणक्रीतं देयमेकं त्रिमासतः॥

Bṛihaspati Sm. 487

2. अमंगलेभ्यः सर्वेभ्यो विधवा स्यादमंगला।
विधवादर्शनात्सिद्धिः क्वापि जातु न विद्यते॥

Skandapurāṇa III. 7. 51.

3. उत्सृष्टमामिषं भूमौ प्रार्थयन्ति यथा खगाः।
प्रार्थयन्ति जनाः सर्वे पतिहीनां तथा स्त्रियम्॥

Mbh, I, 158, 10 (B).

4. न हीदृशं भयं किंचित्कुलस्त्रीणामिहोच्यते।
भयानामपि सर्वेषां वैधव्यं व्यसनं महत्॥

VII, 45, 43.

when the Satī custom was unknown and remarriage were allowed, her lot was somewhat better; nevertheless she was regarded as inauspicious. Later on, it became positively unbearable. It was a remarkable amount of fortitude and resignation, strengthened by the solace of religion and the belief in Karman, which enabled the Hindu widow to pass through her dreary life. A vast majority of them dedicated themselves to religious and spiritual pursuits. Service of the family and society was their motto. They were a source of inspiration to all around them on account of their self-sacrifice, disinterested service and devotion to spiritual pursuits. Some, however, found this ideal too difficult to follow, and it was a great pity that society should have failed to take proper steps to facilitate their remarriage. The spirit of the times, however, rendered such a move impossible.

CHAPTER VI

WOMEN AND PUBLIC LIFE

We have so far dealt with the position of women with reference to their family life. Modern readers, however, would be naturally anxious to know what facilities were afforded to women in ancient India to take part in public life and activities. Could they at all come out in public, or were they condemned to a Purda[1] life ? If they were allowed to move freely in society, what were the spheres in which they used to take an active part ? Were there any careers open to them ? If so, which ? Could they take any part in the administration of the country ? We shall now proceed to discuss these questions.

PURDA SYSTEM

Considerable discussion has been going on as to whether the Purda system was prevalent in ancient India or not. There is a divergence of opinion on the point. Some hold that it was quite unknown in the pre-Muslim days. Others maintain that Hindu ladies used to wear veils even before the advent of the Mahomadens. The available evidence on the point is of a dubious nature, and can be manipulated to support either view. It therefore requires a very careful scrutiny.

There is no doubt whatsoever that the Purda was unknown down to *c.* 100 B.C. In Indo-Iranian times women could move quite freely in society, and manage the family farms if necessary.[2] The same was the case in the Vedic age. We have shown already how girls were often educated along with boys (*ante*, p. 14.) We have also shown how love marriages would take place not infrequently, and how youths could approach their sweethearts to win their love, and how both would often go together to see

1. The Anglo-Indian spelling 'Purdah' is not followed in this work.
2. Dowson, *The Ethical Religion of Zoraster*, p. 153.

shows and sports (*ante*, pp. 66-8). All this would not have been possible if the Purda system had been observed in society by maidens.

Nor did the things change after the marriage. The Vedic marriage hymn requires the bride to be shown to all the assembled guests at the end of the marriage ritual.[1] The hope was further expressed that the bride should be able to speak with composure in public assemblies down to her old age.[2] The presence of ladies in social and public gatherings was a normal feature in the Vedic times. It was quite welcome to society.[3] Whenever anything charming or graceful is to be described, Vedic poets usually think of the gaily attired lady, going out for a function, as the standard object of comparison (*R. V.*, IV, 58, 7; X, 168, 2; etc). From the *Nirukta*, (*c.* 500 B.C.), we learn that ladies used to go out to courts of law to establish their claims of inheritance (III, 5). There is no reference to any Purda arrangement being made for their attendance. Nor does *Ṛigveda* I, 167, 3 contain any reference to the Purda system.[4] The laddle, now being dipped into the ghee pot and then being taken out and brought forward to pour its contents into the sacrificial fire, is compared in this verse to a lady, now remaining in the privacy of her house, and then coming out in public to attend a meeting.

The earliest reference to the Purda system is to be found in the present version of the epics (*c.* 100 B.C.). There we see that some kind of Purda was observed in certain royal families, which felt,

1. सुमंगलीरियं वधूरिमां समेत पश्यत।
सौभाग्यमस्यै दत्वायायास्तं वि परेतन॥
R. V., X., 85, 33.

2. वशिनी त्वं विदथमावदासि।
Ibid, X, 85, 26.
अथ जिर्व्रिविदथमावदासि॥
A. V., XIV, I, 21.

3. जुष्टा नरेषु समनेषु वल्गुः।
A. V., II. 36, 1.

4. मिम्यक्ष यषु सुधिता घृताची हिरण्यनिर्णिगुपरा न ऋष्टिः।
गुहा चरन्ती मनुषो न योषा सभावती विदथ्येव सं वाक्।

probably on account of a notion of prestige, that royal ladies should not come within the gaze of vulgar eyes. At the time when Sītā set out with her husband for the forest through the public thoroughfares of Ayodhyā, a regret is expressed in the *Rāmāyaṇa* that a lady, who had so far not been seen even by the spirits of the sky, should now become the object of public gaze.[1] A similar observation occurs in the *Mahābhārata* also at the time of Dhṛitarāshṭra's departure to forest.[2] The *Rāmāyaṇa further* observes that there is no objection if women come out in public on the occasions of marriages, *svayaṁvaras*, sacrifices and public calamities.[3] It would follow from this that they should remain in Purda in normal life.

It would appear that all the three passages above referred to, are interpolations of a later age, when the Purda system was introduced in a few royal families. For the other data in the epics themselves go against the prevalence of the Purda. Thus when Kauśalyā, Kaikeyī and Sumitrā go out to Chitrakūṭa to induce Rāma to return to Ayodhyā, they move in public without any veil. Sītā herself feels no embarrassment of a Purda lady, when she is going out through the streets of Ayodhyā. In the forests too, which were infested with demons and enemies, she is moving about without any veil. Were she using a veil, her beauty could not have been seen by Śūrpanakhā and reported by her to her brother Rāvaṇa. So the poet's observation that Sītā had not been seen even by the spirits of the sky is simply a poetic exaggeration made to heighten the pathos of her banishment to forest life. Draupadī's public appearance in the gambling hall presupposes an entire absence of the Purda. She no doubt shows some reluctance

1. या न शक्या पुरा द्रष्टुं भूतैराकाशगैरपि।
तामद्य सीतां पश्यन्ति राजमार्गगता जनाः॥
II, 33, 8.

2. या नापश्यच्चन्द्रमा नैव सूर्यो रामाः काश्चित्ताः स तस्मिन्नरेन्द्रे।
महावनं गच्छति कौरवेन्द्रे शोकेनार्ता राजमार्गं प्रपेदुः॥
XV, 16, 13.

3. व्यसनेषु च कृच्छ्रेषु नो युद्धे नो स्वयंवरे।
न क्रतौ न विवाहे च दर्शनं दुष्यति स्त्रियः॥
VI, 116,28.

to go there, not because she was observing the Purda, but because she was in the monthly period. Neither Kuntī nor Gāndhārī is seen to be observing it. In the story of king Poshya, narrated in the Mahābhārata (I, 1-3), we find the student Uttaṅka proceeding to the queen in her harem in order to beg her earings for presenting them to his teacher's wife. This would not have been possible, if there were Purda in the king's palace. Apart from the verses referred to in the last paragraph, the epics show no acquaintance with the Purda system. They are therefore likely to be later additions, made with the desire to heighten the pathos of the departure of Sītā and Dhṛitarāshṭra to forest.

It would however appear that soon after the beginning of the Christian era, a section of society began to advocate a greater seclusion for women. This was more particularly the case in royal families, where the notion began to prevail that royal ladies should not come within the public gaze. In some Jātakas, we find queens moving in covered carriages (V. 439, VI, pp. 31, 33, 167, 498), but in others we see them moving freely and talking with ministers and other officers (VI. pp. 23 9, 300). Purda makes its appearance in some dramas of Bhāsa (*c.* 200 A.D.). In his *Pratimā* we find Sītā coming on the stage with a veil, though subsequently Rāma asks her to remove it in order to allow the weeping citizens to have a parting glance of the princess, whom they adored so much. The widowed queens of Daśaratha are also seen in this drama to be moving with a veil, when they go out to see the gallery of royal statues. This prevents even Bharata from recognising them. In the *Svapnavāsavadattā*, Padmāvatī does not observe any Purda during her maidenhood, but after her marriage she does not like that her husband should receive the ambassador from Ujjayinī in her presence. The king, however, overrules her objection, pointing out that the *elite* of the society would feel offended, if the Purda was observed by the queen in their presence.[1]

1. राजा:—कलत्रदर्शनार्हं जनं कलत्रदर्शनात्परिहरतीति बहुदोषमुत्पादयति। तस्मादास्यताम्।

Act VI.

The *Nāgānanda* of Harsha (625 A.D.) also shows that maidens were expected to wear no veil; it was donned only after the marriage.[1] The commentary on the *Dhammapada* (*c.* 300 A.D.) shows that ladies were covering their faces when out on travel and that the girls of marriageable age were also segregated and not allowed to be approached by male servants.[2] In the *Mahāvīracharit* of Bhavabhūti (*c.* 750 A.D.), we find Rāma advising Sītā to put on a veil, when she was about to approach Paraśurāma to pay him her respects.[3] Some medieval poets like Māgha observe how the beauty of the faces of ladies could be visualised only for a moment, when their veils happened to slip accidentally.[4]

It would therefore appear that by about 300 A.D. some royal families were beginning to think it desirable that their ladies should be seen only by the select few; when moving in public they should put on a veil. The royal example was being imitated by a few families in higher and fashionable society; in the *Mṛichchhakaṭika* we find the courtesan Vasantsenā being offered a veil, when she was raised to the status of a respectable lady at the end of the drama.

This view was, however, shared only by a small section of society, perhaps confined to Northern India. It appeared as altogether irrational to women in general, who began to oppose it with all their might. From the *Lalitavistara* we learn that when Gopā, the bride-elect of the Buddha, was betrothed to him, she was advised to wear a veil. She refused to follow the course observing that the pure in thought require no such artificial

1. विदूषकः—भो वयस्य कन्यका खल्वेषा तत्किं न प्रेक्षावहे।
राजाः—को दोषः। निर्दोषदर्शना हि कन्यकाः॥
Act I.

2. Vol. I, p. 391; II, p. 217 and III, p. 24.

3. रामः—प्रिये गुरुरयं परशुरामः। तदपसृत्य कृतावगुंठना भव।

4. त्रस्तावगुण्ठनपटाः क्षणलक्ष्यमाणवक्त्रश्रियः सभयकौतुकमीक्षते स्म।
V. 17.

protection.[1]

This rational opposition, which the Purda system was receiving from spirited ladies, resulted in the system not becoming popular for several centuries. It may have been prevailing in a few royal families, but their number was very small. It was probably confined to a few royal houses of northern India. Sculptures and paintings of the first millennium of the Christian era do not at all disclose any veils over ladies' faces. The sculptures at Sanchi in Central India, for instance, show that the women of the 2nd century B.C. could see a procession from the balconies of their houses without covering their faces with veils (Plate I). The same was the case in the Deccan during the 5th and 6th centuries A.D., as may be gathered from several paintings at Ajanta.[2] This is clearly incompatible with the Purda system. Ajanta supplies further and more significant evidence to show that the Purda was altogether unknown in the Deccan at this time. We find queen Māyādevī seated in the open court without any veil, when astrologers are being consulted about the implications of her dream.[3] The wise minister Vidhura Paṇḍita delivers his sermons to royal ladies, none of whom cares to veil her face in his presence.[4] Both at Sanchi and Ajanta we come across mixed throngs of men and women moving together in streets,[5] and participating in worship at public temples (Plate II); women are, however, not to be seen wearing any veils. To show a veil round the face may be rather difficult for a sculptor, but not at all for a painter. If therefore we see even married women moving about in public without any Purda in Ajanta

1. गोपा शाक्यकन्या न कंचन दृष्ट्वा वदनं छादयति स्म।

Her argument was:--

ये कायसंवृता गुप्तेन्द्रियाः सुनिवृताश्च
मनः प्रसन्ना किं तादृशानां वदनं प्रतिछादयित्वा

Canto XVI.

2. Yazdani, *Ajanta*, Part II, Pl. XXIV.
3. *Ibid*, Pl. XXI.
4. *Ibid*, Plates XXXIV, XXXIX.
5. *Ibid*, Plates XXIV, XXV; Cunningham, Pl. XXVII.

paintings, the conclusion is irresistible that it was hardly much in vogue even in the higher and fashionable sections of society.

The evidence of sculptures and paintings is corroborated by the data of Dharmaśāstra and classical Sanskrit literature. Several Smṛitis like those of Manu and Yājñavalkya lay down detailed rules about the life of women, but they nowhere lay down that women were not to go out except when properly veiled.

In most of the Sanskrit dramas, we do not find any traces of the Purda system. The plots of the *Śākuntala* and the *Mālatī-Mādhava*, for example, would not have been possible in a Purda-ridden society. In the first Act of the *Śākuntala* the maidens do not cover their faces with veils, even when they see and converse with Dushyanta.[1] In the *Mālatī-Mādhava* the heroine and her numerous friends go out to the temple without any veil whatsoever; the hero is thus able to perceive the maddening beauty of the heroine and falls in love with her. Similarly in the *Kādambarī* of Bāṇa, neither Mahāśvetā nor Kādambarī, nor any of their numerous friends and attendants observe any Purda. From the *Meghadūta* (I, 26) we learn that women of Ujjayinī used to go to the Siprā for sport in water at the time of bath. This would not have been possible if the Purda were in vogue there. Yuan Chuang has given an intimate picture of the Hindu society of the 7th century A.D., but he nowhere refers to the Purda system. We learn from him that Rājyaśrī, the widowed sister of Harsha, used to come out without a veil in her brother's court. The *Rājataraṅgiṇī* gives a detailed account of the life in the Kashmir court and palace during the period 700-1150 A.D.; but we can nowhere get any references to the Purda in it. Abu Zaid, an Arabian traveller of the early 10th century, has noted that in most of the courts in India queens appeared in public without any veils (Elliot and Dowson, I, P. 11). It is there-

1. In the V Act, the heroine no doubt appears with a veil, but that is because she had donned it as a protection against the dust and weather during her journey. It was not doffed by her for some time owing to her sense of bashfulness and embarrassment at her first public appearance before her husband. Her veil in the V Act therefore does not prove the existence of the Purda system.

fore clear that the Purda was confined to a very small section of the ruling classes down to the 10th century A.D.

Though in Hindu society as a whole there was nothing like the modern Purda system in existence, there were certain restrictions on the movements of women. They could go out to visit their friends and relations, but decorum required that they should not stay at their houses for the night, or when their business was over. They were to observe a certain amount of reserve in the presence of strangers. They could speak with merchants and doctors and transact the necessary business, but they were to be circumspect while dealing with unknown persons.[1] They could receive male guests, but they were relieved of this duty, if there were male relatives in the family to discharge it. There were here and there some jealous husbands, who would not allow their wives to go out without their permission to see shows and amusements (*Arthaśāstra*, III, 3), but they were the exception rather than the rule.

Though there was no Purda system, women who felt themselves to be in a rather helpess condition, would often avoid going out in public. Such was the case of widows and maidens without proper guardians, and of married women, whose husbands had gone out on a journey.[2] Thus in the *Svapnavāsavadattā* of Bhāsa, queen Padmāvatī observes that it was but natural for Tāpasī to avoid strangers, because her husband was out on a journey[3]. If it was necessary for such women to work for their bread; Kauṭilya lays down that the Superintendent of the Weaving Department should make arrangements to send cotton to their homes for being spun into thread. They were not required to go to his office, unless they chose to do so (II, 23).

1. न परपुरुषमभिभाषेत अन्यत्र वणिक्प्रव्रजितवैद्येभ्यः।
Śankha in Aparārka on *Yāj.*, I, 83.

2. क्रीडां शरीरसंस्कारं समाजोत्सवदर्शनम्।
हास्यं परगृहे यानं त्यजेत्प्रोषितभर्तृका॥
Yāj., I. 84.

3. प्रोषितभर्तृका परपुरुषदर्शनं परिहरत्यार्या।
Act VI.

When they moved out, or had to converse with strangers, they used to put on a veil. When their guardians returned, they used to discard it.

To conclude, we find that even in pre-Muslim times there was a section in society from *c.* 100 B.C. which advocated the use of the veil for royal ladies for the purpose of increasing their prestige. There is, however, no evidence to prove that a large section of royal families observed this custom during the Hindu period. Women of richer classes led a more sheltered life than what would be welcomed by the educated ladies today. This is shown by the terms *antaḥpuram* 'inner apartment' and *avarādha* 'place without access' used to denote the harem in the palace. Strangers were not expected to enter it. Women themselves would often retire into seclusion, when they found that their natural guardians were not with them. With their return, they would again begin to move out as usual, of course with due regard to decorum and propriety.

Even in the *Kathāsaritsāgara*, written towards the end of the 11th century A.D., there are hardly any traces of the Purda. In the story of Arthalobha (III, 286) we find a lady participating in mercantile business. Polygamous kings occasionally attempted to introduce some seclusion in their harems, but they were strongly and successfully opposed by their queens. Thus in the story of Ratnaprabhā, we find the heroine protesting to her husband against his view that even his own friends should not enter her apartments. 'I consider', says she, 'that the strict seclusion of women is a folly produced by jealousy. It is of no use whatsoever. Women of good character are guarded only by their own virtue and nothing else.'[1]

There are absolutely no traces of any Purda observed within the family in the Hindu period. It was the regular duty of a

1. आर्यपुत्र प्रसंगेन वदामि तव तच्छृणु।
रक्षा चान्तःपुरेष्वीदृङ नैवमेतन्मतं मम॥
नीतिमात्रमहं मन्ये स्त्रीणां रक्षा नियन्त्रणम्॥
36, 6-7.

daughter-in-law to pay her respects to elderly relations by bowing at their feet. There is nothing whatsoever in our tradition or literature to suggest that the father-in-law or the elder brother-in-law could not see the face of a daughter-in-law or a younger sister-in-law, as is the case now under the Purda system in northern India.

The general adoption of the Purda system by the ruling and aristocratic families of Hindu community is subsequent to the advent of the Muslim rule. It was accepted by Hindu society partly in imitation of the manners of the conquerors, and partly as an additional protection for the women folk. In the Muslim ruling families the Purda was so strict that a message had to pass through three intermediaries before it could reach the desired person in the zenana (*J. A. S. B.*, 1935, p. 246). The Hindu chiefs and nobles followed the example of their overlords in their own harems. This happened almost universally in northern India, where the Muslim rule and culture were in ascendancy for a long time. In the Deccan, the Muslim influence was superficial, and so the Purda system got no footing in the Hindu society there. It was, however, introduced in their families by the Maratha rulers with a desire to render themselves as respectable as the Muslim kings whom they had supplanted.

There were some further causes to facilitate the general adoption of the custom at about 1200 A.D. As a rule Hindu women at this time were illiterate and inexperienced. The times were unsettled, there was a general feeling of insecurity and Hindu life and honour did not count for much in the eyes of the conquerors. The Purda afforded some additional protection to beautiful women while out on journey from the covetous eyes of an unscrupulous soldiery. It was therefore welcomed by Hindu women. They did not protest against it as Ratnaprabhā, a heroine in the *Kathāsaritsāgara*, had done before. (p. 174).

The Purda system became quite common among rich Hindu families of Bengal, Bihar and U. P. in the 15th and the 16th centuries. Both Vidyāpati and Chaitanya refer to it. When the wives of Raja Rudra Pratap Singh of Puri came to see

Chaitanya, they travelled in covered litters. In Rajputana the custom became universal in the ruling families. It was regarded as an essential insignia of respectability and high breeding. As a consequence, down to the present century, persons who had risen in wealth and importance were anxious to introduce Purda in their family in order to command respectability. Women of the peasant and working classes could of course not afford to remain in seclusion; they had to move out for their daily work. They used to move the lapel of their *saris* slightly over their faces when a stranger passed by them.

The above survey of the history of the Purda system would show that it was confined to small sections of Hindu society down to the beginning of the 11th century A. D. In most strata of the community, there was no seclusion of women and they could take a fair part in the social life around them. They could move about with a fair degree of freedom in the earlier period. They could visit temples and monasteries to listen to religious discourses. They could go to see shows in the company of their friends and lovers. These visits afforded convenient opportunities to young people, anxious to settle in matrimony. In urban areas women could go out to public parks for sport and recreation. A fifth century inscription describes the parks of the city of Mandsore in Central India as full of young ladies singing gleefully.[1] In the *Rāmāyaṇa* we are told that when peace and order prevail in society, maidens go out in the evening to gardens for play and recreation (II, 67, 17). Ladies in high families could even take part in dramas that were to be shown to a limited audience.

The situation gradually changed with the lowering of the marriage age. Inexperienced and uneducated wives became incapable of taking part in many of the activities mentioned above. Naturally husbands began to claim and excercise a greater control over them which proved detrimental to their

1. अजस्रगाभिश्च पुराङ्गनाभिर्वनानि यत्र समलंकृतानि ॥
C. I. I., III, No. 18.

participation in the social and public life and activities. Jealous husbands with narrow outlook would not allow their wives to mix freely with the outside world. This created an atmosphere favourable for the spread of the theory that women should lead a life of seclusion. During the Hindu period, however, the theory found acceptance only in a very small number of ruling families. With the advent of the Muslim rule it gained a powerful impetus owing to the culture and example of the conquerors. Women were ill-fitted to fight for their earlier freedom on account of their inexperience and ignorance and submitted to the new order.

It may be, however, pointed out that seclusion of women was not confined to India alone. In Athens at *c*. 500 B.C. women could not meet their husband's guests, or go outside the house without proper guards (*E. R. E.*, Vol. V, p. 735). A bridegroom could not see his bride before marriage in the cultural capital of ancient Greece owing to the strict conventions under which women lived (*Ibid*, Vol. VIII, p. 445). A character in one of the plays of Menander says, 'A free woman should be bounded by the street door'. At Sparta women had separate apartments and could not be present at a banquet. In ancient Assyria veil was worn by all married women, harlots and concubines being regarded as ineligible for it. In Persia also seclusion of women had become quite common before the beginning of the Christian era. The Bible lays down that women should not speak in public at the Church. If they had any difficulties, they were to ask their husbands at home, for 'it is a shame for women to speak in the Church' (I Corithians, 14, 34-5). Early Church Fathers held similar views. Tertullian says, 'For a virgin of virtuous habits every public appearance with an unveiled face was equivalent to suffering a rape'.[1] Clement of Alexandria says, 'Let the woman be entirely covered, unless she happens to be at home. She will not invite another to fall into a sin by uncovering her face'.[2] In Russia soon after the intro-

1. Quoted by M. Lyer in *Family*, p. 229.
2. Quoted by Davies in *A Short History*, p. 223.

duction of Christianity the Terem system was introduced, which shut out women from friends and foes alike. In the 16th century wives and daughters of noblemen could not be seen even by their own brothers and other near relations (Halle, *Women in Soviet Russia*, p. 11).

To come to modern times, we find that in the west also women lived under strict conventions till quite recent times. Down to 1850 A.D. in England a woman could not take a walk, much less a journey, alone; nor could she ask a fellow worker to visit her, unless that fellow worker happened to be not only a girl, but also a member of familiar family. It was almost scandalous for a woman to address a public meeting. When two ladies spoke at a meeting convened for the purpose of supporting the women's cause in 1869, a member of Parliament said, 'Two ladies, wives of members of this Parliament, had recently disgraced themselves by speaking in public.' When the House of Commons was built in 1844, it was with great difficulty that a Ladies' Gallery was sanctioned. It was, however, decided to put a grille before it in order to screen the occupants from the public gaze. This grille was removed only in 1918.[1]

The above survey of the Purda system shows that the seclusion of woman was quite common in most of the eastern and western civilisations down to quite recent times. Owing to the continuance of the medieval atmosphere and the advent and dominence of the Muslim civilisation, India has continued to cling to the custom down to modern times. In recent years, however, the Purda custom has begun to beat a precipitate retreat. Social reformers and medical practitioners have been long pointing out its evil consequences. The education, which women have now begun to receive in larger and larger numbers, is proving fatal to the custom. Strange though it may apppear at first sight, the Non-Cooperation and Civil Disobedience movements have helped a good deal in the annihilation of the Purda. They inspired many Purda ladies to come out in the public to

1. Ray Strachy, *The Cause*, pp. 79, 118, 362.

take part in the political movement, and their example had a magnetic influence. It may be confidently prophesied that in a generation the Purda custom would be completely banished from Hindu society.

CAREERS FOR WOMEN

We have seen above that for a long time there was no Purda in Hindu society and women used to receive education of a fairly advanced type. Let us see now whether they could follow any careers, if urged by a natural inclination or forced by adverse circumstances.

In the Vedic period the Aryans were mostly occupied in military or semi-military activities, as they were engaged in the task of subjugating the country. They had therefore to rely upon a greater degree of cooperation from women than was necessary in later times. Women used to take an active part in agriculture and in the manufacture of bows, arrows, and other war material. Saṁhitās also refer to famale workers in dying, embroidery and basket-making. It is interesting to note that the Vedic Saṁhitās have special words to denote female workers in the above crafts, which have disappeared in the later literature. This circumstance would show that women even in higher circles were manufacturing bows and arrows, cloth and baskets in the Vedic period, but gave up these plebian professions in later times. Women in the lower strata of society, however, continued to weave cloth, prepare baskets, and participate in agriculture as before.

In the post Vedic period there were two or three professions open to women in the higher sections of society.

The teaching career was the most common. This is quite clear from the coining of a separate word to distinguish a lady teacher from a teacher's wife. The latter was by courtesy called. Āchārāṇyī,' but if a woman was herself a teacher, she was to be designated 'Āchāryā'. As we have already shown, some of these lady teachers would specialise even in abstrause and difficult branches like theology and philosophy. Lady teachers teaching grammar, poetry and literature must have been more common. It is not improbable that among their pupils, occasionaly there might have been male students as well. Some of the lady teachers were remarkable for their eloquence and depth.

Women were admitted into Buddhism and Jainism as nuns and were allowed to preach. Some of them like Dhammadinnā developed into remarkably eloquent and successful preachers, as can be inferred from the unstinted encomium showered upon them by the Buddha.

Medical career was selected by some women. Among the works translated into Arabic in the 8th century A.D. there was one on midwifery written by a Hindu lady, whose name appears as Rūsā in the Arabic grab. Lady doctors in the past, like those in the modern age, seem to be usually specialising in midwifery. It is, however, difficult to make an exact estimate about their number in society. Even at present there are several lady doctors in moffusil treating patients on Ayurvedic lines. Their number in the past could not have been a negligible one.

In the realm of business we find that women had no disabilities. They do not figure in the list of persons declared incompetent for entering into a valid contract. Women in lower classes and commercial and industrial circles used to take an active part in carrying on the business transactions of their families. They could even pledge their husband's credit and enter into contracts on their behalf (*Yāj*. II, 47; *Vishṇu*, VI, 31). We have unfortunately no evidence to show what part ladies in higher circles used to take in the business of their families. Probably, then as now, they lagged behind their humbler sisters.

We have seen in Chapter I that music was cultivated by ladies in cultured families since very early times. Ladies, who could sing or dance, were much admired. Was then music open as a career to ladies in respectable families ? The answer is probably in the negative. We nowhere come across respectable ladies as music teachers. Girls in royal and rich families were usually coached either by male musicians or by dancing girls. It may be further pointed out that when early marriages came into vogue, it was not possible for ladies in cultured families to get the necessary proficiency in music before their marriage. Music as a career was not possible after the marriage owing to the progressively stringent ideas about decorum and seclusion.

When child marriages became the order the day, women in cultured families ceased to be connoissours of or even aquainted with the arts of vocal and instrumental music and dancing. These fine arts became the exclusive accomplishments of the courtesan class.

Courtesans had a peculiar position in ancient India. As persons who had sacrificed what was regarded as specially honorable in a woman, they were held in low estimation. But society treated them with a certain amount of consideration as the custodians of fine arts, which had ceased to be cultivated elsewhere in society. Men, who had a liking and love for music and dancing, could not find delight in the company of their own wives, who ceased to possess these accomplishments from *c.* 400 B. C. Though despised in one sense, courtesans began to be respected for their achievements in fine arts. Famous capitals like Vaiśālī and Rājgṛiha had chief courtesans of their own, who were often formally installed in their position by the state with due pomp and ceremony. Ambapallī, the chief courtesans of Vaiśālī (in northern Bihar) in the days of the Buddha, excited considerable admiration in the contemporary society. Noted for her beauty and accomplishments, possessed of considerable wealth, her pomp and pageant was in no way inferior to that of a member of the Senate of the Lichchhavi Republic. The Buddha did not deem it inappropriate to accept her invitation for a lunch and the gift of a mango groove for his Order. Sālavatī, Ambapallī's contemporary and competitor at Rājagṛiha (in Southern Bihar), enjoyed an equally high status. These chief courteasans had their own train of singers and dancing girls and were as extravagant in charging fess as in spending their earnings. Stories in Jātakas further show that besides being good artists, they were often noted for their constancy as well. One

Jātaka narrates how a courtesan became very poor because she waited for three years for a youth, who had paid her 3000 rupees. During this long period she did not accept even a betel leaf from another man (IV 248-9). Vasantasenā in the *Mṛichchhkatika* is another example of character and constancy among girls born in the courtesan families. Probably the majority of this class did not possess these virtues; nevertheless they enjoyed a certain status because men of wealth and position, who had aesthetic tastes, could find delight only in their company.

The numerical strength of the class of singing girls was fairly strong. Throughout her history India has been studded with small princes and princelings, who have been accustomed to extend a liberal patronage to singers and dancers. In the royal courts of the ancient and medieval periods a large number of singing girls were engaged as *Chauri*-bearers, betel-carriers, fan servants, etc. Besides the nominal duties indicated by their names, most of these women used to sing, dance and even stage dramas at the court. Dancing girls were also employed as spies by the Secret Service Department.

Some women also served as parasol-bearers, door-keepers, guards and hair-dressers in royal courts. But these careers were probably not open to women from higher classes.

When temples of Hindu gods came to be built and endowed on a magnificent scale, some people began to feel in course of time that there should be singing girls attached to shrines to play music on the occasions of the different services and worships of the day. The custom of the association of dancing girls with temples is unknown to Jātaka literature. It is not mentioned by by Greek writers; the *Arthaśāstra*, which describes in detail the life and duties of dancing girls, is silent about it (II, 27). The custom, however, had come into vogue by about the 3rd century A. D., for Kālidāsa refers to dancing girls present in Mahākāla temple of Ujjayinī at the time of the evening worship (*Meghadūta*, I, 35). Several Purāṇas also recommend that arrangements should be made to enlist the services of singing girls to provide vocal and instrumental music at the time of divine services. These singing girls were usually prostitutes, and we are pained to find that some of the Purāṇas should have gone to the extent of recommending the purchase of beautiful girls for their dedication to temples.[1] One Purāṇa goes to the extent of saying that the best way to win Sūryaloka is to dedicate a bevy of prostitutes to a solar temple.[2] Childless parents would often vow to dedicate their first born child to a temple, thus increasing the number of temple girls.[3]

This custom probably became quite common in the 6th century A. D., when most of the Purāṇas, containing a reference to it, seem to have been composed. In the 7th century Yuan Chwang saw numerous singing girls in the temple of the Sun at Multan. The *Rājataraṅgiṇī* (IV 31) attests to the existence of this custom in Kashmir from about the 7th century A. D. The famous temple of Somanātha is said to have employed 500 dancing girls in order to provide music before the deity continuously throughout the day and night. Several incriptions from south India prove the association of dancing girls with temple service from about the 9th century A. D. When king Rājarāja built the Tanjore temple in the 10th century A. D., he provided for a temple service by no less than 400 dancing girls.

The introduction of dancing girls in temples tended to lower their moral and spiritual atmosphere. Some people began to visit shrines not so much to pay their respects to deities, as to carry on their love intrigues with the singing girls employed there. To judge from a reference in the *Kuṭṭinīmatam*, we have to conclude that sometimes this used to happen even in the famous temple of Viśvanātha at Banaras.[4] The custom, when introdu-

1. क्रीता देवाय दातव्या धीरेणाक्लिष्टकर्मणा।
कल्पकालं भवेत्स्वर्गो नृपो वासौ महाधनी॥
Padmapurāṇa, Srishṭikhaṇḍa, 52, 97.

2. वेश्याकदंबकं यस्तु दद्यात्सूर्याय भक्तितः।
स गच्छेत्परमं स्थानं यत्र तिष्ठति भानुमान्॥
Bhaviśhyapurāṇa., I. 93, 67.

3. *Ancient Account of China and India*, p. 88.

4. Vv. 743-755.

ced, was therefore vehemently opposed by all the champions of social purity like Brāhmaṇas and ascetics. Alberuni refers to this opposition and says that it proved of no avail, because the custom was championed by kings and members of the aristocracy (II, p. 157). A 10th century inscription from Rajapuatana confirms the statement of Alberuni. It records the express instructions of a chieftain to his descendants that if the arrangement that he had made about the services of dancing girls at different temples was interfered withby ascetics and Brāhmaṇas, they should be at once stopped (*E. I.*, XI, p. 28). It is therefore clear from this record that the opposition of the majority of the Brāhmaṇas and puritanical thinkers to the association of dancing girls with temples was so strong down to the 10th century that even kings were afraid that their arrangements may fail owing to the success of the puritanical crusade. It is thus clear that the Purāṇas, which recomend the employment of dancing girls in temples, represent the view of a minority of the Brāhmaṇa community, which in its zeal to provide pomp and splendour at temple service, failed to realise the natural effects of the new practice on the moral and spiritual atmosphere of divine shrines. All the moral and religious leaders of the community, however, fought against this innovation. Their oppostion, however, proved of no avail. The royal support eventually succeeded in making the custom general and popular.

The modern Hindu public opinion is deadly opposed to the association of dancing girls with temple service. The dedication of girls to temples was legally prohibited first in Madras State; it is not permissible now in any part of the Indian Republic. The custom has now disappeared from all parts of the country.

Before concluding this section it is necessary to point out that the association of dancing girls with temples was fairly common in several countries in ancient time. In Egypt temples of Osiris and Isis were crowded with dancing girls. At Corinth in Greece thousands of women used to dedicate themselves to Venus and sell their bodies for the benefit of the temple. The custom was prevalent among the Herbrews and Babylonions as well.

WOMEN AND PUBLIC ADMINISTRATION.

Let us now see what part women took in the administration of the country. Political thinkers were not unanimous as to whether it is desirable to permit women to become rulers of the state. One school saw no objection in allowing them to ascend the throne. There is a proposal in the Rāmāyaṇa to offer the crown to Sītā, when Rāma was banished to the forest.[1] It could not materialise owing to Sītā's determination to accompany her husband in his banishment. Bhīshma advised Yudhishṭhira to sanction the coronations of the daughters of those kings, who had died in the war and left behind no male issues.[2] In one Jātaka, we find a king of Banaras renouncing the world and his queen assuming the reins of administration at the request of the subjects (IV, p. 487). In Orissa when king Lalitābharaṇadeva and his son died towards the end of the 9th century A.D., the widowed queen mother was requested by the feudatories to accept the sovereignty. In compliance to their request, we are told, she ascended the lion-throne like Kātyāyanī and ruled till the birth of a grandson.[3] Queen Diddā of Kashmir ruled that state for twenty two years, not as a regnant, but as a full sovereign.

The examples of queens reigning independently in their own rights are however few. This is to be attributed to the fact that the school of the political thinkers, which like the Salique law, opposed the accession of women to the throne, was representing

1. आत्मा हि दारा सर्वेषां दारसंग्रहवर्तिनाम्।
आत्मेयमिति रामस्य पालयिष्यति मेदिनीम्॥
II, 37, 38.

2. कुमारो नास्ति येषां च कन्यास्तत्राभिषेचय।
XII, 32, 33.

3. तदधुनापि प्रसीद। नाथवत्सुचिरं धारयेनाम्। क्रियतां लोकानुग्रहः स्वीक्रियतां प्रक्रमागता करराज्यश्रीः॥
J. B. O. R. S, II, pp. 422-3

the general opinion of society. It held that women should not be made rulers, for on account of their natural limitations, they cannot become efficient administerators.[1] We hardly come across any queens like Diddā of Kashmir ruling independently in their own right. Megasthenes had no doubt heard of queen rulers in Pāṇḍya country, but that was because of the matriarchal system prevailing in Malabar and the territory around. Hindu princess, even when entitled to the throne in their own rights, did not usually like to become the legal heads of their states in supersession of their husbands, whom they revered intensely. Their consorts usually became *de jure* as well as *de facto* heads of the government. Thus when Gaurī, a Raṭṭa princes who was an heir to a fiefdom in Karnatak, married a prince of Banahaṭṭa family in the 10th century, her husband became the ruler over her principality (*J. B. B. R. A. S.*, X, p. 77). The Gupta history provides perhaps the only exception to the rule. The founder of the dynasty, Chandragupta I, was ruling the kingdom jointly with his Lichchhavi queen Kumāradevī. The names and effigies of both the king and the queen appear on their coins, along with the name of the Licchhavi clan from which the queen was descended. The same is the case with the coins of William III and Mary II, who were jointly ruling over England from 1689 to 1694. Political reasons, however, were responsible for this joint rule; in the case of the first Gupta emperor the Lichchhavis were too proud to allow their state to be marged in the Gupta empire on the marriage of their princess with Chandragupta; and so a compromise was arrived at, under which both the king and the queen were regarded as equal and joint rulers of the state. Normally, however, when a princess with her own right to the throne married, her husband became the *de jure* ruler as well.

1. अनवकाशं यमित्थी राजा अस्स चक्कवर्तो।
M. N., III, 65-66.

यत्र स्त्री यत्र कितवो बालो यत्रानुशासिता।
मज्जन्ति तेऽवशा राजन्नद्यामश्मप्लवा इव ॥
Mbh, V, 38, 92

Though queens usually did not assume the reins of government when their husbands were alive, they did not hesitate to assume full control of the administration as regents, when their husbands died or sons were minors or taken prisoners. During the captivity of king Udayana of Kauśāmbī, his mother had taken full charge of the administration. The way in which she discharged her duties excited the admiration of even experienced ministers.[1] Many dowager queen regents also are known to ancient Indian history. The queen of Masaga was directing the attack against Alexander the Great, when her husband was killed in the battle with the invader. In the second century B.C. queen Nayanikā was at the head the administration of the extensive Sātavāhana empire of the Deccan during the minority of her son. In the 4th century A. D. Prabhāvatīguptā was directing the Vākāṭaka administration in Madhya Pradesh for more than 10 years after her husband's death as the Queen Regent for her minor son. In medieval Kashmir queen Sugandhā was actively governing the country after the death of Śankaravarman. In Rajput history there are several instances of widowed queens carrying on the administration efficiently during the minority of their sons even in troublesome times. Thus when her husband Sāmarasī died on the battlefield along with Pṛithvīrāja in 1193 A. D. Kūrmādevī took the administration of Mevad in her own hands, and fought at the head of her troops resisting the invasion of Kutbu-d-din.[2] Karṇavatī, one of the widows of Rana Sang, took a prominent part in the defence of Chitor, when it was attacked by Sultan Bahadur Shah of Gujrat. Her moving and inspiring address rekindled patriotism in a sullen and alienated nobility, which as a consequence immediately mustered strong in the defence of the famous fort. The odds, however, were too heavy against the gallant defenders. Undaunted by the inevitable defeat that was starting them in the face, Jawahirbai, another queen of King Sanga, fought at the head of the army and died on the battle-field while defending

1. *Pratijnāyaugandharāyaṇa,* Act I.
2. Tod, *Annals*, vol. I, pp. 303-4.

the castle.[1] Many other similar instances of able queen regents can be given from the medieval Rajput history.

In the Maratha history Tarabai of Kolhapur, Anubai of Ichalkaranji, Ahalyabai of Indore and Lakshmibai of Jhansi are well known for the skill, diplomacy, efficiency and bravery with which they carried on the government during their regencies. In spite of the most adverse circumstances Tarabai, the founder of the Kolhapur ruling family, showed remarkable grit and statesmanship in continuing and organising the Maratha opposition to Aurangzeb after the death of her husband Chhatrapati Rajaram in 1700 A. D. The fact that her opponent had the resources of the whole of India at her command did not deter her from her patriotic duty. During her regency of 30 years (1745-1775 A.D.), Anubai Ghorpade of Ichalkaranji (near Kolhapur) conducted most efficiently the administration of her state. She used to participate in many of the campaigns of the Peshwas with her own forces. She was in fact the maker of her state and had inherited all the qualities of her illustrious father, Peshwa Balaji Vishvanath. Ahalyabai Holkar of Indore was entrusted with administrative duties by her father-in-law, Malharrao Holkar, when she was only 24. Her regency during 1766-1795 A. D. covered a critical and troublesome period of Indian history. She, however, managed to steer the ship of her state clear of all shoals and rocks. While the rest of the country was torn by wars, her dominions enjoyed peace and prosperity. Her extensive and judicious charities, her repairs and reconstrucitons of old and demolished temples, illustrated to the whole country how the Maratha rule stood for the revival and progress of Hindu culture. Queen Lakshmibai of Jhansi was a lady of ideal character and great administrative abilities. She was a trained soldier and a born general; the skill, bravery and generalship which she showed in fighting with the English against heavy odds have excited the admiration of friends and foes alike.

1. Todd, *Annals*,, I, p. 362.

Hindu kingdoms under lady regents were usually well governed. An Anglo Indian officer of long standing had observed to J. S. Mill that if a Hindu principality was vigilantly and economically governed, if order was preserved without oppression, if cultivation was extending and people prosperous, in three cases out of four he found it to be under a woman's rule. This high praise would show that Hindu queen regents were not mere figure heads of government, but used to actively guide and supervise the state administration.

Queens used to excercise a good deal of influence on the administration even when their husbands were ruling. They were often entrusted with most delicate missions and their advice was eagerly awaited. When Duryodhana was adamant in his resolution to go to war with his cousins, the last effort to dissuade him from his resolve was entrusted to his mother queen Gāndhārī. The influence which the masterly mind of Draupadī exercised upon the Pāṇḍavas and their policy is well known. Kuntī sums up her inspiring and eloquent message to her sons by asking them to follow the advice of Draupadī. This shows how great was the confidence which was placed in her judgment by all her relatives.

Inscriptions testify to several queens and princesses taking an active part in the administration. This was particularly the case with the Deccan. Thus Vijayabhaṭṭārikā, the senior queen of king Chandrāditya of the Chālukya family, was ruling over a portion of the Bombay Deccan by the middle of the 7th century. We have got a charter given by her in the 5th year of her reign (*I. A.*, VII, p. 163). In 786 A. D. we find Śīlamahādevī, the crowned queen of the Rāshṭrakūṭa king Dhruva, making a land grant on her own authority (*E. I.*, XXII, p. 98). Obviously she felt that being the crowned queen, she had an inherent right to issue routine administrative orders without any reference to her husband; or, the latter may have expressly invested her with certain ruling powers, including the important power of making land grants. Revakanammaḍi, a daughter of the Rāshṭrakūṭa king Amoghavarsha I and wife of Erraganga, was the governor of the district of Edetore in 837 A. D. Malilādevī, a queen of Someśvara Chālukya, was governing the extensive province of Banavāsī in 1053 A. D. Ketalādevī, another queen of the same king, was the governor of the *Agrahāra* of Ponavad. Akkādevī, an elder sister of Jayasimha III, was ruling over the district of Kinsukad in 1022 A. D. Kumkumadevī, a sister of Vijayāditya, was ruling over a portion of Dharwar district in Karnatak in 1077 A. D. Lakshmīdevī, the chief queen of Vikramāditya VI, (1075-1125 A. D.), was in charge of the administration of 18 religious endowments.[1] Bammaladevī, queen of the Hoysala king Vishṇuvardhana, was ruling over Asundi district in *c.* 1125 A. D. Guntur district was being governed by Kākatīya queen Rudrambā at the time of the visit of Marco Polo towards the end of the 13th century A. D. We have already referred to the great influence which Rajput wives and mothers used to exercise over the internal and external policies of their husbands and sons. They often used to show remarkable originality and presence of mind in the face of grave danger. Thus it was queen Padmiṇī who suggested the device which secured the release of her husband.

Let us now see what part ordinary women took in the administration of the country. There were democratic assemblies in the Vedic age. The marriage hymn expresses the hope that the bride would be able to speak with composure and success in these public assemblies down to her old age.[2] It is thus probable that some ladies used to take an effective part in the public discussions of the democratic assemblies of the age. In the later Vedic period, the state of affairs changed; a text expressly informs us that women do no longer go to public assemblies.[3] Later on popular representative bodies at the seats of central and provincial governments disappeared. Village,

1. Altekar, *The Rāshṭrakūṭas and their Times*, p. 154.

2. वशिनी त्वं विदथमावदासि।

R. V., X., 85, 26.

3. तस्मात्पुमांसः सभां यांति न स्त्रियः।

M. S., IV, 7, 4.

town and guild assemblies remained the only popular bodies known to the later period (*c.* 200 B. C. to 1200 A. D.). Rules about the administration of these bodies given in Smṛitis and south Indian inscriptions do not show that women were usually among their members. Female education was on the decline; marriage had become obligatory for women, and it was taking place very early in their life. Ordinary women of this period did not naturally feel much interest in the problems discussed in these bodies. Child marriages led to maternity at an early age, and most women were naturally too much engrossed in family duties and responsibilities to find leisure to take part in public affairs. During the last two thousand years, therefore, ordinary Hindu women have not been taking any part in public administration. It may be pointed out that the same was the case in the west till quite recent times.

We shall now take a brief survey of the position of women in public life during the last seventy five years. They hardly figured in it down to the beginning of the present century. This was but natural, for women were for a long time unable to get the benefit of western education, which was mainly responsible for creating a new social and political consciousness. Mrs. Anandibai Joshi, Pandita Ramabai, Mrs. Ramabai Ranade and a few coworkers of theirs braved the public opinion and courageously proceeded with the work of female emancipation. Things however changed when female education began to become more widely diffused since the beginning of the present century. Lady workers in the public life began to become more numerous. In the beginning they were naturally engaged in tackling the problems mainly concerned with their own sex, like female education, maternity welfare, widow remarriage, the abolition of the Purda custom, etc. From about the time of the Non-cooperation movement of 1920 they began to figure in the political movements as well. Several of them distinguished themselves as platform speakers and hundreds of them went to jail to win freedom for their motherland in the Civil Disobedience Movement of 1930 and the Quit India Movement of 1942. One

Hindu lady, Mrs. Sarojini Naidu, adorned the chair of the Indian National Congress, which was then the highest honour in the gift of the Indian people

The sphere of women's activity in public life has been gradually increasing since in 1935. When provicial autonomy was introduced in 1937, some of them became Parliamentary Secretaries, Depity Speakers and even Ministers. With the advent of Freedom in 1947 their participation in public life has become still more extensive; the number of women who are members of legislature, Parliamentary Secretaries and Ministers has been continuously increasing. One lady Mrs. Sarojini Naidu served with distinction as the Governor of U. P. and another Mrs. Vijyalakshmi Pandit has distinguished herself as a successful ambassador.

In order to co-ordinate and direct the different movements connected with their welfare, women have organised Indian Women's Congress, which has been regularly meeting every year since 1926. In order to afford a forum to women in all stations of life, this conference used to eschew all political questions from its deliberations and discussions down to 1938. After that date this restriction was withdrawn.

In the matter of franchise, Indian women have been very fortunate. They have got it almost without asking. The angle of vision of looking at the question changed profoundly subsequent to the Great War, and the British Parliament granted franchise to British women in 1918. The Parliament took up the question of Indian Reforms soon thereafter, and decided to leave the question of the enfranchisement of Indian women to provincial legislatures. The latter bodies showed a liberal spirit and Indian women thus got their franchise without having recourse to breaking of windows and courting of imprisonment. The Government of India Act of 1935 introduced a differential lower franchise for women in order to enfranchise a large number of them. It also reserved a few seats for them in every provincial legislature. These principles have been given an extended application in the constitution of Free India.

As far as professions are concerned, women have made good progress in the medical and teaching lines. There are also a few lady advocates, but women have not yet begun to shine at the bar. There is extensive unemployment among educated men at present, but educated women are yet better off in this respect. Of course things may change when the supply becomes greater than the demand.

The number of women engaged in professions is still very small. Whether it will ever rise to anything like the proportion that we see in England or America is doubtful. In the first place the scope of employment even for educated men is very limited in India. Then we have to note that family life still appeals to the average Hindu woman as the proper sphere of her activity. It is true that modern education may gradually change the traditional viewpoint in this respect, and educated wives may not like to confine their activities only to their hearths and homes. Wholesale desertion of the home by the wife in pursuit of a career is, however, not desirable from several points of view. The development of the practice of part-time employment would afford a good solution of the problem; it would not much interfere with the home life of the educated wife and would afford sufficient facilities to her to usefully employ her spare time and make her own contribution to the family budget.

CHAPTER VII.

WOMEN AND RELIGION

Let us consider in this chapter the status and privileges which Hindu religion accorded to women. In the present age when religion is gradually losing its hold on popular mind, the subject may appear as of no great importance to some of our readers. The case, however, was quite different in the past. Religious rights and privileges were valued most highly; even political and proprietary rights faded before them in importance. The social status of an individual was vitally connected with the place which religion accorded to him in its rites and rituals. Privileges accorded or denied to women by religion will therefore throw valuable light on their position in society.

In his early history man is seen excluding woman from religious service almost everywhere because he regarded her as unclean, mainly on account of her periodical menstruation. During this period the woman was the object of the greatest dread. The case is on record of an Australian aborigine going stark mad because he had unknowingly touched the blanket used by his wife during her period, and then killing first his wife and then himself under the influence of his frenzy. The dread which this Australian felt was shared by the average man in his early history, when he did not know the physiological causes of the mysterious phenomenon, which he feared so much.

The Aryans also regarded the woman as untouchable during her monthly period. This was the case as early as the Indo-Iranian age. Like the Hindus, the Iranians also used to segregate women during this period and regard them as religiously impure (Vendidad, 16). The Vedic age assigned this temporary impurity of women to their taking over from Indra one third the sin of Brāhmaṇa murder, which he incurred when he had killed Vṛitra (*T. S.*, II, 5, 1, 5-7). During this period, therefore,

Hindu society has been regarding women as extremely impure and temporarily untouchable. Even the sight of their person and the sound of their voice were to be avoided. Hygienic rules often appear in the form of religious taboos in Hindu culture, and there can be no doubt that the complete isolation of women that was insisted upon during this period was partly due to the desire of ensuring complete rest which is so desirable for them during this period.

Child bearing was regarded as the special function of women, and evil spirits were believed to be very anxious to visit them during their periods to prevent conception. In the Vedic age brides were grown up in marriage and its consummation took place usually on the 4th day. One Vedic stanza in the marriage hymn prays that the bride should have no evil eye, and hopes that she would not be the cause of the sudden death of her husband.[1] We can understand this strange prayer only if we note the belief of the early times that evil spirits, haunting the person of the bride, render her touch and sight very dangerous to her husband. One stanza of the marriage hymn expressly refers to a female spirit taking possession of the bride and attempting to do harm to her husband through her person.[2] The prayer, above referred to, praying that the bride may not be the cause of her husband's death is a magical formula intended to immunise the husband from the possible consequences of his contact with the evil spirits, haunting his bride at the time of the menstruation and consummation.

From the Vedic time downwards women have been regarded as impure during the time of confinement also. The phenomenon of menstruation is repeated at the child-birth. It was besides apprehended that evil spirits would be haunting the mother during her confinement on account of their eagerness to kill new-born babies.

1. अघोरचक्षुरपतिघ्नी एधि।

R. V., X, 85, 44.

2. कृत्यैषा पद्वती भूत्वा जाया विशते पतिम्॥

R. V., X, 85, 29.

Apart from the periods of menstruation and confinement women were not regarded as impure by religion. It is true that a ceremony to purify the wife before her participation in sacrifices has been enjoined (Ś. *Br.*, V, 2, 1, 8-10); we cannot however, attach much importance to it, for a similar purification has been prescribed for men also (*T. Br.*, 1, 3, 7). In the Vedic age women enjoyed all the religious rights and privileges, which men posseseed. In Chapter I we have seen that women used to receive Vedic education. Some of them were even the authors of Vedic hymns (*ante*, p. 10). They therefore could recite Vedic *mantras* as a matter of course. Some women, especially unmarried ones, are seen offering Vedic sacrifices all by themselves. In one place we find a maiden taking a shoot of the Soma shrub while returning from her bath, and straightway offering it in sacrifice to Indra, when she reached home.[1] In another place we find a lady, named Viśvavārā, getting up early in the morning and starting the sacrifice all by herself[2]. In the Vedic age there were no images to worship or temples to visit. The Bhakti school, advocating simple prayer to God by mere songs of devotion, was yet to come into prominence, as also the Jñāna theory recommending merely the contemplation of Brahman or Ātmā. So the offering of sacrifice was the only popular and well-established method of worshipping divine powers. Naturally therefore it could not be interdicted to women, especially because they were all initiated into Vedic studies after their *upanayana*. All of them therefore could offer sacrifices after their initiation.

Marriage, and not renunciation, was the ideal recommended to society by Vedic religion. The woman therefore was not an impediment in the path of religion; her presence and co-operation were absolutely necessary in religious rites and cere-

1. कन्या वारयावती सोममपि स्रुता विदत्।
अस्तं भरन्त्यब्रवीदिन्द्राय सुनवै त्वा॥
VIII, 91, 1.

2. एति प्राची विश्ववारा नमोभिर्देवाँ ईडाना हविषा घृताची॥
V, 28, 1.

monies. This naturally increased her religious value. Man could not become a spiritual whole, unless he was accompanied by his wife;[1] gods do not accept the oblations offered by a bachelor.[2] The husband alone cannot go to heaven; in the symbolical ascent to heaven in the sacrifice, he has to call his wife to accompany him on the occasion (Ś. *Br*., V, 2, 1, 8). A son was indispensable for spiritual well-being in the life to come, and he could be had only through the wife. She was thus indispensable from the spiritual and religious points of view. This circumstance was responsible for ensuring her a religious status as high as that of her husband.

Normally, religious prayers and sacrifices were offered jointly by the husband and the wife. There are several references to couples waxing old in their joint worship of gods.[3] The wife used to take an active and real part in family sacrifices. Like the husband, she too had to perform a special *upanayana* on the occasion of some sacrifices. She had her own hut in the sacrificial compound, and also her own cow to provide her with sacred milk during the sacrifice (Ś. *Br*., X, 2, 3, 1; XIV, 3, 1, 35). In the early Vedic period, the duty of chanting musically the Sāma songs seems to have been usually performed by the wife;[4] later on it came to be entrusted to a special class of male priests called Udgātṛis. The wife used to pound the sacrificial rice, give bath to the animal that was to be immolated and lay in bricks, when altar was to be built (Ś. *Br*., VI, 5, 3, 1; III, 8, 2, 1-6). She participated with her husband in the preparation of the offering, the consecration of the fire, the offering of the

1. तस्मात्पुरुषो जायां वित्त्वा कृत्स्नतरमिवात्मानं मन्यते।
A. Br. I. 2. 5

2. अयज्ञीयो वै एष योऽपत्नीकः।
S. Br., V. 1, 6, 10.
A similar view is expressed in Avesta also.

3. बृहद्वयो बृहते तुभ्यमग्ने धियाजुरो मिथुनासः सचन्तः।
R. V., V, 53, 15.
प्रत्वा ततस्रे मिथुना अवस्यवः।
Ibid, I, 133, 3. See also I, 72, 5.

4. पत्नीकर्मैव एतेऽत्र कुर्वन्ति यदुद्गातारः।
Ś. Br., XIV, 3, 1, 35.

oblations and the concluding ceremonies. She herself had to recite some formulae. It is true that sometimes these had to be dictated to her;[1] but the case was probably the same with her husband also with reference to the prayers in many of the sacrifices. Women's participation in Vedic sacrifices was thus a real and not a formal one; they enjoyed the same religious privileges as their husbands.

If the husband was away on a journey, the wife alone performed the various sacrifices, which the couple had to offer jointly. This was the case in the Indo-Iranian period as well (Erpatistan, Fargard 1). This practice continued down to the Sūtra period (*c.* 500 B. C.).

Indrāṇī in one place proudly claims that she had started some rites and retuals.[2] Gods and goddesses are usually fashioned after the human model. We may therefore well infer that a few lady theologians may have made some contributions to the development of the Vedic ritual. What Indrāṇī did might well have been possible for some of the cultured ladies of the Vedic age, whose songs have been honoured by their inclusion in the Vedic Saṁhitā. We have, however, no direct evidence on the point.

There were some sacrifices which could be offered by women alone down to *c.* 500 B. C. Sītā sacrifice, intended to promote a rich harvest was one of them. Rudrabali was another; it was intended to ensure prosperity and fecundity among the cattle (*P. G. S.*, II, 17; III, 8, 10). Rudrayāga, intended to secure goodluck to maidens in marriage, was a third one. The last mentioned sacrifice could of course be performed by women alone; in the case of the earlier two, it is possible that the exclusive association of women with them was due to the theory that since they are intended to promote rich harvest and fertility,

1. तां वाचयति नमस्ते आतान इति।
Ś. Br., III, 8, 2, 4.

2. वेधा ऋतस्य वीरिणीन्द्रपत्नी महीयते।
R. V., X, 86, 10.

they should be performed by women alone, who are their visible symbols.

If the cooperation of the husband was unavailable for any reason, the wife could offer the sacrifices all alone. On the morning of Rāma's installation as the crown prince, Kauśalyā is seen performing all alone the Svastiyāga to ensure felicity to her son;[1] she was the neglected wife, and probably she felt that it would be too much to expect her husband to come to participate in the sacrifice. At that time he was as a matter of fact engaged in assuaging the wrath of his favourite wife Kaikeyī. Similarly Tārā is represented by Vālmīki as performing alone the Svasti sacrifice, when her husband Vāli was about to issue out to fight with Sugrīva. This was probably because Vāli was then too busily engaged in equipping himself to find time to participate in his wife's sacrifice. These instances show that in the early period women's participation in sacrifices was a real one; nay, very often husbands used to leave the whole affair to the exclusive charge of their wives, when they were otherwise very busy. The normal practice, however, was that the couple would joinltly perform the various sacrifices.

Intercaste *anuloma* marriages were permitted during this period. What then was the religious status of a wife who belonged to a lower caste? Could she participate in sacrifices? Later writers like Manu no doubt ordain that only the wife of the same caste could be associated with the husband in the sacrifices. The view of the earlier age was different; it allowed a *dvija* wife of the lower caste also full religious privileges, if she were the only wife of the husband.[2] A Śūdra wife, or a wife for whom a bride-price had been paid, was however not entitled to any religious rights and privileges.

1. सा क्षौमवसना देवी नित्यं व्रतपरायणा।
अग्निं जुहोति स्म तदा मंत्रवत्कृतमंगला।
II, 20, 15.

2. मिश्रासु (बहुभार्यासु) कनिष्ठयापि सवर्णया (धर्मकार्यं कुर्यात्)। समानवर्णाया अभावे त्वनन्तरयैव चापदि च। न त्वव द्विजः शूद्रया।
Vishṇu, Ch. XXIV; see also *Manu*, IX, 87; *V. D. S.* XVIII, 17.

The participation in sacrifices presupposed Vedic study, and we have shown already in Chapter I how girls used to devote themselves to it during their maidenhood (*ante*, p. 10-11). The Initiation Ceremony (*upanayana*) of girls used to take place as regularly as that of boys at the normal time. This was the case as early as the Indo-Iranian age. The Parsis have still preserved this custom; Naojot ritual, which corresponds to Hindu *upanayana*, is even now performed by them regularly in the case of girls as well. In India, the initiation of girls used to take place regularly down to the beginning of the Christian era. The Vedic age held that Brahmacharya discipline and training was as much necessary for girls as it was for boys.[1] It was apprehended that if the most important religious Sanskāra of *upanayana* was not performed in the case of girls, women would be automatically reduced to the status of Śūdras; how then could Brahmaṇas, Kshatriyas and Vaishyas be born of them ?[2] *Upanayana* of women was absolutely indispensable, if the cultural tradition of the different Aryan classes was to be preserved.

After their *upanayana* girls used to follow a discipline more or less similar to that of boys. They were, however, shown certain concessions. They were not to grow matted hair. Like boys, they were not to go out to beg their daily food. As far as possible, they were to be taught by their near relations like the father, the uncle or the brother. They were permitted to discontinue their course, when their marriages were settled at about the age of 16 or 17. A few, however, continued their studies for a much longer time and were known as Brahmavādinīs.[3] It is a great pity that most of the above rules about the

1. ब्रह्मचर्येण कन्या युवानं विन्दते पतिम् ॥

A. V., XI, 5, 18.

2. न हि शूद्रयोनौ ब्राह्मणक्षत्रियवैश्या जायन्ते ।

Hārita XXI, 20 quoted at *Par. Mād.*, Vol. I, part 2, p. 48.

3. तत्र ब्रह्मवादिनीनामग्नीन्धनं वेदाध्ययनं स्वगृहे च भैक्षचर्येति ।
सद्योवधूनां तूपस्थिते विवाहे कथंचिदुपनयनमात्रं कृत्वा विवाहः कार्यः ।
पुराकल्पे तु नारीणां मौंजीबंधनमिष्यते ।

P. T. O.

upanayana of girls should have to be gathered from works written at a time when the custom was rapidly going out of vogue, or had already ceased to be followed. We therefore get only very scrappy and insufficient information on the subject.

We have seen already (*ante*, pp. 12-13) how after their *upanayana* women used to specialise in Vedic theology and philosophy. Nay, some of them figure among the authors of Vedic hymns, the very reading of which was going to be prohibited to their sex by a later age. Women held that they were inherently entitled to study the Vedas; we find a sweetheart flatly declining to marry her lover, when she suspected that he was disinclined to reveal to her some of his Vedic dogmas and theories (*T. Br.*, II, 3, 10). When *upanayana* of girls was common, it is needless to add that women used to offer morning and evening prayers as regularly as men; the *Rāmāyaṇa* twice discloses Sītā discharging this religious duty.[1]

During the age of the Brāhamaṇas (*c.* 1500 to 1000 B. C.), the volume of Vedic studies became very extensive, as a number of subsidiary sciences were developed and lengthy commentaries were written on Vedic texts. The spoken dialect of the age had begun to differ considerably from the language of the Vedic hymns, and the theory had found universal acceptance that to commit a single and even a most minor mistake in the recitation of a Vedic Mantra would produce disastrous consequences to the

(*Continued from the last page.*)

अध्यापनं च वेदानां सावित्रीवचनं तथा।
पिता पितृव्यो भ्राता वा नैनामध्यापयेत्परः।
स्वगृहे चैव कन्याया भैक्षचर्या विधीयते।
वर्जयेदजिनं चीरं जटाधारणमेव च॥

Hārīta and Yama quoted in *V. M. S.*, p. 402.

1. वाग्यतास्ते त्रयः संध्यां समुपासत संहिताः (ते त्रयः रामलक्ष्मणसीताः)
II, 87, 19.

सन्ध्याकालमनाः श्यामा ध्रुवमेष्यति जानकी।
नदीं चेमां शिवजलां सन्ध्यार्थे वरवर्णिनी॥

V, 14, 48.

reciter.[1] As a natural consequence, society began to insist that those who wanted to undertake Vedic studies must be prepared to devote a fairly long period, of about 12 to 16 years to the task. We have seen above (*ante*, pp. 49-51) that at this time women used to be married at about the age of 16 or 17, and could thus give only 7 or 8 years to their Vedic studies. So short a period was quite insufficient for an efficient grounding in the Vedic lore in the age of the *Brāhmaṇas*. Society was not prepared to tolerate dilettante Vedic studies, and as a consequence, lady Vedic scholars began to become rarer and rarer.

Vedic sacrifices also became very complicate at this time; they could be properly performed only by those who had studied their minute intricacies very carefully. As a consequence, the participation of women in sacrifices gradually became a mere matter of formality. For some time wives continued to perform the duties that were formerly allotted to them in sacrifices, but gradually a tendency arose to allot most of the sacrificial work to males. Many sacrificial duties that could be once discharged by the wife alone, came to be assigned to male substitutes in the age of the Brāhmaṇas.[2] In some rituals like the Srastarārohaṇa, women continued to take a prominent part and recite the Vedic Mantras down to *c.* 500 B. C. (*P. G. S.*, III, 2), but the practice became gradually unpopular. The wife was originally entitled to offer oblations in the Gṛihya fire in the absence of the husband; now a son, or a brother-in-law began to act in her place (*S. G. S.*, II, 17, 13)). She continued to perform the evening sacrifice down to the beginning of the Christian era, but the recitation of the Vedic Mantras was prohibited to her on

1. मंत्रो हीनः स्वरतो वर्णतो वा मिथ्याप्रयुक्तो न तमर्थमाह।
स वाग्वज्रो यजमानं हिनस्ति यथेन्द्रशत्रुः स्वरतोऽपराधात्॥

Pāṇiniśikshā, 52.

2. तद्धस्मैतत्पुरा जायैव हविष्कृदुपतिष्ठति। तदिदमप्येतर्हि य एव कश्चनोपतिष्ठति।

Ś Br., I, 1, 4, 13.

the occasion.[1]

As amateurish Vedic studies could not be encouraged, and as women had now to take a purely formal part in sacrifices, the *upanayana* of girls began to become a mere formality in course of time. At *c*. 500 B. C., as we learn from Hārīta, only a few Brahmavādinīs used to devote themselves seriously to Vedic studies after their *upanayana*; in the case of the vast majority of girls the formality of the sacrament was somehow gone through just before their marriage.[2] A few centuries rolled on in this way and then writers like Manu began to advocate that girls' *upanayana* may be performed, but no Vedic Mantras should be recited on the occasion.[3] This development may be placed at about the beginning of the Christian era. *Upanayana* without Vedic Mantras being recited in and taught after the ritual was a contradiction in terms, and so later writers like Yājñavalkya began to advocate the more honest and straightforward course of prohibiting the ceremony altogether in the case of girls (I, 13)). A theory was started that the marriage ritual in the case of girls really served the entire purpose of *upanayana*; service of the husband corresponded to the service of the preceptor, and household duties were a fit substitute for the service of the sacrificial fire.[4] *Upanayana* therefore was unnecessary for girls. It may have been prescribed for them in a former age, but that rule was a dead letter in the present one. It is interesting to see how later writers like Medhātithi proceed to explain away clear passages in earlier texts permitting women's *upanayana* (on *Manu*, V, 155). Eventually medieval digest writers

1. सायमन्नस्य पक्वस्य पत्न्यमन्त्रं बलिं हरेत्।

Manu, III, 121.

2. Ante, p. 200, n. 3.

3. अमंत्रिका तु कार्येयं स्त्रीणामावृदशेषतः।

Manu, III, 66.

This verse occurs after the description of *upanayana*.

4. वैवाहिको विधिः स्त्रीणां संस्कारो वैदिकः स्मृतः।
पतिसेवा गुरौ वासो गृहार्थोऽग्निपरिक्रिया॥

Ibid, II, 67.

like Mitramiśra made wonderful discoveries of stray passages from lost Purāṇas, which boldly declared that women have the same status as that of the Śūdras and are therefore altogether ineligible for *upanayana*.[1]

Minor religious rituals like the Jātakarma, Nāmakaraṇa, Chūḍa, etc. were originally performed just as regularly in the case of girls as they were in that of boys. When *upanayana* was discontinued in the case of girls, it began to be advocated that other rituals also should be permitted to them, only if they were performed without the recitation of the Vedic Mantras. This position has been taken up by almost all the Smṛiti writers.

The prohibition of *upanayana* amounted to spiritual disenfranchisement of women and produced a disastrous effect upon their general position in society. It reduced them to the status of Śūdras. We have seen how in the earlier age women could, if necessary, perform sacrifices all by themselves. But now Manu came forward to declare that a pious Brāhmaṇa should not attend a sacrifice, which is performed by women (IV, 205). There were many Śruti texts which clearly declared that the husband and the wife were to perform the Vedic sacrifices jointly. When the *upanayana* of women became a mere formility at about 200 B. C., there arose a school which advocated that wives should not be associated with their husbands even formally in the performance of Vedic sacrifices. It argued quite seriously that the references in sacred texts to the sacrifices in the dual number did not refer to the husband and the wife, but to the sacrificer and the priest (*P. M.*, 1, 1, 2, 2) !

This new theory was opposed by the orthodox tradition, as it was all along accustomed to see sacrifices being jointly performed by the husband and the wife. The wife's participation had no doubt become a formal one, but society was not prepared to stop it altogether. Jaimini was the spokesman of the orthodox school, and he has explained very clearly how the references

1. वदन्ति केचिन्मुनयः स्त्रीणां शूद्रसमानताम् ।
Purāṇāntara quoted by Mitramiśra in *V. M.*, Paribhāshā, p. 40.

to the sacrificers in the dual number can denote only the husband and the wife. While doing so, however, he emphatically declares that a woman alone is quite ineligible to perform any sacrifice. 'The woman can stand no comparison with man. The sacrificer is learned, his wife is ignorant'.[1] The new theory took some time to popularise. In Jaimini's own time queen Nayanikā of the Deccan performed a number of Vedic sacrifices during her widowhood, and there was no dearth of learned Brāhmanas to accept her handsome gifts on the occasion.[2] The practice of women performing sacrifices by themselves, however, died down by the beginning of the Christian era. As pointed out already, Manu is seen condemning it sternly in his code.[3] The Smṛiti school on the whole was inclined to curtail the earlier religious rights and privileges of women, mainly because *upanayana* was no longer performed in their case. Those, who had not undergone this Vedic Sanskāra were naturally held to be incompetent to offer Vedic sacrifices.

The prohibition of Vedic sacrifices to women did not, however, produce any long standing hardship; for these sacrifices themselves soon went out of vogue. Neither men nor women were eager to perform them from about the beginning of the Christian era. What however did infinite harm to women was the theory that they were ineligible for them because they were of the status of the Śūdras. Henceforward they began to be bracketed with Śūdras and other backward classes in society. This we find to be the case even in the *Bhagavadgītā* (IX, 32).

It must be here pointed out that the exclusion of women from

1. अतुल्या हि स्त्री पुंसा। यजमानः पुमान् विद्वांश्च। पत्नी स्त्री चाविद्या च।

P. M., VI, 1, 24.

2. गृहतापसाय चरितब्रह्मचरियाय दिखव्रतयंञसुदाय यंञा हुता आगधेय...अनारभनीयो राजसूययंञो...असमेधो....गर्गतिरतो.... ।

A. S. W. I., V, p. 88.

3. नाश्रोत्रियतते यज्ञे ग्रामयाजिकृते तथा।
स्त्रिया क्लीबेन च हुते भुंजीत ब्राह्मणः क्वचित्॥

IV, 205.

Vedic studies and sacrifices was not due to any deliberate plan to lower their status. Custodians of the Vedic lore honestly believed that no one should be allowed to recite and use the Vedic Mantras who had not studied them properly. Women found it impossible to devote the necessary time for this purpose on account of their early marriages. It was therefore but fair that they should not be allowed to invite on themselves and their relations those dreadful calamities, which were honestly believed to result from an incorrect recitation of the Vedic stanzas.[1] The desire was not to humiliate women, but rather to save them from dire consequences.

When the Vedic Karmamārga gradually went into background, its place was taken by the new Bhakti and Pauranik schools, which rose into prominence at *c.* 500 A.D. The leaders of these movements had a catholic outlook and threw open their doors to all, irrespective of sex and caste. This was a welcome development for women. Their religious disenfranchisement had created a vacuum; it was filled by the Bhakti-Pauranik religion. In fact they became its *de facto* custodians.

Women are by nature more religious and devotional than men. They can visit temples with greater regularity, perform sacred rites with higher faith and submit to religious fasts with more alacrity than men. The Pauranik religion which came into prominence by *c.* 500 A. D., made ample provisions, for the religious requirements of women. As early as the 3rd century B.C., women were already accustomed to perform a number of vows and fasts (*vratas*), which were unknown to Śrutis and Smṛitis. They are referred to by Aśoka in his Rock Edict No. IX,[2] and the Vimānavatthukathā in the *Dhammapada* refers to a lady, who being anxious to devote herself to some Vrata without being disturbed by her gay husband, paid him some money out of her own Strīdhana, so that he may get his pleasure elsewhere (I, 15). Vratas therefore were quite common even before the beginning

1. See, *ante*, p. 200 n. 2.

2. अबफजनियो च बहु च बहुविधं च खुदं च निलठियं मंगलं करोति।

of the Christian era. The reorganisers of the Pauranik religion increased their number, spread them evenly over the whole year and invested them with a moral fervour by associating a number of ethical and edifying stories with them. Hinduism, as it is known to and practised by the masses today, is not the Hinduism of the Śrutis or Smṛitis, but the Hinduism of the Purāṇas, and women have been its most devoted followers and patrons. Most of the women in society at this time were uneducated and therefore incapable of understanding or appreciating subtle intellectual arguments like those advanced by the Vedānta school. The new religion, however, mostly relied on an appeal to faith and devotion. It therefore appealed to women immensely. Being certain that the sections of society, which were its devoted followers, had an inexhaustible fund of credulity, the writers of Purāṇas, did not take much care to offer a reasonable or rational explanation in every case. Very often virtues were so much exaggerated that they assumed the garb of vice. Vices were sometimes condoned because they were associated with some heroes or demi-gods. Hindu women, who went on performing the Vratas and listening to the stories contained in the Purāṇas, became by temper and training very credulous and devotional. Most of them became strangers to rationalism based upon discriminative reason under the influence of the new religion. The same, however, was the case with men at this time, if perhaps to a slightly less extent. It however cannot be denied that the continuance of the old religious vein, moral fervour and spiritual tradition is largely due to the zeal, sincerity and devotion of women. Thus those very women, whom religion had once regarded as outcastes, eventually enabled it to tide over most difficult times. They were the most faithful custodians of its spirit and traditions.[1]

BUDDHISM AND JAINISM

Let us now see what place and position was assigned to

1. स्त्रीभ्यः सर्ववर्णेभ्यो धर्मशेषान्प्रतीयादित्येके।
Ap. Dh. S., II. 29. 16.

women in Buddhism and Jainism. Both these were ascetic re- religions, and they have not devoted much attention to the duties and ideals of lay women. The founders and leaders of both these movements shared the indifference to, or contempt of women, which is almost universal among the advocates of the ascetic ideal. The Buddha was reluctant to admit women to his Church, and the Digambara Jains hold that women can never get salvation except by first being reborn as men. It may be added here that Buddhism did not subscribe to this dogma.

Owing to the pressing entreaties of his foster mother, the Buddha eventually decided with great reluctance to admit nuns into his Church. Mahāvīra is not known to have raised any objection in the matter. But both Buddhism and Jainism placed nuns under a more rigorous discipline than monks. Some of the restrictions placed upon the nuns were no doubt reasonable ones; thus it was laid down that they should not stay alone without the protection of monks; that they should avoid the company of men of doubtful character; that only monks of unquestioned purity and integrity should be allowed to preach before nuns; that they should always live together in groups of twos and threes, etc. Some other rules, however, betray a lack of confidence in the character and judgment of women. Thus the admission of a new nun was to be sanctioned by a joint meeting of the monks and nuns; new monks, however, could be admitted without consulting the nuns at all. Nuns were to go out to beg only when led by an experienced matron. The climax is, however, reached by the rule which lays down that a nun, though 100 years old, must stand in reverence before a monk, though he may have been just initiated in the Church. The reader will not now be surprised to learn that a nun could never preach before a congregation of monks, though the selected ones among the latter could preach before a congregation of nuns.[1] It may be here added that early Christian Fathers

1. *Vinaya*, Chullavagga, X, i, 4; *Mūlachāra* of Vaṭṭakera, pp. 177-97.

shared similar views; they held that it was contrary to nature that women should be allowed to preach. The Council of Laodicea closed the doors of the preaching career to women in 365 A. D., and not all the feminist agitation has succeeded even now (1956 A. D.), in getting them reopened for them. Islam permits women to read the Koran, but not to preach from it.[1]

The above rules betray that inherent air of superiority, which man usually finds it difficult to renounce with reference to women. Not all of them were, however, followed in practice; thus the theory that nuns could under no circumstances preach to monks did not stand in the way of Rājīmatī, the wife of Neminātha, in delivering a stirring sermon to her brother-in-law Rathanemi, when the latter had lost self-control under the influence of tempting circumstances (*Uttrādhyayanasūtra*, No. 22).

In spite of some discriminative rules, referred to above, the permission that was given to women to join the Church by Jainism and Buddhism raised a new and respectable career before them. In Brahmanical religion also there were some nuns like Sulabhā and Gārgī Vāchaknavī; their number, however, seems to have been much larger in Buddhist and Jain circles. Buddhism declared that womanhood was no bar to salvation,[2] and Śvetāmbara Jains concurred with the view. Marriage was not necessary for women; nay, it was a fetter which women were advised to avoid. They were therefore urged to become nuns without entering into matrimony. Among the nuns of the *Therigāthā* the majority consists of women, who had renounced the world during their maidenhood. The career of preaching and evangelising that was thus opened before women by Jainism and Buddhism attracted a large number of talented ladies, who distinguished themselves as teachers and preachers. Several inscriptions show that senior nuns had their own female disci-

1. J. L. Davies, *A Short History*, p. 238.

2. इत्थिभावो नो किं कयिरा चित्तम्हि सुसमाहिते।
ञानम्हि वत्तमानम्हि सम्माधम्मं विपस्सतो॥

Therīgāthā, 61

ples and novices and used to possess influence sufficient to collect funds necessary for the maintenance of their establishments. We find rich heiresses, refusing tempting marriage offers and joining the preaching army of the new religions. Such, for instance, was the case of Guttā, Anopamā and Sumedhā, who eventually became very famous preachers (*Therigāthā*, 54, 56, 73). Similar was the case of Saṅghamitrā, the daughter of Aśoka, who went to far off Ceylon, to spread the gospel of the Buddha. Jayantī, a daughter of king Sahasrānīka of Kausāmbī, doffed her royal robe and became a devout nun, the moment her questions about the nature of the individual soul, the ideal of life, etc., were satisfactorily answered by Mahāvīra. Some ladies like Abhirṁpā Nandā and Sumaṅglā no doubt joined the Church as a welcome escape from household tyranny, but their number does not seem to have been large.

When discipline became slack and unworthy persons began to be admitted into monasteries and nunneries, the tone of moral life deteriorated. It hastened the process of the downfall of Buddhism. Later Hinduism took a lesson from what it saw in Buddhist monasteries and nunneries and declared women to be ineligible for renunciation (*Saṁnyāsa*). It maintained that not renunciation but due discharge of family responsibilities was the most sacred duty of women.[1] Nuns therefore have disappeared from Hinduism during the last 1500 years.

The reader has already noted the main religious disabilities of women. In the modern feminist movement in India, we hardly notice any effort made to get them redressed. This is natural. When men themselves have given up Vedic sacrifices, women naturally feel no inclination to agitate for the right to perform them. The Aryasamaj, which has revived these sacrifices, has extended the right to perform them to women as well. In the modern materialistic world, the average woman feels no grievance for being deprived of the right to become a nun. She

1. स्त्रियाः श्रुतौ वा शास्त्रे वा प्रव्रज्या न विधीयते।
प्रजा हि तस्याः स्वो धर्मो सवर्णादिति धारणा॥

Yama in *SCV.*, p. 596

looks with a contemptuous smile on a dogma, which would declare that she is ineligible for spiritual salvation because of her sex. *Upanayana* has become a meaningless formality even in the case of boys; women naturally feel that they have nothing to gain by becoming re-eligible for it. It is true that the religious disenfranchisement that resulted from the ineligibility for *upanayana* produced a disastrous consequence upon the general status of women in society; but women have realised that improvement in this direction in modern days depends mainly upon the spread of education and the acquisition of economic rights and independence. They therefore naturally feel no inclination for initiating an agitation for the restoration of their old religious rights and privileges.

It would be, however, in the interest of Hindu society if it remains constantly alive to the full implications of the Vedic theory that the husband and the wife are equal and necessary partners in divine worship. The principle implies that men and women have equal rights and responsibilities in matters temporal as well. Since the spiritual disenfranchisement of women, men have become accustomed to regard them as their inferiors in all the spheres of life. This outlook must disappear. We must remember that women have done greater service to religion than men by preserving the old religious tradition, moral fervour and spiritual vein in Hindu society. These constitute a priceless heritage, and men ought to be graetful to women for preserving it. If an effort is made to spread a rational knowledge of the fundamental principles of Hinduism among women, they would undoubtedly become much better representatives of our culture and religion than what men are to day.

CHAPTER VIII.

PROPRIETARY RIGHTS DURING COVERTURE.

The study of the evolution of the proprietary rights of women is a very fascinating subject. It has a vital importance to the historian of the woman, for economic independence and prosperity have usually an important bearing on the well-being of a class. The reader is already aware how the general position of women went on deteriorating after the beginning of the Christian era. He will now be surprised to learn that, in spite of this general setback, their proprietary rights were gradually becoming more and more extensive in course of time.

In early times proprietary rights of women were recognised very tardily in almost all civilisations. This was the case specially in patriarchal societies. For a long time there was no question of the woman holding any property; she herself was an item in the moveable property of the husband or the patriarch. This was the case among the Teutons. The Frisians used to give their women and children in payment of their taxes to Rome, when they had no other means to discharge their liabilities. At Rome the husband could sell his wife in early times, the right being taken away only at the beginning of the Christian era. For a long time the wife was under the tutelage of her husband and could possess no separate property at all, if she was married according to the orthodox religious rites. Even after the husband's death she did not become a *sui jure*, but passed under the tutelage of other male relatives. During the feudal age in Europe, women could no doubt inherit and hold even landed property. This was, however, a nominal right. Women were really pawns in the hands of kings. Land was for military service, which women were incapable of rendering. So the emperor would take immediate steps to marry the daughters or widows of his barons or knights to whomsoever he liked. When in his Spanish campaigns a number of his noblemen died, Charlmaigne immediately married their widows to the barons of his own choice. He was anxious that land should not be under the ownership of those who could not fight in his wars. Whether the widows concerned wanted to marry, and if so, whether they had approved of the proposed new husbands, was a matter which he did not stop to enquire. Women were a sort of vitalised deed of conveyance. They were hardly as important as horses, which were so useful in war, save as living titles to landed property.[1]

In India too in very early times women were regarded as chattel. They were given away as gifts in the Vedic age, as would appear from several hymns, which glorify the gifts of generous donors.[2] In the *Mahābhārata* we find Dhṛitarāshṭra proposing to give hundred female slaves of Kṛishṇa as a token of his regard for him.[3] The husband was deemed to have a natural proprietary right in the wife. It is on this undisputed assumption that Hariśchandra proceeds to sell his wife to the Domb at the Banaras Ghat and Dharma proceeds to stake Draupadī in the gambling hall. It may be further pointed out that even this proud and haughty queen does not think of disputing this right of her husband, when she is dragged to the court of Dhṛitarāshtra. She does not at all maintain that she has not lost her freedom because the husband has no right to sell or stake away his wife. She only wants to know whether her husband was a free man, when he had staked her.[4] In the *Ṛigveda* also in the famous gambling hymn, we find the wife being staked away by the husband (X, 34).

1. The reader will get more information on the points discussed in this para from George, *Story of Woman* and Müller Lyer, *Family*.

2. उप मा श्यावा स्वनयेन दत्ता वधूमन्तो दश रथासोऽस्युः।
I, 126, 3

3. दासीनामप्रजातानां शुभानां रुक्मवर्चसाम्।
शतमस्मै प्रदास्यामि दासानामपि तावताम्॥
V. 86, 8.

4. किंतु पूर्वं पराजैषीरात्मानमथवा नु माम्।
II, 89, 19.

The *Mahābhārata*, however, states that the assembly began to hiss loudly when Dharma proceeded to stake his wife.[1] It would therefore appear that though the husband's proprietary right in the wife was theoretically recognised, its actual exercise met with a stern social disapprobation. It was felt that only intoxicated or inhuman persons could think of exercising it.[2] In the Vedic age also, it was only a confirmed gambler who would sometimes stake his wife. In cultured circles the wife was regarded as the co-owner of the family property along with her husband, as the term *dampatī* would show.

Apart from the rather exceptional cases, referred to above, which really reflect the state of society in prehistoric times, there is no evidence of women being regarded as chattel in ancient India. The Dharmaśāstra writers of the first and the second centuries A. D., leave no scope for an enterprising husband to utilise the results of his research in prehistoric social customs and institutions to the disadvantage of his consort; they have definitely declared that women and children cannot be objects of gift or sale under any circumstances.[3]

Let us now consider the proprietary rights of the wife, *vis-a-vis* her husband. The theory approved by the Hindu culture as early as the Vedic age was that the husband and the wife should be the joint owners of the household and its property. The husband was required to take a solemn vow at the marriage that he would never transgress the rights and interests of his wife in economic matters.

The theory of the joint ownership of the couple should have led to a number of important corollaries, and fortified the position of the wife against an unreasonable or vicious husband.

1. एवमुक्ते तु वचने धर्मराजेन धीमता।
धिग्धिगित्येव वृद्धानां सभ्यानां निसृता गिरः॥
II, 86, 40

2. को हि दीव्याद्भार्यया राजपुत्रो मूढो राजा द्यूतमदेन मत्तः।
II, 89, 17.

3. स्वं कुटुंबावरोधेन देयं दारसुतादृते।
Yaj., II, 175

This, however, does not seem to have taken place. One Dharmasūtra writer concludes from the joint ownership theory that the wife is entitled to incur normal expenditure on the household during her husband's absence.[1] Another concedes to her a third share of the husband's property, in case she was superseded unjustly.[2] But no further deductions were drawn.

The theory of joint ownership helped the wife only in securing a number of minor rights and privileges. It invested her with an absolute right of maintenance against the husband. A verse attributed to Manu, but not to be found in the present *Manusmṛiti*, goes to the extent of declaring that the husband ought to maintain the wife, even if there were no family property. He may have recourse even to questionable means, if there was no other alternative.[3] The husband could not proceed on a journey without making proper provision for her maintenance and the household expenditure. If he married a second time, the first wife had to be properly provided for. If the wife had the misfortune of being assaulted, the liability of the husband to maintain her did not come to an end.[4] Early jurists no doubt held it improper for a wife to vindicate her claims against the husband in a court of law; later jurists like Vijñāneśvara, however, differed from this view and maintained that if a husband abandons a

1. पाणिग्रहणत्वाद्धि सहत्वं कर्मसु...द्रव्यपरिग्रहेषु च। न हि भर्तुर्विप्रसवासे नैमित्तिके दाने स्तयमुपदिशंति।

A. D. S., II, 6,14,16-20.

2. आज्ञासंपादिनीं दक्षां वीरसूं प्रियवादिनीम्।
त्यजन्दाप्यस्तृतीयांशमद्रव्यो भरणं स्त्रियाः॥

Yāj., II, 76.

3. वृद्धौ च मातापितरौ साध्वी भार्या सुतः शिशुः।
अप्यकार्यशतं कृत्वा भर्तव्या मनुरब्रवीत्॥

4. स्वयं विप्रतिपन्ना वा यदि वा विप्रवासिता।
बलात्कारोपभुक्ता वा चोरहस्तगतापि वा॥
न त्याज्या दूषिता नारी नास्यास्त्यागो विधीयते॥

V. D. S. 28. 2, ff.

virtuous wife, or wilfully misappropriates her property and refuses to restore it, she can move a court of law to get her grievances redressed.[1]

The theory of the joint ownership of the couple secured only the above minor advantages to the wife. It was not pressed to its logical conclusion in order to secure her an absolute equality with the husband in the ownership of the family property. Hindu jurists were not prepared to entertain such a claim on behalf of the wife. Only one amongst them, Yājñavalkya, permits her to claim a one third share, if she is unjustly superseded.[2] But this claim does not appear to have been either actually conceded in practice by society, or sanctioned by other jurists. The wife had no right to incur any substantial expenditure during her coverture without her husband's permission. Even the *Mitākshara* expressly declares that she can spend out of the family property only with the concurrence of the husband.[3] Hindu jurists have further failed to protect the wife's right to a maintenance or a share; they do not invalidate a sale or a mortagage of the family property by the husband, if it was prejudicial even to her right of maintenance. They would have regarded such a procedure as immoral and reprehensible; they have however failed to make it invalid *ab initio*.

General circumstances in society were very unfavourable to the theory of the joint ownership being utilised to invest the wife with the above powers and rights. Landed property was for a long time being owned either by village communities or by large joint families. Individual ownership was but slow

1. यत्तु गुरोः शिष्ये पितुः पुत्रे दंपत्योः स्वामिभृत्ययोः। विरोधे तु मिथस्तेषां व्यवहारो न सिध्यति तदपि अत्यंतव्यवहारनिषेधपरं न भवति। यदि दुर्भिक्षादिव्यतिरेकेण स्त्रीधनं व्ययीकृत्य विद्यमानधनोऽपि याच्यमानो न ददाति तदा दंपत्योरिष्यत एव व्यवहारः।

Mit. on *Yāj.*, II, 32.

2. See *ante*, p. 215 n. 2.

3. तस्माद्भर्तुरिच्छया भार्याया अपि द्रव्यविभागो भवत्येव न स्वेच्छया॥

Ibid on Yāj., II, 52.

in coming into general recognition even in the case of males. By the time individual coparceners could assert their individual rights in the estate of the family, the husband had come to be deified; so it became very difficult for jurists to invest the wife with any susbstantial rights as against the husband. The joint ownership of the husband and the wife thus practically remained a legal fiction. In effect the husband was the sole owner of the family property and the wife had no legal remedy, if he proceeded to squander it and defeat her right to a maintenance or a share. The modern law courts also have not come forward to afford any protection to the wife in such cases. It is only in Portugese India, where the Code Napoleon prevails, that the consent of the wife is a condition precedent to any valid disposal of the family property by the husband. It is now high time that the Indian Legislature should proceed to amend the Hindu Law, and invest the wife with full powers over her own share of the family estate, rendering its sale without her express consent illegal. The old Vedic theory of the joint ownership of the husband and the wife will fully justify such a legislation.

It was only with reference to immoveable property that Hindu society was for a long time unwilling to invest the wife with full or exclusive ownership. The reasons for this have been already indicated. As far as moveable property like ornaments, jewelry, costly apparel, etc. was concerned, women's right to own it was recognised at a very early date. All this property went under the category of Strīdhana or Women's Special Property. The story of its development is a very interesting chapter in the history of Hindu law.

It is very difficult to define Strīdhana precisely; Hindu jurists only proceed to describe its different varieties. Suffiice it to state that the term is used to denote property over which women are allowed to have their own more or less absolute sway in normal times.

In its origin, Strīdhana was vitally connected with the custom of the bride-price (*śulka*). We have already shown (*ante*, pp. 39-41) that this custom is of hoary antiquity, and that it continued to persist for a long time in spite of its vehement denunciation. The custom was no doubt a bad one, but it had one relieving feature. It helped the development of Strīdhana. Owing to the affection, which parents naturally felt for their daughters, they used to return usually a part, and sometimes even the whole of the bride-price to the bride, to be enjoyed by her as her separate estate during her own life. If she died leaving some children behind, her father would not object to the property devolving upon them, as they were also his own grand-children. If, however, the daughter left no issue behind, her father would claim the property back from the son-in-law, who was expected to contract a fresh marriage in due course. Smṛiti writers expressly declare that the Strīdhana of a woman, married according to the Āsura form of marriage, where bride-price has to be paid by the husband, would revert to her parents or brothers, if she left behind no issues.[1] This rule makes it quite clear that one of the ingredients of Strīdhana was a portion of the bride-price, returned to the bride by her father. The husband therefore had to recognise his bride's ownership in it. The bride used to spend this gift usually in the purchase of ornaments for herself and utensils and furniture for her new household.[2]

Even when no bride-price was paid, the bride used to receive some wedding gifts in the Vedic age. *Pāriṇāhya* was the term used to denote them, and Vedic texts declare that the wife was to be their owner.[3] Gifts given on such occasions usually consisted of ornaments and clothes that could be worn by women alone. Men could have utilised them only by sale. In Hindu society there is, however, a deep prejudice against this procedure in connection with ornaments and clothes worn on auspicious

1. अप्रजस्त्रीधनं भर्तुर्ब्राह्मादिषु चतुर्ष्वपि।
दुहितॄणां प्रसूता चेच्छेषेशु पितृगामि तत्॥

Yāj,. II, 145.

2. The Gerade of the Saxons, which corresponded to Strīdhana, also usually consisted of women's dress, ornaments and household furniture.

3. पत्नी वै पारीणाह्यस्य ईशे।

T. S., VI, 2, 1, 1.

occasions. Women therefore were naturally allowed to own these gifts. Whether the Vedic age allowed them to dispose of these articles without their husbands' consent, we do not know. Probably such a procedure was not permitted.

In course of time the scope of Strīdhana was enlarged. Gifts given by the husband even subsequent to the marriage were included in it. These were often extensive and would sometimes include even the whole of the husband's property. Women came to be gradually invested with full powers over the property thus conveyed to them. At the time of his impending retirement Yājñavalkya proceeds to divide his whole property equally between his two wives. Under similar circumstances Dharmadinnā was informed by her husband that she could take away as much of his property as she liked, and retire to her parents' house (*Thg.*, 12). In both these cases the clear intention was to convey full rights of ownership to the wife over the whole of the family property.

That women could exercise absolute control over such gifts, which constituted their Strīdhana, was a principle that came to be recognised fairly early in Hindu society. There were no doubt archaic texts which declared that wives, like sons and slaves, could own no property; whatever they acquired would be the property of their husbands.[1] Commentators, however, boldly declared that these texts had no application to the present age. It is interesting to note that even writers like Baudhāyana, who refuse to recognise the wife's right of inheritance, freely concede her title to Strīdhana[2]. Manu also does the same, though he does not recognise the widow as an heir to her husband. It is needless to add that writers like Vishṇu and Yājñavalkya, who recognise the widow as an heir, naturally

1. भार्या पुत्रश्च दासश्च त्रय एवाधनाः स्मृताः।
यत्ते समधिगच्छन्ति यस्य ते तस्य तद्धनम्॥

Manu, VIII, 416.

2. मातुरलंकारं दुहितरः सांप्रदायिकं भजेरन्नन्यद्वा॥

B. D. S., II, 2, 44.

concede proprietary rights to women over Strīdhana. All later writers do the same.

The Vedic literature is silent about the precise scope of Strīdhana. We get an idea of its scope only from the Dharmaśāstra works. Manu is the earliest writer to give a comprehensive description of Strīdhana. According to him it consists of six varieties; (1-3) gifts given by the father, the mother and the brother at any time; (4) gifts of affection given by the husband subsequent to the marriage; (5-6) and presents given by anybody either at the time of the marriage, or at the time when the bride is taken to her new home.[1] Gifts under most of these categories would consist usually of ornaments and costly apparel, and Manu is very vehement in denouncing those who would deprive women of these presents after their husbands' death.[2] Vishṇu (XVII, 18) adds three more categories to Strīdhana, (1) gifts given by the son (2) or any other relation; (3) and the compensation given to the wife at the time of her supersession on the occasion of her husband's second marriage. The above distinction in the different varieties of Strīdhana are not of great importance; suffice it to say that it mainly consisted of gifts given by relations, either at the time of the marriage or subsequent to it.

It is interesting to note that gifts given by non-relatives subsequent to the marriage, and the wages earned by the wife

1. अध्यग्न्यध्यावहनिकं दत्तं च प्रीतिकर्मणि।
भ्रातृमातृपितृप्राप्तं षड्विधं स्त्रीधनं स्मृतम्॥
IX, 194.

2. स्त्रीधनानि तु ये मोहादुपजीवन्ति मानवाः।
नारीयानानि वस्त्रं वा ते पापा यान्त्यधोगतिम्॥
III, 52.

पत्यौ जीवति यः स्त्रीभिरलंकारो धृतो भवेत्।
न तं भजेरन्दायादा भजमानाः पतंति ते॥
IX, 200.

for her work are not included in Strīdhana. The exclusion of these two items is not difficult to understand. It was not advisable to encourage women to elicit presents from outsiders, for it would have led to serious complications in families presided over by jealous husbands. Inclusion of wages in Strīdhana would also have been unfair. They were usually earned only by the women of the working classes, whose budgets can never be balanced even today without including the earnings of women and children. Under these circumstances it would have been manifestly unfair to credit the wife's wages to her Strīdhana and call upon the husband to shoulder the entire burden of the family. Hindu jurists felt that the earnings of both the husband and the wife should be dedicated to the needs of the family. They have, however, failed to provide relief to the wife in case her husband were to squander his own earnings and compell the wife to support the family by her own wages. The law is still defective on this point and requires to be amended.

From about the 7th century A. D., we find a general tendency to enlarge the scope of Strīdhana. Devala is seen including maintenance and accidental gains under it.[2] But it was left to Vijñāneśvara to propose most extensive additions to the scope of Strīdhana. Taking advantage of the word *ādyam* 'etcetera' which Yājñavalkya has used at the end of the enumeration of the usual six varieties of Stridhana, this commentator declares that the expression in question is used in order to include the property acquired by inheritance, purchase, partition, chance, and adverse possession.[3] This amplified definition of Strīdhan is

1. प्राप्तं शिल्पैस्तु यद्वित्तं प्रीत्या चैव यदन्यतः।
भर्तुः स्वाम्यं तथा तत्र शेषं तु स्त्रीधनं स्मृतम्॥

Kātyāyanasāroddhāra, v. 736.

2. वृत्तिराभरणं शुल्कं लाभश्च स्त्रीधनं भवेत्॥

3. आद्यशब्देन रिक्थक्रयसंविभागपरिग्रहाधिगमप्राप्तमेतत्स्त्रीधनं मन्वादिभिरुक्तम्॥

On *Yaj.*, II, 143.

so comprehensive that it will include every type of property in the possession of a woman, howsoever it may have been acquired by her.

There can be no doubt that the original verses in *Yājnavalkya-smṛiti*, which are quoted in the foot note below,[1] did not contemplate the inclusion of any of the categories mentioned by Vijñāneśvara within the scope of Strīdhana. It is even doubtful whether the crucical term *ādyam*, which is Vijñāneśvara s sole justification for the amplification of the definition of Strīdhana, really occured in the original verse of Yājñavalkya. Jīmūtavāhana contends that the correct reading is '*Ādhivedanikaṁ chaiva*' and not *Ādhivedanikādyam cha*'. The word '*ādyam*' is generally used in Sanskrit at the end of an enumeration, so it should have come not after '*ādhivedanika*' in v. 143, but after, '*anvādheyakam*' in v. 144, which is the last specific category of Strīdhana mentioned by Yājñavalkya. Aparārka, who is one of the earliest commentators of Yājñavalkya, also reads *chaiva*, which seems to be the genuine reading of the verse.

But even supposing that the reading of Vijñaśvara is the genuine one, we have to concede that Yājñavalkya could hardly have intended to include items like inheritance and share at partition under the term 'etcetera'. These were very important items, which not only increased extensively the woman's rights, but circumscribed those of the coparceners. Yājñavalkya would surely have specifically and prominently mentioned them in his description of Strīdhana, instead of smuggling them surreptitiously under the term 'etcetera.' The word etcetera, if at all used by him, must have been obviously intended to include items like bride-price, gifts from grand-father and other relations, and presents received after the marriage, which are mentioned in the immediately following line.

1. पितृमातृपतिभ्रातृदत्तमध्यग्न्युपागतम् ।
आधिवेदनिकाद्यं च स्त्रीधनं परिकीर्तितम् ॥
बन्धुदत्तं तथा शुल्कमन्वाधेयकमेव च ॥
II, 143-144.

The above discussion will show that Vijñāneśvara has used one of the usual devices of Sanskrit commentators in order to enlarge the scope of Strīdhana. The credit of liberalising the law of Strīdhana therefore belongs to him and not to Yājñavalkya.

Hindu jurists of medieval times are divided as to the acceptability of the extended definition of Stridhana, as propounded by Vijñāneśvara. Majority of them, however, concur with him; Aparārka, Nanda Paṇḍita Mitramiśra and Kamalākara are prominent among them. Some, however, have refused to recognise his interpretation; Viśvarūpa, Devaṇabhaṭṭa and Jīmūtavāhana are the chief among them.

This clevage in the opinions of the jurists shows that society was following no uniform practice in the matter of recognising the scope of Strīdhana. There are, however, no actual recorded cases to show how far the items mentioned by Vijñāneśvara were actually included within the scope of Strīdhana in medieval times. The fact, however, that a large number of his successors uphold his opinion, would show that society was to a great extent following his lead.

Let us now consider the extent of the power which women possessed over their Strīdhana. We have no discussion about this point in early works. Vedic literature, for instance, is silent as to whether the wife could dispose of her property (Pāriṇāhaya) without her husband's permission. As secular law and its literature developed in course of time, the question began to be discussed by jurists. Early Smṛiti writers were not prepared to invest the woman with full powers over her Strīdhana. Manu for instance, declares that a wife ought not to alienate even her own property without her husband's sanction.[1] In course of time it was felt that this prohibition was not equitable. With a view to be fair to all the parties, later jurists divided Strīdhana into two categories, *saudāyika* and *asaudāyika*. Free gifts

1. न निर्हारं स्त्रियः कुर्युः कुटुम्बाद्बहुमध्यगात्।
स्वकादपि हि वित्ताद्धि स्वस्य भर्तुरनाज्ञया॥

IX, 299.

of affection given by relations like the father, the mother, or the husband were included in the first category[1] and were declared to be under the complete control of women.[2] The rest of the Strīdhana was *asaudāyika* Stridhana; women could not alienate it, but only enjoy its usufruct during their life time.

Originally Strīdhana consisted usually of ornaments and costly clothes. In course of time landed property also began to be conveyed to women as Strīdhana property. Jurists of the 7th and the 8th centuries discuss the question as to whether women possess full powers of ownership over the immoveable property so acquired. As may be expected, opinion was divided on the point. Kātyāyana holds that women possess the power of sale and mortagage even over the immoveable property included in their Strīdhana.[3] Nārada differs from him and declares that women can dispose of only the moveables in their Strīdhana.[4] Medieval writers generally concur with this view.[5]

The reason why women were not granated full rights over the landed property included in their Strīdhana are not difficult to understand. In the vast majority of cases, it used to be a gift from the husband, and so it originally belonged to the property of

1. ऊढया कन्यया वापि पत्युः पितृगृहेऽथवा।
भ्रातुः सकाशात्पित्रोर्वा लब्धं सौदायिकं स्मृतम्॥

Kātyāyana in *Dāyabhāga*.

2. सौदायिकं धनं प्राप्य स्त्रीणां स्वातंत्र्यमिष्यते।
यस्मात्तवानृशंस्यार्थं तैर्दत्तं तत्प्रयोजनम्॥

Kātyāyana in *Dāyabhāga*.

3. सौदायिके सदा स्त्रीणां स्वातंत्र्यं परिकीर्तितम्।
विक्रये चैव दाने च यथेच्छं स्थावरेष्वपि॥

Kātyāyana in *Dāyabhāga*.

4. भर्त्रा प्रीतेन यद्दत्तं स्त्रियै तस्मिन्मृतेऽपि तत्।
सा यथाकाममश्नीयाद्द्याद्वा स्थावरादृते॥

Quoted in *Vyavahāramayūkha*, p. 97.

5. एवं च सौदायिके स्थावरेतरप्रीतिदत्ते च स्त्रीणां स्वातंत्र्यमन्यत्र तु स्त्रीधनेऽपि अस्वातंत्र्यमिति मन्तव्यम्॥

S. C. V., p. 656

the joint family. It was not in the interest of the latter to allow a coparcener to fritter away its resources by allowing him to make an unconditional gift to his wife from the family property. The gifts were regarded as valid only during the life of the donees. The latter were not allowed to alienate them to any of their cognatic relations. Similar considerations operated when the property in question was received by the woman from her father. The latter's agnatic relations were not prepared to tolerate his conduct, if he proceeded to permanently alienate a portion of the immoveable property of the family. Patriarchal joint families in ancient times were too much attached to their ancestral possessions to allow their transfer to a cognatic relation.

The question of the power of alienation of the Strīdhana property was approached by the Bengal school of the medieval times on different lines. Its famous exponent Jīmūtavāhana felt that it was illogical to increase the scope of Strīdhana, and then to curtail women's powers of disposal over it. He argued that it would be proper to describe only that much property as Strīdhana, which women are allowed to dispose of according to their own free will. He therefore limited the scope of Strīdhana by refusing to recognise its amplified definition, as given in the Mitāksharā school, but conceded to women full proprietary rights over its time-honoured six varieties.

Did Vijñāneśvara intend to invest women with full proprietary rights over the whole of his amplified Strīdhana ? It is a great pity that he should not have specifically discussed this important question. We are therefore driven to mere inferences. It is possible to argue that there is nothing improbable in Vijñāneśvara having intended to give full rights to women even over the landed property acquired by inheritance or partition, and included in their Strīdhana. Women will get property by inheritance, usually when their husbands had separated from the joint family and died without leaving any male issues. The husband's action in effecting a separation from the joint family had put an end to its interest in his separated share; Vijñāneśvara might well have felt that the widow should be allowed to have full powers over it. The most probable course, which the widow will usually adopt in such cases, would be to gift her Strīdhana to her daughters. These were also the next heirs., even if the property was not regarded as her Strīdhana. Her husband had already effected separation from the joint family, and so after the death of the widow, daughters were the next normal heirs. So there was no reason for Vijñāneśvara to curtail the powers of women over the property they had acquired by inheritance. As far as the share at partition is concerned, it must be noted that a woman could get it only when her husband or sons had themselves proceeded to divide the family property. When a share was given to the wife by the husband or to the mother by the sons, it was clearly intended that it was for her special and exclusive use. Society would have regarded it as an immoral procedure, if sons had proceeded to put fetters on the power of their aged and revered mother with reference to the share, which they had freely and voluntarily given to her. It is also significant that Vijñāneśvara while concluding his discussion about the widow's right of inheritance, introduces a number of carefully worded qualifying clauses; but none of them even suggests that she was to be a limited heir.

It is however very doubtful whether Vijñāneśvara really intended to invest the widow with the right of disposal over the landed property included in her Strīdhana, but acquired by inheritance or partition. He was not prepared to concede even to the male manager of the joint family the full power to alienate the immoveable property that he may have himself acquired.[2] Could he then have ever dreamt of investing women with a right, which he was not prepared to grant even to the male manager? His silence on the point may be simply due

1. तस्मादपुत्रस्य स्वर्यातस्य विभक्तस्यासंसृटिनो धनं परिणीता स्त्री संयता सकलमेव गृह्णाति।

On *Yāj.*, II, 136.

2. स्थावरे तु स्वार्जिते पित्रादिप्राप्ते च पुत्रादिपारतंत्र्यमेव।

On *Yāj.*, II, 113.

to the fact that he tacitly accepted the general principle that women are limited heirs, a principle which was approved even by Bṛihaspati, the most well known advocate of women's rights. Radical jurists, who advance new theories to popularise a much needed reform in a conservative society, do not always accept all the deductions that can be legitimately drawn from their own premises. The Privy Council was therefore right when it declared that the property acquired through inheritance by a woman, though included in her Strīdhana, cannot be disposed of by her, and will revert back to the next heirs of her husband, instead of devolving upon the peculiar heirs of Strīdhana in its narrower sense. How far the law should now be changed in this matter will be discussed in the next chapter, where the question of the right of inheritance of the widow will be considered.

We have seen above that there was a school of jurists which was opposed to the recognition of the amplified definition of Strīdhana. The main reason for this was not its hostility to the rights of women, but the peculiar mode of devolution of the Strīdhana property. If this property had devolved upon the next heirs of the husband, it is quite probable that all the jurists would have agreed to the amplification of Strīdhana proposed by Vijñaneśvara. As will be soon shown, Strīdhana however used to devolve usually either upon female heirs or upon the parents or brothers of women. So the Strīdhana property usually went out of the husband's family. The joint family institution was naturally opposed to a course, which was calculated to diminish its resources.

Hindu jurists were, however, unanimous in giving to women full proprietary rights over the Strīdhana in its narrower sense. They have expressly declared that the husband has no right to lay his hands upon it. If he was compelled to utilise it for his own purposes, he had to return it with interest.[1] If, however,

1. वृथादाने च भोगे च स्त्रियै दद्यात्सवृद्धिकम्।

Devala, quoted in *Vyavahāramayūkha*, p. 98.

the family was in great distress, the husband could utilise his wife's Strīdhana to tide over the difficulty. No other member of the family, however, could do so. Jurists differ as to whether the Strīdhana utilised by the husband to meet abnormal times was to be returned back to the wife. Yājñavalkya thinks that it need not be repaid.[1] Kātyāyana holds that if the husband had promised to return it, he ought to keep his word.[2] An agreement by husband to give some property as Strīdhana was binding on his estate; if he died without completing it, his next heirs were required to carry it out.[3] Adverse possession could not deprive a woman of her title to Strīdhana.[4]

It is only rarely that we come across a discussion of the effects of unchastity on the right to Strīdhana. Devala has discussed this topic and declared that an unchaste woman forfeits her title to Strīdhana.[5] This seems to have been the general view. British courts, however, refused to follow it and recognised women's title to Strīdhana inspite of her unchastity.

The scheme of the inheritance of Strīdhana is a very complicated one and it has many provincial variations. We need not

1. दुर्भिक्षे धर्मकार्ये च व्याधौ सम्प्रतिरोधके।
गृहीतं स्त्रीधनं भर्त्ता न स्त्रियै दातुमर्हति॥

Yāj., II, 147.

The *Mitāksharā* explains:—
भर्तृव्यतिरेकेण जीवन्त्या धनं न केनापि दायादेन ग्रहीतव्यम्।

2. व्याधितं व्यसनस्थं च धनिकैर्वोपपीडितम्।
ज्ञात्वा निसृष्टं यत्प्रीतया दद्यादात्मेच्छया तु सः॥

Quoted in *SCV.*, p. 659.

3. भर्त्रा प्रतिश्रुतं देयमृणवत्स्त्रीधनं सुतैः।

Kātyāyana in *SCV.*, pp. 658.9.

4. स्त्रीधनं च नरेन्द्राणां न कथंचन जीर्यते।
अनागमं भुज्यमानं वत्सराणां शतैरपि।

Nārada, III. 83.

5. अपकारक्रियायुक्ता निर्मर्यादार्थनाशिका।
व्यभिचाररता या च स्त्रीधनं न च सार्हति।

Quoted in *VMV.*, p. 98.

discuss the details of the problem here, as they would interest only the professional lawyer; it is sufficient for our purpose to refer to general principles. If a woman dies without leaving any issues, and if her marriage had taken place by any of the unapproved forms of marriage like the Āsura, Rākshasa, etc., her Strīdhana reverts to her parents or brothers.[1] The reason for this rule is the general presumption that the Strīdhana in such cases must have mainly consisted of the bride-price, which was voluntarily returned by the father to his daughter for her use during coverture. If she dies leaving some issues behind, her Strīdhana would devolve upon them. Her father or brother would not naturally mind allowing the property to be inherited by them; but if she died issueless, the Strīdhana or the bride-price was demanded back. The law at present presumes that all marriages take place by the approved forms, and so this rule of inheritance of Strīdhana is only of historical interest. Strīdhana now reverts to the husband, if the wife dies without issues.

A vast majority of jurists from early times lay down that Strīdhana should devolve upon daughters. It usually consisted of ornaments and clothes, which could be used by women alone; so it was deemed to be in the fitness of things that they should be inherited by daughters. It is true that if they had devolved upon sons, their wives could very well have utilised the articles concerned. But women feel a greater affection for their daughters than for their daughters-in-law, and this circumstance determined the line of the succession. Among daughters, unmarried ones were to be preferred to married ones, and among the latter, the first claim was of those who were not well-to-do.[2] This devolution is governed just by those principles, which

1. अप्रजस्त्रीधनं भर्तुर्ब्राह्म्यादिषु चतुर्ष्वपि।
दुहितॄणां प्रसूता चेच्छेशेषु पितृगामि तत्॥

Yaj., II, 145.

2. तत्र चोढानूढासमवाये अनूढैव गृह्णाति। तदभावे परिणीता। तत्रापि प्रतिष्ठिताऽप्रतिष्ठितासमवायेऽप्रतिष्ठिता गृह्णाति। तदभावे प्रतिष्ठिता।

Mitāksharā on *Yāj.*, II, 145.

would appeal to an impartial and affectionate mother. In some schools, if there were no daughters living, the Strīdhana devolved upon daughter's daughters. Such cases, however, were few in practice.

In patriarchal societies there is a general prejudice against property passing to female heirs; so this principle of allowing Strīdhana to devolve on daughters did not appeal to a large section of Hindu community. As long as Strīdhana consisted of a few gifts given at the time of the marriage, its devolution upon daughters did not meet with much opposition. In course of time, however, gifts given by the husband during the married life came to be included in Strīdhana. The motive of the husband was no doubt to provide the wife against a rainy day, but he rarely intended to do so at the cost of his sons. His usual expectation was that the property should pass on to his sons after the death of his wife. Some jurists therefore felt that the most equitable course was to allow both the sons and the daughters to inherit the Strīdhana of their mother. This course is recommended by Manu;[1] we may well presume that he is very probably referring to the Strīdhana property given by the husband, though he does not say so in so many words. The Bengal, Mithilā, Madras and Gujarat schools of the Hindu Law rely upon the above view of Manu, when they lay down that Strīdhana consisting of gifts received from the husband subsequent to the marriage should devolve equally upon daughters and sons.[2]

There are many other minor details about the inheritance of Strīdhana. As they do not throw any light on the position of women, they are of interest only to the practising lawyer. We therefore need not discuss them here.

The above survey of the history of Strīdhana shows that it

1. जनन्यां संस्थितायां तु समं सर्वे सहोदराः।
भजेरन्मातृकं रिक्थं जनन्यश्च सनाभयः॥

IX, 192.

2. *Dāyabhāga*, IV, 9-12, *Mayūkha*, IX; *SCV.*, p. 656.

was recognised very early in the history of Hindu civilisation. Maxims of prehistoric times declaring that women can hold no property independently of their husbands were no doubt included in law books down to the 5th century A. D.; but they were not allowed to affect the development of Strīdhana. Its scope went on gradually increasing, till eventually, in some schools at least, it came to include all the varieties of property that a woman may happen to own. It is probable that the jurists, who included in Strīdhana even the property acquired by inheritance and partition, did not intend to invest women with the right of its alienation. Nevertheless it is indisputable that they allowed them at least a life estate in it; this concession was indeed a remarkable one for the age. Over Strīdhana in its narrower sense women possessed absolute ownership; they could dispose of it at their own will, and their husbands had no right over it. It is true that in times of exceptional difficulties Strīdhana could be used for the general needs of the family, but that was a liability that could not be equitably avoided. It is worth noting that some jurists have laid down that Strīdhana spent even on such occasions ought to be refunded to women on the return of prosperity to the family.

The survey of the scope and the development of Strīdhana discloses that a considerable regard was shown to the economic needs of the weaker sex. The law, as it was developed by Vijñāneśvara, was no doubt remarkably liberal for his age, for it included all property, howsoever acquired, under the category of Strīdhana. It is true that Vijñāneśvara probably did not intend to give women the full right of disposal over the immoveable property, acquired through inheritance or partition. Women, however, had no right to complain in the matter, for male coparceners also had no such unrestricted right even over their own self acquired property.

This history of Strīdhana is undoubtedly a proud and glorious chapter in the story of Hindu civilisation. It discloses a constant and continuous tendency in Hindu society to increase the scope of Strīdhana, usually at the expense of mens' rights.

Women were also invested with the right of its independent disposal; even the husband could not touch it save under exceptional circumstances. This state of affairs compares very favourably with that in England, where down to 1870 A.D., marriage suspended the very legal existence of the wife, whose entire property, whether inherited or self-acquired, automatically passed under the husband's control at the very moment of her marriage, unless secured by a previous settlement.

Only a few words are necessary in connection with the future development of the Strīdhana law. All the categories included in Strīdhana by Hindu jurists have been recognised by modern courts. They however hold that the property, which the widow inherits from her husband, is not Strīdhana in the technical sense, and that she cannot therefore dispose of it at her own free will. How far the law should be changed in this respect will be considered in the next chapter, where the widow's right of inheritance will be discussed in detail.

Smṛitis have laid down that any income, which a wife will acquire by her own exertions, will not be her Strīdhana, but will be merged in the general income of the family. We have already shown above (*ante*, p. 220-1) how this apparently unreasonable rule came to be laid down. Circumstances have, however, changed now. It is but fair to admit that what an educated wife earns as a teacher, or a professor, or a doctor, or an uneducated wife as a field labourer or a factory worker, should be primarily regarded as her own property. The husband should have no right over it. It should be left entirely to the wife, as to what portion of her earnings she would devote to the general family expenditure. In actual practice it would be found that a woman factory worker, for instance, will spend a lesser amount on herself than her husband would do, out of the wages they receive from their employer. The modern woman has developed her own individuality and would not like to surrender the ownership over her own earnings even to her husband.

Married women, who earn a livelihood, are however few. Gifts received at the time of marriage are not many or valuable in the present age and they are not useful for daily expenditure. Strīdhana obtained as an heir to the husband after his death becomes available during widowhood when a woman has hardly any enthusiasm to utilise it. In stead of enlarging the scope of the old items in Strīdhana, the modern woman would desire the recognition of a new item, viz., a share in the monthly or annual income of her husband.

In spite of the spacious theory of the joint ownership the husband is usually the *de facto* controller of the family purse. The present age is an individualistic one and the modern wife, whether educated or uneducated, often feels that it should not be necessary for her to get the sanction of her husband for every little expenditure that she may have to incur on her behalf. In order to get over the embarrassing situations often arising on such occasions, she often feels that it would have been much better if she had a share in her father's property, the income of which she could have spent at her own free will. There are, however, several serious difficulties in the way of giving the daughter a share in the patrimony, as will be shown in the next chapter (Section I). It has, however, to be admitted that owing to inherited traditions, the husband is often inclined to assume a patronising air when sanctioning any expenditure for the wife which is not relished by him. It has further to be recognised that whether in the west or in the east, there is not yet a proper appreciation of the unpaid work for the household, which the wife ungrudgingly does for the common welfare of the family. Gifts from the husband form an important item in the Strīdhan as envisaged by Hindu jurists, and its scope went on gradually increasing in course of time. The difficulties of the modern sensitive wife, above referred to, will disappear if the law enjoined that a small percentage of the monthly income of the husband shall be given to the wife as her Strīdhana, to be spent by her at her own sweet will, either for her own sake or for the sake of the family. An orientation in the development of Strīdhana on this line is necessary in the modern individualistic age. It will immensely help in increasing the happiness of many a family.

CHAPTER IX

PROPRIETARY RIGHTS :

INHERITANCE AND PARTITION.

We shall continue here our story of the development of the proprietary rights of women. We surveyed in the last chapter the position of the wife, *vis-a-vis* her husband, regarding the ownership of the family property, and discussed the evolution of Strīdhana. It was all along a story of gradual but continuous progress. In this chapter we shall discuss the rights of inheritance and partition, which are undoubtedly more important than the right to Strīdhana. As already shown in previous chapters, the angle of vision with which the daughter, the wife and the widow were looked upon varied in different ages. Naturally therefore, the development of their rights of inheritance and partition proceeded on different lines. It would be therefore convenient to discuss it separately. The present chapter is therefore divided into four sections; the first three deal with the rights of inheritance of the daughter, the widow and other female relations respectively, and the last one with the rights at partition.

SECTION I.

Daughter's Right of Inheritance

A reference has been already made to an old saying that a son, a wife and a slave can own no property independently of the father, the husband and the master (*ante*, p. 219, n. 1). The daughter is obviously intended to be included here under the son. In more than one place in the later Vedic literature we come across the view that women have no right of inheritance.[1]

1. तस्मात्स्त्रियो निरिन्द्रिया अदायादीः।

T. S. VI, 5, 8, 2.

ता (स्त्रियः) नात्मनश्चैशत न दायस्य चैशत।

Ś. Br., IV, 4, 2, 13.

There is no doubt that in very early times there was a general prejudice against property devolving upon female heirs by inheritance. The daughter formed no exception. She was often expected to increase the assets of her father's family by bringing a bride-price. That she should get a share in and decrease the corpus of her father's property would have appeared as very preposterous to men at the down of civilisation. The very conception of Strīdhana shows that women could normally get property only by way of gifts from their relations at or subsequent to their marriage. There was no possibility of their acquiring any estate either by inheritance or by partition.

Among the female heirs the brotherless daughter was the first to succeed in establishing her right of inheritance. Circumstances were more favourable for the recognition of her right than that of the wife or the widow. As shown in the last chapter in the patriarchal atmosphere the wife could advance no claim in competition with her husband. The widow often used to marry or get a son by Niyoga; so the problem of her inheritance did not arise in society in any acute form. We have already shown (*ante*, pp. 10-11) how the daughter in the Vedic age was well educated and possessed full religious privileges. Probably she could not heself offer funeral oblations to the manes, but she could get this done by her son. For all religious purposes the Vedic father could thus regard a daughter to be as good as a son.[1] He had a strong prejudice against adopting a son.[2] He therefore preferred property passing to his own daughter in preference to a stranger, who by a religious fiction, was to be regarded as an adoptive son. He could also usually arrange for

1. It is true that in Dharmaśāstra literature, generally the son of a Putrikā is classed as a substitute for a real son; in early times, however, in some localities the daughter herself and not her son was regarded as the substitute. Thus *V. D. S.*, XVII, 15 states तृतीया पुत्रिका and not पुत्रिकापुत्र. A similar conclusion can be drawn from *Manu* IX, 134. From the *Rājataraṅgiṇī* we find that Queen Kalyāṇadevi, wife of King Jayāpiḍa, was herself regarded as a Putrikā by her father. A 19th century Pandit of Kashmir had done the same at the same time of Dr. Bühler's visit to that state.

2. न हि प्रभायारणः सुशेवोऽन्योदर्यो मनसा मन्तवा उ।

R. V., VII, 4, 8.

the perpetuation of his own family by making an agreement with the son-in-law that he should send back his first son to continue his maternal grandfather's family.

Amongst women, a brotherless daughter was thus the first to get her right of inheritance recognised. This happened as early as the time of the *Ṛigveda*, for there is no doubt that one of its early hymns refers to a brotherless daughter getting her share of patrimony.[1] This right of inheritance, however, was not an unmixed blessing. The Vedic age put a high premium on the son, and sons-in-law were unwilling to allow their first-born son to revert back to the families of their maternal grandfathers. In the present age there is a keen competition for the hand of a maiden, who is her father's heir; in the Vedic age she found it not always easy to marry and had often to remain a spinster.[2] Even when the father of a brotherless daughter gave an assurance that he did not regarded her as a Putrikā and would not claim her son, prospective bridegrooms feared that there might be a mental reservation behind the promise.[3] They would usually refuse to accept the daughter and her estate.

There is evidence to show that the right of a brotherless daughter to inherit her father's estate continued to be recognised down to *c.* 400 B.C. In the *Therīgāthā* we come across an interesting incident. We find a mother trying to dissuade her daughter Sundarī from entering the nunnery by pointing out that she had become a full heir to her father's extensive estate as the latter had become a monk; she should therefore think of marriage and

1. अभ्रातेव पुंस एति प्रतीची गर्तारुगिव सनये धनानाम्।
R. V., I, 124, 7.

2. अमूर्याः सन्ति जामयः सर्वा लोहितवाससः।
अभ्रातर इव योशास्तिष्ठन्तु हतवर्त्मनः॥
A. V., I, 17, 1.

यास्क **comments**:—अभ्रातृकाया अनिर्वाह औपमिकः।
III, 5.

3. अभिसंधिमात्रात्पुत्रिकेत्येके।
G.D.S., XXIX, 17; see also *V.D.S.*, XV, 5.

pleasure, and not of nunnery and penance.[1] It is clear from this story that a brotherless daughter was recognised as an heir in north-eastern India during the 5th century B.C.

By about 200 B.C. girls ceased to be educated and began to be married at an early age. There was a general deterioration in the status of women, who were gradually losing their religious privileges. All this tended to adversely affect the proprietary rights of the daughter. A school came into existence which opposed her right of inheritance, even when she had no brothers. Āpastamba reluctantly allows daughter to inherit, but only if there is no *sapiṇḍa* or teacher or pupil to claim the property. This was a very remote possibility, for agnates include relations upto the 7th degree. He would rather prefer the property to be given to a public cause than to a daughter.[2] Vasishṭha (XV, 7) and Gautama (XXVIII, 21) do not mention the daughter in the list of their heirs. The same is the case with Manu.[3]

The majority of jurists, however, wanted to continue the old tradition, and allow the daughter to inherit her patrimony, if there were no son. The *Mahābhārata* in one place maintains that it would be manifestly unfair and inequitable to allow a subsidiary son to get an inheritance, when there was a daughter to claim it.[4] She must at least get half the property, if not the

1. पिता पब्बजितो तुम्हं भुंज भोगानि सुन्दरि त्वं दायादिका कुले।
Thg., No. 327.

2. पुत्राभावे यः प्रत्यासन्नः सपिण्डः। तदभावे आचार्यः। आचार्याभावे अन्तेवासी हृत्वा धर्मकृत्येषु योजयेत्। दुहिता वा।
II, 14, 2-4.

3. न भ्रातरो न पितरः पुत्रा रिक्थहराः पितुः।
पिता हरेदपुत्रस्य रिक्थं भ्रातर एव च॥
IX, 185.

Kullūka takes the expression पत्नीदुहितृरहितस्य as understood in the second line in order to support his view that Manu admits the daughter as an heir to her father. There is nothing in the text or context to support this assumption.

4. यथैवात्मा तथा पुत्रः पुत्रेण दुहिता समा।
तस्यामात्मनि तिष्ठन्त्यो कथमन्यो धनं हरेत्।
XIII, 80, 11.

दुहितान्यत्र जाताद्धि पुत्रादपि विशिष्यते।

whole.[1] Kauṭilya is also inclined to recognise the daughter as an heir, though perhaps to a smaller share (III, 5).

Yājñāvalkya, as may be expected, warmly champions the cause of the daughter and lays down that she should be the next heir after the son and the widow (II, 135). Bṛihaspati tries to disarm the opposition by sweet reasonableness. He points out that the daughter springs from one's own body just like the son; how then can anyone inherit the property, when she is still alive (XXV, 55) ? Nārada advances a similar argument. Is not the daughter as much the child of her parents as the son[2] ? How then can her right of inheritance be defeated in the absence of the latter ?

There was a school of jurists which suggested that a brotherless daughter should be regarded as an heir only till she was married and well settled in life. Kātyāyana was its chief exponent.[3] Hindu society, however, refused to accept this opinion, and the school of Yājñavalkya, Nārada and Bṛihaspati eventually carried the day. From *c.* 500 A. D. nobody has called into question a daughter's right to inherit her father's property in the absence of a brother. The right has been recognised also by the modern courts.

The estate which a daughter inherits is usually a limited one. It is an absolute one only in the Bombay State. Everywhere else she acquires only a life estate. The Bombay custom of allowing the daughter to become an absolute owner of her patrimony is at least as old as the 13th century. An inscription of this period, discovered in Kolhapur, refers to the sale of a piece of land by a woman, who had inherited it from her

1. अभ्रातृका समग्राहाँ चार्धार्हेत्यपरे विदुः।
XIII, 88, 22.

2. पुत्राभावे तु दुहिता तुल्यसंतानकारणात्।
XIII, 50.

3. पत्नी पत्युर्धनहरी या स्यादव्यभिचारिणी।
तदभावे तु दुहिता यद्यनूढा भवेत्तदा॥
Quoted in the *Mitākshara* on *Yāj.* II, 135-6. See also *SCV.*, p. 687.

father.[1] The Bombay law on this point has been working smoothly and has caused no havoc in the joint family. It is now high time that it should be extended to other states as well.

DAUGHTERS WITH BROTHERS.

Let us now consider the rights of inheritance of a daughter who has brothers. Patriarchal traditions were reigning supreme at the dawn of the Aryan history, and they were not favourable for the recognition of a daughter's right of inheritance in competition with a brother. From *c.* 300 B.C. marriage became obligatory for girls, and society felt that they should get proprietary rights in the families of their husbands and not in those of their fathers.

In the earlier period, however, girls were fairly well educated, and very often they would remain unmarried either by choice or by the force of circumstances. In such cases it was recognised that they ought to be allowed to have a share in their fathers' property. A Vedic stanza expressly refers to an old maiden claiming her share in her patrimony.[2] Usually, however, daughters married, and then they did not get any share in their patrimony. A Vedic poet expressly informs the brother that he should not give any share to his sister; she is after all to migrate to a different family.[3]

It has been argued that there was a school of jurists, no doubt representing a small minority, which favoured the recognition of the right of inheritance of the daughter along with the son as early as *c.* 500 B.C. The only evidence for this view is a passage in the *Nirukta*, where arguments are undoubtedly ad-

1. सोमेश्वरभट्टस्य दुहितुः सकाशाद्गृहीत्वा पूर्वोक्तब्राह्मणेभ्यो दत्तवान् ।
E. I., Vol. III, p. 215.

2. अमाजूरिव पित्रोः सचा सती समानादा सदसस्त्वामिये भगम् ।
कृधि प्रकेतमुप मास्या भर दद्धि भागं तन्वा येन मामहः ॥
R. V., II, 17, 7.

3. न जामये तान्वो रिक्थमारैक् चकार गर्भं सनितुर्निधानम् ।
R. V., III, 31, 2.

vanced to support the daughter's claim. The passage in question is, however, a clear interpolation. We may nevertheless examine here the arguments advanced in it. We find that the champions of the daughter's claim were mainly relying on the authority of two old verses. The first of these occurs in the *Ṛigveda*.[1] Unfortunately it is a very obscure stanza difficult to interpret with certainty. It appears to refer to an agreement by the father of an only daughter with his son-in-law to the effect that his first son will revert to the maternal grand father to continue his family. At any rate it does not refer to any right of inheritance of a daughter, who had brothers as well. The second authority relied upon by this school is a stanza, which it attributes to Manu.[2] This verse does not, however, occur in the present *Manusmṛiti* and it contradicts its views on this point enunciated elsewhere in the book. Further, it has to be pointed out that it does not at all support a daughter's right to inherit along with sons. To argue that the term *mithunānām* in this verse governs the word *putrā ṇām*, the joint expression *mithunānām putrāṇām* meaning childre n of both the sexes, is a procedure that can hardly be justified. The expression *mithunānām* refers to parents, and the author of the verse opines that parents should divide their estate equally among their sons, without assigning a special share to the first-born, as recommended by some early jurists.

It therefore appears that if there was really a school of jurists in the 6th century B.C., which wanted to champion the cause of daughters' inheritance, even when they had brothers, it could adduce no really authoritative texts in its support. The passage in the *Nirukta*, where this discussion occurs, is very probably a

1. शासद्वह्निर्दुहितुर्नप्त्यं गाद्विद्वाँ ऋतस्य दीधितिं सपर्यन्।
पिता यत्र दुहितुः सेकमृञ्जन् संशग्म्येन मनसा संदधन्वे॥

III, 31, 1.

2. अविशेषेण पुत्राणां दायो भवति धर्मतः।
मिथुनानां निसर्गादौ मनुः स्वायंभुवोऽब्रवीत्॥

Nirukta, III, 4.

later interpolation. It is therefore extremely doubtful whether any such school at all existed in early times.

The general opinion of Hindu society was that sisters should get no share in the patrimony, if they had brothers. This is the opinion of the Dharmaśāstra literature, and Kauṭilya concurs with it.[1] There is only one writer, who assigns a small share to the daughter along with sons. It is Śukra. Śukrāchārya, the famous teacher of the Asuras, loved his daughter Devayānī dearer than his own life. It is therefore in the fitness of things that he should have been the only Smṛiti writer to assign a small share to the daughter, even when she had brothers.[2]

Śukra lays down that if a person divides his property in his own life time, he should assign one share each to his wife and sons, half a share to his daughters, and one fourth a share to his daughters's sons. If the division took place after his death, the sister was to get one eighth the share of the brother.[3] In actual practice the division of property usually takes place after the death of the father; so even under Śukra's dispensation, the daughter got only a very small share in the patrimony.

Śukra seems to be the only jurist, who has championed the cause of a daughter's share in her patrimony, even if she were not brotherless. Vishṇu[4] and Nārada[5] also apparently seem to

1. अयादा दुहिता ।

III, 6.

2. *Śukranīti* as a whole is as late as about 1300 A. D., and it is not impossible that its scheme of inheritance, which assigns the daughter a share equal to half that of the son, may be due to the influence of the Muslim law.

3. समानभागा वै कार्याः पुत्राः स्वस्य च वै स्त्रियः ।
स्वभागार्धहरा कन्या दौहित्रस्तु तदर्धभाक् ॥
मृताधिपे तु पुत्राद्या उक्तभागहराः स्मृताः ।
मात्रे दद्याच्चतुर्थांशं भगिन्यै मातुरर्धकम् ॥

IV, 5, 299-300

4. मातरः पुत्रभागानुसारेण भागहारिण्यः । अनूढा दुहितरश्च ।

XVIII, 34.

5. ज्येष्ठायांशोऽधिको देयः कनिष्ठायावरः स्मृतः ।
समांशभाजः शेषाः स्युरप्रत्ता भगिनी तथा ।

XIII, 13.

have recommended the same course; but their intention does not appear to have been to allow the daughter to take away her share after the marriage. Nārada expressly declares that the daughter's share in the patrimony was intended only for her maintenance till her marriage.[1]

Though Śukra was in a hopeless minority, his scheme of inheritance appealed to some sections of the community. There is evidence to show that some fathers used to follow the principle recommended by Śukra and divide their property both among their sons and daughters. This was probably the case when the property was self-acquired. We actually come across such a case in a Mysore epigraph. An inscription, dated 1188 A.D., refers to a gentleman named Māchi, partitioning his landed property both among his sons and daughters. The sons of the latter encroached upon the lands of the sons of the former; the epigraph refers to the settlement of the dispute.[2]

Smṛitis and inscriptions, which attest to a daughter being assigned a share in the patrimony, are exceptions and not the rule. The general opinion of society was that women should get shares, directly or indirectly, in the property of their husbands and not in that of their fathers. Marriages had become obligatory for girls by *c.* 300 B. C., and so the cases of spinsters remaining unprovided did not at all arise in society in the subsequent period.

Since marriages had become obligatory for girls, it was naturally laid down that reasonable expenses in connection with them should be a charge on the family property. If a father died before his daughters had been wedded, the sons were bound to spend reasonable amounts for their suitable marriages out of the family estate. What precise amount a brother ought to spend for his sister's marriage could not obviously be laid down

1. या तस्य दुहिता तस्याः पित्र्योंऽशो भरणे मतः।
आसंस्कारं भजेरंस्ताः परतो बिभृयात्पतिः॥
XIII, 27.

2. *E. C.*, VI, Mudgere No. 24.

in the law books; it used to vary with the status and circumstances of each family. A general rule, however, has been laid down that a brother should spend for his sister's marriage an amount equal to a one fourth share[1]. The language used in this connection is rather vague, and is capable of the following three divergent interpretations. (1) Each brother should forswear one fourth the share he has received, and the amounts so pooled together should be equally divided among the sisters and spent for their marriages. In practice this principle was likely to lead to anomalies, if the sons and daughters in a family were not equal in number. Thus if there was only one sister and she had four or more brothers, her marriage portion was bound to be greater than the individual share of her brothers. If the above ratio of the brothers and sisters were reversed, the marriage share of a sister would have been very inadequate; it would have been one sixteenth the share of the brother or even less. (2) A second interpretation of the rule suggested that the property should be divided into as many shares as there are children, and daughters should be given one fourth of the share thus ascertained. This arrangement also is likely to produce anomalies similar to those mentioned in connection with the first interpretation. (3) A third school therefore has pointed out that the real intention of the jurists in laying down this rule is that the patrimony should be so divided that ultimately the resulting marriage share of each sister should be equal to one fourth the share of each brother. This interpretation is probably the one intended by our jurists.[2]

Hindu jurists, however, declare that their intention is not so much to assign a one fourth share to the daughter, as to make

1. असंस्कृतास्तु संस्कार्या भ्रातृभिः पूर्वसंस्कृतैः।
भगिन्यश्च निजादंशाद्दत्वांशं तु तुरीयकम्॥

Yāj., II, 124.

See also *Manu*, IX, 118.

2. See *SCV.*, pp. 625 ff; *VMV.*, pp. 581 ff.

adequate provision for her marriage.[1] To get his sister married was the sacred duty of the brother, and if her one fourth share was insufficient for the purpose, the brother was required to spend an amount even equal to his own share.[2] Some jurists go to the extent of laying down that even if there were no family estate, the brother ought to meet the marriage expenses of his sister from his self acquired property.[3] If, on the other hand, the family property was extensive and the reasonable expenses of a suitable marriage did not amount to the legal one fourth share, the sister was not to take away with her the balance unspent.[4] It will be thus seen that while anxious to make adequate provision for the marriage of a sister, Hindu jurists have disapproved of the principle that she should inherit a share along with her brothers, and carry it away with her after the marriage.

The reasons for this attitude are not difficult to understand. Marriage had become absolutely necessary for daughters. So there was no possibility of spinsters remaining unprovided. There was a general prejudice against the introduction of an outsider among the land-holders of a village since early times. This, however, was inevitable if the daughter, who was usually married to some outsider either in a near or a distant village, was allowed to claim a share. We must further remember that down to the middle of the 19th century, communications were difficult and

1. कन्याभ्यश्च पितृद्रव्ये देयं वैवाहिकं वसु।

Devala in *SCV.*, p. 625.

2. यदि संस्कारपर्याप्तमपि पितृधनं नास्ति तदा पुत्रसमभागितैव दुहितॄणाम्।

VMV., p. 582.

3. अविद्यमाने पित्रर्थे स्वांशादुद्धृत्य वा पुनः।
अवश्यकार्याः संस्कारा भ्रातृभिः पूर्वसंस्कृतैः॥

Nārada, XIII, 34.

4. तस्मात्संस्कारोपयुक्तद्रव्यस्यैव दानमात्रं विवक्षितम्।

VMV., p. 582.

अनूढा इति विशेषोपादानाच्च विवाहार्थं पुत्रभागानुसारिभागहरणं न पुनर्भ्रातॄणामिव दुहितणां दायविभागार्थमिति गम्यते।

SCV., p. 625.

expensive, and it was not easy for a daughter or her husband to manage her landed property situated in a distant village. To give a share to the daughter in immoveable property was thus not a feasible proposition. As far as the moveables were concerned, she used to get a fair share in them as presents at the time of her marriage, or as an heir to Strīdhana estate. Hindu society therefore felt that the best way to provide for women was to invest them with proprietary rights in their husbands' estates, and not in their fathers' property.

Circumstances have however now changed, and the law of inheritance requires some alterations with regard to the daughter. Marriage is no longer a necessary event in the life of every woman. A class of educated women is coming into existence who, either owing to the desire for social service or through the force of circumstances, do not get married. These ladies cannot obviously get any proprietary rights through the husband. The law, as it stands today, does not allow them any share in their fathers' property as well. So they remain altogether unprovided for. As we have shown above (*ante*, p. 239), such women used to get a share in their patrimony in Vedic times. We should revive this right today. As these women lead a single life, their family responsibilities would be naturally less than those of their married brothers; their share in the patrimony should be smaller than that of a married brother, who will have a family to provide for. It is therefore reasonable to suggest that the share of the unmarried sister should be half that of her married brother.

Should a daughter, who gets married, also receive a share in her patrimony even when she has a brother? In 1936 a bill was introduced in the Imperial Legislative Assembly, which *inter alia* sought to give the daughter the same share in the patrimony as the son. This clause, however, had to be withdrawn, as the public opinion was not in its favour. Later on a draft by the B. N. Rao Committee proposed, as suggested in the 1st edition of this work, that an unmarried daughter should get half a share; but this measure also could not pass. The same was the fate of a third bill (1952) which sought to give to the daughter half a share unconditionally. The Hindu Code Bill, now before the Parliament (Feb. 1956) seeks to give even to the married daughter a share in the patrimony equal to that of the brother. Opinion in society and the Parliament is sharply divided on this point and it is difficult to state whether the Bill will pass, if free voting is allowed.

A careful analysis of the whole situation will show that on the whole it will not be in the interest of society to grant this right to the daughter. In the first place she will find it difficult to exercise it. Division of the family property usually takes place after the death of the father. A daughter, who has been married, say ten years before this event, will not be having a precise idea of the moveable property of her paternal family, as she will be spending most of this time in her new home. It may be that during this period her father's family may have sold part of its ornaments to tide over some difficulties. If, as a consequence of these transactions, which are usually kept secret, the moveable property brought forward at the time of the partition is less than what it was at the time of her marriage, the daughter would feel that her brothers have conspired to cheat her of her legitimate share. On the other hand, it is very easy to conceal cash, jewellery and ornaments, and crafty brothers can easily defeat their sisters' rights by producing only a part of them. There are very few families that keep their moveable property in the form of cash balances in banks. Misunderstanding and heartburning will therefore be difficult to avoid between brothers and sisters at the time of partition.

The allotment of a share in the immoveable property is also frought with difficulties. Holdings of land in India are already very small and uneconomic; their size will be reduced to half, if the daughter receives a share in the patrimony equal to that of the son. This will be a national calamity. It may be argued that the rights of the weaker sex should not be sacrificed even for avoiding a national economic calamity. There is a force in this argument. But we would point out that there are further difficulties in the way. The daughter after her marriage will usually go away to a different village or town to live with her husband. She will therefore be an absentee land-lord. The absentee land-lord is already being expropriated in Bombay, and other States will soon adopt the same course. The daughter will thus not materially benefit by a share in the lands of her father.

It has further to be admitted that soon after her marriage, the centre of interest and affection of the daughter naturally shifts to her new home. She becomes more and more immersed in her own family and children, and has no opportunities as before of noticing the financial transactions of her father's family. It would be unfair to saddle her with any liabilities which her parents' family may have incurred as a consequence of certain steps taken after her marriage and without her knowledge. To suggest that the consent of the daughter should be previously obtained on such occasions is impracticable. For usually the members of a family do not like its transactions like sale or mortgage of family property to be discussed by or communicated to even their near relations.

The present situation, however, is very unfair to the woman. She has no share in her patrimony and her condition becomes pitiable, if her husband abandons her and contracts a second marriage or takes to a vicious life. He can even escape his liability to give her a maintenance on the plea that she refuses to live with him. And what woman of self-respect will welcome her husband's home, if she is to be treated there merely as an unpaid and unwanted maid-servant ? The best way, however, to meet the situation is not to assign a share to the woman in her patrimony, but to improve and enlarge her economic rights in her new family, of which she becomes an important member, and with the interests of which she becomes absolutely identified. It should no longer become possible for a husband to institute a suit for the restitution of conjugal rights, and escape his liability to maintain his wife on the plea that she refuses to obey the decree of the court to live with him. If it is proved that the wife has to stay away from the husband for no fault of her own, she should become entitled to get not merely a maintenance, but also a share equal to that of a son. It may be recalled that Yājñavalkya allows the wife a one third share in the husband's property under such circumstances.[1] As marriages usually take place between families of approximately equal financial status, the share which the wife will receive in her husband's property is not likely to be smaller than the one which she would have obtained as a daughter from her patrimony.

If the present law is amended on the above lines, it will not become necessary to complicate matters by giving the daughter a right to a share in her patrimony, which may be of doubtful benefit to her in actual practice, and which may also sometimes land her into financial liabilities. If her father dies after contracting debts subsequent to her marriage, she will be called upon to pay its share. Her liability will of course be limited by her share, but she will have to face a litigation. Serious difficulties may arise in the marriages of girls from poorer families. Would-be bridegrooms accepting daughters from poor families now know that they will receive few or no presents at the marriage; they are sure that there is no liability. When the daughter gets a share, they must be prepared to face the music of a civil litigation after the death of their fathers-in-law. All would-be sons-in-law may not welcome this eventuality.

Normally speaking, more than 90 per cent couples can pull on well with each other, and there would be no necessity in such cases for the wife to demand a separate share from her husband. Unnecessary fragmentations of holdings, which would become necessary if all daughters are given a right of inheritance in their patrimony, will thus be avoided. In the few abnormal cases above referred to, where the condition of women at present becomes pitiable on account of their having no share in the patrimony, they would obtain the necessary relief

1. आज्ञासम्पादिनीं दक्षां वीरसूं प्रियवादिनीम्।
त्यजन्दाप्यस्तृतीयांशमद्रव्यो भरणं स्त्रियाः॥
I, 76.

by getting definite rights in their new families available even against the husband during the coverture.

For several centuries the Hindu wife has been occupying a position of subordination to her husband on account of her illiteracy and want of general knowledge and experience. There is an unconscious tendency in the average husband, both in the east and in the west, to assume a slightly condescending air when any money is to be sanctioned for the normal or special needs of the wife. Educated wives naturally resent this tendency and feel that they should have an income of their own, which they should be able to spend at their own free will. The best way to avoid this difficulty and consequent unpleasantness is not to grant a share in the patrimony, but to create a new variety of Strīdhana from the husband's income, which the wife should be at liberty to spend without his sanction. As a natural corollary of the principle that the husband and the wife are the joint owners of the family property, and as a recognition of the valuable unpaid work which the wife ungrudgingly does for the household, she should be entitled to receive a small percentage, say 5%, of the income of the family as her own Strīdhana, to be spent by her at her own sweet will, either for her own sake or for the sake of the family. An orientation in the development of Strīdhana on this line will remove the difficulties of the modern sensitive wife. It will also render unnecessary the creation of the new right to a share in patrimony, which in practice will be difficult to exercise, and will lead to unnecessary and harmful fragmentations of land-holdings.

To conclude, the following changes are desirable in the law of inheritance, as far as the daughter is concerned:—

(1) The daughter should have the right to demand that the same amount from patrimony should be spent on her education as is spent in her brother's case.

(2) Education expenses apart, the daughter should have the right to a share equal to half that of her brother, if she remains unmarried. The usual presumption should be that the normal expenses of a daughter's proper marriage are equal to half

the share of her brother in the patrimony. So a daughter who marries after the partition will not have to pay anything back after her marriage. This will avoid any devesting of the property subsequent to the marriage of the daughter.

SECTION 2

Widow's Right of Inheritance

The proprietary rights of the wife during the coverture have been already considered in the last chapter. We shall discuss now her rights during widowhood. Let us first take up the question of her right to inherit her husband's property.

We have already seen that there was a general prejudice in early times against allowing women to hold property. Even the wife, who was regarded as the husband's joint-owner in the family property, had only very limited rights as against her consort. It is then no wonder that for a long time widow's right to inherit her husband's property should have remained unrecognised. Vedic texts, which declare women to be incapable of inheriting any property,[1] are particularly aimed against the widow. Joint family of the patriarchal type was the order of the day; males alone could be coparceners in it, women being allowed only a maintenance. In early times the custom of Niyoga was very common; so widows without sons were very few. A vast majority of widows therefore used to get their husband's shares, if not directly as their heirs, at least indirectly as the guardians of their minor sons. Very often they used to marry, and so the question of giving them a share in their dead husbands' property would not arise at all. The refusal to recognise the widow as an heir to her husband was thus causing not much actual hardship in society.

1. तस्मात्स्त्रियो निरिन्द्रिया अदायादीः।
T. S., VI, 5, 8, 2.

ताः (स्त्रियः) नात्मनश्चनेशत न दायस्य चनेशत।।
S. Br., IV, 4, 2, 13.

तस्मात्पुमान् दायादः स्त्री अदायादी।
M. S., IV., 6, 4.

We therefore find that down to *c.* 300 B. C., the right of the widow to inherit her husband's property was not recognised by any jurist. Vedic texts were definitely opposed to this right. Most of the Dharmasūtra writers adopt the same attitude. Baudhāyana expressly rejects the widow's claim on the authority of the Vedic texts referred to in the last para. Āpastamba lays down that in the absence of the son the property should devolve, not upon the widow, but upon the nearest *male sapiṇḍa.* If none such within seven degrees is in existence to claim the property, it should devolve upon the preceptor. If he also is dead, then it should be taken over by a disciple of the deceased to be spent for charitable purposes.[1] This detailed scheme of Āpastamba about the devolution of property nowhere mentions or provides for the widow. The same is the case with Manu. He lays down that the property of a sonless person will first devolve upon his father, then upon his brother, and finally upon a *sapiṇḍa* and a *sakulya* in accordance to his propinquity. When none of these is forthcoming, first a preceptor, then a disciple, and finally the king should take it away.[2] Elsewhere he recognises the mother also as an heir;[3] the widow is, however, nowhere mentioned as possessing any rights of inheritance. It is true that Kullūka, a 15th century commentator no doubt contends that in *Manu smṛiti* IX, 185, though not expressly mentioned, the widow is intended to

1. पुत्राभावे यः प्रत्यासन्नः सपिण्डः। तदभावे आचार्यः। आचार्याभावेऽन्तेवासी हृत्वा धर्मकृत्येषु योजयेत्। दुहिता वा।

II, 14, 2-4.

2. पिता हरेदपुत्रस्य रिक्थं भ्रातर एव च॥
अनन्तरः सपिण्डाद्यस्तस्य तस्य हरेद्धनम्।
अत ऊर्ध्वं सकुल्यः स्यादाचार्यः शिष्य एव वा॥

X, 185, 187

3. अनपत्यस्य पुत्रस्य माता दायमवाप्नुयात्।

IX, 217

be understood as an heir after the son;[1] he is however obviously reading later ideas in the earlier text. There can be no doubt that Medhātithi, the 9th century commentator of Manu, is correct when he maintains that Manu has not recognised the widow as an heir at all.[2]

At about the beginning of the Christian era, both the Niyoga and the widow remarriage fell into disrepute as shown in Chapter V (*ante*, p. 146; p. 153). It was deemed to be more honorable for a widow to spend her remaining life in penances of religion than in pleasures of the family life. Leaders of society began to feel that if the widow was not to marry or get a son by Niyoga, she ought to be assigned a definite share in the family property. Early Dharmasūtra writers, however, were inclined to assign only a maintenance to the widow. This is the case with Kauṭilya also, who makes the widow's maintenance a charge upon the husband's estate, when it was resumed by the state.[3]

It was, however, being felt that this was not a satisfactory arrangement. Jurists gradually began to come forward to plead for a better recognition of the widow's claim. Gautama puts forth a modest proposal that the widow should be regarded at

1. न भ्रातरो न पितरः पुत्रा रिक्थहराः पितुः।
पिता हरेदपुत्रस्य रिक्थं भ्रातर एव च॥

While commenting upon this verse Kullūka says :—

अविद्यमानमुख्यपुत्रस्य पत्नीदुहितृरहितस्य च पिता धनं गृह्णीयात्।

It will be noticed that there is nothing in the verse to justify the words पत्नीदुहितृरहितस्य ।

2. Medhātithi's commentary on this important verse is lost; we know of his views only from Kullūka's reference to them; cf :—

अतो यन्मेधातिथिना पत्नीनामंशभागित्वं निषिद्धमुक्तं तदसंबद्धम्। पत्नीनामंशभागित्वं बृहस्पत्यादिसंमतम्। मेधातिथिंनिराकुर्वंश्च प्रीणाति सतां मनः॥

On *Manu*, IX, 187.

3. अदायादकं राजा हरेत्स्त्रीवृत्तिप्रेतकार्यवर्जम्।

III, 5.

least as a coheir with other *sapiṇḍas*.[1] In course of time the opinion in favour of the recognition of the widow's right began to grow stronger. Why should she get only a portion of the husband's estate, and not the whole of it ? It was felt that she ought to be the sole heir and not a co-heir. This view has been for the first time advocated by Vishṇu at about the beginning of the Christian era. He definitely lays down that the widow shall inherit the whole estate on the failure of sons.[2] About a couple of centuries later Yājñavalkya joined Vishṇu in championing the widows' right; it is his verses which were mainly relied upon by British courts, when they recognised the right of inheritance of the widow on the failure of sons.[3] It may be pointed out that the Upanishadic sage Yājñāvalkya had divided all his property between his two wives, when he had renounced the world. It would therefore appear that the Yājñavalkya school was since early days more favourably inclined to recognise women's rights than was the case with other jurists.

The proposal of Vishṇu and Yājñavalkya to recognise the widow as an heir was a sensational one. It affected the vested interests of male coparceners and therefore immediately provoked considerable and determined opposition. During the

1. पिण्डगोत्रर्षिसम्बन्धा रिक्तं भजेरन्स्त्री चानपत्यस्य। If we read here स्त्री वानपत्यस्य (in stead of स्त्री चानपत्यस्य) as is done in the Ānandāśrama edition of the work, the widow will be an alternative heir, and not a coheir.

2. अपुत्रस्य धनं पत्न्यभिगामि। तदभावे दुहितृगामि॥

XVII, 43.

In the *Pürva-Mīmansā*, VII, 6, 14, Jaimini recognises the right of the wife to hold property. He is, however, probably referring to wives with husbands living, who alone were eligible to perform sacrifices according to him. It does not seem that Jaimini was inclined to recognise the widow as an heir to her husband. *Vishṇusmṛiti* would therefore be the first work to recognise this right, as stated in the text above.

3. पत्नी दुहितरश्चैव पितरौ भ्रातरस्तथा।
तत्सुता गोत्रजा बंधुशिष्यसब्रह्मचारिणः॥
एषामभावे पूर्वस्य धनभागुत्तरोत्तरः।
स्वर्यातस्य ह्यपुत्रस्य सर्ववर्णेष्वयं विधिः॥

II, 135-6.

period 400-1000 A.D. jurists were divided into two schools, the orthodox one, which was not prepared to recognise the widow as an heir and the reformist one, which was bent upon agitating for the popularisation of its new reform.

Nārada, Kātyāyana and king Bhoja of Mālwā (*c.* 1015 to *c.* 1055 A.D.) were the chief advocates of the orthodox view. Nārada lays down that if a man dies without any issue or heir, his property should ultimately escheat to the king, who was to provide only a maintenance to the widow.[1] It is clear that Nārada did not mind property escheating to the crown; he would not, however, allow it to be inherited by the widow. Kātyāyana apparently held an identical view.[2] Bhoja would allow the widow to be an heir only if she submitted to Niyoga. This virtually amounted to denying her the right of inheritance, for Niyoga had become very obnoxious since 500 A.D., and no woman would have agreed to be a party to it. And even if she had consented, her ownership would have been a short-lived one; it would have terminated with the birth of the expected son.

There were several thinkers who recognised this state of affairs as unsatisfactory, but had not the necessary courage to

1. अन्यत्र ब्राह्मणात्किन्तु राजा धर्मपरायणः।
तत्स्त्रीणां जीवनं दद्यादेष धर्मः सनातनः।

XIII, 52.

2. अदायिकं राजगामि योषिद्भृत्यौर्ध्वदेहिकम्।
अपास्य श्रोत्रियद्रव्यं श्रोत्रियेभ्यस्तदर्पयेत्॥

Quoted by Vijñāneśvara on *Yāj.*, II, 136.

Kātyāyana and Bṛihaspati exist only in quotations and we often come across verses attributing contradictory views to them. Thus Vijñāneśvara at the above place also attributes the following verse to Kātyāyana, which clearly supports the widow's right:—

पत्नी पत्युर्धनहरी या स्यादव्यभिचारिणी।
तदभावे तु दुहिता यद्यनूढा भवेत्तदा॥

Similarly Devaṇabhaṭṭa ascribes a verse to Bṛihaspati, which concedes only a partial right of inheritance to the widow. See below p. 255 n. 2. It would appear that these books were not very carefully preserved and interpolations were often made in them by interested parties to support their own views.

recommend that the widow should be recognised as a full heir. They proposed half way measures. Some of them recommended that the wife should be allowed to inherit property worth about 2,000 or 3,000, in addition to any Strīdhana that may have been given to her by her husband.[1] Others thought that she should be permitted to inherit the moveables only.[2] A third view was that the widow may be a deferred heir; she should be allowed to inherit on the failure of brothers-in-law, if her parents-in-law had no objection to the property devolving on her.[3]

The school of reformers, however, was not prepared to accept any such compromises. It insisted that the widows's right to inherit the full share should be recognised. It based its case on logic and reason. Bṛihaspati pointed out that the Vedas, the Smṛitis and sages of antiquity have unanimously declared that the husband and the wife are the joint owners of family property and together constitute one legal personality. A man there fore cannot be said to be completely dead as long as his wife is alive. How then can property pass on to another in the life

1. द्विसाहस्रः परो दायः स्त्रियै देयो धनस्य वै।
भर्त्रा यच्च धनं दत्तं सा यथाकालमाप्नुयात्॥

Vyāsa in Aparārka, p. 752.

Silver Paṇa, roughly equal to a six anna piece, is the coin referred to in the verse. Its purchasing power at that time was equal to that of Rs. 2 today. Property worth 2,000 would be thus equal to property worth about Rs. 10,000 today.

Mahābhārata, XIII, 82, 24 puts the limit at 3,000.

2. यद्विभक्ते धनं किंचिदाध्यादि विविधं स्मृतम्।
तज्जाया स्थावरं मुक्त्वा लभेत मृतभर्तृका॥
वृत्तस्थापि कृतेऽप्यंशे न स्त्री स्थावरमर्हति।

Bṛihaspati in *SCV.*, p. 667.

This text of Bṛihaspati is opposed to a number of other verses attributed to him, and may be of doubtful authority.

3. स्वर्यातस्य ह्यपुत्रस्य भ्रातृगामि द्रव्यम्। तदभावे पितरौ हरेयाताम् ज्येष्ठा वा पत्नी।

Śaṅkha in *Mit.* on *Yaj.*, II, 136.

time of the widow[1] ? Vṛiddhamanu points out that the widow can offer funeral oblations to her husband, and so she should be allowed to inherit his property.[2] To remove any doubt in the matter, Prajāpati lays down that the widow has a natural right to inherit all her husband's property, including moveables, immoveables, bullion, ornaments, stores, etc. Her right is not in the least affected even if her elderly relations, male or female, are alive. She will of course show them proper reverence, but hold the property in her own possession. If any male relation obstructs her peaceful enjoyment of the estate, it is the bounden duty of the king to punish him as a thief.[3]

It is perhaps Jīmūtavāhana, who argues the widow's case in the most masterly fashion. 'There is no authority to hold that the ownership in the husband's property, which the wife acquires at the marriage, terminates with the husband's death. How then can it be argued that the wife's right is destroyed the moment she is widowed? Nor can it be maintained that she is to utilise just as much of the income as may be necessary for her bare maintenance. Vishṇu says that the property of a person

1. आम्नाये स्मृतितन्त्रे च पूर्वाचार्यैश्च सूरिभिः।
शरीरार्धं स्मृता भार्या पुण्यापुण्यफले समा॥
यस्य नोपरता भार्या देहार्धं तस्य जीवति।
जीवत्यर्धशरीरे तु कथमन्यः स्वमाप्नुयात्॥

Quoted in *Dāyabhāga*, Section XI,

2. अपुत्रा शयनं भर्तुः पालयन्ती पतिव्रता।
पत्न्येव दद्यात्तत्पिण्डं कृत्स्नमंशं हरेत च॥

Quoted in *Mit*, on *Yaj*, II, 135-6,

3. स्थावरं जंगमं हेम कुप्यं धान्यरसांबरम्।
आदाय दापयेच्छ्राद्धं माससंवत्सरादिकम्॥
पितृव्यगुरुदौहित्रान्भर्तृस्वस्त्रीयमातुलान्।
पूजयेत्कव्यपूर्ताभ्यां वृद्धानाथातिथींस्तथा॥
तत्सपिण्डा ब्राह्मणा वा ये तस्याः परिपंथिनः।
हिंस्युर्धनानि तान् राजा चौरदण्डेन शासयेत्॥

Quoted in *Parāśaramādhava*, Vol. III, p, 536.

These verses have been attributed to Bṛihaspati in the *Dāyabhaga*, Section XI.

dying without sons will first devolve upon the widow, and then upon the daughter, parents, etc. Now it is admitted that in the above text the term property denotes the whole income of the estate, when construed with all other heirs like the daughter, the brother, parents, etc. How then can it have a restricted meaning when it is construed with the widow alone[1]?

We have seen already how there were early texts, which did not recognise the widow as an heir and allowed her only a maintenance. The new school cleverly explained them away as referring to concubines or unchaste wives. The chaste widow, it was argued, could never be deprived of her inherent right to inherit the entire property of the husband.[2] Now there can be no doubt that this interpretation, though ingenious, is altogether unjustifiable; earlier writers did undoubtedly intend to exclude from inheritance not only concubines and unchaste wives, but also chaste widows. Later champions of women's rights could not follow the straightforward course of refusing to accept the opinions of their predecessors; they had to devise some means, whereby they could explain away the earlier contrary texts without showing any disrespect to their writers. Reform in Hindu social customs and institutions has usually taken this peculiar course owing to the great conservatism of the race.

1. परिणयनोत्पन्नं भर्तृधने पत्न्याः स्वामित्वं भर्तृमरणान्नश्यतीत्यत्र च प्रमाणाभावात् सति पुत्रे तदधिकारशास्त्रादेव पत्नीस्वत्वनाशोऽवगम्यते।......। न च वर्तनोपयुक्तधनमात्राधिकारार्थं पत्नीवचनमिति वाच्यम्। 'अपुत्रस्य धनं पत्न्यभिगामि तदभावे दुहितृगामि तदभावे पितृगामि' इत्यत्र सकृच्छ्रुतस्य धनपदस्य पत्न्यपेक्षमकृत्स्नपरत्वं कृत्स्नपरत्वं च भ्रात्राद्यपेक्षमिति तात्पर्यभेदस्यान्याय्यत्वात्।

Dāyabhāga, Section XI.

2. यदुक्तं 'स्त्रीणां तु जीवनं दद्याद्' इति संवर्धनमात्रवचनं तद्दुश्शीलाधार्मिकसविकरायौवनस्थपत्नीविषयम्।

Kullūka on *Manu*, IX, 186.

यदपि नारदः तत्स्त्रीणां जीवनं दद्यात् इति तदवरुद्धास्त्री परं पत्नीपदाश्रवणत्।

VMV., Sapratibandhadāya section.

Let us resume our subject. The new school maintained that the widow's right of inheritance was an inherent one. The only circumstance that could defeat it was unchastity. When we note the ideas current on the subject at that time, this condition would not appear to be an unexpected one. The modern law on this point is very peculiar. It allows an inheritance to devolve upon a widow, only if she is chaste at the time of its opening. Her subsequent unchastity, however, does not devest the estate.

In spite of the able advocacy of the cause of the widow by the reform school, it took several centuries for her right to be recognised throughout India. The Deccan was more advanced in this respect than northern India. A writer of the 6th century B. C. observes that it is customar for the southerners to recognise the proprietary rights of women.[1] Among the champions of widows' rights the provenance of Bṛihaspati, Vyāsa and Prajāpati is not known, but Yājñāvalkya was a southerner, and his commentator Vijñāneśvara hailed from the Deccan, as he was the Chief Justice of the Chālukya emperor Vikramādiya VI. That the widow's right of inheritance, so enthusiastically advocated in the *Mitākshara*, was actually recognised in contemporary Deccan can be proved from epigraphical evidence. A 12th century inscription from Karnatak, while describing the scheme of devolution of property current in a certain village, mentions the widow as the heir immediately after the son (*E. I.*, V, p. 28). An inscription from Tanjore district, belonging to the same century, declares that a lawfully wedded wife inherits the whole property of the husband, including land, cattle, slaves, jewels and other valuables (*S. I. E. R.*, for 1919, pp. 79-8).

The causes for this earlier recognition of the widow's right of inheritance in the Deccan can only be inferred. As shown before in Chap. VI, Women were taking an active part in the administration in the Deccan even as governors of districts and towns. It is quite

1. गर्तारोहिणीव धनलाभाय दक्षिणाजी ।

Nirukta, III, 5

likely that many of the princesses, who were acting in these capacities, were themselves widows. If society had no objection to widows being governors and collectors, it could also reconcile itself to the recognition of the widow's right of inheritance as well. The existence of matriarchy in some communities may also have helped to liberalise the views of the Deccan society in this respect.

The widow's right of inheritance came into recognition in northern India somewhat later. In the days of Kālidāsa (*c.* 400A. D.), if a person died without leaving a son, his property used to escheat to the king, who had to provide merely a maintenance to the widow. This is quite clear from the Śākuntala episode of the merchant dying in the shipwreck, whose property was proposed to be immediately resumed by the zealous ministers of king Dushyanta. In Gujarat the widow's right of inheritance was not recognised down to *c.* 1200 A. D. King Kumārapāla of that province (1144-1173) admits frankly that his subjects were justified in their impression that their king always desired his rich subjects to die issueless, so that he may resume their property.[1] A poet of his court tells us that it was this king who showed a magnanimity of mind, shown not even by kings born in the golden age like Raghu and Nahusha, and voluntarily forswore his right to the property of the 'weeping widow'.[2] It would be thus seen that this reform met with considerable opposition from the governments of the day, because it adversely affected their revenues. As a partial compensation, some of them introduced a death duty on the property of persons dying without sons (Graham, *Kolhapoor*, p. 333).

1. निष्पुत्रं म्रियमाणमाढ्यमवनीपालो हहा वाञ्छति।

Mohaparājya, Act III.

2. न मुक्तं यत्पूर्वं रघुनहुषनाभागभरतप्रभृत्युर्वीनाथैः कृतयुगकृतोत्पत्तिभिरपि। विमुञ्चसन्तोषात्तदिह रुदतीवित्तमधुना कुमारक्ष्मापाल त्वमसि महतां मस्तक-मणिः॥

Kumārapālapratibodha, p. 43.

Most of the digest writers, who wrote subsequent to *c.* 1200 A. D., have recognised the widow's right of inheritance. We may therefore conclude that by *c.* 1300 A. D., the right had come to be sanctioned throughout the whole country.

The Mitākshară school recognised the widow's right of inheritance, only if her husband had separated from the joint family before his death.[1] An examination of the context of the verse in which Yājñavalkya mentions widow as the next heir, makes it clear that he intended to recognise her right, only if her husband was not a member of the joint family at the time of his death. This conclusion becomes further irresistable from v. 138, where Yājñavalkya lays down that when members of a family have reunited after separation, the surviving male coparceners will succeed the deceased, and not his wife.[2] Vijñānesvara is therefore correct in holding that according to Yājñavalkya only the widow of a separated coparcener can become an heir to her husband. Of course he could have liberalised the law still further by drawing further deductions from the text of Bṛihaspati, which declares that none can touch the property of a person as long as his wife is alive. He could have argued that whether the deceased was a member of the joint family or not, was an immaterial question. As long as the wife was alive, the husband ought to be to regarded as living; the inheritance will not open at all till the death of the wife. She must be therefore allowed to enjoy the property of her husband irrespective of the consideration, whether he had separated from the family or not before his death.

Vijñāneśvara, however, was not prepared to take this step. He had included inherited property under Strīdhana, and he was probably reluctant to sanction a scheme of succession,

1. तस्मादपुत्रस्य स्वर्यातस्य विभक्तस्य असंसृष्टिनो धनं परिणीता स्त्री संयता सकलमेव गृहणाति इति स्थितम्।

On *Yaj.*, II, 136.

2. संसृष्टिनस्तु संसृष्टी सोदरस्य तु सोदरः॥

II, 138.

whereunder extensive property would have automatically and very frequently passed out of the family to female Strīdhana heirs. He probably felt that if a coparcener effected a separation from the joint family, its members should have no grievance if his separated share passed as Strīdhana to his daughter. If, however, no separation had been effected, and the share of an undivided coparcener were still allowed to devolve on his wife, it would have passed out of the family with an alarming frequency, since unlike the Dāyabhāga school, the Mitāksharā school had declared this share as the Strīdhana of the wife. Most of the medieval jurists agree with the Mitāksharā and recognise the widow's right of inheritance only when her husband was not a member of the joint family at the time of his death.

To Jīmūtavāhana, the founder of the Dāyabhāga school, belongs the credit of liberalising the law still further in favour of the widow. We have seen above (*ante*, p. 225) that he would not include inherited property under Strīdhana. This was so, because he wanted to disarm society's opposition to his revolutionary proposal to make the widow an heir to her husband, even when the latter was a member of the joint family at the time of his death. While anxious that every widow should inherit her husband's share in the joint family property, he wanted to prevent it from going outside the family to Strīdhana heirs. He therefore did not include it under her Strīdhana.

The Dāyabhāga law undoubtedly marks a further step in the expansion of the widow's rights. It lays down that the widow can get her husband's share in the family property, even if he happened to be a member of the joint family at the time of his death. Jīmūtavāhana relies upon a text of Bṛihaspati, which is silent about separation and declares that the property of a person can devolve upon his brother, only when he dies without leaving a son or a widow behind.[1] He further points

1. यदा कश्चित्प्रमीयेत प्रव्रजेद्वा कथंचन।
न लुप्यते तस्य भागः सोदरस्य विधीयते।
अनपत्यस्य धर्मोऽयमभार्यापितृकस्य च।
Quoted in Section XI.

out that even when brothers are living as members of a joint family, according to his conception of this institution, each one has got his own share clearly determined, though not specifically separated by metes and bounds; it is then but fair that it should be earmarked for his wife.[1] There is further nothing to prove that the wife's co-ownership in the husband's property, that arises at the marriage, automatically terminates at his death, if it happens while the family is still joint.[2] It is therefore but fair that she should be allowed to inherit her husband's share irrespective of the consideration as to whether he had separated from the joint family or not.

If the texts, on which Jīmūtavāhana had relied, had been utilised to their fullest capacity, they would have easily enabled him to declare that the estate which the widow inherits is an absolute and not a limited one. The widow is the living half of the husband, says Bṛihaspati; and therefore no one can get the right to inherit the deceased's property as long as she is alive. Now Jīmūtavāhana could have easily argued that the powers of the surviving half (the widow) cannot be less than those of the expired half (the husband), and so the widow's estate would be as absolute as that of her husband, she having the power of sale, mortgage or gift. He however did not take this step, but maintained that the widow had only a life estate in her inheritance. She could utilise its full income in any way she liked, but she could not touch its corpus.

To understand Jīmūtavāhana's reluctance to grant to the widow a full estate in inheritance, we shall have to discuss the history of the question. The early jurists like Vishṇu and Yājñāvalkya, who have recognised the widow as an heir, have nowhere used any expressions to show that they regarded her as a limited heir. It is therefore possible to argue that they intended to invest her with the same full powers which they granted to

1. न हि संसृष्टत्वेऽपि यदेवैकस्य तदेवापरस्यापि किन्तु अविज्ञातैकदेशं तद्द्वयोः न तु समग्रमेव।

Dāyabhāga, XI

2. See *ante*, p. 257 n. 1.

other heirs like the son, the father or the brother, whom they have mentioned along with her. In the long discussion of the subject in the *Mitāksharā*, Vijñāneśvara also nowhere states or hints that the widow was a limited heir, having no right to dispose of the corpus of the property. In the concluding sentence of his discussion he states, 'Therefore the chaste and regularly married wife of a person, who has died without leaving behind any sons, and who had separated from the joint family and not reunited with it, inherits his entire property.[1] He has introduced here several qualifying adjectives, very carefully chosen; but among them there is none to suggest that he regarded the widow's estate as a limited one.

A number of other jurists, however, declare definitely that the widow is a limited heir. An authority quoted by the *Mahābhārata* states that the widow can only utilise the income of the property she has inherited; she can under no circumstances dispose of it.[2] Kātyāyana states that the inheritance will revert to reversioners after the death of the widow, she having no power to dispose of it.[3] Bṛihaspati, we have seen, was a fervent champion of the widow's rights, but even he expressly declares that her powers over her inheritance are limited; she cannot sell, mortgage or gift it away. He, however, permits a gift for religious purposes, which presumably was to be of a small portion only.[4] Nārada declines to concede full powers to the wife even

1. तस्मादपुत्रस्य स्वर्यातस्य विभक्तस्यासंसृष्टिनो धनं परिणीता स्त्री सकलमेव गृह्णाति।

On Yāj., II, 136.

2. स्त्रीणां स्वपतिदायाद उपभोगफलः स्मृतः।
नापहारं स्त्रियः कुर्युः पतिवित्तात्कथंचन॥

XIII, 82, 25.

3. अपुत्रा शयनं भर्तुः पालयन्ती पतिव्रता।
लभेतामरणात्क्षान्ता दायादा ऊर्ध्वमाप्नुयुः॥

Quoted in *SCV.*, p. 677.

4. मृते भर्तरि भर्त्रंशं लभेत कुलपालिका।
यावज्जीवं हीनस्वाम्यं दानाधमनविक्रये॥
व्रतोपवासनिरता ब्रह्मचर्ये व्यवस्थिता।
धर्मदानरता नित्यमपुत्रापि दिवं व्रजेत्॥

Quoted at *Ibid.*

over her Strīdhana, if it comprised of any immoveable property. The wise have declared, says this sage, that transaction of landed property like sale, mortgage or gift, if made by women, are, automatically invalid.[1]

To conclude, we find that even some of the warmest champions of the widow's right of inheritance like Bṛihaspati definitely declare her to be a limited heir, while others like Yājñavalkya and Vishṇu are merely silent on the point. No one specifically invests her with the power to dispose of the immoveable property in her inheritance, gifts for religious purposes being the only exception. It is therefore clear that down to the 12th century, the widow was intended to be given only a limited power over her inheritance. Society was, as shown already, very reluctant to recognise the widow as even a limited heir; it would have summarily rejected the case of her champions, if they had suggested that she should be invested with absolute powers over her inheritance.

Late medieval period, *c.* 1200-1800 A. D., was the most conservative one in the history of Hindu customs and institutions. It, however, can claim the credit of attempting to extend the widow's powers over her estate in one direction. We have seen above how down to *c.* 1200 A. D., jurists were unwilling to concede to the widow the right to alienate her estate. Writers of legal digests after that date are seen to encourage the tendency to recognise this right under certain circumstances. There was a text of Bṛihaspati which, as pointed out already, permitted the widow to gift away a portion of her property for religious and spiritual purposes.[2] Medieval writers like Devaṇabhaṭṭa and Nīlakaṇṭha particularly emphasise on this right. The former states that when sale or mortgage of the

1. भर्त्रा प्रीतेन यद्दत्तं स्त्रियै तस्मिन्मृतेऽपि तत्।
सा यथाकाममश्नीयाद्द्याद्वा स्थावराद्वते॥
स्त्रीकृतान्यप्रमाणानि कार्याण्याहुर्मनीषिणः।
विशेषतो गृहक्षेत्रदानाधमनविक्रयाः॥
I, 26-27.

2. See *ante*, p. 263 n. 3.

immoveable property was prohibited to the widow, what was meant was that she should not gift it away in one form or another to persons of questionable character like singers, dancers and actors[1]. The latter maintains that women have inheritent powers to make gifts for spiritual purposes[2].

Neither Devaṇabhaṭṭa nor Nīlakaṇṭha however states whether the consent of the next reversioners was necessary for validating such a transaction. The language which they have used would suggest that if the gift was a bonafide one for religious purposes, the widow could give it herself without the consent of the reversioners. The actual practice seems to have varied considerably. We have no recorded cases for northern India, but south Indian inscriptions of the medieval period show that the silence of the authorities was interpreted differently by different persons and localities.

There was one view that the express permission of the reversioners was an essential pre-requisite for such a transaction. It would be therefore better if the gift was formally made jointly by the widow and the reversioners. Some inscriptions from south India show that this opinion was acted upon in practice on several occasions. Thus a 10th century epigraph from Mysore records a gift of land given by a widow and her brother-in-law (*E. C.*, IX, Holkere No. 33). The brother-in-law is obviously introduced here to show that the transaction had the full consent of the next reversioner. The widow alone could not have sold the property. A 12th century inscription from the same state records the donation given by a widow to a temple along with her brother-in-law and Śrīvaishṇavas. Here it is clear that the consent of not only the next reversioner but of the whole caste was deemed necessary to validate the transaction (*Ibid*, X, No.

1. मृते भर्तरीत्यस्मिन्दृष्टदानप्रतिरोधः। अदृष्टार्थदानविधानात्तदितरदृष्टार्थनर्तकादीनां दानादौ अस्वातन्त्र्यप्रतिपादनार्थमिति मन्तव्यम्। एवं च धर्मदाने स्वातंत्र्यमस्त्येव। अपुत्रा शयनमादिकात्यायनोक्तमविभक्तदशाविषयम्।
S. C. V. pp. 667-7.

2. अदृष्टार्थदानतदुपयोग्याधमनादि भवत्येव।
Vyavahāramayūkha p. 86.

100 A). A 13th century inscription from Madura district narrates how two childless widows wanted to give a garden to a temple, how their relations would not sanction the transaction, and how eventually they could achieve their object only by securing the permission of some other reversioners (*S. I. E. R.*, 1916, No. 401). It is quite clear from the above cases that the widow's estate was regarded as a limited one. The permission of the next reversioner, if not of the whole caste, was necessary to enable her to gift it even for a religious purpose.

There are, however, other records equally numerous and hailing from the same part of the country, which record sales or gifts of landed property by widows made for religious purposes, but which are silent about any permission of the reversioners. A 12th century inscription from Trichiniopoly district records the gift of a piece of land by a Brahmana widow made in favour of a temple; a 13th century inscription from Kolar district refers to a sale by a widow of her own share in her landed property; a 15th century record mentions a Brahmana widow building a temple and giving to it a gift of land for the spiritual benefit of herself and her husband; a 17th century inscription describes how a Brahamana lady gifted away a whole village to a temple. In none of these records it is anywhere mentioned or suggested that any of the widows had obtained the consent or permission of any reversioner for disposing her landed property. Had any such permission been received, it would have been surely mentioned, as was done by the persons who drew up the documents referred to in the last para. It is to be noted that these epigraphs were lithic deeds of title, intended to last for centuries; it is natural to presume that they would have carefully mentioned all relevant circumstances that would have been necessary to prove that the transactions recorded were valid ones, and the donees had acquired full and unquestioned titles.

The epigraphic evidence then shows that the custom differed

1. *I. M. P.* III, p. 1544; *E. C.*, X, Kolar No. 103; *I. M. P.*, I. p. 56; *E. C.*, XI, Holkere No. 80.

with different castes and different localities in south India. Some sections of society felt that the permission of the reversioners was necessary to validate even a religious gift; others thought that it might be dispensed with. When we note that our jurists all belonged to the priestly class, it need not be wondered that their general tendency should have been to give the widow an unrestricted power in the matter.

While pleading for an unrestricted power to the widow to make gifts for religious purposes, Mitramiśra, a 17th century jurist of Uttara Pradesh, uses some expressions, suggesting that he was half inclined to sanction bonafide sales or gifts made even for non-religious purposes. 'To those who contend' says he, that women have no right to sell or gift away their husband's inheritance, we ask; do you mean to maintain that even if the gift or sale in question has already become an accomplished fact, it would become invalid merely because it was made by a woman ? This is unfair...Texts prohibiting sales etc. refer to the disposal of landed property made to vicious persons with the malicious purpose of defeating the rights of coparceners. They do not invalidate gifts etc. properly made. *Ownership gives the right of disposal as much over the immoveables as over the moveables, and an accomplished transaction cannot be unsettled even by a hundred sacred texts* . This principle would have undoubtedly invested the widow with full rights of disposal even over immoveable property. But Mitramiśra not only does not draw its natural corollary, but proceeds immediately to circumscribe its application. For he concludes his discussion with the observation,

1. संमुखमेव वचनार्थमादाय नास्त्येव स्त्रिया भर्तृरिक्थे दानविक्रयाद्यधिकार इत्याहुः। तत्रेदं वाच्यम्। किं तस्य तया कृतेऽपि दानादौ तत्स्वरूपानिष्पत्तिरेव। मन्वादिवचनैः सकलभर्तृधनग्रहणे तस्या उक्ते सति तस्या अस्वतंत्रस्वत्वे दानादिस्वरूपानिष्पत्तेर्बाधितत्वात्.........। दानादिप्रतिषेधवचनानि दुर्वृत्तं पुरुषं प्रति कुटुम्बदुःखदानार्थमेव दानक्रियादिप्रवृत्तिनिषेधकानि न तु दानादिस्वरूपानिष्पत्तिप्रतिपादकानि। ......यथेष्टविनियोगार्हत्वलक्षणस्वत्वस्य द्रव्यान्तर इव स्थिरेऽप्यविशेषाद्वचनशतेनापि वस्तुनोऽन्यथाकरणाशक्त्या तत्प्रतिपादनानुपपत्तेरिति निरूपितम्।

VMS., p. 628-9

"It therefore follows that a widow can dispose of her immoveable property either for making a religious gift or for maintaining herself or for other proved necessities:[1] he does not add 'or for any other purpose she may like'. In spite of his liberal principles Mitramiśra was thus prepared to invest the widow just with those powers, which have been recognised in modern courts. It is clear that society was not yet prepared to grant the widow an unrestricted power over her immoveable inheritance.

Should we now change the law and invest the widow with full powers over the immoveable property inherited by her ? This is a question on which opinion is divided at present. Dr. Deshmukh's bill, introduced in 1936 in the Imperial Assembly sought to invest the widow with this power, but the effort failed. The educated woman naturally feels it an insult that she should not have a power over her inheritance, which is conceded to the most illiterate and inexperienced villager. We must, however, note that even at present the widow can sell or mortgage her property for genuine necessities. The disability is that her powers in this connection are not unrestricted. This is of course a disability from one point of view, but also a protection from another. In the Punjab and Palestine, for instance, male peasants had unrestricted powers of alienation; the result was that many of them sold away their valuable lands and eventually became paupers, as they could not properly utilise or invest the sale proceeds. Eventually the governments of these provinces had to restrict these powers in the interests of the peasants themselves. We should not forget that 95 percent widows are still uneducated, inexperienced and altogether innocent of the provisions of law. If they are given the right to dispose of the landed property, many of them will be induced by interested parties to enter into unwise transactions. The money realised

1. तस्माददृष्टार्थे दाने दृष्टादृष्टावश्यकार्यार्थमाधौ विक्रये चास्त्येव पत्न्याः सकलभर्तृधनविषयेऽप्यधिकारः। नियमस्तु नटनर्तकादिदानानावश्यकाधिविक्रियनिवृत्त्यर्थमिति सिद्धम्।

VMS., p. 630

from sale will not last long, and the majority of widows disposing of their property will eventually find that they have lost both the lands and their sale proceeds. Their condition will then become very pitiable. In the present circumstances, therefore, it is not in the interests of the widows as a class that they should have unrestricted power of alienation. A beginning, however, should be made by giving it to those widows, who possess certain minimum educational qualifications. This of course will often adversely affect the prospective rights of reversioners, but they have been already annihilated by the ruling of the Privy Council, which has given the widow in many parts of the country an unrestricted power of adoption. If coparceners cultivate friendly and cordial relations with the widow, there is no reason why she should wantonly defeat their expectations. She would then take as much interest in her husband's family as her coparceners, and would not normally stand in the way of its continued prosperity after her death by selling or willing away her share.

Till 1937 it was only in Bengal where the Dāyabhāga law prevailed, that the widow could inherit her husband's property, even if he had died as a member of the joint family. Outside Bengal, she was recognised as an heir, only if her husband had effected a separation from the joint family before his death. This was the law as it was laid down in the *Mitāksharā* and enforced in modern courts. The latter, however, were anxious to help the widow as much as they could, and sought to facilitate matters in her favour by decreeing that a person should be regarded as being separated from the joint family, not only when he had actually severed his connection, but also when he had merely communicated his intention of doing so to his other coparceners. This used to enable many persons, who did not share the traditional regard for the sanctity of the joint family, to secure the devolution of their shares upon their wives. Those wives, however, who did not advise their husbands to take this rather unpleasant step, got as a reward for their regard for the joint family, the misfortune of losing their right of inheritance to their husbands. This was undoubtedly an undesirable and anomalous state of affairs. The Hindu Women's Right to Property Act of 1937 extends the Dāyabhāga principle to the whole of British India, and invests the widow with the right to inherit her husband's share in the family property, irrespective of the consideration as to whether he had effected a separation from the joint family or not. This is a step in the right direction and widows all over the country now possess this right.

SECTION 3.

Other Female Heirs.

We have considered so far the right of inheritanace of the daughter, the wife and the widow. The cases of remaining female heirs need not be considered in detail in the present work. Only some words will be necessary about a few of them.

The right of the mother to inherit the property of her son was recognised fairly early. Manu, who does not recognise the widow as an heir, concedes to the mother the right to inherit the property of a son dying without any issues (IX, 217). All the jurists concur with Manu in this matter. Some of them do not even allow sons to partition family property as long as the mother is alive. In practice the widowed mother was regarded as the sole controller of the estate, though the sons were its legal heirs and owners. Hindu culture held the mother in very high reverence; so her right of inheritance came to be recognised much earlier than that of the wife or the widow. In every day life, however, occasions were very few when property passed to a mother as the next heir of an issueless son. The recognition of this right did not therefore give rise to many exceptions to the general view of early times that women should not be recognised as heirs. The grandmother's claim to inherit her grandsons' property was also recognised very early for reasons similar to those which operated in favour of the mother. In actual practice, however, not even one grand-mother in a million could have got an opportunity of being benefited by this concession. For she was a fairly distant heir and came only after the parents and brothers of the deceased. The recognition of the widow, on the other hand, as the next heir to an issueless husband was a revolutionary step, as it was sure to give rise to a large number of female heirs in actual practice. A long time therefore had to elapse before it could be taken.

We have seen above that the Deccan was the pioneer in recognising women's rights of inheritance. She continues her lead even today, for the Bombay school recognises a larger number of female heirs than any other school of Hindu Law. It is the only school which gives the right of inheritance to the widows of the agnates (Gotraja Sapiṇḍas). It is interesting to note that even the *Mitākshară* does not support their claim to inheritance.[1] In Bombay Presidency, however, the right of the widows of agnates was recognised, mainly because local enquiry showed that it was actually conceded in practice. The courts were also influenced to some extent by a wrong translation of a passage in *Manusmṛiti* by Sir William Jones. He had translated the line in question as 'To the nearest Sapiṇḍa, *male or female*, the inheritance next belongs.' The italicised words are not in the original text at all;[2] Sir William Jones had added them on the authority of Kullūka, who has explained the term Sapiṇḍa as *pumān strī vā*, 'either male or female'. It will be seen from this incidence how adventitious circumstances connected with early translations have in some cases considerably affected the development of Hindu Law in modern times.

The sister has been placed much higher in the line of succession in the Bombay school than anywhere else. She comes immediately after the grand-mother, mainly on account of an ingenious argument advanced in the *Mayūkha*.[4] It is clear that Nīlakaṇ-

1. The *Mitākshară* does not at all mention the paternal uncle's wife or her daughter-in-law as an heir. Neither Devaṇabhaṭṭa nor Mitramiśra recognises Gotraja Sapiṇḍa widows as heirs. *SCV*., p. 694; *VMV*., p. 671.

2. Cf :—अनन्तरं सपिण्डाद्यस्तस्य तस्य हरेद्धनम् ।
IX, 187.

3. 7 *Indian Appeals*. pp. 212-239.

4. तस्या अपि भ्रातृगोत्रे उत्पन्नत्वेन गोत्रजत्वाविशेषाच्च ।
P. 89.

ṭha is here trying to justify a known usage with the help of some spacious arguments.

Among the heirs of the descending order, Hindu jurists have been the hardest on the widowed daughter-in-law. Only one among them, Nanda Paṇḍita (*c.* 1575 A. D.), recognises her as an heir.[1] The rest found it difficult to grant her any relief. The reasons are easy to understand. The Mitāksharā recognised the widow as an heir only when her husband had already separated from the joint family. It was regarded as highly indecorous for a son to separate from his father or grandfather; so there were hardly any widowed daughters-in-law in society who could claim a share under the Mitākshara scheme of succession. Under the Dāyabhāga law, the separation of her husband from the family was no doubt not necessary for a widow to get a share; there was, however, another fatal difficulty in the way of the widow of the predeceased son. Under the Dāyabhāga scheme, the son could get no right in the family property till after the death of the father; the widowed daughter-in-law could claim no share in the family property, because her husband himself was entitled to none at the time of his death. Thus both the Mitākshara and the Dāyabhāga schools could extend no relief to the widow of a predeceased son. The British courts followed faithfully the medieval authorities on this point, and were therefore unable to liberalise the law in her favour. The situation has changed in 1937 with the passing of Hindu Women's Right to Property Act; now the widow of a predeceased son can get a life estate in the share to which her husband would have been entitled.

It is not necessary to consider the rights of inheritance of any more female heirs for the purpose of our present work. We therefore now pass on to consider women's rights at partition.

1. Cf :—श्वश्रूमरणे श्वश्रूस्नुषयोः स्वत्वसाम्येन श्वश्रूमरणे स्नुषाया एव साधारणसाम्यात् ।

Nanda Paṇḍita bases his case for the widowed daughter-in-law on Bṛihaspati's dictum,

जीवत्यर्धशरीरे तु कथमन्यः स्वमाप्नुयात् ।

Kane, *History of Dharmaśāstra Literature*, I, p. 212

SECTION 4

Partition

The theory of joint ownership should have invested the wife with the right to demand a partition against her husband in case it became impossible for her to live with him. No such right was however recognised. Yājñavalkya lays down that a wife should get a third share in her husband's property, if she is unjustly superseded.[1] He is, however, the only jurist to recognise such a right, and it is quite possible that in actual practice, husbands may have managed to escape this liability under the plea that the wives superseded were disobedient ones. It may be, however, pointed out that to demand a partition was regarded as a very unbecoming procedure; even a grown up son could not ask for it, if his father were living jointly with his grand-father or other elderly collaterals. The wife thus suffered from the same disabilities as against her husband, as the son suffered as against the father. It is however high time to invest the wife with an incontestible right to demand her full share in the property, if she is compelled to live separately owing to her husband's misdemeanour. In such cases, she ought to get a share equal to that of a son.

Let us now consider normal cases of partition and women's rights on such occasions. The Vedic literature occasionally refers to a partition made by the father during his life time;[2] there is, however, nothing to indicate whether the wife used to receive a share on such occasions. Very probably, in spite of the general prejudice against allowing a share to women in inheritance, the father must have assigned an adequate share to his wife, if she were living at the time. In actual practice, the assigning of a share to the wife must have merely amounted to

1. आज्ञासंपादिनीं दक्षां वीरसूं प्रियवादिनीम्।
त्यजन्दाप्यस्तृतीयांशमद्रव्यो भरणं स्त्रियः॥
I, 76.

2. पितुर्न जिव्रेर्वि वेदो भरन्त।
R. V., I, 70, 5; see also *T. S.*, III, 1,9,4-5.

the patriarch reserving two shares for himself as against one assigned to each son. The wife probably got no independent control over it.

While describing partition, many of the Dharmaśāstra writers expressly include the mother, the wife and the daughter among the parties entitled to a moity. Among these the case of the daughter has been already considered (*ante*, pp. 239 ff.). As far as the wife is concerned, both Yājñavalkya and Kātyāyana allow her a share. If the partition had taken place during the husband's life time, very probably the wife must be allowing her husband to be in possession of her share; it must have therefore merely increased her husband's moity. It is interesting to note that Nārada allows two shares to the husband at partition[1]; the second one was probably intended for his wife.

Yājñavalkya allows the widowed mother a share equal to that of her son.[2] Śukra allows her only a one fourth share (IV, 5, 297), but his view is not shared by the vast majority of jurists, who insist that the mother should receive one full share. Some writers attempted to curtail the full share allowed to the mother by suggesting that the expression 'equal share' is not to be interpreted literally; it is really intended to mean just as much money as may be necessary for her maintenance. The *Mitāksharā*, however, rightly points out the utter unreasonableness of this interpretation and maintains that the widowed mother must get a full share[3]. Most of the jurists have accepted this view, as also

1. द्वावंशौ प्रतिपद्येत विभजन्नात्मनः पिता।
XIII, 12.

2. यदि कुर्यात्समानंशान्पत्न्यः कार्याः समांशिकाः।
न दत्तं स्त्रीधनं यासां भर्त्रा वा श्वशुरेण वा॥
I, 115.

पितुरूर्ध्वं विभजतां माताप्यंशं समं हरेत्।
II, 123

3. अथ 'पत्न्यः कार्याः समांशिका' इत्यत्र 'माताप्यंशं समं हरेत्' इत्यत्र च जीवनोपयुक्तमेव धनं स्त्री हरतीति मतं तदसत्। अंशशब्दस्य समशब्दस्यच आनर्थक्यप्रसंगात्।

On *Yāj.*, II, 136.
See also *V. D. S.*, XVIII, 34, *Kātyāyana-matasaṁgraha*, v, 693.

the modern law courts. The latter, however, had given the ruling that the widow could get this share only if her sons sued for a partition; she could not herself bring the suit. This was clearly against the spirit of the Hindu law. Manu and Kauṭilya do not even permit brothers to effect a partition during the mother's lifetime;[1] they would have been shocked to be told that the mother could get her share only if her sons chose to effect a partition. The law therefore needed a change in the direction of allowing the mother to sue for her share, in case she could not pull on well with her sons. This desideratum was achieved by the Hindu Women's Right to Property Act passed in 1937 by the Indian Legislature.

We have now finished the history of the proprietary rights of women. It has no doubt detained us rather long, but it has made many interesting disclosures. We found that it did not take long for Hindu society to set aside primitive theories about women being mere chattel. It recognised their right to Strīdhana fairly early and went on expanding its scope, till eventually by the 12th century A.D., all varieties of property were included in it all over India, except in Bengal. In normal times the husband was not allowed to touch this property of his wife. The only development necessary in modern times in this connection is the recognition of the right of the wife to a small percentage in the husband's income as her *bhartṛidatta strīdhana*, in recognition of the joint ownership of the family property and her valuable service in the household management. This would remove the difficulties of the modern sensitive wife, who does not like that for every little expenditure which she may have to incur, she should have to secure expressly or impliedly the permission of her husband.

The position of the wife *vis-a-vis* the husband was not satisfactory. She could not enforce a partition against him, if he persistently misbehaved or embarked upon a second marriage. Yājñavalkya, no doubt, allowed the wife a one third share in

1. *Manu*, IX, 104; *Arthāśāstra*, III, 5.

the family property, if she was unjustly superseded. He was, however, in a hopeless minority. We must, however, now follow his lead and allow the wife to claim a share at least equal to that of a son, if she is forced to live separately for no fault of her own. This would remove the proprietary disabilities from which such wives suffer at present on account of their having no share in the patrimony. We must further render it impossible for the husband to mortgage or sell his wife's share in the family property without her express consert.

Hindu jurists held marriage to be indispensable for the daughter, and therefore felt that they should merely provide for it. They went to the extent of laying down that a brother should provide for his sister's marriage even if there were no ancestral assets for the purpose. They were, however, opposed to give her a right of inheritance in the patrimony along with her brothers. The religious theory was that the marriage completely transfers the bride to the new family, and the jurists therefore felt that she should be provided for from its assets. We have shown above (*ante*, pp. 245-8) how on the whole this is a reasonable and satisfactory arrangement. There are many difficulties to encounter and few benefits to accrue from giving a daughter the right of inheritance along with her brothers. The present law gives rise to certain anomalies in some abnormal cases, but the correct remedy is to enlarge the wife's rights as against the husband on the lines indicated above. Of course, as far as daughters who remain unmarried are concerned, they should be given a share in patrimony equal to half that of their brothers. The Hindu Code Bill is however seeking now (Feb. 1956) to give them a full share, and a section of the Hindu community is in favour of this innovation.

The brotherless daughter has been regarded as an heir since very early times. In Bombay presidency she takes the property as an absolute heir. This law should now be extended to the whole of the country.

For a long time the widow was not recognised as an heir, mainly because she usually possessed some kind of son, as a guardian for whom she could hold her husband's share in the family property. When the custom of Niyoga disappeared and the childless widow came on the scene, Hindu society soon became alive to the necessity of recognising her as an heir. The fervour and zeal with which the battle of her right of inheritance was fought, are creditable for Hindu culture. The widow was no doubt regarded as a limited heir. She could, however, utilise the full income of the property, howsoever large it may be; only she could not alienate it without sufficient cause. When we consider how the vast majority of Hindu widows were illiterate at this time, the limitation must be pronounced to have been more a protection than a disability. The time has not yet come when we can effect a wholesale change in the law on the point. A beginning should, however, be made by allowing women the right of alienation, if they possess certain minimum educational qualifications.

The Bengal school was most liberal to the widow; it allowed her to become an heir, even if her husband had not separated from the joint family. This principle has been extended to the whole country since 1937; so a legitimate grievance, from which the widows under the *Mitāksharā* law were suffering, has been now removed.

It will be thus seen from the above survey that the proprietary rights of women have been developing fairly satisfactorily. As circumstances changed, they were being enlarged by Hindu jurists without any agitation whatever on the part of women. Society was actuated by a genuine desire to improve their economic lot, and did not hesitate to adopt measures that considerably curtailed the time-honoured rights of male coparceners. The courage that was shown in investing the widow with the right of inheritance, even when her elderly relations like brothers-in-law were alive, was really of a high order, when we consider the prevailing patriarchal atmosphere in society. The progress made cannot be of course regarded as adequate by the modern woman, but we must recognise that each age has its own limitations and cannot easily rise above them. Modern Hindu society has been showing a keen desire to enlarge the proprietary rights of women; the legislatures in India both Provincial and Central, began to champion measures to liberalise the law since 1936. The States of Baroda and Mysore led the way in the matter under the inspiration of their enlightened rulers. And now (Feb. 1956) we have a measure before the Indian Parliament, sponsored by the Government, which seeks to give the married daughter a share in patrimony equal to that of the brother. What will be the fate of this measure cannot be anticipated; but it seems to be reasonably certain that at least the unmarried daughter will get a share in the patrimony equal to half that of her brother.

CHAPTER X.

DRESS AND ORNAMENTS.

A detailed study of the dress and ornaments worn by Hindu women of different classes age by age would be out of place in this work, which discusses their position in society mainly from the sociological point of view. It would require a separate volume, profusely illustrated. We propose to treat the subject here only in its braod outlines, so that the reader may get a general idea about it. In a book which professes to discuss the position of women in an exhaustive manner, a chapter on their dress and ornaments is perhaps indispensable.

Dress.

The dress of women in the Indus Valley civilization, as disclosed by its terracottas, consisted of a *sari* fastened by a girdle. A garment to cover the torso does not make its appearance. In some cases a fan-like head-dress is seen on the terracotta figurines; it is doubtful whether it was in general vogue.

The Vedic literature supplies us with very little information about the dress of the women of the age. The vocabulary itself of the period has got no separate words to denote women's clothes. The same words are used to denote the different clothes worn both by men and women. An under-garment (*vāsaḥ antaram*) and an upper garment (*paridhānam*) were in general use among the members of both the sexes. A waistband was used round the lower garment (*Ś. Br.*, 1, 3, 3, 6). Probably both the garments were usually coloured in the case of women, for the Vedic literature refers to the dyer (*V. S.*, 30, 12). In addition to the two garments, mentioned above, kings used to wear a gorgeous mantle (*drāpi*) on ceremonious occasions. Queens also probably had the counterpart of this mantle in the form of an embroidered shawl, though there is no definite evidence on the point. In one place goddess Indrāṇī is described as wearing a headdress (*ushṇīsha*, *Ś. Br.*, XIV, 2, 1, 8); it is probable that the well-to-do ladies of the Vedic age were also doing the same.

Probably this *ushṇīsha* was something like a *pagree* and not merely a piece of cloth for covering the head like the modern *oḍhṇī*. It was not very common, for the usual custom for the ladies was to arrange the hair in different artistic plaits, (*A. V.*, X. 114. 3; *V. S.*, XI. 56), the grace of which could not be properly revealed, if the head was covered by a head-dress or *oḍhṇī*.

We get no information or clue as to how the lower garment or *sari* was worn in these days. The art of weaving was well developed, and it is fairly certain that the *sari* was a long piece, about five or six yards in length. A portion of it was therefore very probably used to cover the upper part of the body as well, as is done in modern times all over the country. The additional upper garment (*paridhānam*) was probably used only on ceremonious occasions. The same was probably the case with the head-dress.

The epics show that the dress of women continued to be more or less of the above type for a long time. Draupadī's remarks, when summoned to the gambling hall, make it clear that to go out without an upper garment properly covering the entire bust was regarded as indecorous.[1] At home, however, only one *sari* was worn, but it used to cover the shoulders and bosom as well; Draupadī, when dragged out by her garment by Duśśāsana, is described as having the upper part of her *sari* falling down.[2] The additional upper garment was not absolutely necessary to cover the bust. It only formed part of the ceremonial dress. Sītā therefore could dispense with it when she wanted a piece of cloth to tie her ornaments in order to drop them down to Sugrīva, when she was very anxious to leave behind a clue about her abduction, as she was being carried away through the air by Rāvaṇa.

The fashion of wearing a head-dress, which was sometimes

1. एकं च वासो मम मन्दबुद्धे सभां नेतुं नार्हसि मामनार्य ॥
II, 89, 44.

2. प्रकीर्णकेशी पतितार्धवस्त्रा दुःशासनेन व्यवधूयमाना ॥
II, 89, 47.

followed in the Vedic age, became rarer in later times. Women are rarely seen wearing a *pagree* in Bharhut or Sanchi sculptures. Curiously enough, sometimes nuns appear with a head-dress at Sanchi. At Ajanta women's head-dress rarely makes its appearance.

Though a pre-fabricated head-dress or *pagree* went out of fashion, women used to cover their head by an *oḍhṇī*, or piece of cloth, which used to cover their head and fall gracefully over their shoulders and back. This fashion was popular in Central India and Mālwā, for ladies sculptured at Bharhut and Sanchi are invariably seen wearing graceful *oḍhṇis* (Pl. III). Apparently it was not popular in Eastern India, Śūrasena (Mathura area) and Deccan, for the Didarganj statue of Yakshiṇi (*c.* 300 B. C.), the ladies sculptured at Mathura (*c.* 100 A. D.) and Nagarjunikonda (*c.* 200 A.D.) and paintings at Ajanta (*c.* 300-500 A.D.) are seen without any *oḍhṇis*. It would appear that opinion was divided; ladies of fashion wanted to fully exhibit their coiffure by discarding the *oḍhṇi*; others preferred to heighten their charms by costly *oḍhṇis* worn in graceful fashions, partly revealing and partly concealing the coiffure. Gradually both *oḍhṇis* and head-dresses became unpopular; we do not come across them in the medieval sculptures. Orthodox women found it more convenient to cover their head with a portion of their *saris*. Fashionable ladies did not like to conceal from view their elaborate and artistic coiffure.

The classical Sanskrit literature supplies us with meagre and disappointing data about the dress of women during the first millennium of the Christian era. It no doubt grows very eloquent in several places in describing in detail the beauty of young ladies and their attractive and numerous ornaments, but it rarely describes the constituents of their dress or the precise manner in which it was worn. The scanty available evidence shows that women normally required two garments during this period also. The upper garment or shawl was used only on ceremonial occasions. Goddess Lakshmī, who appears seated on numerous Gupta coins, is seen invariably wearing a shawl, which completely covers her bosom, bust and arms down to the wrist (Allan, *Catalogue of Gupta Coins*, Pl. I. Nos. 6, 10, 13). When in standing posture, ladies used to wear the shawl in different ways. Sometimes it used to cover their entire person down to the ankles (ibid., Pl. III, no. 6); but when they were standing akimbo, they often used to fold the garment and pass it over their shoulder and let it hang down to the ankles through the arm cavities (ibid., Pl. No. 5). At home the *sari* alone was sufficient, for part of it could decently cover the upper body as well. Women used to take a part of their *sari* over their shoulders so as to completely cover the navel and the breasts. Their waistband, for instance, could become visible only if the upper part of the *sari* happened to slip down. This could usually occur either when a woman was beside herself, being confounded or overpowered with terror,[1] or when she was anxious to disclose the charms of her person when bent upon winning over a haughtly sage or an indifferent lover. Normally the upper part of the *sari* covered not only the bust, but it also reached down to the knees. Rājaśekhara is explicit on the point. Dharmaśāstra writers also lay it down that women should be so dressed that their navel should never become visible and legs should be covered down to the ankles.[3]

The sculptural evidence, however, seems to be partly in conflict with the above observations, based mainly on the data of literature. In the early sculptures of the Punjab and the North-Western Frontier Province (*c.* 100 B.C. to c. 300 A. D.) we undoubtedly come across several female statues, whose busts are covered with part of their *saris*, as described in the epics and

1. Compare, for instance, the description of Gopīs given by Bhāsa when they were terrified by Kṛishṇa's fight with Kāliyā serpent:—

संभ्रान्ता गलितोत्तरीयवसनास्त्रस्ताकुलव्याहृताः।

Bālacarit, IV, 1.

2. Compare, for instance, Aśvaghoṣa's description of one of the damsels sent to dissuade prince Siddhartha from renouncing the world:—

मुहुर्मुहुर्मदव्याजस्रस्तंनीलांशुकापरा।
आलक्ष्यरशना रेजे स्फुरद्विद्युरिव क्षपा॥

Buddhacarit, IV. 133.

3. न नाभिं दर्शयेदागुल्फाद्वासः परिदध्यात्। न स्तनौ विवृतौ कुर्यात्॥

Śaṅkhasmṛiti.

classical Sanskrit literature. Such, for instance, is the case with the numerous statues of Hārīti[1]. Māyādevī, seated by her husband's side when listening to the prophesy about her new-born babe, and a beautiful standing Nāgī in human form (Plate V, A) are both shown covering their shoulders and breasts with a part of their *saris.*[2] The same is the case with several female statues at Mathurā[3].

But the sculptures in Central and Southern India and the paintings at Ajanta and Bagh caves have quite a different tale to tell. In the sculptures at Bharhut (*c.* 150 B. C.) the *sari* is generally seen covering the body below the navel; no part of it is taken round the bust so as to cover the breasts and shoulders. (Plate III B). A separate upper garment is often worn by ladies, but it does not at all cover their bosom (Plate III A.). The same is the case with the sculptures at Sanchi and Amaraoti[4] and paintings at Ajanta, which cover the first four or five centuries of the Christian era.

How are we to explain this phenomenon of women appearing without any clothing over their upper person in the sculptures and paintings of Central and Southern India ? Several explanations have been offered in this connection. Cunningham thought that nudity conveyed no sense of indecency in India prior to the advent of the Muslims; so women in sculptures and paintings naturally appear in a nude or semi-nude condition (*Tree and Serpent Worship*, pp. 102-3). This theory, however, ignores the data of the Gandhāra sculptures, where women appear fully dressed, and is in conflict with the evidence of contemporary literature, which makes it quite clear that it was regarded as highly indecorous for a woman to move out without completely covering her upper person. How then are we to explain this apparent conflict between the data of sculptures and the evidence of literature ?

Cunningham did not make proper allowance for the circums-

1. Bachhoffer, *Early Indian Sculpture*, Pl. 150 B; Gründwedel, *Buddhist Art in India*, (Eng. Trans.), fig. 55, p. 104.
2. Hargreave, *The Buddha Story in Stone*, Pl. VIII; Bachhoffer, Pl. 150.
3. Agrawal, *Mathurā kī Bauddhakalā*, Pl. XIV.
4. Cunningham, *The Stupa of Bharhut*, Plates XIII an XXI.

tance that many of the carvings are not now left in the same condition in which they were, when finished by the artists. Havell has pointed out that the exaggerated thinness of the legs in the human figures at Amaraoti makes it clear that the sculptures had their finishing coat of plaster (*Indian Sculpture and Painting*, p. 104)) Late Balasaheb Pantpratinidhi, Rajasaheb of Aundh, who was a distinguished artist and art critic, has adduced further evidence in support of the above theory. He has pointed out that in some bas-reliefs at Amaraoti (e.g. Cunningham, *Tree and Serpent Worship*, Pl. LXIX), ladies are to be seen having the *sari* at the waist and also at the feet rolling in folds. At their back also we see some folds hanging down. But the thighs and legs are bare (Plate VI). Now it is clearly impossible to so wear a *sari* that it should cover the waist and feet, but leave the legs and thighs bare in front. The only possible explanation is the one offered by the Rajasaheb, viz. in order to produce an effect of transparent garment the limbs of the body, such as the thighs etc., were first carved nude and then given the finishing touch of coating and colouring.[1]

It is therefore clear that in Amaraoti sculptures at any rate nudity was not the order of the day; the *saris* were shown partly in carving and partly in plastering and colouring. The upper body therefore may have been covered by that portion of the *sari* which was to be shown in plastering and colouring. In one place in carving also we do actually get the example of a female taking a portion of her *sari* across her bust and over her shoulders, so as to completely cover her bosom.[2] This was the normal dress of the ladies of the age and province.

It must be, however, admitted that this explanation of the dress being shown partly in carving and partly in colouring does not hold good of many schools of sculpture in ancient India. Such is particularly the case with the sculptures at Bharhut and Sanchi in Central India. Here, unlike at Amaraoti, the whole of the *sari* covering the waist, the thighs and the legs is shown in

1. *A. B. O. R. I.*, Vol. III, p. 19.
2. Cunningham, *Tree and Serpent Worship*, Pl. LIX.

carving; the method of its wearing also shows that no part of it was intended to be taken over the shoulders so as to cover the bust (Plate III A and B). It is therefore not possible to argue that the breasts of women in the sculpture at these places were intended to be subsequently covered by a garment that was to be shown partly in plastering and partly in colouring. This process would have been also a costly one, for the sculptures at these places were intended to be exposed to the rain and sunshine throughout the year. Replastering and recolouring would have been frequently necessary, and the monks at these monasteries could not have found it always easy to get generous donors to defray the necessary expenditure. Are we then to conclude from the evidence of the plastic art that the women in central India used to move about with their breasts uncovered in the early centuries of the Christian era ?

Nor can it be argued that the upper person of the women in these sculptures is bare, because the sculptors were not skilful enough to show the same *sari* as covering both the lower and the upper part of the body. They could have avoided this difficulty by using a separate upper garment to cover the bust. As a matter of fact at both these places ladies of position are often seen wearing an upper garment, but it does not cover the breasts[1] (Plate III, A). In the case of the Ajanta paintings at any rate the excuse of inefficiency cannot be advanced. The artists were experts and they could easily have shown their women wearing the *sari* in such a way as to cover both the upper and the lower parts of the body. But they have not done so. It is true that most of the women at Ajanta, whose breasts appear uncovered, are in the privacy of their inner apartments where they may not perhaps be expected to wear their full dress. But in some Ajanta frescoes we find women moving about even in public streets, with the same insufficient dress. In one scene, for instance, we see a queen moving in a procession in the state carriage along with her husband; she is, however, shown as wearing neither a jacket

1. Cunningham, *The Stupa of Bharhut*, Pls XIII, XXI.

nor a bodice, nor is her *sari* covering her breasts (Herigham, (*Ajanta*, Pl. XXIV).

Shrimant Balasaheb Pantpratinidhi, the late Rajasaheb of Aundh, suggested that we can account for this insufficient dress of women at Elora and Ajanta on the assumption that the artists were Dravidian in culture.[1] He points out that even to-day very few women in Kochin and Malbar wear any upper cloth. So Dravidian artists have shown their women folk as wearing just the dress that was current in Dravidian society. The Rajasaheb held that the artists at Bharhut and Sanchi, on the other hand, were following the Aryan tradition, and so have shown their women as wearing an upper garment which covers the breasts and falls over the left shoulder.[2]

This theory also is not free from difficulties. It may be at the outset pointed out that the distinction sought to be drawn between the so-called Dravidian artists at Ajanta and Elora and the so-called Aryan artists at Bharhut and Sanchi is not supported by actual data; for the artists of the latter places are as indifferent in covering the breasts of their women as those at the former[3] (Pl. III B). Sometimes they show their ladies wearing an upper garment, but it is so worn as not to cover the breasts at all[4] (Pl. III, A).

It is further very doubtful whether all Dravidian women were actually accustomed to move about without covering their breasts. It is true that till quite recently women in Malabar used to regard a bodice or an upper garment as not very necessary. But the Malbar practice was probably a primitive one and cannot be regarded as typically Dravidian. At any rate the ladies in Tamil and Telugu provinces were not accustomed to move about without properly covering their upper person. In this connection the *Saptaśati* of Hāla, which undoubtedly reflects the Dravidian life during the early centuries of Christian era, supplies conclusive

1. B. S. Pantpratinidhi, *Elora*, p. 100.
2. *Ibid*, p. 97.
3. *The Stupa of Bharhut*, Pl. XXII. 3; XXIII. 3.
4. *Ibid.*, Pls IXIII & XX.

evidence. Three verses in this anthology make it quite clear that Dravidian women used to cover their breasts with adequate clothing.[1] The first of these clearly refers to the breasts being covered by the upper garment. The anthology further shows that Dravidian women not only used to cover their upper person with a part of their *sari* or by a separate shawl, but that they also wore a bodice or *Kanchukī*. Its ends were tied together between the breasts,[2] and it was not entirely removed even in the privacy of the bed-room.[3] It is not therefore possible to argue that the women at Elora and Ajanta do not cover their breasts because they are the representatives of Dravidian culture. The *Saptaśati* shows clearly that the Dravidian ladies in contemporary times used to cover their upper person with a bodice and an upper garment; the so-called Aryan artists at Sanchi and Bharhut are as careless about covering the breasts of their women as are so-called Dravidian fellow workers at Elora and Ajanta.

The real explanation of women appearing without covering their busts properly in the sculptures and paintings of Southern and Central India seems to be the artistic convention of the age. Breasts are the most significant symbol of motherhood and the artists of these provinces probably felt that they may be shown uncovered in works of art, though they may be normally concealed in actual life under a bodice or a part of the *sari*. This convention facilitated the task of fully exhibiting the beauty of the female form without suggesting any indecency. It also gave

1. रक्तदुकूलान्तरितः स्तननखलेख इव नववध्वाः।
VI, 69.
बलादाकृष्टवस्त्रार्धान्तप्रस्थिते मंथरं त्वं व्रज।
II, 62.
नीलपटप्रावृतांगीति मा खल्वेनां त्वं परिहर।
VI, 20.
Sanskrit renderings of the Prakrit verses is being quoted here.

2. द्व्यंगुलकपाटपिनद्धसविशेषनीलकञ्चुलिका।
दर्शयति स्तनस्थलवर्णिकामिव तरुणीं युवजनेभ्यः॥
VII, 20.

3. ग्रामतरुण्यो हृदयं हरन्ति विदग्धानां स्तनभारवत्यः।
मदने कुसुम्भरागयुक्तकञ्चुकाभरणभ्रान्ताः॥
VI, 45.

the artists an opportunity to show the different beautiful ornaments worn on the chest, the neck and the shoulder (Pl. I). This would become quite clear from several statues like those of Indrāṇī and Nārasimhī discovered at the Sutna residency, and now exhibited in the Indian Museum, Calcutta. In the case of these images the lower and upper rims of their shawls can be clearly seen at the elbow and shoulder respectively. But the intervening space as well as the entire bust are shown altogether uncovered by the shawl, obviously with a view to display the ornaments worn at the neck, the chest and the shoulder. There was nothing unusual in this procedure, for the art convention everywhere prescribes a much scantier dress for women than is actually used by them in normal life. This will be quite evident to all the students of ancient and modern sculptures and paintings of European countries. Just as we cannot conlcude that women in modern Europe move about in a nude condition in society because they appear entirely uncovered in some works of art, so also we cannot maintain that women in ancient India moved about in public without covering their upper person, because their breasts are shown uncovered in sculptures and paintings of Central and Southern India. The fact is that the dress in sculptures and paintings is not always a faithful copy of the dress actually in vogue in everyday life. The non-recognition of this truth will lead to strange deductions. We shall have to conclude that the Buddha allowed a much ampler dress to the nuns of his Order than was ever worn by ladies of fashion. The former were allowed to have three pieces of cloth, while the latter in sculptures are seen to be wearing only one or two. We shall have to admit that maid-servants used to wear richer dresses than the princesses they served; for at Ajanta the former are seen wearing gaudy and striped bodices which are never seen on the bodies of the latter. We cannot therefore ignore the conclusive evidence supplied by contemporary literature and conclude that women were not properly covering their breasts and busts in ancient India either by a bodice or by a portion of their *sari*. The standard of decorum universally accepted in Dharmaśāstra and in literature required a woman not only to wear a bodice, but also to cover her bust with an upper garment.

To conclude, the artists of Central and Southern India held that the unfolding of the beauty of the female form by showing the bust uncovered in a work of art need not and should not give rise to any indecent thoughts, if the woman concerned were a lady of virtuous character. To the spectator she would strike as a mother. If, however, she was a dancing or singing girl, there would not be this sacred atmosphere round her. The artist, therefore, felt that she should not be shown displaying the charms of her uncovered bust. As a consequence we usually find dancing girls appearing with a full dress covering their entire person from their necks to ankles. They are seen covering their breast with jackets, blouses or frocks. This would become quite clear from the dancing scenes at Bharhut, Bagh caves and Sarnath.[1]

There are different fashions of wearing the *sari* current at present in different parts of India. The same was the case in the past. At present women of the higher classes of the Deccan wear the *sari* in the *sakachchha* fashion, i.e. by passing a part of it in between their legs and tucking it up behind at the waist. In Gujarat, Bengal and Uttara Pradesh, on the other hand, the *sari* is worn in the *vikachchha* fashion, i.e. round the legs without any portion of it being tucked up behind.

The women of the Gangetic plain were, generally speaking, following the *vikachchha* fashion which is still current there. This is made quite clear from the Didarganj statue of the *chauri*-bearer from Bihar (Plate II) and the statue of Hārīti from Mathura in U.P.[2] That the same fashion continued to be in vogue in U. P., Bihar, Bengal and Orissa throughout the ancient and medieval period is made quite clear by numerous statues of Tārā, Māyā, Mahishāsuramardinī, female attendants on Vishṇu figures etc. that have been discovered in these provinces and are now

1. Cunningham, *Bharhut*, Pl. XV M Pl. E; Sahani, *Catalogue of the Museum of Archaeology of Sarnath*, Pl. XXIII, A.
2. Vogel, *La Sculpture*, Pls. XI. XII.

preserved in the Indian Museum, Calcutta.

The present Maharashtrian fashion of wearing the *sari* may be seen obtaining in the Punjab and North-Western Frontier Province during the early centuries of the Christian era. A statue of goddess Hārīti in the Peshawer Museum executed by a Gandhāra artist shows the *sari* worn in the *sakachchha* fashion; its upper end is passed over the left shoulder and let down hanging from the right, as is done at present by the Maharashtrian ladies.[1] The same is the case with a goddess appearing on a coin of king Azilises ruling over the Punjab in the 1st century B.C.,[2] and with numerous female figures from the same province now preserved in the Indian Museum, Calcutta. The statue of a Nāgī[3] in human form is remarkable in this respe ct (Plate V, A).

In Maharashtra itself we find quite unexpectedly the *vikachchha* fashion of the Gangetic plain prevailing down to the 7th or 8th century A. D. This is rather strange, but the evidence of sculpture is quite convincing on the point. In most of the Ajanta frescoes we find both ladies and maid-servants usually wearing their *saris* without a *kachchha*.[4] The same is the case with ladies sculptured at Nagarjunikonda in Telugu country; it is only maid-servants who occasionally appear there with a *sakachcha sari*.[1] It is after about 900 A.D. that we begin to get images of goddesses in the Deccan wearing the *sari* in the *sakchchha* fashion. We may, therefore, presume that this fashion became popular in the Deccan at about the end of the first millennium of the Christian era. It was, however, adopted only by the ladies of the upper classes; women of lower classes still continue to adhere to the old *vikachchha* fashion.

The Deccan ladies seem to have borrowed this fashion from their sisters in Mālwā and Central India. The sculptures at Sanchi and Bharhut show that the *sakachchha* fashion was the order of the day in this part of India since early times. This becomes

1. *Handbook to the Sculptures in the Peshawer Museum*, Pl. VII, p. 334.
2. *Catalogue of the Coins in the Punjab Museum*, Vol. I, Pl. XIII.
3. Bachhoffer, Pl. 130 left.
4. Heringham, *Ajanta*, Pls. IIa, X, XI, XIV, XVIII.
5. *A. S. I. A. R.*, 1930-34, Pls. 39 and 40.

clear beyond all doubt from some of the bas-reliefs, where the back of women is visible, showing clearly the *kachchha* tucked up behind at the waist.[2] (Plate VII). This central Indian fashion eventually spread to the Deccan. It had penetrated to South Bihar also in the 2nd century B.C., as would appear from the sculptures found at Bodhagaya (*Ars Asiatica*, XVI, Pls. VI, XI, XIV, etc). It did not, however, appeal to the ladies in Gujrat and Northern Bihar, who continue to wear their *saris* in the old *vikachchha* fashion. In Maharashtra too the *sakachchha* fashion was adopted only by the upper classes; women of the lower classes still continue to adhere to the old *vikachchha* style

The poet Rājaśekhara supplies some further details about the way in which the ladies of different provinces used to dress themselves in the 10th century A.D. In Bengal the upper part of the *sari* was taken over the head so as to cover the coiffure. In Uther Pradesha the upper garment or the upper part of the *sari* was wound round the bust and used to reach down to the knees. In Malbar the *sari* hung down from high above the navel, its knot being tied under the armpit. It is not very clear how exactly this was done.[2] In ancient times, as in modern days, the fashion of the provincial capitals had a great influence in determining the toilet, the coiffure and the fashion of the dress of the women in the interior.[3]

Let us now ascertain the role which stitched clothes played

1. Cunnigham, *Bharhut*, Pls. VIII, XIII, XLV 3; *Tree and Serpent Worship* Pls. XXV 2, XXXVII 2.

2. See *Kāvyamīmānsā*, pp. 8 and 9. Cf.

सीमन्तचुम्बिसिचयः स्फुटबाहुमूलः।(वेषः) for Bengal;

आश्रोणिगुल्फपरिमण्डलितोत्तरीयं वेषं नमस्यत महोदयसुन्दरीणाम्। for U. P;

कक्षानिवेशनिबिडीकृतनीविरेष वेशश्चिरं जयति केरलकामिनीनाम्॥

for Malbar.

3. यो मार्गः परिधानकर्मणि गिरां या सूक्तिमुद्राक्रमे।
भंगिर्या कबरीचयेषु रचनं यद्भूषणालीषु च।
दृष्टं सुन्दरि कान्यकुब्जललनालोकैरिहान्यच्च यत्
शिक्षन्ते सकलासु दिक्षु तरसा तत्कौतुकिन्यः स्त्रियः॥

Bālarāmāyaṇa, X.

in the dress of women. There is one view which holds that the art of sewing was unknown to the Hindus before the advent of the Muslims. It is, however, altogether untenable. The needle and the process of sewing are both referred to as early as in the Ṛig Veda;[1] there is a passage in the *Aitareya Brāhmaṇa* which clearly refers to two pieces of cloths being joined together by the needle.[2] The Buddha had forbidden monks to do sewing work for nuns.[3] The *Amarakoṣha* expressly mentions the tailor[4] and the Chinese pilgrim I-tsing informs us that shirts and trousers were quite common in Kashmir and the Punjab during the 7th century A.D., though they were not in vogue in the plains.[5] The fact is that in the hot plains of northern India stitched clothes are very inconvenient, and so for the greater part of the year both men and women could go on without them. That seems to be the reason why they are so rarely referred to in literature.

We may discuss here the controversial question as to whether stitched clothes were in vogue in the Vedic age. In the Indo-Iranian times the Aryans were undoubtedly living in a cold climate, where stitched clothes would have been welcome; but then they had not probably sufficiently advanced in civilization to begin their use. The Ṛig Veda refers to Varuṇa as wearing a *drāpi* while sitting in his heavenly court (I, 26, 13). But whether this was a mantle or an overcoat we do not know. In the marriage hymn the bride is described as wearing a *śāmulyam* on her wedding night, which was discarded the next morning. This may have been the *sari* rather than a short. According to the *Kātyāyana Śrauta Sūtra* (p. 866, Weber's edition) the wife of the sacrificer was given a *chaṇḍātaka* or *dahara* to wear, when she had to ascend by a very high step to the top of the sacrificial pillar.

1. सीव्यत्वपः सूच्या अच्छिद्यमानया। II, 32, 4.

2. यथा सूच्या वासः संदधीयात्। एवमेवैताभिर्यज्ञस्य च्छिद्रं संदधेत्। III, 18.

3. यो पन भिक्खू अञ्ञातिकाय भिक्खुनिय चीवरं सिब्बेय सिब्बापेय्य वा पाचित्तियंति। p. 86.

4. II, 10, 6.

5. I-tsing, P. 68.

While doing so, the thighs were likely to be exposed if there was no underwear, as the *sari* was very probably used in the *vikachchha* fashion. So a *chaṇḍātaka*, which has been expressly described as a short by the commentator,[1] would have been very desirable. The original Vedic passages, where this ceremony is described, do not, however, refer to any *chaṇḍātaka* being worn by the wife on the occasion; the word is also not known to Pāṇini, Patañjali and Amara. Kātyāyana is therefore probably referring to an innovation of his age, when he refers to the short or *chanḍātaka*, being worn by the wife on the occasion. In the Vedic age very probably only a *dahara* or *kaupīna*, that is a strip of cloth to be worn on a girdle in between the legs, was used on the occasion. Though, therefore, sewing was known in the Vedic age, as is made clear by references quoted above, there is no evidence of stitched clothes having come into general vogue at the time.

The help of the art of sewing seems to have been first taken for preparing the bodice. This took place even before 600 B.C., for Buddhist and Jain nuns are enjoined to use it. Its traces can be seen below the breasts of the statue of Chaṇḍā Yakshiṇī at Bharhut (*Cunningham*, Pl. XXII, fig.3). If the bodice is not shown on the other female statues of the peace, the desire to show off the ornaments on breast may have been the obvious reason. The bodice did not require much tailoring like the modern blouse. It had short sleeves but no buttons, and it was secured in its proper place by its ends being tied together in between the two breasts.[2] On one of the coins of Samudragupta, Lakshmī can be seen wearing the bodice precisely in this way. We can see both the knot and the two ends hanging down in its continuation. (See Pl. V, B). From Kālidāsa, however, we learn that sometimes the ends of the bodice were tied in a knot on the shoulder;[3]

1. अर्धोरुकं विलासिन्या वासश्चण्डातकं विदुः।

2. Cf. Mahāvśnetā's descrition.

स्तनयुगुलनिबद्धग्रंथिना कल्पतरुलतावल्कलेन कृतोत्तरीयाम्।

Kādambari, p. 248.

3. इदमुपहितसूक्ष्मग्रंथिना स्कन्धदेशे स्तनयुगपरिणाहाच्छादिना वल्कलेन।

Śākuntala I, 19.

what was the make up of this type of bodice and how it was tied on the shoulder is rather difficult to understand. The bodice required very little tailoring and women used to stitch it at home. It could be easily taken out, if necessary, to protect onself against the lunar or solar rays (*Śriṅgāraśataka*, 17). A narrow breast band was also used across the bosom in the Deccan and Ceylon. This fashion did not spread to northern India.[1]

Jackets, blouses and frocks seem to have come into vogue in the plains of northern India, when they were included in the dominions of the Scythians, the Kushaṇas and other Central Asian invaders. As these conquerors hailed from a very cold region, they were accustomed to wear shirts, trousers and overcoats. This is quite clear from the evidence of their coinage. Kushāṇa kings like Kanishka and Huvishka are invariably seen wearing a trouser and an overcoat on their coins.[2] In the Mathura and Gandhāra sculptures, which belong to the period of Kushāṇa supremacy (*c*. 50. A.D. to *c*. 300 A.D.), women begin to appear in blouses and frocks. In one bas-relief at Mathura even *Sapta Mātṛikās* are seen wearing frocks.[3] In Ganddhāra sculptures, which mostly hail from the N. W. F. Province, blouses and jackets are fairly common. In one place we find Hārīti wearing a blouse of long sleeves[4]. A Nāgiṇī in human form is also seen doing the same (See Pl. V. A). In another sculpture, Māyādevī is shown wearing a frock over her *sari*.[5] On one of the coins of the Scythian ruler Azilises even goddess Lakshmī standing on a lotus is represented as wearing a blouse and a trouser[6].

Uttara Pradesh, Central India, Gujarat and Maharashtra were under Scythian rule for different periods during the first four centuries of the Christian era. This circumstance

1. Smith, *History of Fine Arts in India and Ceylon*, Pl. LVII, Gopinath Rao, *Hindu Iconography*, I, ii, Pl. 99.
2. In the early period of their coinage Gupta kings also are seen wearing this foreign dress; it took a few decades for them to discard it in favour of the national Hindu dress.
3. Agarwal, *Mathurā kī Buddhakalā*, Pl. 21.
4. Bachhoffer, Pl. 150. B
5. Indian Museum, Calcutta; Gandhār gallery exhibit No. 13.
6. *Punjab Museum Coin Catalogue*, Vol. I, Pl. XIII, No. 332.

very probably facilitated the spread of the fashion of stitched clothes in Hindu society. The tendency to imitate the dress of the rulers is not peculiar to the modern times. It existed in the past as well.

Society, however, had a general prejudice against stitched clothes, and women were for a long time reluctant to take to jackets, blouses and frocks. We find only dancing girls adopting the new fashion in dress in the beginning. This would become quite clear from the fact that it is only women of this class, and not ladies of rank, who are seen wearing jacket and blouses at Bharhut, Bagh and Sarnath. At Ajanta we sometimes find maid-servants wearing shorts and jackets; ladies of position, however, are still seen avoiding their use. It is quite possible that greater stitching was introduced in the bodice (*kañchukī*) at this time, but the prejudice against full fledged jackets, blouses and frocks remained unabated. These became common among a section of ladies only in the Muslim period. They continued to be regarded as a foreign innovation, and women in orthodox families engaged in religious duties used to remove them for the time being.

We may passingly refer here to the dress of the Buddhist nuns. They were permitted the three pieces of cloth allowed to the monks, *samghāṭī*' (for the lower part), *antarvāsaka* (for the upper part), and *uttarāsaṅga*, (the covering garment). *Kañchuki* or bodice was also prescribed especially for the young nuns. Jainism permitted a larger number of clothes to its nuns, especially by way of shorts and underwares.

The kind of cloth used by women for their dress differed with their status. Maidens and women in coverture used to wear gay and embroidered cloth. The ladies of the 4th and 5th centuries A.D. used to prefer dotted, striped gauzy and embroidered muslims for their bodices. This is quite clear from several paintings at Ajanta.[1]

Widows do not appear to have used any bodices. The colour of their *saris* was plain white in the early period. The widowed

1. Smith, *A History of Fine Arts*, p. 288, fig. 207.

daughters-in-law of Dhṛitarāshṭra are described as wearing white garments, when they went to see their old father-in-law in the forest.[1] The orthodox practice of Deccan widows to wear reddish *saris* seems to be due to the influence of the colour of the garments of Buddhist nuns. The Gujarat practice of giving black garments to the widow seems also to be a post-epic development. Like the poeple in the west Gujaratis held that black was the proper colour for a person in mourning and therefore for the dress of the widow, who was to be in a perpetual mourning. In Bengal and northern India, however, the old custom continues and widows still wear white plain *saris* without any borders.

The *lahaṅgā*, which is so common in Rajputana and northern India at present, was altogether unknown for a long time. We meet it for the first time in some rare Mathura sculptures of the 2nd century A.D., where only maid servants or milkwomen are seen using it.[2] It became popular in higher society only in medieval times after the establishment of the Mahomaden rule. It is not referred to in literature, nor seen in paintings and sculptures of the Hindu period. It however became quite common after a few centuries of Muslim rule. In northern India it even became an indispensable constituent of the traditional bridal dress. In south India the Muslim influence was less felt and so the *lahaṅgā* or *parakara* became common only among small girls. Grown up women did not take to it.

The paintings of the Mogul period give a fairly accurate idea of the dress of Hindu women, who had come under the influence of the new fashions brought into vogue with the advent of the Muslim rule. These ladies used to wear a *lahaṅgā* or *pyjamā* down from their waist. The former was sewn in different artistic designs, and nothing was usually worn over it. The *pyjamā*, however, was a simple one, and usually a short *sari* was worn over it. The bust was covered by a bodice or a jacket. An upper garment or *oḍhṇī* was also in vogue; it hung down from the head covering a

1. शुक्लोत्तरीया नरराजपत्न्यः !

Mbh. XV, 27. 16.

2. Motichandra—*Bharatiya Veshabhushā*, p. 125.

portion of the back. In rural areas and orthodox circles the old dress continued to be current.

Women are naturally more conservative than men, and so the British domination for 150 years did not effect any revolution in their dress. They continue to use their old dress consisting of a *sari*, a bodice and a shawl, even when their husbands have begun to don suits, neckties and collars. The bodice, however, is becoming more and more artistic and fashionable. Shorts and frocks have become common among girls in urban areas, but there are yet no indications that grown up ladies would take to them large numbers. With increasing facilities in communications women are in a better position to observe the dress prevailing in neighbouring States, and there is a tendency among educated and fashionable ladies to borrow some fashions current in other parts of the country. Thus the *vikachchha* mode of wearing *sari* is now becoming common among the fashionable ladies in the urban areas of the Deccan. The dress of the average Hindu women, however, still continues to be the old traditional one of her province. The *lahaṅgā* is the only exception. The main reason for this conservatism is the fact that the traditional dress is on the whole well suited for the climate of the country.

Ornaments

The reader must have seen that on the whole the dress of Hindu women was simple. Simplicity, however, did not characterise their tastes in the realm of ornaments. Since very early times they have been fond of wearing very brilliant and artistic ornaments in quantities that cannot be described as meagre. Men, however, are to a large extent responsible for the development of this taste among women; for a reader of the Vedic literature or a student of ancient sculptures and paintings will find it difficult to decide as to who was fonder of ornaments, men or women. Men used to vie with women in the number of ornaments to be worn on their person. They seem to have lagged behind them only in the case of the ornaments on the forehead, which were generally used by women alone. This fondness for ornaments was to some extent a natural consequence of the general prosperous condition of our motherland in these days.

In the Vedic age bangles were worn both on hands and feet by men and women.[1] Their number was probably a large one; whether they reached right up to the elbow or the knee, as they did in the case of one figurine discovered at Mohenjo Daro[2] and in numerous images and sculptures of the ancient and medieval period, we do not know. Rings were used on fingers. Shoulders were not neglected; they had their own ornaments, which must obviously have been large in size.[3] Necklaces of gold and precious stones were used on the neck; they used to reach down to the chest.[4] Earings (*karṇaśobhana*) are also referred to.[5] An ornament called *kumbha* was worn on the head; we do not know its precise size or nature.[6]

Gold, silver and precious stones were the chief material for these ornaments. Pearls are referred to in one passage in a very late Brhamaṇa work.[7] The Aryans could have become familiar with them only when they reached the sea in course of time. It is intersting to note that glass bangles are not referred to in Sanskrit literature before *c.* 1,000 A.D.[8]

Sculptures, paintings and the *Nāṭyaśāstra* of Bharata throw a flood of light on the nature and number of different ornaments used by our women in the early centuries of the Christian era. It is not at all possible to describe them in detail in words. One can get an adequate idea of them only from their representations in sculptures and paintings. More than half a dozen different ornaments, partly made of gold and partly of pearls,

1. *R. V.*, *V.* 54, 11; I, 1168, 3.
2. Kramrisch, *Indian Sculpture*, pl. I, 4.
3. अंसेष्वा वः पप्रथेषु खादयः।

   R. V., I, 166, 9.
4. *R. V.*, V, 54, 11; I, 122, 14.
5. *Ibid.*
6. कुरीरमस्य शीर्षणि कुम्भ चाधिनिदध्मसि।

   A. V., VI, 138, 3.
7. *Shaḍvimśa Brāhmaṇa*, V, 6.
8. They are mentioned by Someśvara in his *Surathobsava* cf,

   का च काचवलयावलिशब्दैराजुहाव हृदयं दयितास्य।

and variously described as *śikhāpāśa*, *śikhājāla*, *muktājāla*, etc., were used to adorn the head and the forehead. One can get an adequate idea of their nature and gracefulness only by studying them in Ajanta paintings. The designs of earings were very graceful. The variety in the nature of necklaces of gold and pearls is indeed striking. The *Nāṭyaśāstra* refers to four types of zones (XXIII, 27); but sculptures prove beyond any doubt that the old sage Bharata was not up-to-date in his knowledge on the point. A gauzy pearl ornament was used over the breasts. Bharata refers to an ornament to be worn over thighs called *pādapatra* (XXIII, 141); it seems to have been made of pearls, as may be gathered from a painting of Māyādevī in Cave No. 2 at Ajanta.[1] This ornament seems to have now gone out of fashion. Shoulders were adorned with *keyūras*, of which there were several types. Nor was the portion just above the elbow neglected. The number of bangles worn on the hand was very large; in Bengal they were often joined together so as to form a composite ornament reaching almost to the elbow.[2] The fashion at Ajanta, however, prescribed only a few bangles for the hand. They were often set with pearls or diamonds. The number of bangles worn on the feet was a large one; some of them used to produce a gingling sound, when their wearers were in motion.

The fashions of dressing the hair were as numerous as graceful. An examination of the paintings at Ajanta will be an eye-opener even to the most fashionable ladies of the present generation. These fashion can be better seen in the original than described in words. It is customary at present to talk of Orissa as a backward province. The fashions of hair dressing current there twelve hundred years ago were, however, so varied and graceful, that even the most fashionable cinema stars of Bombay and Calcutta may immensely add to their popularity by imitating some of them. Six of these fashions have been illustrated on the accompanying plate (See Pl. VIII), which has been prepared with the help of some of the woodcuts published by the late Dr. Rajendralal

1. Yazdani, *Ajanta*, part II, Pl. XX.
2. Bhattasali, *Iconography*, Plates XIX, XX.

Mittra in his *Indo-Aryans*, Vol. I. A glance at the plate will show that the beauties of Orissa were not content with the quantity of hair, which nature had given to them; they used to add some padding or stuffing or false or borrowed hair to increase its mass, so as to render the different hair-arrangements possible. Some ladies used to arrange the hair in gradually receding tiers (See Pl. VIII, A), some used to turn them up in a fantastic cone, curling and twisting upwards behind the head and kept in its position, probably by means of a wire concealed (See Pl. VIII, B). Some used to arrange them in two artistic bundles hanging on either side of the head (See Pl. VIII, C), while others used to add a third one perched just at the top of their crown (See Pl. VIII, D). Pearl strings were liberally used to help the hair to retain its new shape and configuration (See Pl. VIII, A, B, C, D, E). But perhaps the most interesting fashion is the one illustrated by Pl. VIII, F. Here we find the hair arranged into six braids and then twisted up into six rays, kept into an erect position either by means of wax, or with the help of sticks or wires enclosed within. The Mathura fashions two thousand years ago were equally interesting. Some ladies arranged the hair in two tiers separated by flower gardens (Pl. IX), others beautified them by tassels, hanging down beautifully (Pl. X) Pl. XI shows a simple but artistic knot of the hair beautified by flower wreaths and gold plaques.

Ointments were used not only for the eyes but also for the lips and teeth.[1] Sandal paste and saffron powder were used for the face and the breasts. Different types of dyes and ointments were used for decorating hands, feet, fingers and toes. Ornamental linear figures were drawn on cheeks and breasts to heighten their charms. A streak of Sindhūra on the head or a circular mark of Kumkuma on the forehead was made by maidens and women in coverture. This was regarded as an indispensable sign of *saubhāgya* or married bliss. Inscriptions often describe how valorous kings used to kill their opponents and deprive their

1. नेत्रयोरञ्जनं कार्यमधरस्य च रञ्जनम् ।
दन्तानां विविधा रागाश्चतुर्णां शुक्लता तथा ॥ *Nāṭyaśāstra*, 23, 20.

wives of the use of Sindhūra.[1] Women were leading a simple ascetic life during their widowhood. The use of ornaments or embroidered clothes was therefore out of question for them. While describing the achievements of their heroes, the authors of inscriptions often state how the bracelets of the wives of their enemies dropped off along with their necklaces.

It is interesting to point out here that among the numerous ornaments described by poets and illustrated by sculptors and painters, the nose-ring and toe-ring are conspicuous by their absence. This is rather surprising, because both of them are at present regarded as indispensable for a woman with her husband living. The omission of the toe-ring may have been accidental, as it is otherwise not a very prominent or valuable ornament. But the case of the nose-ring is quite different. It is a very important ornament. It is in use in all provinces at present. It is regarded as a sign of *saubhāgya* or married bliss. Till recently every bride used to get it at the time of her marriage. Women of the old fashion would never go out without wearing it. And yet we find that Bharata does not mention it in his exhaustive list of the ornaments of women given by him in the 23rd chapter of his *Nāṭyaśāstra*. Ornaments for almost every limb are to be found in this list, but there is no mention of the nose-ring for the nose. This is also true of the list of ornaments given in the *Amarakosha* also. Sanskrit poets and dramatists also show no acquaintance with the ornament. In fact there is no word in Sanskrit language to denote it. Words for the ornament in modern vernaculars cannot be derived from any Sanskrit original. The word *vesara* used for the ornament by a section of Hindi-speaking population is of unknown origin. The word *vāḷi* used by the Gujaratis is of a secondary origin; it originally denotes a *valaya* or circular ornament, and is secondarily used to denote the nose-ring because of its roundish shape. The words *natha*, *nathia*

1. यस्यानने शरदखण्डशशिप्रसन्ने कोपं व्यनक्ति हृदयस्थमरिप्रियाणाम्।
सिन्दूरभूषणविवर्जितमास्यपद्ममुत्सृष्टहारवलयं कुचमण्डलञ्च ॥
Khajuraho Inscription, 953 A. D., *E. L.*; I, p. 129

nathni, *naththā*, *nathnag*, etc., which are used to denote the ornament in different vernaculars of India, are all derived from the Prakrit word *natthā*, which denotes the string passed through the nose of an animal in order to control it with ease. It does not denote any nose ornament at all in any Prakrit or Apabhramśa language. It has no prototype of its own in Sanskrit.

At Udayagiri and Bhuvanesvara in Orissa, at Bodhagaya and Patna in Bihar, at Bharhut and Sanchi in Central India, at Mathura in U. P., at Taxila in the Punjab, at Ajanta, Elora and Badami in the Deccan, at Amaravati in Madras presidency, we have found several sculptures and paintings of women who are over-loaded with a rich variety of ornaments all over their body. The nose-ring is, however, nowhere to be seen (See Pls. III, and IV). These sculptures and paintings are spread over almost all the centuries of the first millennium of the Christian era. It is therefore clear that the nose-ring was unknown throughout the whole of India during the entire Hindu period. Hindu sculptures of Puri and Rajputana of the post-Muslim period and mural paintings in the Padmanābhasvāmi temple at Trivendrum of the 14th century begin to show the nose-ring from the 13th century. Both the positive and the negative evidence thus shows that the nosering is not a Hindu ornament. It seems to have been clearly borrowed from the Mahomadens. It is indeed a mystery how this ornament of foreign origin should have come to be regarded as the most important insignia of *saubhāgya*.

The above conclusion, however, is not accepted by some scholars[1], who point out how the nose-ring is clearly referred to in several poems (*stotras*) of the great Śaṅkarāchārya, who cannot be placed later than *c.* 800 A. D. It cannot be denied that Śaṅkarāchārya clearly refers to this ornament in the *Saundarya-laharī*, V. 61; *Yamunāshṭaka*, V. 7; *Tripurasundarīmānasapūjā*, V. 45 and *Devīchatushṭayopachārastotra*, V. 20. We give below in the foot-

1. E. g. Dasgupta, *Calcutta Review*, May, 1937.

note the first two of the above verses.[1] It may be observed in reply that a very large number of poems (*stotras*) have been popularly ascribed to the great Śankarāchārya, but his authorship of all of them is by no means certain. The above poems may have been composed by a late medieval writer, and been later ascribed to Śaṅkarāchārya. Of it may be that the nose-ring had become current in Malbar by the 8th century, the practice being adopted from that of the Arabs, with whom the Malabaris came into fairly close contact from the 7th century owing to their maritime activity. Arabs probably borrowed the ornament from the Hebrews, as it is mentioned in the old Testament.[2]

The modern economist may perhaps regret that so much money should have been locked up in the unremunerative investment in ornaments. It is, however, to be noted that there were not many safe and productive sources of investment in the past. It may be further pointed out that from the purely woman's point of view, the habit of investing a large part of family saving in ornaments was a desirable development. For a long time women were denied the right to have a share in the immoveable property of the family, as shown already in Chapter VIII (*ante* pp. 267-8). As far as the moveables like ornaments and jewelry were concerned, they were allowed to have a complete sway over them. Ornaments worn by a woman during coverture, and intended really for her alone, constituted her Strīdhana, and could not be taken away from her by coparceners.[3] The more the amount invested in the ornaments, the stronger therefore became the economic position of the wife. The hardships of a

1. असौ नासावंशस्तुहिनगिरिवंशध्वजपरि
त्वदीयो नेदीयः फलतु फलमस्माकमुचितम्।
वहन्नतर्मुक्ताः शिशिरतरनिश्वासघटितम्
समृद्धयापस्तासां बहिरपि च मुक्तामणिधरः ॥ सौन्दर्यलहरी, ६
करिवरमौक्तिकनासिकभूषणवातचमत्कृतचंचलिकके। यमुनाष्टक, ७

2. *New Indian Antiquary*, 1943-3, p. 25.

3. पत्यौ जीवति यः स्त्रीभिरलङ्कारो धृतो भवेत्।
न तं भजेरन्दायादा भजमानाः पतन्ति ते ॥

Manu, IX, 200.

scheme of inheritance under which the widow was for a long time not recognised as an heir to her husband's immoveable property, were considerably neutralised by this habit of investing a large part of the family savings in ornaments. Ornaments in fact were in the past what an insurance policy is in modern days. The large amounts invested in them have enabled thousands of Hindu women to tide over difficult times.

We have now finished our general survey of the dress and ornaments of Hindu women. To some extent it will be also helpful in understanding the general position of women in society. Nature has endowed women with a more artistic and aesthetic temperament than men. All over the world they therefore generally take immense interest in personal decoration by wearing attractive dress and fine ornaments. Hindu society had recognised this fact and given full latitude to women in this respect. Hindu women had never any ground to complain that their natural tastes and inclinations in the sphere of dress and ornaments were thwarted by an insufficient provision in the family budget. The atmosphere in society was such that the Hindu wife could generally carry out most of her plans about the purchase of ornaments and jewelry, even if her husband were somewhat lukewarm in the matter. The theory of her perpetual tutelage, which we shall discuss in detail in the next chapter, did not stand in her way in this matter.

CHAPTER XI.

GENERAL ATTITUDE TOWARDS WOMEN

In the course of the last ten chapters, we have surveyed different sides and activities of women's life. We are now in a position to ascertain and understand the general attitude of Hindu society towards the fair sex. The problem is, however, a complicated one. We have seen already that the general position and status of women were changing from age to age, and so naturally the attitude of society towards them could not remain the same in different periods. We have therefore to note and account for the vicissitudes in the attitude of society. A further difficulty of a more serious type arises from the nature of the data on which we have to rely. In the same century and in the same province, we sometimes come across diametrically opposite views about the worth, nature and importance of women. One school is seen declaring that the woman is the highest gift of God to man, while the other is seen asserting that the best way to reach God is to avoid woman. It is not an easy task to determine which of these contending views represented the opinion of the community. And we cannot exclude the possibility of the views of the average man not being adequately expressed in the din of this wordy warfare between the extremists of the opposite camps.

Perhaps one of the best ways to ascertain the attitude of society in this matter would be to find out its angle of vision towards women overtaken by the misfortune of falling in the hands of ruffians or enemies. Such a situation is the real touch stone to test the genuineness of society's sympathy towards the weaker sex; it enables us to find out how far man is prepared to rise above the prejudices of his sex and judge the woman by an equitable standard. The present attitude of Hindu society in this matter is very stiff and unsympathetic; if a woman has the misfortune of falling into captivity even for a short time, she finds it impossible to get readmission into her family and society. In this respect we are following the example of Śrī-Rāmachandra, who refused to accept back Sītādevī after the overthrow of Rāvaṇa. He informed her that all his efforts to kill Rāvaṇa were only for the purpose of avenging the wrong done to him; he had no idea whatsoever of accepting back a wife, who had stayed so long in the house of the enemy.[1] Sītā points out in reply that being in captivity, she was no longer the master of her person; she could command only her mind and that was always faithful to her husband.[2] This explanation did not satisfy Śrī-Rāma; he accepted Śītā only when a superhuman agency vouchsafed her continuous chastity.

A critical student of the *Rāmāyaṇa*, however, finds it difficult to believe that the sentiments above expressed really represented the views of Śrī-Rāma. He knew from Jaṭāyu within an hour of Śītā's abduction that she was taken into captivity by Rāvaṇa. There are several passages in the epic to show that Śrī-Rāma wanted to recover Sītā not so much to avenge a wrong done to him, as to restore to happiness a cherished wife, whom he continued to love intensely and respect very highly for her

1. विदितश्चास्तु ते भद्रे योऽयं रणपरिश्रमः।
स तीर्णः सुहृदां वीर्यान्न त्वदर्थं मया कृतः॥ १५॥
रक्षता तु मया वृत्तमपवादं च सर्वशः।
प्रख्यातस्यात्मवंशस्य न्यङ्गञ्च परिरक्षता ॥१६॥
कः पुमान् हि कुले जातः स्त्रियं परगृहोषिताम्।
तेजस्वी पुनरादद्यात्सुहृल्लेख्येन चेतसा ॥१७॥
रावणांकपरिभ्रष्टां दृष्टां दुष्टेन चक्षुषा।
कथं त्वां पुनरादद्यां कुलं व्यपदिशन्महत् ॥२०॥

Rāmāyaṇa, VI, 118, 15 ff.

2. न तथास्मि महाबाहो यथा त्वमवगच्छसि।
प्रत्ययं गच्छ मे येन चारित्रेणैव ते शपे॥६॥
यद्यहं गात्रसंस्पर्शं गतास्मि विवशा प्रभो।
कामकारो न मे तत्र दैवं तत्रापराध्यति॥७॥
मदधीनं तु यत्तन्मे हृदयं त्वयि वर्तते।
पराधीनेषु गात्रेषु किं करिष्याम्यनीश्वरा॥८॥

Ibid, VI, 119, 6-8.

voluntary resolution to share his miseries of the forest life[1]. Later on when Śrī-Rāma reaches the ocean along with his army, and the bridge is being built, he is once again overpowered by the thoughts about his beloved. He regrets very much that he could not reach in time to respond to his wife's pathetic call for help when she was being carried away by force, and shows an intense anxiety to be once more united in her loving arms.[2] There is not the slightest indication in any of these passages that Śrī-Rāma intended to spurn away his wife, because she was remaining in the captivity of Rāvaṇa. His cruel address to Sītā, when she is actually brought before him after the victory over Rāvaṇa, therefore comes as a great surprise to the reader. It is very probably a later interpolation, introduced to facilitate the incorporation of the superhuman proof of Sītā's unbroken chastity.

Whether the passage in question is a genuine one or not, one thing is quite clear; our Smṛiti writers have refused to prescribe for average women the unreasonable standard of purity attributed in it to Śrī-Rāma. They perhaps thought that it was a good ideal, but too high to be followed in actual life. They felt that it was necessary and equitable to treat women in Sītā's plight with much greater sympathy and reasonableness than what is

1. श्यामा पद्मपलाशाक्षी प्रिया विरहिता मया।
कथं धारयति प्राणान्विवशा जनकात्मजा ॥१०३॥
किं नु वक्ष्यामि राजानं धर्मज्ञं सत्यवादिनम्।
सीताया जनकं पृष्टः कुशलं जनसंसदि ॥१०८॥
या मामनुगता मन्दं पित्रा प्रव्राजित वनम्।
सीता सत्पथमास्थाय क्व नु सा वर्तते प्रिया ॥१०९)॥
गत्वा लक्ष्मण पश्य त्वं भरतं भ्रातृवत्सलम्।
न ह्यहं जीवितुं शक्तस्तामृते जनकात्मजाम् ॥१११॥

IV, 1, 103 ff.

2. तन्मे दहति गात्राणि विषं पीतमिवाशये।
हा नाथेति प्रिया सा मां ह्रियमाणा यदब्रवीत् ॥७॥
कदा नु चारुबिम्बोष्ठं तस्याः पद्ममिवाननम्।
ईषदुन्नम्य पास्यामि रसायनमिवातुरः ॥१३॥
कदा नु खलु मां साध्वी सीता सुरसुतोपमा।
सोत्कण्ठा कण्ठमालंब्य मोक्षत्यानन्दजं पयः ॥२०॥

VI, 5, 7 ff.

shown in the present version of the *Rāmāyaṇa*. With a broad-mindedness that is indeed admirable, a number of Smṛitis and Purāṇas declare that women, who had the misfortune of being made prisoners, or of being assaulted criminally, should be treated with sympathy, and not with contempt, and be accepted back by their families after they had performed certain purificatory rituals. Thus Vasishṭha declares that if a woman is taken into captivity by an enemy, or spirited away by thieves, or ravished against her will, she ought not to be abandoned by her family. The same is the view of Atri, who points out that one such misfortune ought not to be allowed to ruin the whole life of a woman.[2] An ordinary penance ought to be quite sufficient. Parāśara advocates a similar considerate treatment[3]. The *Matsyapurāṇa* points out that it would be absurd to condemn a woman, because she is overpowered and ravished; in such a case the assaulter alone is guilty and ought to be punished with death[4]. Bṛihaspati avers that even if defiled in the worst manner, a woman should not be abandoned; there is always an appropriate penance for her proper purification.[5]

1. स्वयं विप्रतिपन्ना वा यदि वा विप्रवासिता ॥
बलात्कारोपभुक्ता वा चोरहस्तगतापि वा ॥
न त्याज्या दूषिता नारी नास्यास्त्यागो विधीयते ।
पुष्पकालमुपासीत ऋतुकालेन शुध्यति ॥
V. D. S., XXVIII., 2-3.

2. सकृद्भुक्ता तु या नारी म्लेच्छैर्वा पापकर्मभिः ।
प्राजापत्येन शुध्येत ऋतुप्रस्रवणेन च ॥
V. 35.

3. बन्दिग्राहेण या भुक्ता हृत्वा बद्ध्वा बलाद्भयात् ।
कृत्वा सान्तपनं कृच्छ्रं प्राजापत्येन शुध्यति ॥
सकृद्भुक्ता तु या नारी नेच्छन्ती पापकर्मभिः ।
प्राजापत्येन शुध्येत ऋतुप्रस्रवणेन च ॥
X, 26-7.

4. बलात्संदूषयेद्यस्तु परभार्यां नरः क्वचित् ।
वधो दण्डो भवेत्तस्य नापराधो भवेत्स्त्रियः ॥
227, 126.

5. अत्यंतदूषिता वापि न परित्यागमर्हति । सर्वेषां निष्कृतिः प्रोक्ता
P. T. O.

What is to be done if the criminal assault is unfortunately followed by a conception? Our Smṛitis recognised that in the case of criminal assault, conception was an accidental circumstances, and it would not be equitable to refuse to readmit its victim merely on that score. They have therefore laid down that such a woman should be admitted to her former position as soon as she had delivered the child. The child was to be given to somebody else for rearing up, and was not to be admitted as a member of the family. Atri and Devala are typical advocates of this view; the latter avers that once the child is delivered, the woman becomes as pure and flawless as ever before.[1]

The liberal views of Atri and Devala were accepted by Hindu society down to about the 9th century A.D. During the first half of the 8th century thousands of men and women were taken into captivity by the Muslim invaders of Sindh; those of them who could effect their escape were accepted back in their families and society (Elliot and Dowson, I. p. 126).

From about the 11th century society began to change its attitude towards these unfortunate women and refused to admit them back. Women carried into captivity by force could no longer entertain any hope of regaining their old position in Hindu society. The advice of the Smṛitis, which recommended a contrary course, was silently brushed aside and the door of Hinduism was once for all closed to such women. The establishment of the Muslim rule in the country might have been partially responsible for this development. Under the Islamic law apostacy was puni-

(*Continued from the last page*).
नारीणां तु विशेषतः ॥ बलात्कारोपभुक्ता वा चोरहस्तगतापि वा। स्वयं विप्रतिपन्ना वा अथवा विप्रमादतः ॥

Aśaucha Chap. 53-54, *G. O. S.* Edition.

1. असवर्णेन यो गर्भः स्त्रीणां योनौ निषिच्यते।
अशुद्धा सा भवेन्नारी यावच्छल्यं न मुञ्चति ॥
विनिसृते ततः शल्ये रजसो वापि दर्शने।
तदा सा शुध्यते नारी विमलं काञ्चनं यथा ॥
स गर्भो दीयतेऽन्यस्मै स्वयं ग्राह्यो न कर्हिचित्।
स्वज्ञातौ वर्जयेद्यस्मात्संकरः स्याद्यतोऽन्यथा ॥

5?-2.

shable with death, certainly in the case of men and probably in the case of women (*E. R. E.*, Vl. I., p. 625). Under Muslim rule it was thus not an easy proposition to reclaim to Hinduism women who had been once captured and married by Muslims. It may be, however, pointed out that large parts of Rajasthan and the Deccan were under nominal Muslim rule; but there is no evidence to show that Hindu society was willing to readmit violated women. New notions of purity were mainly responsible for the refusal of society to admit back such women, though this course was clearly recommended by earlier Smṛitis.

This changed attitude produced a disastrous consequence on the strength and solidarity of Hindu society. Out of the thousands of women that were forcibly carried into captivity by Muslim invaders from the 11th century onwards, almost all would certainly have liked to come back to their old homes and society. But they knew that their fate was sealed once for ever, the moment they had fallen into the hands of the enemy. No return was possible; they had to adjust themselves to their captors and new surroundings. It was because of this consciousness that Kamalādevī, the queen of king Bhīma of Gujarat, when captured and forcibly married by Alla-ud-din Khilji, eventually not only reconciled herself to her lot, but urged her new husband to capture and bring her daughter to Delhi, so that she should be married to the Crown Prince. Had this unfortunate lady known that she would be accepted back in her family, she would have tried to effect her escape or avenge her wrong. We have seen already (*ante*, p. 22) how spirited Kshatriya ladies used to take revenge for the wrongs done to themselves or their families by having recourse to the sword. Not a single Rajput princess, however, among those who were forced into Muslim harems against their wish, is known to have followed their example. They did not lack in courage or military spirit; but they knew that even if they took revenge and effected their escape, they could hope to have no honorable position in their own families and society. They had to reconcile themselves to the inevitable.

Down to the 11th century, however, Hindu society was keeping its door open to women taken prisoners in war. They had always the hope that they would be taken back into their families, if they escaped from their captivity; so they would usually try to effect their escape or wreak their vengeance on their captors. Well known is the strategem by which princesses Sūryadevī and Pramālādevī, daughters of king Dahir of Sindh, took their revenge upon General Kasim for the miserable plight to which he had reduced them and their mother, along with thousands of their sisters in Sindh. They were sent by the general to Baghdad for being presented to the Khalifa. The princesses were very young, for they had not yet reached their teens; but the fortitude and ingenuity which they showed in very trying circumstances were very remarkable. When eventually produced before the Khalifa, they declared that though intended for him, Kasim had kept them with him for three days. This enraged the Khalifa, who immediately sent orders to Kasim to put himself, wherever he may be, in raw leather immediately and come back to him. When as a result of the execution of this order, the corpse of Kasim reached Baghdad, it was proudly shown to the princesses by the Khalifa. When they found that their plan to wreak vengeance had succeeded, they declared that they had not been even touched by Kasim and that they had told a lie in order to encompass the ruin of one, who had brought slavery and dishonour to thousands of their sisters in their kingdom. The Khalifa was exasperated and he ordered them to be immured in a wall. The princesses gladly welcomed this escape from life and dishonour.[1] It is to be noted that in later times no princesses even of the Rajput stock sought to wreak vengeance on their captors. They knew that they had no place in their society, even if they escaped back after wreaking their vengeance. They had to reconcile themselves to the inevitable. Had the views of Atri and Devala ultimately prevailed, were the doors always kept open for women overtaken by misfortune to return to their families and society, the Muslim

1. Al Bilaudari in Elliot and Dowson, Vol. I, pp. 210-2.

population in the once-undivided India would not have risen to nine crores. Hindu society has paid heavily for its narrow orthodoxy; it is high time that we should now take a rational view of the whole situation and cease to penalise women for their misfortune. After all honour or virtue can be lost only by a distinct act of volition, and not by an accident or misfortune. There is a growing tendency at present to accept this rational view; it must be strengthened and made quite universal.

Generally speaking in all climes and times men have laid down a much higher standard of sexual mortality for women than what they were themselves prepared to accept. Hindu society has been no exception to this rule. Men found guilty of the breach of the marriage vow have been treated with a relative leniency. It is no doubt true that some authorities lay down that a husband, who becomes unfaithful to his wife, commits a sin for which there is no adequate penance[1]. Āpastamba declares that such a husband should be compelled to wear donkey's skin with hair turned outside, and made to beg alms in that uniform for six months. At every door he was first to announce his crime and then accept alms if offered.[2] There is no doubt that this punishment must have exposed the delinquent to a terrible humiliation, but it may be well doubted if an appreciable percentage of guilty husbands ever received it in actual practice. Had the punishment been a reality, the crime would have become very rare. The deterrent effect of the rule was nullified by the dictum of later Smṛitis, that a wife ought to revere as God even that husband, who has repeatedly transgressed his marriage vows (*ante*, p. 109).

The early Hindu thinkers recognised that the phrase, it is human to err, is as much applicable to women as to men, and they were prepared to treat lapses of women from the marriage vow with

1. एवं भार्यास्त्यजतां नराणां नास्ति निष्कृतिः।
Mbh., XIII, 58, 13.

2. दारव्यतिक्रमी खराजिनं बहिर्लोम परिधाय दारव्यतिक्रमिणे भिक्षामिति सप्तागाराणि चरेत्। सा वृत्तिः षण्मासान्।
1, 9, 18.

a fair amount of sympathy and commiseration. In the Vedic period we find that women who had gone astray, were allowed to take part even in religious service, provided they confessed their error.[1] Early Dharmaśāstra writers also were fairly lenient; Vasishṭha, for instance, has no objection to the readmission of a woman who had voluntarily gone astray, provided she really repented and submitted to a proper penance (*ante*, p. 308 n. 1). Parāśara recommends that a woman should be abandoned, only if she is a confirmed sinner (X, 35). Yājñavalkya would advise this step only if adultery had resulted in conception (1, 72). The same is the view of the *Mahābhārata*, which further points out that man is usually more to blame in such offences than woman.[2] Other writers have suggested that a woman should be driven out of the house only if her associate were a person of very low caste[3]. Otherwise she was to be segregated in the house and excluded from religious functions and privileges.[4]

After about the 11th century A.D. lapses of women began to be treated with greater sternness. The earlier authorities, which had permitted the re-admission of women who had casually gone astray, were taken to be referring to the cases of mental and not physical adultery.[5] This was an altogether unjusifiable procedure, as the context and wording of the passages concerned clearly show. A few medieval thinkers like Mādhavā-

1. प्रतिप्रस्थाता पत्नीमुदानेष्यन् पृच्छति न चरसीति। ....। निरुक्तं चैनः कनीयो भवति सहृचं भवति।

S. Br., II. 5, 2, 20.

2. तस्मात्तु पुरुषे दोषो ह्यधिको नात्र संशयः।
विना गर्भं सवर्णेषु न त्याज्या गमनात्स्त्रियः॥

XIII, 58-5.

3. चतस्र एव संत्याज्या पतने सत्यपि स्त्रियः।
श्वपाकोपहता या तु भर्तृघ्नी पतिपुत्रगा॥

Chaturviṁśatimatam in *Par. Mād.*, on X, 28.

4. Cf. *Mitāksharā* on *Yāj.*, I., 72
त्यागश्चोपभोगधर्मकार्ययोर्न तु निष्कासनं गृहात्तस्याः।

5. Aparārka, while commenting on *Yāj.*, I, 72
'व्यभिचारे ऋतौ शुद्धिर्गर्भे त्यागो विधीयते'। says एतच्च मानसे व्यभिचारे।

chārya[1] continued to advocate a humane treatment of women, who had happened to go astray for a while; they realised that to drive out such women from their homes was to compel them to lead a life of sin and shame for ever. Society, however, would not follow their lead and began to insist upon a much higher standard of sex morality in the case of women, than what it was prepared to tolerate in the case of men. A single lapse came to be regarded as fatal for the woman, while even a moral wreck was to be revered as God by his dutiful wife. This last statement is no doubt hyperbolic and is not to be taken literally. Nevertheless, it clearly shows that lapses of men were very leniently treated, while women had no chance if they had committed a single mistake. This was highly inequitable, and it has made reclamation work next to impossible at present. Hundreds of women, who once in a while become guilty of misdemeanour, are being eternally lost of Hindu society, because it refuses to treat them with human sympathy. This again has led to a considerable swelling of the non-Hindu and low class population in India. We must once more begin to follow the liberal lead of Vasishṭha, who has recommended the acceptance of such women, provided they show genuine repentance.

The concern which a society feels for the welfare of its women is also shown by the rules that are laid down for the conqueror about the treatment of women captured in war. In early times these unfortunate women had very often to enter the harem of the conqueror, as is clearly shown by the recognition of the Rākshasa or Kshātra form of marriage. When Manu allows each soldier to retain such women as he may have himself captured, he is obviously referring to this old barbarous practice (VII, 70). Society's sense of morality and fairplay was getting refined, and it began to be felt in course of time that such barbarism should be no longer tolerated. We accordingly find social thinkers coming forward to declare that the conqueror ought to treat honorably all women captured in war, and set

1. *On Parāśarasmṛiti*, V, 2.

them at liberty. It was left for the Pauranic age to enunciate this liberal doctrine; we find it specifically advocated by the *Agnipurāṇa*[1]. The great Shivaji was following this meritorious tradition when he honorably sent back to her relatives the beautiful wife of the commander of the fort of Kalyan, who was presented to him by his soldiers, who had taken her a captive.

The historian is, however, compelled to observe that in a large number of cases this rule about the chivalrous treatment of women was disregarded by Hindu commanders and soldiers long before the advent of Islamic armies. When the Maukhari king Grahavarman was defeated and killed in war in 605 A. D., his wife Rājyaśrī was put in prison with heavy fetters on her feet. Medieval inscriptions often refer to several cases of the ill-treatment of women seized in war. A Chola king of the 11th century had taken captive the mother of his Ceylonese contemporary; he cut her nose because her son had invaded his country and laid it waste[2]. In the heat of the struggle when every one was crying for vengeance, it is clear that the rules of chivalrous treatment were often completely ignored. Medieval inscriptions from south India contain several other cases of the ill-treatment of women; we very often come across the victor carrying away the treasures and wives of his enemies into his own harem.[3] It is however somewhat consoling to find that persons guilty in this respect were often realising that their conduct was sinful and would sometimes proceed to perform a penance (*S. I. E. R.*, 1918, No. 73).

In the later medieval period warfare became more inhuman as a consequence of the contact with the barbarous hordes that came pouring into India almost every century. In Rajasthan

1. संप्राप्य विजयं युद्धे देवान्विप्रांश्च संयजेत् ।
रत्नानि राजगामीनि अमात्येन कृते रणे ।।
तस्य स्त्रियो न कस्यापि रक्ष्यास्ताश्च परस्य च ।।

Ch. 235, 62-3.

2. *E. C.*, IX, Devanhalli, No. 75.

3. Khajuraho inscription, *E. I.*, I, p. 145; *E. C.*, VI, Chikkamanglur, No. 160; *Ibid*, XII, Chikkanayakanhalli No. 565,

interminable internecine warfare was going on during this period; but Rajputs failed to observe a code of warfare, which would respect the honour of captive women. Conquerors often carried the wives of the conquered to their harems.[1] This, however, was inevitable, for the practice had become universal in India since the advent of Islamic armies. We cannot therefore sufficiently admire Shivaji for rising above the morals of his age and treating captured women with great respect and consideration.

We have so far considered the attitude of society towards women in abnormal circumstances. Let us now see what its attitude towards them was in ordinary daily life.

From very early times Hindu society used to show its concern for women in a variety of ways. Its chivalrous feeling secured several privileges and concessions for the fair sex. The killing of a woman was regarded as a very disgraceful offence since very early times. In the Vedic literature it is pointed out that a woman ought not to be killed.[2] Rāma very reluctantly killed Taṭīkā, only when he was convinced that there was no other alternative open for him; he had to protect the sages, hundreds of whom had been already killed by the ogress.[3] It is interesting to note that even in spite of the universally accepted divinity of Rāma, there were critics like Bhavahūti in later times who ventured to fearlessly censure his conduct in killing Tāṭikā.[4] Bhīshma allowed himself to be killed, because he did not want to fight with one, who had been born as a woman, though subsequently changed into a man. Rāvaṇa thought of killing Sītā

1. Tod, *Annals*, II p. 741 (Crooke's edition).

2. स्त्री वैषा यच्छूर्नि वै स्त्रियं घ्नन्ति।

S. Br., XI, 4, 3, 2.

3. न ह्येनामुत्सहे हन्तुं स्त्रीस्वभावेन रक्षिताम्।
वीर्यं चास्या गतिं चापि हनिष्यामीति मे मतिः॥

I, 27, 3.

4. वृद्धास्ते ह्यविचारणीयचरितास्तिष्ठन्तु किं वर्ण्यते।
सुन्दस्त्रीदमनेऽप्यखंडयशसो लोके महान्तो हि ते॥

Uttararāmacharit, Act V, 34.

on more than one occasion, but he was dissuaded from his plan by the thought that it is unchivalrous to kill a woman (VI, 93, 60). When the tutelary deity of Laṅkā proceeded to stop the entry of Hanumān, he merely gave her a blow; he had realised that the exercise of a more than minimum force would be blameworthy, as his opponent was a woman.[1] The *Mahābhārata* has declared in several places that like Brāhmaṇas and cows, women also ought not to be killed. In the famous story of the demon Baka the house-wife presses her husband to send her to the demon for being devoured; she fondly hopes that though a demon, Baka would never think of killing a woman.[2]

For the offence of killing a woman Manu has prescribed the capital punishment.[3] To die in the defence of a woman is declared to be the surest way of ensuring a seat in heaven.[4] In some of the Smṛtis it is no doubt stated that the sin of killing a woman is equal to that of killing a Śūdra; this however does not refer to the gravity of the crime, but to the theological dogma that the status of women was equal to that of the Śūdras, both not being entitled to the privilege of the sacred initiation (*upanayan*). This little incident will make it clear how great and far-reaching were the consequences of losing religious privileges in ancient times.

Hindu society has sought to show its concern for the woman in a variety of ways. On crowded streets way was to be made for her. If she was in difficulties in her journey, it was the duty of every cultured person to help her in overcoming them. She

1. स्त्री चेति मन्यमानेन नातिक्रोधः स्वयं कृतः।
V, 3, 39.

2. अवध्याः स्त्रिय इत्याहुर्धर्मज्ञा धर्मनिश्चये।
धर्मज्ञाद्राक्षसान्प्राहुर्न हन्यात्स च मामपि॥
I, 172. 41.

3. स्त्रीबालब्राह्मणघ्नांश्च हन्याद्द्विट्सेविनस्तथा।
IX, 232.

4. ब्राह्मणार्थे गवामर्थे स्वाम्यर्थे स्त्रीकृतेऽथवा।
स्थानार्थे यस्त्यजेत्प्राणांस्तस्य लोकाः समाहिताः॥
Pānchatantra, Mitrabheda, 5th story.

was to be exempted from the ferry tax. If she had no proper guardians, the state was to look after her interest and property. To accept a bride-price was a very great sin. The marriage expenses of a daughter were a charge on her father's property, and brothers were expected to meet them, even if there were no ancestral assets. For the same offence law courts were usually to impose a lighter punishment upon women than upon men (*Arthaśāstra*, IV, 12). Merit was to be always honoured, whether it was found in men or in women[1].

Within the house every one was to show the highest solicitude for the woman. She was to be honoured like the Goddess of Prosperity. The patriarch was warned that his family would prosper only if the ladies under his charge were cheerful; it would surely come to grief if the women folk were in sorrow. Women have their own innocent fancies and hobbies; they ought to be respected. Women are the support of the universe; it exists on account of and through them. One can therefore never do too much for them. Woman and prosperity are not two different things; woman brings prosperity when she is properly treated and respected. The holiest object in the world is a good woman; a tear of sorrow rolling down from her eye will be a great portent even for a mighty tyrant.[2]

1. गुणाः पूजास्थानं गुणिषु न च लिंग न च वयः।

Uttararāmacharit, Act, II, 2.

2. The following texts are the authorities for this para:—

श्रिय एताः स्त्रियो नाम सत्कार्या भूतिमिच्छता।
लालितानुगृहीता च श्रीः स्त्रीर्भवति भारत॥

Mbh., XIII, 81, 15.

शोचन्ति जामयो यत्र विनश्यत्याशु तत्कुलम्।
न शोचन्ति तु यत्रैता वर्द्धते तद्धि सर्वदा॥

Manu, III, 57.

स्त्रियः साध्व्यो महाभागाः संमता लोकमातरः।
धारयन्ति महीं राजन्निमां सवनकाननाम्।

Mbh, XIII, 78, 23.

पृथिव्यां यानि तीर्थानि सतीपादेषु तान्यपि।

Brahmavaivartapurāṇa, 83, 119.

प्रवादः सत्य एवायं त्वां प्रति प्रायशो नृप।
पतिव्रतानां नाकस्मात्पतन्त्यश्रूणि भूतले॥

Rāmāyaṇa, VI, 114, 65.

The above passages no doubt express very fine and chivalrous ideas about women. There are, however, a large number of passages in Sanskrit literature, both religious and secular, which are of an opposite nature, and cast serious reflections upon women and their character. We shall now proceed to consider them, and try to find out what is their precise implication.

The context clearly shows that many of the passages, where women in general have been decried, merely express the views of men in the throes of bitter disappointment. The exigencies of the situation are often responsible for such opinions, and they ought not to be taken at their face value. Thus a passage in the *Ṛigveda* declares that women are very fickle[1]; the speaker, however, is Purūravas, who was bitterly disappointed to find that his beloved Urvaśī had left him, because he was unable to keep the terms of the agreed contract. Another passage in a later Saṁhitā observes that women are falsehood incarnate; the context, however, shows that the reference is to women of bad character.[2] In the Rāmāyaṇa Laskshmaṇa observes that women are cruel and malicious by nature, but that was because he was quite unjustly rebuked by Sītā, who compelled him to go in search of Rāma against his better judgment[3]. In another passage in the same epic, it is stated that women are wicked and selfish, but it is immediately added that the remark is intended to apply only to Kaikeyī (II, 12, 99). In a third place in the same work the sage Agastya says that women combine the fickleness of the lightning, the sharpness of the weapon and the swiftness of

1. न वै स्त्रैणानि सख्यानि सन्ति सालावृकाणां हृदयान्येता।
X, 95, 15.

2. अनृतं स्त्री अनृतं वैषा करोति या पत्युः क्रीता सती अथान्यैश्चरति।
M. S., I, 10, 11.

3. उत्तरं नोत्सहे वक्तुं दैवतं भवती मम।
वाक्यमप्रतिरूपं तु न चित्रं स्त्रीषु मैथिलि ॥२७॥
स्वभावस्त्वेष नारीणामेवं लोकेषु दृश्यते।
विमुक्तधर्माश्चपलास्तीक्ष्णा भेदकराः स्त्रियः ॥२८॥
स्त्रीत्वं दुष्टं स्वभावेन गुरुवाक्ये व्यवस्थितम् ॥३१॥
III, 45.

the eagle[1]; the sage makes this observation, not because he genuinely believed in its truth, but because he wanted to emphasise that Sītā, whom he was praising, had none of these defects and drawbacks. The Buddha in one place holds up for admiration the wife of the slave type; we must however remember that he is there giving advice to a recalcitrant daughter-in-law (*Ang. Nik.* IV, p. 91))

Some of the uncomplimentary remarks about women are further due rather to a light-hearted cynicism than to a deep-rooted conviction. 'Even Indra has observed,' says the *Ṛigveda* in one place, 'that women cannot control themselves[1].'[2] One of the later Saṁhitās observes that women can be easily won over by one who is fair in form and expert in singing and dancing[3]. In some of the writings of modern feminists, we come across similar semi-frivolous and semi-cynical observations about men. They are not intended to be taken seriously. In one Jātaka story a woman of 120 is represented as falling in love with a youth of 20. This is frivolity and nothing else. It has its counterpart in many of the present day magazine stories, where we often find old men of seventy marrying tender girls of seven.

From about the beginning of the Christian era we begin to come across passages, which were deliberately written for the purpose of blackening the character of women. In one place in the *Mahābhārata* we are told that sensual enjoyment is the sole aim of woman's existence.[4] In another place a woman herself

1. शतह्रदानां लोलत्वं शस्त्राणां तीक्ष्णता तथा्।
गरुडानलयोः शैघ्र्यमनुगच्छन्ति योषितः॥
इयं तु यवतो भार्या दोषैरेतैर्विवर्जिता।
श्लाघ्या च व्यरदेश्या च यथा देवी तचरुन्धती॥

II, 13, 6-7.

2. इन्द्रश्चिद्ध तदब्रवीत् स्त्रिया अशास्यं मनः।

IV, 33, 17.

3. तस्माद्य एव नृत्यति यो गायति तस्मिन्नेवैता निम्लिष्टतमा इव।
S. Br., III, 2, 3, 6. Compare also
सुलापा वै दर्शनीयेन स्त्रियः।

4. असंभोगो जरा स्त्रीणाम्।

Mbh., IV, 39, 78 (B).

is made to narrate a story illustrating how her sex is fickle and faithless by its very innate nature (XIII, 73-8). We are gravely informed that the sex urge in women is so great that they will eagerly unite with the meanest of men.[1] Nearest consanguinity would be no effective bar. If a woman has remained virtuous, it is simply because she could not get a proper cover, place and opportunity.[2] A man with a hundred tongues would die before finishing the task of lecturing upon the vices and defects of women, even if he were to do nothing else through out a long life of hundred year.[3] Similar uncharitable sentiments about women occur in Pali literature also.[4]

The above passages are no houbt written deliberately with a view to blacken the character of women. But it is not be assumed that the sentiments they express found general acceptance in society. Yudhishṭhira, for instance, refused to accept the theory that women are by their very nature vicious and wicked; he pointedly enquired from Bhīshma that if such were really the case, how could scriptures have laid down that religious duties should be performed only in association with the wife? Bhīshma, unable to give a rational reply, contented himself by narrating a cock and bull story, in which he made a woman herself declare that her sex was vice incarnate (*Mbh*, XIII, 73-8). Such fantastic stories can, however, carry no conviction to any reasonable person. Varāhamihira has subjected the case of the misogynist to a very critical and searching analaysis and cross-examination. He at the outset points out that all the defects

1. नासां कश्चिदगम्योऽस्ति नासां वयसि संस्थितिः।
विरूपं वा सरूपं वा पुमानित्येव भुञ्जते॥

Ibid, XIII, 73, 17.

2. स्थलं नास्ति क्षणं नास्ति नास्ति प्रार्थयिता नरः।
तेन नारद नारीणां सतीत्वमुपजायते॥

Padmapurāṇa, Sṛishṭikhaṇḍa, 49, 20.

3. यदि जिह्वासहस्रं स्याज्जीवेच्च शरदां शतम्।
अनन्यकर्मा स्त्रीदोषाननुक्त्वा निधनं व्रजेत्॥

Mbh, XIII, 74, 74, 8.

4. Baden, *Women in Buddhism*, pp. 42-50.

that have been attributed to women exist in men as well. Women however try to remove them, while men are supremely indifferent in the matter. Marriage vows are equally binding on the couple. Men treat them lightly, while women act up to them. Who suffers more from the sex urge, men who marry even in their old age, or women who lead a chaste life, even if widowed in the prime of their youth ? Men no doubt go on talking of their love to their wives while they are alive, but contract second marriages soon after their death; women, on the other hand, feel grateful to their husbands and decide to follow them on the funeral pyre, urged by the promptings of their conjugal love. Who then is more sincere in his love, man or woman ? For men to say that women are fickle, and faithless is the height of impudence and ingratitude; it reminds one of the audacity of clever thieves who first send away their loot and then challenge innocent persons demanding from them the stolen articles.[1]

The above masterly and just indictment of Varāhamihira shows clearly that the case of the misogynist is very weak; how is it then that it ever came to be advanced ? It appears that some Hindu writers have painted the woman in very black colours, not so much because they believed in what they said, but because they were anxious to dissuade men from marriage and family life. Varāhamihira expressly states that the Renunciation (*Saṁnyāsa*) School was accustomed to decry women

1. प्रब्रूत सत्य कतमोऽगनानां दोषोस्ति यो नाचरितो मनुष्यैः ॥६॥
दंपत्योर्व्युत्क्रमे दोषः समः शास्त्रे प्रतिष्ठितः।
नरा न तमवेक्षंते तेनात्रा वरमंगनाः ॥१२॥
न शतेनापि वर्षेणामपैति मदनाशयः।
तत्राशक्त्या निवर्तन्ते नरा धैर्येण योषितः ॥१४॥
पुरुषश्चटुलानि कामिनीनां कुरुते यानि रहो न तानि पश्चात्।
सुकृतज्ञतयांगना गतासूनवगूह्य प्रविशन्ति सप्तजिह्वम् ॥१६॥
अहो धाष्टर्यमसाधूनां निन्दतामनघाः स्त्रियः।
मुष्णतामिव चोराणां तिष्ठ चोरेति जल्पताम् ॥१७॥
Bṛihatsamhitā, Ch. 76, 4ff.

with the above end in view.[1] Of course there were a few writers in this school too, who have taken a balanced view of the whole situation and given due praise to women for the invaluable assistance which they give to their husbands in the realisation of temporal and spiritual goals of life. This, for instance, is the case with one section of the *Yogavāshisṭha*.[2] Such thinkers were, however, in a small minority. As a rule, in order to induce men to adopt a life of renunciation, which they honestly believed to be essential for salvation, the writers of the Saṁnyāsa School felt that they might indulge in hyperbolic language in describing the faults, drawbacks and vices of woman, who is the centre and attraction of family life for man.

Varāhamihira's theory is indeed true to a very great extent. The monastic life was a very difficult one; a person could lead it honorably only if he could control his passions effectively. One way of enabling him to do so was to emphasise that the pleasures of the home life were ephemeral and worthless, and the woman who formed the centre thereof, was the most detestable object in the world. In one passage of the *Yogavāsisṭha* Rāma when anxious to renounce the world is made to observe that the woman is the mine of all imperfections and the cause of all sorrows. His arguments advanced in this connection are very interesting. 'Desire for enjoyment will arise only when one has a wife, otherwise one would be free from it. If a man renounces the wife, he renounces the world; if he renounces the world,

1. येऽप्यंगनानां प्रवदन्ति दोषान् वैराग्यमार्गेण गुणान्विहाय ॥
ते दुर्जना मे मनसो वितर्कः सद्भाववाक्यानि न तानि तेषाम् ॥

Ibid, 74, 5.

2. यथैताः स्नेहशालिन्यो भर्तॄणां कुलयोषितः ।
सखा भ्राता सुहृद् भृत्यो गुर्मित्रं धनं सुखम् ॥
शास्त्रमायतनं दासः सर्वं भर्तुः कुलांगनाः ।
सर्वदा सर्वयत्नेन पूजनीयाः कुलांगनाः ॥
लोकद्वयसुखं सम्यक्सर्वं यासु प्रतिष्ठितम् ।
निरिच्छायाः प्रयातायाः परं संसारवारिधेः ॥

VI A, 109, 26-29.

he would surely be happy'.[1] One can hardly think of a more falacious argument. The *Mahābhārata* observes that prosperity and women would never be steady and faithful, howsoever assiduously one may work for them, simply because it desires its readers to turn to Dharma in preference of Artha and Kāma.[2] We learn from I-tsing that there was a monk at Nālandā, named Rāhulamitra, who would never see any women except his mother and sister. He told I-sting, 'I am naturally full of worldly attachment. Without doing this, I cannot stop its source.' A person somewhat weaker than Reverend Rāhulamitra would have agreed with Manu and declared that one should be careful about oneself even when one is in the company of one's own mother, sister or daughter.[3] Persons brought up with such notions will naturally regard women merely as snares for the temptation of men.[4] They have not the fairness to recognise that women so appear to men, not because they are really 'the seed of the tree of existence,' or 'the living torch illuminating the way to Hell'[5] (as the Jain saint Hemachandra descri-

1. सर्वेषां दोषरत्नानां सुसामुद्रिकयानया।
दुःखभृङ्गलया नित्यमलमस्तु मम स्त्रिया॥
यस्य स्त्री तस्य भोगेच्छा निस्त्रीकस्य क्व भोगभूः।
स्त्रियं त्यक्त्वा जगत्त्यक्तं जगत्त्यक्त्वा सुखी भवेत्॥
I, Ch. 21. vv. 23, and 35.

2. धर्मे मतिर्भवतु वः सततोत्थितानां स ह्येक एव परलोकगतस्य बन्धुः। अर्थाः स्त्रियश्च निपुणैरपि सेव्यमाना नैवाप्तभावमुपयन्ति न च स्थिरत्वम् ॥
Mbh., I, 2, 392.

3. मात्रा स्वस्रा दुहित्रा वा न विविक्तासनभाग्भवेत्।
बलवानिन्द्रियग्रामो विद्वांसमपि कर्षति॥
II, 25.

4. न हि स्त्रीभ्यः परं पापीयस्तरमस्ति वै।
मानवानां प्रमोहार्थं कृत्या नार्योऽसृजत्प्रभुः॥
Mbh, XIII, 40, 4 (B)

5. बीजं भवस्य नरकमार्गद्वारस्यं दीपिका।
शुचां कन्दः कलेर्मूलं दुःखानां खनिरंगना॥ *Yogaśāstra*, II, 87.

See also *Nītivākyāmṛita*, 221-245 for similar views of another Jain author Somadevasūri. In Chullpaduma Jātaka II. p. 193, the Buddha says:—
मातुगामो नाम अकतञ्जू थद्दहृदया।; see also *Morajātaka*, II, 159.

bes them to be), but because men themselves are unable to control their passions. Men are as a matter of fact a greater snare to weak women than women are to weak men. Tó attribute one's weakness to the wickedness of the other sex is hardly fair. It is interesting to note that this fallacy has not been committed by Jain and Buddhist nuns. Several psalms of the latter have come down to us; nowhere therein do we find them accusing man of being a snare to wòman. Women have in this respect undoubtedly shown a greater fairness, chivalry and balanced judgment than men.

It may be pointed out that this tendency to attribute all real and imaginary faults to women is not confined to the Renunciation School of India alone. The case was the same in ancient Greece. Socrates says, 'Woman is the source of all evil; her love is to be dreaded more than the hatred of man; the poor young men who seek women in matrimony are like fish who go to meet the hook.' Similar sentiments have been expressed by Christian saints. It is true that Christ himself has not indulged in any tirade against women. The Apostles and early Fathers, however, have painted the woman in the blackest colours. St. Paul says, 'It is good for a man not to touch a woman; marriage was a concession, a degradation to avoid fornication' (I Cor. VII, 1). Tertllian says, 'Woman is the gate of Hell, mother of all ills. She should blush with shame at the thought of her womanhood and live in perpetual penance for the sins of Eve.' Another Father has declared, 'I have not felt any calamity more hurtful to man than woman. Oh assembly of women, verily you are mostly of the hell on the day of Resurrection. You are the Devil's gateway. You destroy God's image, Man.' Marbod, a Bishop of Rennes who lived in the 11th century, delivers himself in the same strain. 'Of the numberless snares that the crafty enemy spreads for us over all the hills and fields of the world, the worst and the one which one cannot avoid is Woman; sad stem, evil root, vicious fount, Who persuaded our first parent to taste the forbidden fruit? A woman. Who forced the father to defile his daughter? A woman'.[1]

Most of the faults and vices that have been attributed to women by the Renunciation School are not to be taken seriously. Their aim was more to divert man from woman, than to paint the latter in her true character. Varāhamihira, who points out the patent absurdity of these charges, may be taken to represent the view of the cultured Hindu society upto the 7th century A. D.

It is however true that more writers should have come forward to defend women against such unfair attacks. The absurdity of the charges levelled against them should have been exposed in numerous works. This, however, did not happen. *Pari passu* with the growing popularity of the Renunciation School, education of women declined. Their *upanayana* disappeared and they began to be married at a very early age. Denied the advantages of a liberal education, suddenly transferred to the rather unsympathetic atmosphere of the mother-in-law's house at a very young age, often called upon to bear the unwelcome company of a co-wife, frequently forced to drag on a miserable existence in an interminable widowhood, the character of women as a whole showed some inevitable deterioration after about 200 A. D. Many of them naturally began to show pettiness, narrowmindedness, jealousy and peevishness, as a result of forced repression in some directions and unnatural stimulation in others. So Manu's exaggerated description of the woman's character as possessing the above defects began to appear as partly true.[2] The average man began to feel that there was some truth in some of the charges levelled against women. He therefore began to assume a rather patronising attitude towards them. It cannot be denied that even some of the best writers of the first millennium of the Christian era have often expressed very

1. The above quotations have been taken from Chapter IV of *'A short History of Women'* by J. L. Davies (1927).

2. शय्यासनमलंकारं कामं क्रोधमनार्जवम् ।
द्रोहभावं कुचर्यां च स्त्रीभ्यो मनुरकल्पयत् ॥
IX, 17.

unfair views about women. Thus Kālidāsa, for instance, while no doubt declaring in one place the wife to be the best companion and counsellor of her husband, proceeds to describe her as merely an instrument of physical pleasure on another occasion.[1] Had these authors lived in an age when female education was general and adequate, when lady scholars were making important contributions to the progress of knowledge, when lady poets and authors were not rare in society, when women had not been reduced to the status of Śūdras by their being declared ineligible for *upanayana* and other religious privileges, they would not have made some of their caustic and disparaging remarks about the weaker sex. The illiteracy of women and their general backwardness made the temptation to pass patronising remarks too strong. This tendency will disappear as soon as women take their natural place by the side of men as their honoured, valued and well-equipped coworkers.

One of the natural consequences of the general deterioration in the position of women was the theory of their perpetual tutelage. Let us now examine the precise implications of this famous adage.

It may be observed at the outset that no such theory is ever advanced by any authority down to about 300 B.C., when women were being properly educated in cultured families and married after they had become fairly well equipped for the family life. The decisive part which ladies like Sītā, Kaikeyī, Kuntī, and Draupadī played in the determination of momentous issues makes it quite clear that women had an effective voice even in matters of moment in earlier days. It was only when education of women declined and girls began to be married at an

1. गृहिणी सचिवः सखी मिथः प्रियशिष्या ललिते कलाविधौ।
अपि स्वदेहात्किमुतेन्द्रियार्थाद्यशोधनानां हि यशो गरीयः॥

Raghuvaṁśa, VIII, 67 and XIV, 35.

The last line however cannot be taken at its face value, because Kālidāsa wants to emphasise how Rāma could have sacrificed anything including his life for keeping his reputation unsullied.

immature age, that the theory of the perpetual tutelage of women appeared in the field.

The original idea of those who were responsible for the above theory was not so much to deny freedom to women, they undoubtedly were for its curtailment, as to afford them additional protection. The disability that was imposed was primarily intended for the benefit of women. As a woman herself has observed in the *Mahābhārata*, to be without a proper protector is a great calamity for the fair sex in this world, which is full of wickedness.[1] Manu therefore ordains that the father ought to *protect* a woman while she is a maiden, the husband when she is married, and the sons when the husband is no more; a woman ought not to remain independent. In the immediately next verse Manu points out that the father would be to blame if he does not marry his daughter in proper time, the husband, if he does not look after his wife properly, and the son, if he does not *protect* his mother during her old age.[2] It is thus clear that Manu's aim was not so much to deny all freedom to women as to ensure for them an adequate and continuous protection throughout the life. It cannot be gainsaid that the world being what it is, society cannot take too much care in the matter. Yājñavalkya also enunciates the doctrine of the dependence of women, but with him also it is a natural corollary of the lifelong protection that has to be afforded to them.[3]

1. अनाथत्वं स्त्रियो द्वारं दुष्टानां विवृतं हि तत् ॥
I, 172, 12.

2. पिता रक्षति कौमारे भर्ता रक्षति यौवने।
रक्षन्ति स्थविरे पुत्रा न भजेत्स्त्री स्वतन्त्रताम् ॥
कालेऽदाता पिता वाच्यो वाच्यश्चानुपयन्पतिः।
मृते भर्तरि पुत्रस्तु वाच्यो मातुरक्षिता ॥
IX, 3-4.

3. रक्षेत्कन्यां पिता विन्नां पतिः पुत्रश्च वार्धके।
अभावे ज्ञातयस्त्वेषां न स्वातंत्र्यं क्वचित्स्त्रियः ॥
I, 85.

Cf. also *Smṛityantara* in Aparārka on *Yāj.*, I, 109:—
पक्षद्वयावसाने तु राजा भर्ता प्रभुः स्त्रियः।
स तस्या भरणं कुर्याद् गृह्णीयाच्च पथश्चुलाम् ॥

In course of time, however, the phrase began to be taken out of its context, and people began to interpret it literally. A woman deserves no independence; therefore it follows that she ought not to do anything on her own responsibility and initiative in childhood, youth and even in old age. She must obey the father in childhood, the husband in youth, and sons in old age.[1]

Unfortunately circumstances favoured the further curtailment of the freedom of women, as was inevitable under the influence of the above adage. From about the beginning of the Christian era, as we have shown already, women ceased to receive proper education and began to be married at an early age. As a rule, therefore, they were inferior to men in intelligence, education and the experience of the world. It was therefore natural that some social thinkers should have come forward to emphasise that women have to be protected, not so much because it is the chivalrous duty of the stronger sex to do so, but because they are incapable of standing on their own legs. They must be always under the leading strings of men; they deserve no independence.

It must be, however, pointed out that the maxim 'Women deserve no independence' was not literally interpreted even by those who neglected the protection aspect of the doctrine. Manu, for instance, allows the wife large powers in the management of the household. It was she who was to control its expenditure and supervise the general arrangements of the kitchen, furniture,[2] and periodical religious and secular functions.

1. बाल्ये पितुर्वशे तिष्ठेत्पाणिग्राहस्य यौवने ॥
पुत्राणां भर्तरि प्रेते न भजेत्स्त्री स्वतंत्रताम् ॥

Manu, V, 147.

2. अर्थस्य संग्रहे चैनां व्यये चैव नियोजयेत् ।
शौचे धर्मेऽन्नपक्त्यां च पारिणाह्यस्य चेक्षणे ॥

IX 11.

Cf. also *Kāmasūtra* p. 227
सांवत्सरिकमायं संख्याय तदनुरूपं व्ययं कुर्यात् ।

Nārada, who has emphasised on the perpetual tutelage of women, lays down that at the death of the father, the mother was to be preferred as the guardian of the minor children to any other male relation (1, 37); her perpetual tutelage did not disqualify her for the task. The view that mothers in their old age should be under the control and guidance of their sons, though expressed in some Smṛitis, never found general acceptance in society. As a matter of fact writers like Manu, who have advocated this view, have themselves abandoned it later on. Thus Manu does not allow sons to exercise even their legal right to claim a partition, as long as their mother is alive. It was thus the major sons and not the aged mother, who suffered from want of independence. After the death of the father, even when sons were majors, it was the mother who, in practice if not in theory, guided and controlled the household. We have already seen in chapter VI (*ante*, pp. 187-8) how queen regents used to exercise considerable influence over the general administration of their kingdoms by taking the reins of government in their own hands. The influence continued even when sons used to attain majority. This would be quite clear from the prominent part which Kuntī, for instance, played in shaping the policy of her sons. Every one who knows anything of Hindu society is well aware of the important position which the mother usually occupies in the counsels of the family. The juridical doctrine of the dependence of women vanished before the great reverence that was instinctively shown to the mother by her sons. Hence she occupied an honoured and exalted position in the family. Even foreigners were very often struck by it. Thus Dr. Leitner, the Educational Commissioner in the Punjab during the 3rd quarter of the last century, has observed that the difficult task of mediation in family disputes was best performed by the elderly women of the household.

That the doctrine of the perpetual tutelage of women was not seriously taken by Hindu society will also become clear from the history of their proprietary rights already discussed in Chapters VIII and IX. We have seen how these rights went on expanding *pari passu* with the greater and greater emphasis that was being given to the doctrine of perpetual tutelage. The logical corollary of the doctrine should have been to curtail the property rights of women; why concede these to them when their male gurdians, and not they themselves, were going to exercise them ? The fact, however, was that the doctrine of perpetual dependence of women was never seriously subscribed to by Hindu society, though some of its jurists had solemnly initiated it. Proprietary rights of women went on developing in spite of the doctrine. The only result of material consequence which it produced was to circumscribe women's power to dispose of immoveable property. It has to be noted, however, that the rights of males also were by no means unrestricted in this matter.

It is however necessary to point out here that the doctrine of the perpetual tutelage of women was universally accepted almost everywhere till quite recent times. 'To the average Athenian' says Prof. Gilbert Murray, it was probably rather wicked for a woman to have any character, wicked for her to take part in public life, wicked for her to acquire learning. Even the great philosopher Aristotle thought that like slaves, artisans and traders, women should occupy a subordinate place. Their will is weak, virtue less perfect and self-sufficient, and deliberative faculty rather inconclusive. Male by nature is superior and female inferior. The one rules and the other is ruled, and this principle of necessity extends to all mankind.[1] The Roman Law regarded the wife as the daughter of her husband as far as her juridical status was concerned; for a long time she could not sign a will, make a contract or become a witness. Down to *c.* 200 A. D., even mothers of several children continued to be under the tutelage of their male relations. 'Woman is always dependent,' says Confucius, 'and owes due homage to her father-in-law and husabnd.' In the Christian marriage, the wife has to take the vow of obedience at the time of her marriage; logically speaking this places her under the perpetual tutelage

1. *Politica*, 1254, b, 1260, a.

of her husband. The Bible argues that women should never usrup authority over men, but be always subordinate to them, firstly because Eve, and not Adam, was deceived (I Timothy ii, 9-15), and secondly because the former was created out of a rib of the latter. At the synod of Macon in 585 A.D., the assembled bishops debated with much earnestness as to whether women were human beings at all, and finally concluded that they were. Numberless writers of medieval Europe have emphasised the inherent inferiority of women. Milton, for instance, held that women ought to obey without argument. His Eve says to Adam,

> My Author and Disposer, what thou bidst,
> Unargued I obey, so God ordains;
> God is thy law, thou mine; to know no more,
> Is woman's happiest knowledge and her praise.

Even Rousseau, the apostle of freedom who bewailed the fact that man though born free should be in chains everywhere, condemned women to a servile position. 'Girls,' he argues, 'should be early subjected to restraint. This misfortune, if it be really one, is inseparable from their sex.' Even educated and cultured ladies of the 18th century felt that women could never dream of independence. While writing about the education of girls, Hannah Moore says, 'Girls should be led to distrust their own judgment; they should learn not to murmur at expostulation, they should be accustomed to expect and endure opposition. They should acquire a submissive temper and forbearing spirit. They must endure to be thought wrong sometimes, when they cannot but feel that they are right.'[1] The French Revolution, which stood for Equality, was not prepared to grant it to women. The French National Assembly treated women so contemptuously that it refused even to read their petition (George, p. 186). In the Anti-Slavery Congress held in London in 1840, women delegates from America were not admitted because British representatives felt that it was contrary

1. Davies, *A short History of Women*, p. 357.

to the word of God that women should sit in the Congress. In England there was a determined opposition to the admission of women to the medical course down to 1888 A. D. Oxford University admitted women students, but would not give them any degrees till 1920 A.D. Cambridge, though bantered and ridiculed into granting degrees to women, still refuses to grant them the right to vote at meetings, where men holding corresponding degrees, are allowed to vote. Until the first Great War succeeded in shattering old prejudices and fetters, women did not succeed in winning elementary political rights. They are still without franchise in some countries in Europe.

We should therefore note in fairness that the doctrine of perpetual tutelage of women that came to be advocated in ancient India, when women ceased to be educated and began to be married early in their childhood, was almost universally subscribed till the beginning of the 20th century. The relatively stronger position of men in all the spheres of life, their better education, stronger muscles, leadership in literature and jurisprudence, naturally helped the spread of the notion. Down to the middle of the last century public opinion averred in the West also that men were by nature superior to women mentally, morally and physically; the latter must therefore be ruled by the former. Ambition and independence were unfeminine attributes; women have to cultivate obedience, humility and unselfishness.

To conclude, from about the beginning of the Christian era, Hindu society began to assume a patronising attitude towards women, as was done almost everywhere both in the West and the East till quite recently. While solicitous to increase the scope of their proprietary rights, while anxious to ensure all creature comforts to them, it failed to assess their proper worth with an impartial mind. The tendency to pass disparaging remarks about women in general became commoner. Some thinkers like Varāhamihira no doubt realised its danger and proceeded to nip it in the bud. But they did not get as much support in society as their cause deserved. This, however, need not surprise us. The general position of women had really deteriorated. They were no longer receiving any educaion. Theologically they had been reduced to the status of the Śūdras. Early marriages interfered with the proper development of their character. It could no longer be properly moulded in the loving and sympathetic atmosphere of the parents' house. Girls had to leave it at an early age and migrate to the house of the parents-in-law, where an atmosphere of awe prevailed, and where they had to play the junior to a large number of elders, who were often not sufficiently sympathetic. When they grew old, they had the apprehension of supersession. As a consequence their character suffered from forced repression in some directions and unnatural stimulation in others, as does that of men also under an unsympathetic foreign rule. As a consequence, women began to show greater pettiness, narrowmindedness and peevishness than men. The tendency to pass disparaging and patronising remarks about their character therefore became almost irresistible. Men should have tried to investigate into the causes of this phenomenon with a view to remove them. In stead of doing so, they allowed themselves to succumb to the temptation of merely passing uncharitable remarks about the weaker sex. This weakness, however, was not peculiar to Hindu civilisation, but was shared by it with all other contemporary cultures. The tendency to adopt a patronising attitude towards women will disappear as soon as women take their proper place as valued and well-equipped coworkers with men. This desideratum will be achieved at no distant date, when we consider the rapid strides which female education is taking at present. There is no doubt that men are at present trying their best to help in the physical moral, intellectual and economic development of women. It is to be hoped that our sisters will regard this as a partial compensation for our patronising attitude and sins of ommission and commissions in the past, which were almost unavoidable in an age of darkness prevailing all over the world.

CHAPTER XII

Retrospect and Prospect

We have now finished the task of describing the history and vicissitudes of the status and condition of women in the course of the long history of Hindu civilisation. We saw how the position, power, status and disabilities of the daughter, the wife and the widow went on changing in course of time. Women once enjoyed considerable freedom and privileges in the spheres of family, religion and public life; but as centuries rolled on, the situation went on changing adversely. On the other hand we found that the proprietary rights went on gradually expanding in spite of the growing tendency to regard women as unfit for independence.

The method we have so far followed was the vertical one; we isolated each topic, custom or institution and treated its history and development from age to age. This must have enabled the reader to perceive clearly the evolution of the different stages in the development of different ideas, customs and institutions. The method, however, has one defect ; it does not enable the reader to get a comprehensive and detailed picture of any one period as whole. He will have to consult the different chapters of the work afresh if, for instance, he desires to have a synthetic picture of the position of women as a whole, either in the Vedic or in the Upanishadic period. It is therefore necessary and desirable to follow the horizontal method of narration as well, and proceed to delineate the position of women as a whole in the different epochs of our long history. This will enable the reader to have a full picture of each period and find out how far the position as a whole went on improving or deteriorating.[1] It will be also possible to discuss here the general causes

1. References to original authorities are, as a rule, not given in this chapter, as it is based upon conclusions already proved in the preceding pages.

responsible for the changes at a greater length and in a more connected manner than was so far possible to do in the preceding chapters.

It will be convenient to divide the period we have to survey into four divisions:—

1. The Age of the *Ṛigveda*, from *c.* 2500 to *c.* 1500 B. C.
2. The Age of the Later Saṁhitās, Brāhmaṇas and Upanishads, from *c.* 1500 B. C. to *c.* 500 B.C.
3. The Age of the Śūtras, Epics and early Smritis, from *c.* 500 B. C. to *c.* 500 A. D.
4. The Age of later Smṛitis, Commentators and Digest writers, from *c.* 500 A.D. to *c.* 1800 A. D.

The periods of the last two epochs are chronologically definite; those of the first two are, however, rather vague, and there is as yet no unanimity about their precise duration. The limits suggested for them above are, however, the most probable ones, and are usually accepted by the majority of scholars.

For the purposes of the proposed survey, period by period, it is unfortunately not possible to divide the history into smaller and more numerous periods. The data at our disposal are too scanty for the purpose. The difficulty is further increased by our inability to know the precise dates of many of our authorities. Some of the works are further composite ones; there can be, for instance, no doubt that the present *Mahābhārata* and *Manusmṛiti* contain ideas popular in epochs, which were separated from each other by more than half a millennium. The period-wise survey is therefore beset with considerable difficulties, but has to be nevertheless attempted for the general reader in the interest of clarity.

THE RIG-VEDDIC AGE : *c.* 2500 B. C. TO 1500 B. C.

Our readers know already that the position of women in the Vedic age was far from being analogous to what it usually is in early uncivilised societies. In communities that have not yet emerged from barbarism, there hardly exist any checks on the tyranny of man over woman. Ill-usage, underfeeding and overworking are pushed to the greatest limit, compatible with the preservation of the race. Women are divorced, abandoned, sold or killed at the mere whim of men. They have to carry about children, and also serve as beasts of burden, when the tribe moves from one place to another. The treatment thus meted out to them need not cause any surprise; in primitive life the muscle was an indispensable element in success and the man was stronger in it than the woman. He fought with the animals and enemies to protect women and children; he chased the big game to feed the family. Physical prowess, bodily vigour and muscular strength thus naturally established man's permanent superiority over woman, who besides lacking these qualities, was periodically in a most helpless condition a few weeks before and after her frequent confinements. Man had not yet developed sufficient culture and sensibility to make him feel and realise that women undergo these trials and tribulations for the sake of the race, and therefore deserve to be treated with utmost sympathy and consideration. It was taken for granted everywhere that women as such can have no rights and privileges. They were inherently inferior to men and therefore must be always subordinate to them. This was the case, for instance, in ancient Greece; as a writer has trenchantly put it, 'There was no woman question at Athens because all women were as mere vegetables, and there was no woman question at Sparta because both men and women there were little better than animals.[1] The archaic Roman law granted to the husband the power over the life and the limbs of the wife, and for many centuries matrons with several children continued to be under the tutelage of their male relations. In ancient Palestine the woman was a piece of property to be bought and sold.

The position which women occupied in Hindu society at the dawn of civilisation during the Vedic age is much better than what we ordinarily expect it to have been. There are no

1. Davies, *A short History of Women*, p. 172.

doubt a few indications to show that brides were sometimes sold in marriage or even carried away by force. But the better conscience of society had already begun to assert itself, and condemn these practices as unholy and unworthy. The ideal marriage of the Vedic period was a religious sacrament, which made the couple joint owners of the household. The old tradition that the wife was the property of the husband had not yet completely died down; the famous hymn about gambling in the *Ṛigveda* (X, 34) shows that some times confirmed gamblers would stake away their wives to their opponents. The advice given to the gambler in this hymn, however, shows that social conscience had already begun to disapprove this practice.

On the whole the position of women was fairly satisfactory in the Vedic age. Ordinarily girls were no doubt less welcome than boys, but we must add that there were also some parents in society who would perform special religious rituals for the good luck of getting learned and capable daughters. Girls were educated like boys and had to pass through a period of Brahmacharya. Many of them used to become distinguished poetesses, and the poems of some of them have been honoured by their inclusion in the canonical literature. The marriages of girls used to take place at a fairly advanced age, the normal time being the age of 16 or 17. Educated brides of this age had naturally an effective voice in the selection of their partners in life. Very often there were love marriages, which were later blessed by parents. There was no seclusion of women; they used to move freely in society, often even in the company of their lovers. In social and religious gatherings they occupied a prominent position. Women had an absolute equality with men in the eye of religion; they could perform sacrifices independently and were not regarded as an impediment in religious pursuits. Marriage in fact was a religious necessity to both the man and the woman; neither could reach heaven without being accompanied by his duly married consort. The position of the wife was an honoured one in the family. In theory she was the joint owner of the household with her husband, though in actual practice, she was the subordinate partner. In rich and royal families polygamy prevailed to some extent, but ordinarily monogamy was the rule. If a wife had the misfortune to be widowed, she had not to ascend her husband's funeral pyre. The Satī custom was not in vogue at all; the widow could, if she liked, contract another marriage, either regularly or under the custom of Niyoga. The main disabilities from which women suffered in this age, as well as in the next one, were proprietary ones. They could hold or inherit no property.

Landed property could be owned only by one who had the power to defend it against actual or potential rivals and enemies. Women were obviously unable to do this and so could hold no property. The transition from the communal to the family ownership of land was just taking place; the conception of the rights of the different members of the family, even when males, was yet to crystalise. Naturally therefore women, like many other male members of the family, were incapable of owning property; the patriarch was its sole owner and guardian.

We also do not come across any queens reigning independently or as regents. Considering the general position of women as delineated above, these disabilities come as a great surprise to us, but a little reflection will show that they were natural and inevitable. The Aryans were gradually establishing their rule in a foreign country surrounded on all sides by an indigenous hostile population that considerably out-numbered them. Under such circumstances queens ruling in their own rights or as regents, were naturally unknown.

The position of women on the whole was fairly satisfactory. In the Vedic literature there are no doubt a few observations like 'Women have a fickle mind,' 'Women can be easily won over by one who is handsome and can sing and dance well.' They, however, reflect the light-hearted cynicism of some poets, and do not embody the considered views of the leaders of society. The community as a whole was showing proper concern and respect for women, allowing them considerable freedom in the different activities of the social and political life.

THE AGE OF THE LATER SAMHITĀS, BRĀHMAṆĀS AND UPANISHADS.

(*c.* 1500 to *c.* 500 B.C.)

The changes which took place during this period in the position of women were gradual. Their proprietary rights continued to be unrecognised, the only exception being in favour of marriage gifts of moveable property. In the higher sections of socicty the Sacred Initiation (*upanayana*) of girls was common, and they subsequently used to go through a course of education. Some of them used to attain distinction in the realm of theology and philosophy, and a considerable number of women used to follow the teaching career. There was, however, a gradual decline in female education as the period advanced. The system of sending out girls to famous teachers or centres of education came to be discouraged; it was laid down that only near relations like the father, the brother or the uncle should teach them at home. Naturally therefore religious and secular training became possible only in the case of the girls of rich and cultured families. As a consequence there arose a tendency to curtail the religious rights and privileges of the average woman; many functions in the sacrifice, which formerly could be performed by the wife alone now came to be assigned to male substitutes. Some sacrifices like Rudrayāga and Sītāyāga continued to be performed by women alone, and when the husband was out, the service of the sacrificial fire continued to be entrusted to the wife. In cultured families women used to recite their Vedic prayers morning and evening, and perform sacrifices on their husband's behalf, when they were otherwise preoccupied.

The marriage age of the bride continued to be about 16. In practice, if not in theory, brides had some voice in the selection of their partners in life, and *svayaṁvara* was fairly common in Kshatriya circles. The marriage ideals and the mutual relations and rights of the parties continued to be more or less the same as they were in the earlier age. Divorce was permitted to the wife, though the permission was not extensively availed of.

The Satī custom was altogether unknown, and the widow had the option of remarriage either with her brother-in-law or with an outsider. Naturally there was no tonsure of widows. Purda was altogether unknown, but women had ceased to attend public meetings.

Before we proceed to delineate the picture of the condition of women in the next periods, let us pause a while to consider the causes of this phenomenon of a relatively better condition and status of women in these early centuries, as compared to what it became in subsequent epochs. The reader has already seen in the foregoing pages how there took place a continuous and gradual deterioration in the position of women as a whole during the next two thousand years (*c.* 500 B.C., to *c.* 1500 A.D.). How are we to explain this phenomenon ? Usually we find that the condition of women improves as society advances to modern times. How is it that there is an exception in the case of the position of women in Hindu civilisation ?

The relatively more satisfactory position of women in the two epochs we have just surveyed was due, partly to political and partly to religious causes. As a rule in a community, which is civilised and is moving in search of pastures fresh and new, women occupy an honorable position. Men are mostly engrossed in military or semi-military activities, and they have to rely to a very great degree on the help and co-operation of women in the normal spheres and activities of family life. Under such circumstances women can clearly and convincingly demonstrate to men that they are not parasites, but very useful members of society, whose co-operation is very valuable in securing prosperity in peace and victory in war. It is well known how the First World War worked as a miracle in winning over the most deadly opponents of women's franchise. In July 1914 even Liberal British statesmen would not think of giving franchise to women, although the latter had exhausted all constitutional and unconstitutional means of agitation for securing their objective. In November 1918 there was not a single member in the same old Parliament to oppose the proposal to enfranchise millions of women. The valuable part which women had played in the prosecution of the First World War had disarmed all opposition.

It would appear that the general freedom and better status which women enjoyed in the Vedic age were largely due to men being engrossed in the work of conquest and consolidation. Women used to take an active part in agriculture, and the manufacture of cloth, bows, arrows and other war material. They were thus useful members of society, and could not be therefore treated with an air of patronage or contempt. The cheap or forced labour of the enslaved population was not yet available to the Aryans for the tasks mentioned above.

It may be pointed out that women in the age of Homer (*c.* 1000 B.C.) occupied a much more honorable position in Greek society than they did in the days of Pericles (*c.* 500 B.C.). Causes were more or less similar. In the Homeric age women were productive and valuable members of society. They worked as hard as men, and managed the house-hold without much co-operation from their male relations or slaves. The whole process of garment making was under their supervision in Greece, as it was in India. They brought water, they washed clothes, they cooked food. In the age of Pericles slavery had become an established institution and all manual work in the household was done by slaves. The wife lost nearly all her occupations. She became a parasite and society ceased to respect her.

The exigencies of the political situation in the Vedic period were responsible for the abolition of the prehistoric Satī custom and the sanctioning of Niyoga and remarriage. Like Hitler and Mussolini, Vedic chiefs were anxious for heroes, more heroes, and still more heroes. The gospel they preached to the householder was not of eight sons of the later days, but of ten. The non-Aryans were probably outnumbering the Aryans, and they were anxious to have as strong and numerous an army as possible. Under these circumstances it would have been a suicidical policy to encourage the revival of the obsolete custom of Satī or to prohibit widow remarriages. Society came to the definite conclusion that its vital interests demanded that the custom of Satī should be interdicted, and that widows should be allowed and encouraged to marry and mutliply the stock.

Another factor responsible for the relatively satisfactory position of women was the influence of religion. Asceticism was at a discount in the Vedic age. Maidens and bachelors had no admission to heaven; gods accepted no oblations offered by the unmarried. It was essential to offer the ordained sacrifices to gods for procuring happiness and prosperity both here and hereafter, and they could be properly performed by the husband and the wife officiating together. Wife was not an impediment but an absolute necessity in the religious service. This circumstance naturally helped to raise her status. To enable her to discharge her religious duties properly, it was necessary to ordain that her *upanayana* should be duly performed; this ensured a proper training and education to girls. It required at least half a dozen years to complete the educational course; that naturally rendered early marriages impracticable. When girls were properly educated and married at the mature age of 16 or 17, a considerable regard had naturally to be shown to their own likes and dislikes at the time of the marriage. Love marriages were also inevitable when girls remained ummarried to that advanced age and were moving freely in society.

It will be thus seen from the above discussion how down to about 500 B.C. the custom of Satī and child marriage did not exist to embitter the lot of the woman, how she was properly educated and given the same religious privileges as man, how she could have a voice in the settlement of her marriage and occupy an honoured position in the household, how she could move freely in family and society and take an intelligent part in public affairs, and how it was possible for her to take to a career, if urged by an inclination or a necessity.

THE AGE OF THE SŪTRAS, THE EPICS AND THE EARLY SMṚITIS.

(c. 500 B. C. to *c.* 500 A.D.)

The position of women deteriorated considerably in this

period, and its causes may be conveniently discussed here. Some centuries before the beginning of this period, the Aryan rule had become well established over the greater part of India. The Aryan conquest of the indigenous population and its loose incorporation in the social structure of the victors as members of the fourth Śūdra class, had given rise to a huge population of a semi-servile status. We saw that the introduction of slavery revolutionised the position of women in the classical period of Greek history; they became parasites and lost the esteem of society. The same happened in India, when a definite semi-servile status came to be assigned to the Śūdra class within Hindu society, service of the Aryan conquerors being its only and definite duty. Women, however, did not suffer merely because they ceased to be productive members of society. A greater calamity awaited them from the presence of Śūdra women. In the earlier period of their expansion, the Aryans followed the traditions of ruthless warfare. Indra, we are told, trampled upon the Dasyus in their cave retreats. When, however, the Aryans reached the upper Gangetic plain, they found that the indigenous civilisation there was too deep-rooted to be completely wiped out by them. They had to remain content merely with imposing their sovereignty, very often merely a nominal one, over the original inhabitants, variously described as Dāsas, Śūdras, or Nāgas. When the two races proceeded to live together peacefully, inter-marriages became inevitable. In the age of the Ṛigveda, we do not come across any cases of Arya Śūdra marriages. The Brāhmaṇas and the epics, however, supply ample evidence to show that the Aryan chiefs were freely marrying non-Aryan princesses in the later period. Arjuna married Uḍupī, a Nāga princess-regent. Bhīma married Hiḍimbā, a sister of a Rākshasa chief. The sage Kavasha, who plays an important part in the *Aitareda Brāhmaṇa*, was the son of a slave girl. These examples are only typical and would show that in the concluding half of the later Samhitā period (*c.* 1000 B. C. to *c.* 500 B.C.) the marriages of Aryan men with non-Aryan women were becoming common. It is important to note that the early Dharmaśāstra writers have no objection to an Aryan marrying a Śūdra woman, provided he had another Aryan wife; it is only later writers who proceed to interdict such a procedure with a great vehemence.[1]

The introduction of the non-Aryan wife into the Aryan household is the key to the general deterioration of the position of women, that gradually and imperceptibly started at about 1,000 B. C., and became quite marked in about 500 years. The non-Aryan wife with her ignorance of Sanskrit language and Hindu religion could obviously not enjoy the same religious privileges as the Aryan consort. Association with her must have tended to affect the purity of speech of the Aryan cowife as well. Very often the non-Aryan wife may have been the favourite one of her husband, who may have often attempted to associate her with his religious sacrifices in preference to her better educated but less loved Aryan cowife. This must have naturally led to grave mistakes and anomalies in the performance of the ritual, which must have shocked orthodox priests. The first remedy they must have thought of was to declare the non-Aryan wife to be unfit for association with her husband in religious rituals. 'The black non-Aryan wife may be her husband's associate in pleasure, but not in religious rituals' say several authorities.[2] But a mighty king, mad with love for his non-Aryan beloved, was not to be dictated to by a priesthood dependent upon him for its subsistence. He would insist upon having his own favourite wife by his side at the time of his sacrifices, no matter her race or caste.

1. न ब्राह्मणक्षत्रिययोरापद्यपि हि तिष्ठतोः ।
कस्मिंश्चिदपि वृत्तान्ते शूद्रा भार्योपदिश्यते ॥
शूद्रावेदी पतत्यत्रेरुतथ्यतनयस्य च ।
शौनकस्य सुतोत्पत्त्या तदपत्यतया भृगोः ॥

Manu, III, 14, 16.

2. द्विजस्य शूद्रा भार्या तु धर्मार्थं न क्वचिद्भवेत् ।
रत्यर्थमेव सा तस्य रागान्धस्य प्रकीर्तिता ॥

Vishnu, ch. 26.

कृष्णवर्णा या रामा रमणायैव न धर्माय ।

V. D. S., XVIII, 17.

How then was the situation to be retrieved ? Eventually it was felt that the object could be gained by declaring the whole class of women to be ineligible for Vedic studies and religious duties. There would then be no question of rejecting admission to a non-Aryan wife and granting it to an Aryan one; all would be ineligible and none need be offended. It is Aitiśāyana who is seen advocating this view by about 200 B.C. It is however almost certain that he is merely a typical representative of a powerful school reaching back to a fairly great antiquity. It is not impossible that his school may be as old as 500 B. C., if not even earlier.

The growing complexity of the Vedic sacrifices was another factor that tended to make the wife's association in religious rituals a more and more formal affair in course of time. In the Vedic age, a young maiden would take a Soma stalk and proceed straight to offer it to Indra in a sacrifice performed by her all alone. In course of time the sacrifice became a very complex affair, and the slightest mistake in its performance or in the recitation of its hymns and formulae was regarded as frought with very grave consequences. It required a long training to get the necessary capacity to follow intelligently the minute details of the complicated sacrifice, and the average woman had not so much time to devote for the purpose. In the Vedic age she was married at about the age of 16 or 17; she could thus devote six or seven years to her Vedic studies before her marriage. During this period a girl could equip herself fairly well for her post-marriage participation in sacrifices, as the Vedic literature was then not extensive and could be studied as popular religious poetry. The sacrificial ritual was also simple. Towards the end of the period of the later Saṁhitās and Brāhmaṇas, a maiden could hardly hope to get a full and adequate knowledge necessary for the purpose, unless she remained unmarried till about the age of 22 or 24. This was an impracticable proposition for the average girl. There were new forces in society which were clamouring for early marriages. The Aryans had settled down in a rich and prosperous country and their political supremacy had become unquestioned. Naturally they took to an easy and luxurious life, and the marriageable age of boys and girls began to be lowered. In the Ṛigvedic age the father was anxious to have strong and numerous sons more for secular than for religious purposes; in the days of the later Saṁhitās, the son became a religious rather than a secular necessity. A man comes to this world, it was pointed out, saddled with a threefold debt; the most important one of these was the debt to the manes which could be liquidated only by the birth of a son. Why then not marry a girl as soon as she attains maturity and is in a position to present a son to her husband ? Why wait for three or four years unnecessarily ? It may be noted that when Kaṇva learns that his daughter had contracted a love marriage with Dushyanta, a passage later interpolated in the *Mahābhārata*, represents him as blaming himself rather than his daughter. He practically admits that it was his mistake not to have married his daughter earlier; so many months had passed away uselessly since the time she could have got a son.[1]

Owing to the different causes narrated above, at the beginning of this period (*c*. 500 B.C.), there arose a tendency to lower the marriageable age of girls, and as a consequence, to discourage their *upanayana* and education. Down to aboutt he beginning of the Christian era, in cases of difficulty parents were permitted to keep their daughters unmarried to the age of 16 or 17, but it was emphasised that it would be advisable to get them married soon after the attainment of puberty. The view that women should not be at all allowed to participate in sacrifices was no doubt not accepted by society, but its vigorous advocacy by one school, along with the general lowering of the marriag age, tended to a growing and inevitable neglect of the Vedic education of girls. During the first half of this period a few

1 ऋतवो बहवस्ते वै गता व्यर्थाः शुचिस्मिते ।
सार्थकं साम्प्रतं ह्येतन्न च पाप्मास्ति तेऽनघे ॥
I, 95-65.

maidens continued to specialise in Vedic studies and rituals, but the majority of girls used to go merely through the formality of *upanayana* just before the celebration of their marriage. It is doubtful whether they were in a position to recite their morning and evening prayers. At about 200 A. D., it was felt that this meaningless formality should be discontinued. It was declared that marriage was the substitute for *upanayana* in the case of girls; they need not have any separate sacred initiation.

Upanayana was usually performed at about the age of 9 or 10, and the same age now came to be regarded as the ideal time of marriage for girls. Towards the end of this period (*c.* 500 A. D.), parents could not usually keep their daughters unmarried after the age of 12.

The discontinuance of *upanayana*, the neglect of education and the lowering of the marriage age produced disastrous consequences upon the position and status of women. Early marriage put an effective impediment in the higher education of girls. Brides being too young and inexperienced, ceased to have any effective voice in the settlement of their marriages. *Svayaṁvara* continued to be in vogue in Kshatriya circles, but it came to be condemned by Brahmanical writers. Love marriages became a thing of the past. Child wives with no education worth the name became the order of the day, and they could not naturally command respect from their husbands. Not infrequently parents had to marry their daughters in a hurry, lest the girls should attain puberty before their marriage. The matches arranged under such circumstances were often ill suited, and women were thus often compelled to spend their lives with unsuitable or unworthy partners. It is painful to find that Smṛiti writers should have come forward to preach the gospel that a wife should always revere her husband as God, even if he were a moral wreck.

During the first half of this period widow remarriages and Niyoga continued to be permitted, but the volume of public opinion against these customs was increasing, and they came to be eventually interdicted at about 500 A. D. Marriage was regarded as a religious sacrament in the Vedic period also, and yet society was permitting divorce and remarriage in exceptional cases. During the period under review, marriage became an irrevocable union, irrevocable, however, only so far as the wife was concerned. The husband could discard his wife for the grave offence of not being sufficiently submissive. The wife however could not take a similar step and marry a second time, even if her husband had taken to vicious ways and completely abandoned her. This differential treatment was due to the simple fact that women were no longer able to effectively oppose these absurd theories and claims, most of them being uneducated and quite ignorant of their former status and privileges.

The age of city or small states had gone, and the Hindu kingdoms in this period became fairly extensive. The splendour of royal courts naturally increased, and kings began to keep a much bigger harem than what was ever dreamt of in previous epochs. Their example was imitated by their numerous feudatories and rich subjects. This produced a very unfavourable consequence upon the condition and status of the vast majority of women of the upper classes, and it had its natural repercussions on the status of wives in ordinary families. The dictum, 'The wife ought to revere her husband as a god, even if he were vicious and void of any merit', was probably written with a particular reference to the unfortunate denizens of the harems in rich families; subsequently the advice came to be extended to the whole sex. One can hardly excuse Smṛiti writers for having enunciated this absurd and inequitable doctrine, though one can understand that their motive may have been partly to discourage a hasty tendency to sever the marital tie. They have, however, never dreamt of preaching a similar gospel to the husband; they permit him to discard his first wife on the most flimsy grounds.

The growing harems of the mighty kings naturally made them jealous, and some of them sought to keep their wives in seclusion. The Purda system, however, was yet confined only to a very small section of the royal families; majority of kings did not care to adopt it.

The period of 500 years between 200 B.C. and 300 A. D. was a very dark and dismal one for Northern India. The fertile plains of the Punjab and the Gangetic valley were subjected during this period to one foreign invasion after another. First came the Greeks, who under Demetrius and Menander (*c.* 190-150 B.C.) were able to penetrate right up to Patna in Bihar. Then came the Scythians and the Parthians (*c.* 100 B. C. to 50 A.D.,) whose frightful wars of conquest reduced Hindu population by one half, 25 percent, being killed and 25 percent, being enslaved and carried away.[1] These barbarians were followed by the Kushāṇas, who succeeded in overrunning practically the whole of northern India by the middle of the 2nd century A. D. Political reverses, war atrocities and the decline of population and prosperity naturally produced a wave of despondency in society. It facilitated the spread of the ideal of renunciation (Saṁnyāsa), which though held before society by Upanishadic, Buddhist and Jain teachers, was meeting with stubborn opposition in Hindu comunity. Thus Kauṭilya prescribes a punishment for a person who would renounce the world before his old age, and without providing for his dependents.[2] Early Dhramasūtra writers regard renunciation as a positively anti-Vedic custom.[3] The despondency prevailing in society at about the beginning of the Christian era began to wear down the opposition to the

1. चतुर्भागं तु शस्त्रेण नाशयिष्यन्ति प्राणिनाम् ।
शकाः शेषं हरिष्यन्ति चतुर्भागं स्वकं पुरम् ।
विनष्टे शकाराज्ये तु शून्या पृथ्वी भविष्यति ॥

Gargasaṃhitā, Yugpurāṇa, vv. 54, 84.

2. पुत्रदारमप्रतिविधाय प्रव्रजेतः पूर्वः साहसदण्डः ।
लुप्तव्यवायः प्रव्रजेत् ।

II, 1.

3. त्रैविद्यविद्यानां तु वेदाः प्रमाणमिति निष्ठा । तत्र यानि श्रूयन्ते व्रीहियवपश्वाज्यपयःकपालपत्नीसंबन्धकान्युच्चैर्नीचैः कार्यमिति तैर्विरुद्ध आचार अप्रमाणमिति मन्यन्ते ।

A. D. S., II, 9, 9.

ऐकाश्रम्यं त्वाचार्या अप्रजननत्वादितरेषाम् ।

B. D. S., II, 6, 29.

Saṁnyāsa ideal. There is no doubt a good deal of truth in the observation of Bhīma at one place in the *Mahābhārata* that renunciation appeals only to those who are unsuccessful in life.[1] Just as the renunciation philosophy of the Bhakti school appealed to Hindu society in medieval times owing to the political set-back which it had received at the time on account of the rise of Islam, so also the ascetic ideal of Upanishads, Jainism and Buddhism began to get a real hold over the social mind only at about the beginning of the Christian era owing to the prevailing wave of political and economic despondency.

The new development affected the position of the widow adversely in various ways. It strengthened the hands of those who were opposed to Niyoga and widow remarriage. Both the customs therefore fell gradually into disrepute. Niyoga no doubt deserved to be stamped out, but not so the widow remarriage. It however could not escape a similar fate. It began to be argued that the world was a mirage, and its pleasures were mere snares. The fate was undoubtedly cruel to the widow in carrying away her husband. It had however given her a new opportunity to secure spiritual salvation. It is true that the Vedas have declared that a son was necessary for securing heaven; the childless widow, however, should not think of remarriage in order to get heaven through a son. She ought to aim at the higher ideal of salvation (*mukti*) and not at the lower one of heaven (*svarga*). The former can be best attained by leading a pure and chaste life, as was done by hundreds and thousands of monks and nuns, who had entered the Saṁnyāsa stage direct from the Brahmacharya, without passing through the married life.[2] The widow should therefore never think of remarriage. This advice was, however, a onesided one; Smṛitis do not offer it to

1. श्रिया विहीनैरधनैर्नास्तिकैः संप्रवर्तितम् ।
वेदवादस्य विज्ञानं सत्याभासमिवानृतम् ॥
XII, 10, 20.

2. अनेकानि सहस्राणि कुमारब्रह्मचारिणाम् ।
दिवं गतानि विप्राणामकृत्वा कुलसंततिम् ॥
Manu, V. 159.

the widower. On the other hand, they permit him to remarry immediately after the death of the first wife, 'lest the sacred fires should remain unlit.'

A greater calamity that overtook the widow in this period was the revival of the Satī custom. In the beginning it was confined to the warrior class. It however began to spread wider in society in course of time, as the action of the Satī came to be regarded as a great religious sacrifice, which deserved to be imitated. A school of rationalists opposed the custom vehemently, pointing out its utter futility and stupidity. Its efforts partly checked the spread of the custom for a while.

The only direction in which the position of women improved in this period was in the sphere of proprietary rights. Society had begun to discourage widow remarriages. As a consequence there began to arise a class of childless young widows. In the earlier period, practically speaking this class did not exist, as Niyoga and widow marriages were then in general vogue. Now when both these practices were prohibited, society had to devise an honorable means to enable the widow to maintain herself. She could of course live in the joint family and receive maintenance along with others; but this was not an advisable step in the transition period during which Niyoga was being gradually stamped out. Some writers have laid down that a woman should not be compelled to submit to Niyoga against her wish.[1] It is clear that in uncultured families some of the male relations like the brother-in-law would occasionally force an unwilling widow to submit to their vicious wishes under the specious plea of Niyoga. The childless widow could be saved from this calamity by sanctioning her a life estate in her husband's share, and by permitting her to stay separately.

It thus came to happen that the proprietary rights, which were not recognised in the Vedic age when women were better educated and enjoyed greater freedom, came gradually to be

1. नाकाम्या संनियोज्या स्यात् । *B. D. S.*, II, 1, 20.
नाकामा संनियोज्या स्यात्पुत्रकामां तु योजयेत् ।
Yama in *SCS.*, p. 225.

recognised during this period. It is true that the doctrine of perpetual tutelage of women became popular at this time, and it should normally have proved fatal to the recognition and development of their proprietary rights. But men do not always seriously believe in the solemn theories they haughtily enunciate, nor do they care to draw all possible corollaries from them. Such was the case with the theory of women's perpetual tutelage. Jurists felt no self-contradiction in declaring that women were unfit for independence, and yet investing them with new proprietary rights. They thought that sufficient regard would be shown to the theory of perpetual tutelage by laying down that women could enjoy only the income of their inheritance, but not dispose of its corpus.

It is further true that the tendency to regard women as fragile and of a weak moral fibre was getting stronger in this period. It was, however, only the woman in the abstract that was so regarded. In society, however, the woman in the abstract did not exist; there was the wife or the daughter or the mother, and for every one of them Hindu society felt very tenderly. The daughter and the wife had the father and the husband to provide for them, but there was no such guardian of natural affection to look after the childless widow. A school of jurists therefore arose at the beginning of the Christian era, which advocated that the widow should be recognised as an heir to her husband, if the latter had effected his separation before the time of his death. The new reform was, as usual, vehemently opposed by vested interests, but eventually it began to find greater and greater support in society.

THE AGE OF LATER SMṚITIS, COMMENTATORS AND DIGEST-WRITERS

(*C.* 500 A. D., to *c.* 1800 A.D.)

The only sphere in which the position of women improved in this age was the one of proprietary rights; otherwise she continued to lose all along the line. The right of the widow to inherit the share of her husband came to be eventually recognised all over the country by *c.* 1200 A. D. In Bengal the position was further improved by conceding her this right even when her husband had not separated from the joint family at the time of his death. The scope of the Strīdhana was further extended by the Mitāksharā school by including in it property acquired even by inheritance and partition. The widow's estate continued to be a limited one, but in some parts of south India she was allowed to gift it away for religious purposes without the consent of the reversioners.

Proprietary rights apart, in all other spheres the position of women continued to deteriorate in this period. Most of the causes responsible for women's degradation during the last period continued to operate in this age also. The *upanayana* of women went completely out of vogue. From the theological point of view the woman therefore came naturally to be regarded as of the same status as the Śūdra. This inflicted an incalculable harm on their general status and prestige. The marriageable age of girls was lowered down still further. Towards the end of the former period, it was recommended that girls should be married just before the time of their puberty. It would appear that this did not exclude the possibility of a few negligent parents failing to marry their daughters before that time. To prevent this possibility it now came to be declared that a girl becomes mature (*ṛituprāptā*) not when menses appear at the age of 13 or 14, but at the age of 10 or 11, when some preliminary symptoms of impending puberty manifest themselves. The proper age for marriage was therefore 10. The age of 8, however, was regarded as the ideal one; marriage in the case of girls corresponded to *upanayana* in the case of boys, and the proper age for the latter was 8. In Kshatriya families, however, girls continued to be married at about the age of 14 or 15. Widow marriages had become prohibited at this period. The Satī custom had become common in the fighting classes. The Kshatriya father therefore did not think of marrying his daughter at a tender age, when there was always the possibility of his son-in-law dying before his beloved daughter had come of age in the frequent warfare, that had become common at this time. Many Kshatriya ladies were often called upon to assume the reins of government as regents; so training in administrative duties and military exercises had to be given to them. This also necessitated the postponement of their marriage to a somewhat advanced age.

In the case of non-Kshatriya girls, who were married at the age of 10 or 11, naturally no education worth the name could be imparted. Down to about 1200 A.D., daughters in rich families continued to receive some literary education through special teachers; a few of them used to distinguish themselves as poetesses and critics down to the 10th century A. D. But this tradition died down when the old aristocracy perished or declined in importance after the establishment of the Muslim rule. In ordinary families naturally girls now began to grow in ignorance; no education worth the name was possible before the age of 10 or 11, which had now become the usual marriageable age. At the advent of the British rule the literacy among women was confined only to the class of dancing girls; women in respectable families felt very uneasy if it was suspected that they were literate. Being generally illiterate and inexperienced, women naturally ceased to inspire respect, and the tendency to pass cynical observations about their weakness and worthlessness became more common.

Brides of 8 or 9 could naturally have no voice in the settlement of their marriages; they could also become no proper companions to their husbands owing to their immense intellectual inferiority. Their position therefore *vis-a-vis* their husbands further deteriorated. The Christian theologians were declaring at this time that the husband was the head of the wife, as Christ was the head of the Church. Hindu Smṛitis advocated an exactly similar doctrine, and maintained that the husband was the wife's god and her only duty was to obey and serve him. The evil example of royal harems made polygamy more and more fashionable. Marital faithlessness on the part of the husband became more common owing to the custom of child marriage.

Early marriage was naturally followed by early maternity, which increased the mortality among women between the ages of 14 and 22. Young widowers of 25 or 30 were naturally more eager to follow the rule of Manu, which permitted an immediate remarriage, than to emulate the example of Śrī-Rāmchandra, who declined to marry a second time. Widowers of 25 or 30, however, could get brides of 9 or 10 only. This enormous disparity between the ages of the two parties naturally helped the spread of concubinage in society. Its moral tone was affected, and it began to feel nothing objectionable in allowing dancing girls to sing and dance on holy occasions like those of *upanayana* and marriage, or at the time of the religious service in temples. The opposition of purists to this custom proved of no avail, and eventually the association of dancing girls with sacred Sanskāras and temple worship became quite common in several parts of the country.

Down to *c.* 500 A. D. permission was granted to child widows to remarry, though the widow marriage in general had come to be tabooed. This permission came to be gradually withdrawn during this period. From about 1,000 A. D. no widow in a respectable family could remarry, whatever her age might have been at the time of her husband's death. In the beginning only widows in the higher sections of society suffered from this disability, but in course of time it came to be extended to the widows of those lower classes also, which were anxious to be considered respectable. The prohibition of widow remarriage came to be regarded as the most important criterion of the respectability of a class down to the beginning of the present century. The prejudice against the widow remarriage was so deep-rooted, that the permissive legislation passed in the matter in 1856 A.D. had no appreciable effect on the situation for more than half a century.

We have shown above that at *c.* 500 A. D. the custom of the Satī was meeting with considerable opposition from the thinking sections of our society. That opposition continued unabated for another 500 years, and the majority of Smṛitis went on averring that the custom amounted to a suicide and could bring no spiritual salvation. Eventually, however, owing to the growing appreciation of the ascetic ideals and practices, the custom of the Satī came to be surrounded with a halo and began to make a wider appeal. First it was confined to the fighting classes. Smṛiti writers and their commentators down to about the 11th century declare that it would be sinful for a Brāhmaṇa widow to burn herself on the funeral pyre of her husband. Gradually, however, Brāhmaṇas also began to follow the custom, as they did not like to be excelled by Kshatriyas in the pursuit of ascetic practices. Widows now had a dismal prospect before them. They could not remarry. Some of them who were very young must have felt it to be no easy task to walk straight on the narrow and difficult path of strict chastity. They therefore very often preferred the terrible ordeal of the Satī to the tiresome life of the widow. Most of the widows who ascended the funeral pyres of their husbands did so quite voluntarily. Occasionally, however, an unwilling widow was burnt by her fiendish relatives, who were either afraid that she might eventually misbehave and bring disgrace to the family, or who wanted to appropriate for themselves her share in the family property. The recognition of the right of inheritance was thus not an unmixed blessing to the poor widow

The tonsure of the widow came into vogue by about the eighth century A.D. With the disappearance of Buddhism at this time, the prejudice against the custom gradually disappeared, and it was recommended to the widow as a kind of help and protection to her in her ascetic resolve and life.

We have seen above that women were declared to be of the same status as that of the Śūdras, and so came to be gradually excluded from the study of and acquaintance with higher theology and philosophy. Women, however, are by nature more religious than men, and so a new type of religious literature was evolved to meet their needs and aspirations. This was the remodelled Pauranic literature. It enunciated the principles of Hinduism in a homely, easy and attractive manner, illustrating them with a number of edifying stories. Pious people made provision all over the country for the exposition of Purāṇas to public audiences. Women became very well grounded in the culture of the race by habitually listening to this literature. Faith, almost blind faith, was however held up for high admiration in Purāṇas. It was therefore well developed in women, to the detriment however of rationalism. It must be however noted that reason was at a discount at this period among males also both in India and Europe.

We have seen above that the Purda custom was beginning to get a footing in a few royal families in the last period. There was, however, a staunch opposition to it down to the 12th century. Many royal ladies used to plainly tell their husbands that they would not stand the nonsense of the Purda. As a consequence the custom failed to become popular even among royal families down to about 1200 A.D. The advent of the Mahomadens, however, changed the situation. The customs and manners of the conquerors were imitated with as much zeal in the 13th as they were in the 19th century. In the beginning the Purda entered the families of feudatories and nobles, and then it gradually spread among higher classes in northern India. The Muslim influence was weak in the south and so the Purda found no general acceptance there. It got a footing only in a few ruling families.

Rationalism has been at a discount with Hindu thinkers during the last more than one thousand years; this circusmstance has been responsible for a very unfortunate change in society's angle of vision in a very important matter vitally affecting the well-being of women. Down to about 800 A.D. Smṛitis were emphatic in declaring that women, who were forcibly taken into captivity or dishonoured, should be admitted back to their families. Pseudo-puritanical notions distorted social vision in this matter soon after *c.* 1,000 A.D. Hindu society began to show a surprising callousness to women, who had the misfortune of being carried away into captivity even for a very short time. An outsider like Alberuni could not understand the stupidity of the Hindu community in refusing to readmit men and women, who had been captured and converted by force. If one's hand gets soiled, he argues, one should proceed to cleanse and not to cut it. But Hindu society could not understand this very reasonable proposition. From *c.* 1,200 A. D. it refused to follow the lead of Smṛiti writers and declared that once a woman was converted or taken into captivity, nothing would justify her readmission to her old family and religion. This callous and unreasonable attitude has cost Hindu society very dearly. Had the women, who had been forcibly converted or captured, been readmitted into Hindu society, its population would certainly not have dwindled down to 75% of the population of pre-partition India.

The above survey of the position of Hindu women would show that their condition has been on the whole deteriorating during the last two thousand years. It is no doubt true that women as a general rule received similar and often worse treatment in contemporary times in several other civilisations both in the East and the West. But this can hardly be a sufficient consolation or justification for us. For, we had once already evolved a fairly satisfactory standard about the treatment of women and then failed to act up to it owing to subsequent developments, which we ought to have checked. It is true that there was no female education worth the name even in the West down to the middle of the 19th century, but that would not condone its neglect by us, when we had once seen its benefits and advantages. It may be that early marriages might have been common in many countries in ancient and medieval times; but that would not justify the conduct of later Smṛiti writers in disapproving the earlier custom of post-puberty marriages. It may be that seclusion of women in one form or another was common in several European countries for many centuries; but that would hardly be a sufficient excuse for our resorting to that custom, especially when we were once going on without it.

It has also to be pointed out that some of the grievances from which women were suffering during the last two thousand years were either theoretical or common to both men and women. Thus it was only a handful of Pandits, who under the influence of theological theories, regarded women as being of the same status as that of the Śūdras; to ordinary society, however, women were symbols of purity, religiousness and spirituality. They, and not men, were the custodians of national culture, and determined the details of religious rituals and ceremonies more authoritatively than the professional priest. It is true that literacy among women rapidly declined during the last two thousand years. But the same was the case with men, though no doubt to a lesser degree. Outside priestly and commericial classes, literacy was not of great use either. The printing press was yet to come into existence. Books were very costly and almost unprocurable to men of ordinary means. The usual way of imbibing national culture and traditional wisdom was to listen to the village preacher (*Kathaka* or *Paurāṇika*), and illiterate women had greater facilities and opportunities to do this than literate men. It is true that owing to the lowering of the marriageable age, brides lost all voice in the settlement of their marriages. But the same was the case with the bride-grooms also, who being only 14 or 15, could naturally have no effective say in the selection of their partners in life. It must be added that parents normally took all possible care to make the best possible choice. Moreover, it was an age when parental authority was instinctively obeyed; not even one bride or bride-groom in a million ever dreamt of nursing any grievance for being denied a voice in the settlement of the marriage.

Even during the last two thousand years the average woman continued to lead a happy and contented life, fondled by her parents, loved by her husband and revered by her children. It must be, however, admitted that her cup of happiness was more frequently split in this period than ever before by the prohibition of widow remarriage, the revival of the Satī custom, the spread of the Purda and the greater prevalence of polygamy and supersession. Society's attitude towards her was also one of patronising condescension. It no doubt insisted that she should be properly cared for and attended to, but it did not take any effective steps to check the growing tendency to pass very uncharitable and utterly unjustifiable remarks about her nature and worth. It allowed the husband to trample under foot the marriage vow quite openly, but insisted that it should be followed by the wife, even if her husband were a moral wreck.

As shown already by us in the course of the preceding chapters, there were no doubt some extenuating and often sufficient causes for the spread of many of the above unfortunate tendencies, customs and institutions. But we must now realise that circumstances have radically changed and customs and institutions must follow suit. In a society living in an ascetic atmosphere, it may have been thought desirable to prohibit widow remarriage; in the modern age of morbid talkies and four anna novels, to continue to insist upon that prohibition would be suicidical. Polygamy may have had some justification when a son was genuinely believed to be necessary for spiritual salvation; in a society which no longer subscribes to that belief, it becomes an odious institution. In an age when children were married very young and were accustomed to obey the parents instinctively, no one thought of questioning their sole authority to arrange their wards' marriages; in the new epoch when marriages are taking place at an advanced age and when every adult has begun to claim absolute independence as his birth right, it would be no longer justifiable for gurdians to exercise the same powers as before. Hindu society will have to remove a number of cobwebs in its ancient house and change and even revolutionise some of its customs and institutions in order to accord the proper place, which justly belongs to women.

THE FUTURE

The detailed survey of the position of women that we have made in this work would be of considerable use to us in understanding and solving most of the problems that confront us today. Women began to lose all along the line the moment their education began to be neglected. Early marriages naturally came into vogue when there was nothing to keep girls engaged after the age of 9 or 10. Uneducated brides of very young age naturally ceased to have any voice in the settlement of their marriages and began to be treated in a condescending manner by their husbands, who did not find them their proper companions either in tastes or in attainments. It is true that in spite of their illiteracy and inexperience many Hindu women possessed remarkable wisdom and capacity and could manage their home affairs efficiently, even in times of stress and difficulties. The percentage of such women would have been much greater, if female education had not been discontinued by our society. Luckily the need and advantage of female education is now fully understood. Society has now taken to it seriously in towns and cities and rural areas will follow suit in course of time, as the standard of living of our population and the resources of the Union and State Governments improve. As far as the nature of female education is concerned, we have discussed it already (*ante*, pp. 26-28), and pointed out that it should be a course specially intended for women, calculated to promote a harmonious development of their reason and emotions, enabling them at the same time to become earning members of the family either as part-time or whole time workers in case of need. The step taken by Prof. D. K. Karve in founding a special University for women was a step in the right direction; similar courses are being started in some other universities also like the M. S. University, Baroda. Subjects specially useful for house wives, are being introduced for girl students in several Universities. The second Five Years' Plan makes special provision for female education.

When girls of 17 or 18, equipped with proper education, enter matrimony, they cannot but be treated with instinctive respect and consideration by all the society around. Family responsibility, and not inherent incapacity, would be the normal cause of their not being earning members of their families; they would therefore receive the same respect that is instinctively given to the bread-winner. Their practical attainments would add to the beauty of their households, lead to economy in its expenditure and promote sounder education of the children of the family. This would surely ensure for them an equality of status with their husbands in all cultured families. Knowing that a woman equipped with the above education can earn her living and support her family, if necessary, society would cease to regard her as a parasite; nor would she allow to be looked upon with an air condescension. Economic value, actual or potential, exercises considerable influence upon the status of a class. The dominating position of man has been largely due to his being the chief earning member of the family. The observation of a Sanskrit dramatist that a man becomes a woman when he is economically dependent upon her, and vice versa, is true to a very great extent.[1]

In the sphere of marriage and marital relations some reforms are necessary very urgently.

It is high time now that polygamy should be legally prohibited. There is no doubt that legal recognition of polygamy is working an untold harm to a not negligible number of women, who are superseded by their husbands, especially in uncultured classes. The State of Bombay prohibited polygamy in 1947 and the State of Madras in 1948. It is hopped that 'This prohibition has now been extended to the whole of India by the Hindu Marriage and Divorce Act of 1955.'

It is now high time for us to insist both in the East and the West that there should be no double standard of morality in sexual matters; husbands should be required to remain as faithful to their marriage vows as wives. Any transgression in this respect on the part of the husband should meet with instantaneous and severe social opprobrium. Unfortunately nature's partiality to man renders it very difficult to detect his transgressions even when numerous; a single lapse of woman, on the other hand, is often betrayed by its consequences.

1. मयि द्रव्यपरिक्षीणे स्त्रीद्रव्येणानुकंपितः ।
अर्थतः पुरुषो नारी या नारी सार्थतः पुमान् ॥
Chārudatta of Bhāsa, Act III, v.17.

Marriage should continue to be regarded as a religious bond, normally indissoluble in this life. This world however is an imperfect one, and so would be also its most sacred ties sometimes. We must therefore frankly recognise that cases may sometimes occur, where religion will have to dissolve the tie it had once created. The conditions of divorce should be very stringent, but its necessity in modern times has to be recognised. There are several cases in Hindu society of women being completely forsaken by their husbands, who are compelled to lead a forlorn life of virtual widowhood. They cannot remarry, because their first marriage tie cannot be dissolved. If, however, they change their religion and become Christians or Muslims, they can dissolve their existing marriage and enter into a new wedlock. Should we penalise these unfortunate women for their fidelity to Hinduism by refusing them permission for divorce and remarriage ? We have seen already that ancient Dharmaśāstra writers definitely permit divorce under certain circumstances. The demand for divorce was gaining in volume every day. Bombay passed the Divorce Act in 1947 and Madras in 1948. The Indian Parliament passed the Hindu Marriage and Divorce Act in 1955, permitting divoce to the Hindu community all over India. Generally speaking these Acts allow divorce in the cases of impotency, lunacy, and leprosy, lasting for seven years, and desertion for four continuous years. It also allows the remedy, if the husband keeps and the wife becomes a concubine or a prostitute. No divorce is allowed if the couple has lived the married life for 20 years after attaining majority. The above conditions for divorce are fairly reasonable.

It is urgently necessary for Hindu society to change its angle of vision towards women, who have been criminally assaulted or who have temporarily gone astray owing to a mistake or duress. During the last one thousand years we have been very cruel to such women, and have, as a consequence, driven them either to a life of permanent sin and shame or to the folds of other proselyting religions. We must immediately bring ourselves in line with the enlightened viewpoint of our much maligned Smṛiti writers, who had recognised that the phrase, 'It is human to err,' was as much applicable to women as to men, and have recommended that women, who have been overpowered or misled, should be readmitted to their families and society after a suitable penance. Justice, fairplay and the interest of the community as a whole demand that we should try our best to enable such unfortunate women to start their life afresh in an honorable manner.

Widow remarriage has been already legalised, but the number of widows taking advantage of the legislation is still very small. Widows who spend their remaining life cherishing the memory of their late husbands and devoting themselves to the service of their family, society and country will continue to be revered by society. We should encourage and honour all those, who are genuinely anxious to lead such a life. It cannot be, however, gainsaid that the dread of social opprobrium is still preventing a large number of young widows from marrying, in spite of their desire to enter into a fresh wedlock. More energetic educative propaganda must be carried on to prevent this state of affairs.

Considerable difficulties are experienced in finding suitable matches for widows willing to marry; public opinion must assert itself and insist that widowers should marry widows alone.

In the realm of the property law further liberalisation is necessary. Daughters, with brothers, who cannot or will not marry, are becoming fairly numerous in society; their right of inheritance, should be recognised for a share equal to the half of the full share of the brother. The Hindu Code Bill now before the Parliament (March 1956) proposes to give them a full share.

Opinion is at present sharply divided as to the whether the married daughter, who has brothers, should get a share at all, or whether she should get only half a share or a share equal to that of her brother. This clevage of opinion was also reflected in the various drafts proposed before the legislature. The first draft of the Hindu Code prepared by Rao Committee approvingly referred to the views expressed in the first edition of this work at p. 298 and proposed that a daughter should get a share equal to half that of her brother, if she remained unmarried. Later this position was abandoned; it was feared that it would promote immorality, as daughters may not choose to marry if they were to loose their share in patrimony. The Hindu Code Bill now before the Parliament (March 1956) proposes to give a married daughter a share equal to that of her brother. It is difficult to anticipate whether this particular clause will be passed or not. We have already shown how it would not be a feasible proposition to give the married daughter the same share as that of her brother (pp. 243-5). We hold that a daughter, who is unmarried at the time of the opening of the inheritance, should get a share equal to half that of her brother inclusive of the amount spent on her education. This share should not be required to be surrendered at the time of her marriage. It should be regarded as equivalent to the marriage portion of the daughter.

As a natural corollary of the joint ownership of the husband and the wife in the family property, and as a recognition of the valuable service of the wife in the management of the household, the law should lay down that 10% of the income of the husband should be converted into a new variety of *Strīdhana*, to be entirely at the disposal of the wife. This would remove the difficulties of the sensitive wife by keeping at her disposal a fund of her own in lieu of the share in the patrimony which is denied to her.

A deed of transfer of immoveable property should require the joint consent and signatures of the husband and the wife. This is necessary in order to prevent a vicious or spendthrift husband from ruining his wife by selling away her share in the family property.

The law passed in 1937 has secured to the widow her husband's full share in the joint family property. She is, however, still a limited heir. Time has now come to grant women full rights of ownership in their inheritance. Why should not a widowed lady principal of a college possess a right which is conceded by law to her most illiterate peon. The Hindu Inheritance Bill, now before the Parliament, has proposed to invest women with full right over their shares and inheritance.'

Women have already obtained political rights and privileges, more or less coextensive with those of men. They will figure more prominently in public life when there is a wider spread of education and a further improvement in the economic condition of society.

The few changes that are suggested above are not in any way against the spirit of our culture. This point has been made quite clear in the course of this work. That our code of social and socio-religious rules and regulations has never been a fixed and rigid one must have become quite clear to the reader of the preceeding pages, which show how our customs and institutions have been changing from age to age under the influence of new ideals and environments. This conclusion is forced upon us not only by a study of the history of institutions, but also by a survey of the views of the Smṛiti literature about the sources of our Dharma. It has been definitely laid down by a number of authorities that along with Śrutis and Smṛitis *sadāchāra* or accepted good usages also constitute an important source of Dharma[1]. It is no doubt true that *sadāchāra* is regarded as less authoritative than Śrutis and Smṛitis; but this was only in theory. In practice it exercised an influence as great as that of the latter. As a matter of fact Smṛitis themselves are nothing but *sadāchāra* codified in black and white. There used to be a body of learned and pious Pandits, who used to survey the situation from time to time and guide the society by their opinions as to the advisability or suitability of some of the new changes that were being felt to be necessary under changed circumstances. The considered opinions of such Pandit associations (*parishads*) used to be eventually incorporated in new Smṛitis, which used to be known

1. वेदः स्मृतिः सदाचारः स्वस्य च प्रियमात्मनः ।
एतच्चतुर्विधं प्राहुः साक्षाद्धर्मस्य लक्षणम् ॥

Manu, II, 12

after the names of their presidents.[1] Smṛitis like those of Devala, Bṛihaspati or Kātyāyana and later works like the *Mitākshara* and the *Dāyabhāga*, which proposed important new changes in the then established old practices, were really due to the activities of such learned bodies (*Paṇḍita-parishads*).

It is further important to note that even orthodox Smṛiti writers like Manu have recognised that a time might come when their rules would become obsolete, and have therefore declared that if any rules framed by them are found to be not conducive to the welfare of society, or against the spirit of the age, they should be unhesitatingly abrogated or modified[2]. As a matter of fact they themselves have done so in many cases. The Vedas, for instance, were definitely opposed to women's rights of inheritance; later Smṛitis nevertheless managed to get them recognised. The Vedic age had permitted Niyoga; Smṛitis, however, openly carried a righteous and successful crusade against the custom. Marriage by capture and purchase was approved by the earlier age; Dharmaśāstra writers vehemently condemned both the practices. The main reason for this proreform attitude of our Dharmasāstra writers in these matters was that they had realised that circumstances had changed and therefore customs and institutions must follow suit. We must in our own turn recognise that times have changed, old ideals of extreme asceticism have ceased to appeal, the age of authority has gone and is succeeded by an era of rationalism and equality. We must therefore readjust the position of women to the new situation by introducing the changes suggested above. If this is done, the capacity, efficiency and happiness of Hindu women (and therefore of Hindu men also) will increase, and as a consequence, our community will be enabled to take its rightful place in the comity of nations and make important contributions to the progress and happiness of mankind.

1. See A. S. Altekar: *Sources of Hindu Dharma*, Chaps. I-IV.

2. परित्यजेदर्थकामौ यौ स्यातां धर्मवर्जितौ ।
धर्ममप्यसुखोदर्कं लोकविक्रुष्टमेव च ॥

Manu, IV, 176.

॥ ॐ तत्सद्ब्रह्मार्पणमस्तु ॥

BIBLIOGRAPHY

Only important works are included. The following abbreviations are used:—And.—Ānandāśrama Press; B. S. S.—Bombay Sanskrit Series; ed.—edition or edited by; G. O. S.—Gaekwar Oriental Series; Nir.—Nirṇaya Sāgara Press; P. T. S.—Pali Text Society: S. B. E.—Sacred Books of the East: Trans.—Translation.

Vedic and allied Literature

Atharvaveda, Ajmer ed., 1917.
Ṛigeveda, Ajmer ed., 1917.
Yajurveda, Vājasaneyisaṁhitā, Nir, ed., 1912.
Aitareya Brāhmaṇa, And. ed., Poona, 1896.
Śatapatha Brāhmaṇa, ed. by Weber, London, 1849.
Shaḍviṁśa Brāhmaṇa, Calcutta, 1881.
Taittirīya Brāhmaṇa, And. ed., Poona, 1900-1905.
Taittirīya Āraṇyaka, And. ed., Poona, 1897.
Upanishads, Ten Principal ones, ed. with Śaṅkara's commentary by H. R. Bhagwat, Poona, 1918.
Bhagvadgītā, ed. by Tilak, Poona, 1915.
Avesta, English Trans. by Bleeck, Hertford, 1864.
Pehlvi Texts, Part V, S.B.E., Vol. XLVII, London, 1897.

Epics, Puranas and Tantras

Mahābhārata, Kumbhakonam ed., 1906-9, Kumbhakonam. In a few cases the references are to the Bombay ed. of Ganpat Atmaram; they are indicated by the letter B at the end.
Rāmāyaṇa, Kumbhakonam ed., 1929.
Agnipurāṇa, And. ed., Poona, 1900.
Bhāgavata, Kumbhakonam ed., 1926.
Bhavishyapurāṇa, Venkatesvara Press ed., Bombay, 1897.
Brahmapurāṇa, And. ed., Poona, 1895.
Brāhmavaivartapurāṇa, And ed., Poona, 1935.
Matsyapurāṇa, And. ed., Poona, 1907.
Padmapurāṇa, And. ed., Poona, 1893-4.
Mahānirvāṇatantra, Venkatesvara Press ed., Bombay, 1929.

Buddhist and Jain Works

Aṅguttaranikāya, ed. by Morris, P. T. S. ed., London., 1883-1900.
Dhammapāda with commentary, P. T. S. ed., London, 1906-15.
Jātakas, ed. by Fausboll, London,. 1877-1897.
Majjhimanikāya, P. T. S. ed., London, 1888-1925.
Samyuttanikāya, P. āT. S. ed., London, 1884-1904.
Therīgāthā, P. T. S. ed., London, 1883.
Therīgāthā, English trans. by Mrs. Rhys Davids, London, 1909.
Vinayapīṭaka, S. B. E. ed., Oxfoed, 1881-2.
Bhagavatīsūtra, Bombay, 1917-1933.
Mūlāchāra of Vattakera, Manikchand Digambara Series, 1920-23.
Uttarādhyayanas ed. by Carpentier, Upsala, 1922.

Technical Sciences

Nirukta, Venkatesvara Press ed., Bombay, 1912.
Pūrvamīmānsā, ed. by Sandal, Sacred Books of the Hindus Series, Allahabad, 1925.

Vyākaraṇamahābhāshya of Patañjali, ed. by Kielhorn, B. S. S. ed., Poona, 1880-1909.
Brihatsaṁhitā of Varāhamihira, with Marathi trans., Ratnagiri, 1874.

Dharmaśāstra Literature

Gṛihya Sūtras

Āpastamba G. S., ed., by Winternitz, Vienna, 1887.
Aśvalāyana G. S., ed., by Jivananda, Calcutta, 1893.
Baudhāyana G. S., Mysore University, 1920.
Gobhila G. S., Bibliotheca ed., Calcutta, 1908.
Pāraskara G. S., Leipzig, 1876.

Dharma Sūtras

Āpastamba D.S., B.S.S. ed., Poona 1892.
Baudhāyana D. S., in the Smṛitīnām Samuchchaya of And., Poona, 1905.
Gautama D. S., And . ed., Poona, 1910.
Hārīta D. S., as quoted by later writers.
Vasishṭha D. S., in the Smṛitīnām Samuchchaya of And., Poona, 1905.
Vishṇu D. S., ed. by Jolly, Calcutta, 1881.

Smritis

Atri S., in the Smṛitīnām Samuchchaya of And., Poona, 1905.
Bṛihaspati S., S. B. E., Vol. XXXIII, Oxford, 1889. G. O. S.
Devala S., as in Smṛitīnām Samuchchaya of And., Poona, 1905.
Kātyāyanamatasaṅgraha, ed. by Banerji, Calcutta, 1927.
Laghu-Aśvalāyana S., as in Smṛitīnām Samuchchaya of And., Poona, 1905-6.
Manu S., with six commentaries, ed., by Telang, Bombay, 1886.
Nārada S., with the commentary of Asahāya, ed. by Jolly, Calcutta, 1885.
Parāśara S., with Mādhavā's commentary, B. S.S. ed., Poona, 1893-1911.
Yājñavalkya S., with the Mitāksharā, Nir, ed., Bombay, 1918.
Yājñavalkya S., with the commentary of Aparārka, And. ed., Poona, 1903-4.

Medieval Digests

Dāyabhāga of Jimūtavāhana, ed. by Jivananda, Calcutta, 1893.
Smṛitichandrikā of Annambhaṭṭa, Mysore ed., 1914-20.
Vīramitrodaya of Mitramiśra, ed. by Jivananda, Calcutta, 1875.
Vyavahāramayūkha of Nilakaṇṭha, Gujarati Press ed., Bombay, 1923.

Arthaśastra and Kamaśastra Works

Arthaśāstra of Kauṭilya, ed. by S. Sahstri, Mysore, 1919.
Śūkranītisāra, ed. by Jivananda, Calcutta, 1890.
Kāmasūtra of Vātsyāyana, Kashi Sanskrit Series, Benaras, 1929.
Kuṭṭinīmata of Dāmodara, ed., by Tansukhram, Bombay, 1885.

Classical Sanskrit and Prakrit Literature

Buddhacharit, ed. by Cowel, Oxford, 1893.
Gāthāsaptaśatī, Kāvyamālā ed., Bomaby, 1911.
Kādambarī, Nir. Ed., Bombay, 1910.
Kathāsaritsāgara, ed. by Parab, Bombay, 1903.
Kāvyamīmānsā, G. O. S. ed., Baroda, 1906.
Kumārapālapratibodha, G. O. S. ed., Bardoda, 1920.
Kumārasambhava, Nir, ed., Bombay, 1893.
Lalitavistāra ed. by R. L. Mitter, Calcutta, 1877.
Mālatīmādhava, ed., by R. G. Bhandarkar, Bombay, 1876.
Mohaparājaya, G. O. S. ed., Baroda, 1918.
Mṛichchhakaṭika, Nir, ed., Bombay, 1910.
Raghuvaṁśa, Nir, ed., Bombay, 1910.
Rājataraṅgiṇī, ed. by Stein, Bombay, 1892.

Śākuntala, Nir, ed., Bombay, 1916.
Śaṅkaradigvijaya, And ed., Poona, 1891.
Trivendram dramas of Bhāsa; Avimāraka, Bālacharit, Chārudatta, Pratijñāyaugandharāyaṇa, Pratimā, and Svapnavāsavadattā; ed. by T. Ganpati Sastri, Trivendram, 1912-15.
Uttararārāmacharit, ed. by Kale, Bombay, 1901.

FOREIGN TRAVELLERS

Ancient India, as described by Megasthenes and Arrian, Trans. by. M'Crindle, London, 1877.
Ancient India and its Invansion by Alexander the Great, Trans. by M'Crindle, Westminster, 1896.
On Yuan Chwang, Trans. by Watters, London, 1904.
Alberuni's India, trans. by Sachau, London, 1914.
Ibn Batuta, Trans. and selected by Gibb, London, 1929.
Bernier, Travels in the Moghul Empire, 2nd ed., revised by Smith, London, 1914.
Manucci, Moghul India, trans. by Irvine, London, 1906-8.
Tavernier, Travells in India, Oxford, 1925.

MUSLIM SOURCE BOOKS.

Ain-i-Akbari, ed. by Buchanan, Calcutta, 1873.
History of India as told by its own Historians, edited by Elliot and Dowson, London, 1867-77.

ARCHAEOLOGICAL WORKS

Agarwal, Mathūrā kī Baudhakalā, (Hindi).
Bachhoffer, Early Indian Sculpture, Paris, 1929.
Cunningham, The Stupa of Bharhut, London, 1879.
Cunningham, Tree and Serpent Worship, 2nd ed., London, 1873.
Gopinath Rao, T., Hindu Iconography, Madras, 1916.
Gründewedel, Buddhist Art in India, Eng. Trans. by Burgess, London 1901.
Hargreaves, Buddha Story in Stone, Calcutta, 1918.
,, Handbook of Sculptures in the Peshawe Museum. Calcutta, 1930.
Heringham, Ajanta, Oxford University Press, 1915.
Marshall and others, Bagh Caves, London, 1927.
Pant, B. S., Elora, Bombay, 1930.
Smith V. A., A History of Fine Arts in India and Ceylon, Oxford, 1910.
Whitehead, Catalogue of the Coins in the Punjab Museum, Vol. I, Lahore, 1913.
Yazdani, Ajanta, Parts, I and II, London, 1930 and 1933.
Ancient Indian Inscriptions as published in Epigraphia Indica, Indian Antiquary and other Journals referred to in the text.

WORKS ABOUT WOMEN : INDIAN

Horner, Women under primitive Buddhism, London, 1930.
Meyer, Sexual life in Ancient India, Eng. Trans., London, 1930
Mitter, Justice. Position of Women in Hindu Law, Calcutta, 1913.
Nehru, S., Our Cause, Allahabad, 1936.
Upadhyaya, Women in Rigveda, Lucknow, 1933.
Winternitz, Die Frau, Leipzing., 1920.

WORKS ABOUT WOMEN : EUROPEAN

Davies J. L.,A short History of Woman, London, 1928.
George, The Story of Woman, London, 1925.
Hall, F. W., Woman in Soviet Russia, London, 1936.
Mill, The Subjection of Women, London, 1869.
Muller-Lyer, Family, trans. by Stella Brown, London, 1931.
Soltau, The Free Woman, London, 1923.
Stratchy, The Cause, London, 1929.

Stratchy Our Freedom and its Results, London, 1936.
Wollstonecraft, The Rights of Women, 1792.

GENERAL WORKr

Abraham, English Life and Manners in the late Medieval Ages, London, 1913.
Altekar, Education in Ancient India, Beneras, 1934.
,, Rāshṭrakūṭas and their Times, Poona, 1934.
Banerji G. D., Hindu Law of Stridhana, Calcutta, 1923.
Bhave, Peshvekalina Maharashtra, (Marathi), Poona, 1936.
Dasgupta, Bengal in the 16th Century, Calcutta, 1914.
Dawson, The Ethical Religion of Zoraster, Newyork, 1931.
Geiger, Civilisation of the Eastern Iranians, Eng. trans. by Sanjana, London, 1895.
Glotz, Ancient Greece at Work, London, 1926.
Jolly, Hindu Law, Calcutta, 1883.
Jolly, Hindu Law and Custom, Eng. trans. by B. Ghosh, Calcutta, 1928.
Kane, P. V., History of Dharmaśāstra literature, Poona, 1930.
Kelkar and Khare, Hindudharmaśāstra, (Marathi), Vols. I-II, Poona, 1932.
Mahaffy, Social Life in Greece, London, 1933.
Mill and Wilson, History of British India, London, 1848.
Moreland, India at the Death of Akbar, London, 1920.
Report of the Royal Commission on Divorce and Matrimonial Causes, London, 1913.
Saletore, The Social and Political Life in Vijayanagar Empire, Madras, 1934.
Spencer, Principles of Sociology, Edinborough, 1893.
Steele, Law and Custom of Hindu Castes.
Thomas, F. W., The Mutual Influence of the Mahomedans and Hindus, Deighten, 1892.
Thomson E, The Suttee, London, 1928.
Tod, Annals and Antiquities of Rajasthan, ed. by Grooke, Oxford, 1920.
Tripathi G. M., Marriage Forms under Ancient Hindu Law, Bombay, 1906.
Westermarck, A History of Human Marriage, London, 1921.

SUBJECT INDEX

PLATE I

A ROYAL PROCESSION

A base-relief on the left-hand pillar of the northern gateway at Sanchi (Central India).

Time : *c* 2nd century B.C.

Notice how women are seeing the procession from balconies without wearing any veil.

See p. 171.

[Copyright: Archaeological Survey of India]

PLATE II

THE WORSHIP OF A BODHI TREE

A bas-relief from the inner face of the right-hand pillar of the western gateway at Sanchi (Central India).

Time : *c* 2nd century B.C.

Notice how women are offering worship in a mixed throng of men and women without wearing any veil.

See p. 171.

[Copyright : Archaeological Survey of India]

PLATE III

A

A STANDING YAKSHIṆĪ

B

CHULAKOKĀ DEVATĀ

Sculptures from Bharhut (Central India), now in the Indian Museum, Calcutta.

Time : *c* : 2nd century B.C.

Notice the head-dress and numerous ornaments among which the nose-ring is conspicuous by its absence.

See pp. 283, 285-6, 302.

[Copyright : Archaeological Survey of India]

PLATE IV

A

B

A CHAURI-BEARER

A: Front side. B: Back side.

A statute from Didarganj, now in the Patna Museum.

Time: *c.* 4th century B.C.

It is quite clear from B that the *sari* was worn in the *vikachchha* fashion.

[Copyright : Archaeological Survey of India]

PLATE V

A

IGNĀI IN HUMAN FORM

A Gandhāra sculpture in the Indian Museum, Calcutta.

Time : *c.* 2nd century A.D.

Notice how the *sari* is worn in the *Sakachha* manner. See pp. 290, 294.

B

GODDESS ON A WICKER STOOL

From a gold coin of Samudragupta (enlarged).

Time : *c* 375 A.D.

Inscription : *Samudragupta.*

Kañchukī and the ends of its knot between the breast can be clearly seen.

See p. 293.

PLATE VI

PORTION OF A RECEPTION SCENE
From a medallion on a pillar from Ámraoti (Āndhradeśa).
Time : *c.* 1st or 2nd century A.D.
Saris were represented partly in carving and partly in plastering and colouring.
See p. 284.
[Copyright : Archaeological Survey of India]

PLATE VII

WORSHIP OF A BODHI TREE

A bas-relief from the left hand pillar of northern gateway at Sanchi (Central India).

Time : *c.* 2nd century B.C.

Women sitting in front of the throne are clearly wearing the *sari* in the *sakachchha* fashion.

See p. 291.

[Copyright : Archaeological Survey of India]

PLATE VIII

A

B

C

D

E

F

SOME FASHIONS OF COIFFURE

From sculptures at Bhuvaneshwar, Orissa.

Time : 10th century A.D.

See pp. 299-300.

PLATE IX

FEMALE HEAD WITH GORGEOUS COIFFURE

Kandariya templo, Khajuraho, Madhya Pradesh.

(Western wall of the *Maṇḍapa*)

Time : *c.* 10th century A.D.

See p. 300.

[Copyright: Kumari Minakshi Batcshvarkar]

PLATE X

FEMALE HEAD,
with an interesting fashion of coiffure.
Viśvanātha tempe, south wall, Khajuraho, Madhya Pradesh.
Time : *c.* 11th century A.D.
See p. 300.
[Copyright : Kumari Minakshi Bateshvarkar]

PLATE XI

FEMALE HEAD,
with an interesting fashion of coiffure.
Viśvanātha temple, south wall, Khajuraho, Madhya Pradesh.
Time : *c.* 11th century A.D.
See p. 300.
[Copyright : Kumari Minakshi Bateshvarkar]